Is

Anyone

Else

Like Me?

JEAN POSUSTA

iUniverse®

IS ANYONE ELSE LIKE ME?

iUniverse books may be ordered through booksellers or by contacting:

iUniverse
1663 Liberty Drive
Bloomington, IN 47403
www.iuniverse.com
844-349-9409

ISBN: 978-1-6632-4803-9 (sc)
ISBN: 978-1-6632-4804-6 (hc)
ISBN: 978-1-6632-4811-4 (e)

Library of Congress Control Number: 2022921617

Print information available on the last page.

iUniverse rev. date: 11/30/2022

An old Cherokee is teaching his grandson about life.
"A fight is going on inside me," he said to the boy.

"It is a terrible fight and it is between two wolves. One is evil – he is anger, envy, sorrow, regret, greed, arrogance, self-pity, guilt, resentment, inferiority, lies, false pride, superiority, and ego." He continued, "The other is good – he is joy, peace, love, hope, serenity, humility, kindness, benevolence, empathy, generosity, truth, compassion, and faith. The same fight is going on inside you – and inside every other person, too."

The grandson thought about it for a minute and then asked his grandfather, "Which wolf will win?"

The old Cherokee simply replied, "The one you feed."

Jean Posusta is the author of <u>I See You with My Heart</u>, <u>Hope We Don't Go to Paulette's Again Soon</u> and <u>Twisted Winds of Verango,</u> fiction; and <u>This Just Doesn't Make Any Sense,</u> a book used by Hospice; and a staff writer for RM3 Magazine. She has written a dozen murder mysteries for performance and can be booked through MontanaFunAdventures.com. She has won awards for her articles and poetry. Posusta taught for Montana State University after a 35-year career in human services in the Midwest. Posusta lectures on Grief Recovery and Suicide Prevention.

Dedicated to all the folks I quoted and misquoted. I hope that your egos are gone and you will allow me to use your sage wisdom for others to grow. There, that's the end of those lawsuits. Please.

Reviews

"An uplifting book about some very painful events. Posusta has the gift of using her own experiences and vulnerabilities to help others get through theirs. She is not afraid to tackle some painful true stories head on, helping us realize we are not alone." – Dr. Veronica Burford

Some friends also involved in a program supported me, saying that a side effect of reading these pages had occurred for them - doors seemed to open for them now and they let in the strength which faith allows. They were surprised at their transformation. I got so encouraged.

My intent is to exegete brightness where faith has dimmed, as I had been enlightened. As the book revealed itself to me, I realized my subliminal thinking had altered as did my friend's. My burdens no longer lead me through my week; instead I get to do what God wants me to do.

Mostly, my life had been a series of events that happened TO me and emanated in unhappiness. As I repeated my experience to others, they contemplated joining me in my journey, through my recantation of the principles of the Twelve Steps.

Author's Message

"Come with me where dreams are born, and time is never planned."

- Peter Pan

An author can only hope that the sense of their story dialogues with one other person. The story line here may light up your brain. My history and facts have been romantic but hugely flawed. I pray (and you will see why I say, 'pray') that the dialogue you and I achieve builds your character as it has mine. And I am not done yet. Much scientific research and review of academic data crystalized into this book. Then I added the stories of about 10,000 peoples' experiences. Forgive my tropes, and word creations, but they seem to get the message across.

What follows are the excerpts from my life that helped me to mature after fifty years of living in Cope. Which I now label painfully, in recollection, "The Winter of My Discontent".

I do not begin to think that I can school any other person! My writing is like a philosophical recounting of my experiences. Since I was not on the straight and narrow myself and unhappy and unfulfilled, I thought sharing my experience, strength and hope might be meaningful in someone else's state of unmanageability and unhappiness; to the eventual solution of goodness and peace.

Y/Our Life Needs Work - One Introspection

Let's begin with a transformational thought:

"Higher Power and Inner Spirit, allow me to fully gain harmony in my world by creating my own peace. Help me to create balance by moving away from negative influences and purify my thoughts and communication. Whatever changes are necessary, I want to seek and nurture my knowledge and wisdom. Help me to have inner healing in my ideas and the aspects of my life that deal with health and other folks I meet."

What if every day were your New Year's Day? Maybe our New Year's resolutions do not cut the mustard but think about this; we get to start over any time we want, any day, any minute. Go forth and take a step, but make sure it is in your right direction! Make the kaleidoscope of your hours on earth the best you can.

The reviews of this book include the words "revived and recovered" constantly. While I am not a revival minister, I aspire to be an inspirational host to your world. I plan to test your inner voice and wrench the truth out of you to help you get your share only, of respect, support and love we all cry for. If there were a path to humanitarian extant, this is it.

You will be introduced to techniques, tools, and exercises to coax the living out of you. I will explore, question and propose to you the answers and meditative probabilities you have missed all your life. Imagine your time on this earth connected with a satiated being within, awaiting discovery.

Never a better method to expand our existence.

I want to blow your perceptions of you. These writings are your truth mirror. That's right. We are digging deep in to your core of who you are and making you over. There are some tough aspects we will bring out and argue. I'm gonna unravel your concepts.

Even Einstein in his day, alluded that fear and stupidity are basic reactions that rule most individuals. I will add greed to the thought: Greed, fear and stupidity are great forces that drive our actions. Sick!

I want to add hope to your great force that rules the world. Honesty and truth are forces to fight the above.

I know I can only plant the seed in fertile soil and I cannot help you grow by tugging at the seed in hopes that you will sprout. I can lay before you the Miracle Grow and lots of water and nutrition; then you must do your own progression. Success and achievement and ending the worry about money will be yours but you won't even know how it happened and you will be happy within. Ready for the adventure? Be your own magnanimous legacy.

Who am I with this great power? Do I claim to be your inner psyche? No, actually, I am just one of many who have walked in your boots before you. I had nearly ruined my own potential, denied possible wisdom of a higher level, and nearly suicided.

All I can promise to offer you is my experience and the principles or tools to rebuild character, strength, and knowledge through laying out for you, my veteran walk. We are going to learn principles for relating to others and get along in this world. We are going to learn to put those principles to work above personality quirks.

Did you know that seventy-seven percent of our thoughts are negative? Why would we do that! Brains are watchdogs, in that they file the stronger neural-negative experiences as learning tools for survival. A large part of our thinking is about the future or worry about the future. We can focus on regret of the past incessantly, unless directed toward good mental health. Do you have fear, anxiety, panic, or dis-ease? Fear and worry rob you of today! They can change so quickly into obscure misunderstanding and anger. Do you carry regrets? Sadness, hatred, vengeful thoughts, bitterness, denial, and/or grief? All of those lead to your own deterioration, much more on this to follow. Those are all the past. What just happened to your current moment? Oops. Wrongful use of our time and hearts? When all along we could have the joy of that moment while life flows through us – an epiphanous, pivotal moment.

George Bernard Shaw said:

"This is the true life, the being used for a purpose recognized by YOURSELF as a mighty one; the being thoroughly worn out before you are thrown on the scrap heap; the being a force of Nature instead of a feverish selfish little clod of ailments and grievances complaining that the world will not devote itself to making you happy."

I love George, a man before his time. On this I totally agree, use yourself up, use your highest self, and it is up to only you to do both. And what follows is something I inspire to be and do.

Years of just letting my mind do as it thinks got me into an unhappy mess. The revelations in this book will break your train of thought in ways that it did mine, and put some new cars on the rail.

What if where you live and your financial security had nothing to do with happiness, whatsoever?

Another reality: YOUR MENTAL HEALTH

Only about twenty percent of Americans have a mental illness. Or one could say, "Wow, twenty percent of us in America are diagnosable as mentally ill." Which way do you want to perceive it? That is one in five of us. How many live in your home? How many people work near you? How many in your class? Whew, that's a bunch of THEM. And less than forty percent receive any treatment. That makes my chances of working with, living with, being next to an untreated mentally ill person pretty high at all times; unless it is me? If unfortunately, there is diagnosed mental health disorder requiring long term treatment, the average stay is ten years in an institution. There are places for those of us who are too far gone to not hurt ourselves and others. How many arrests include a temporary insanity plea? How many times have you wondered if you were on an edge to go nutso?

Let me remind you of some of the folks who became great and national leaders who suffered from some form of mental health issues and spent time in sanatoriums:

Edgar Allen Poe	Axl Rose	Mark Twain	Virginia Woolf
Mark Rothko	Beethoven	Hemingway	Jackson Pollock
Francis Ford Coppola	Sylvia Plath	Van Gogh	Robin Williams

Chances are, if you are reading this book, you are not perfect. We, you and I, have deficits even if we are sane. Being cognizant allows us to take a rare look into our own psyche, as to its sanity. Cognizance is the opposite of ignorance and denial or judgement. I had to become aware that my distorted thinking has, in the past kept me in distorted thinking with false security. This is a long-term humanistic therapy approach, self-driven toward new skills for regulating emotion dialectically.

Now remember, I am one of thousands out there who has distorted thinking. I played with the title for this book and liked many, but one that was too negative, however represented my feelings: Unsure of My Worth. Many contributors allowed me to form my own unmanageability. The only way that I know that my experiences have not been the way to live this life God gave me; is that I see genuinely happy people who are nice all the time, who get along with everyone and who find peace within themselves and God. See, I happened to create defects that kept my strengths and hopes from fulfillment for quite a number of years.

This book will have no use to the normal people who absorbed and adopted only good traits, the wonderful people of the world who continued to educate themselves and became wholesome and listen to God. I will say you don't need to read any further if you are one.

We Are Heartsick

———

Do this for a week; and you will find relief from them straight away!

Time for a test: (You will score yourself.)

Score 1 through 5 on how often:

1. I feel sorry for myself
2. I notice my feelings of discomfort
3. I have a pity party
4. I notice my feeling of physical or mental tension
5. I forget things almost as soon as I hear them
6. I can't keep track of all that I should
7. I experience emotion almost unconscious of it
8. I am careless
9. I run into things
10. I worry
11. I lose focus easily
12. I miss noticing things on the way to work
13. I eat without being hungry
14. I think about the future a lot
15. I discover I was not paying attention frequently
16. I do most chores automatically
17. I lament past experiences
18. I do things while someone talks to me

19. I get lost on a route somewhere
20. I focus on my goal so much I forget to notice what I am doing while getting there

There is no total score. This is your cognizance. Any true statements?

Mark Twain once said, *"You can't depend on your eyes when your imagination is out of focus."*

So many of us walk around with the same thoughts, many which are never voiced – the wonderings of it all – we are out of focus, but don't dare say. Imagination and the physical realities of life become a science to study, requiring discussion and research and invention and practice. Perception needs inspection and analysis, like you just did above.

A psychologist with whom I worked closely, whose time was long before Seven Degrees of Connection, Dr. Ward Thayer, said that if we bring up seven topics, we would find a common thread within each of us, a place we have been, someone we know, a hobby, an allergy, etc. Perhaps a disorder we have!

More importantly, the point in this chapter, Ward said, *"Ninety-nine percent of living humans probably have a clinical diagnosis, if tested!"*

"In an ideal world, humans hold themselves to the highest standards of ethics and personal integrity; unfortunately, we have rather, created a vast sea of lies, deceptions, and half-truths. We see things as we are, not as they are." – Dr. Jamal Bryant

See, we are more alike than different. Let that be a base to start, in loving others. To borrow a line from a twelve-step program: "Those are good words to design our relationships around."

Our social construction so far, is built into us as the people we were; we must start to change with deconstruction of harmful behaviors. The task of ridding someone or transcending someone from inherent morals has been previously thought to be nearly onerous. I am out to prove that theory wrong, using you.

Ten Years Ago

I asked him to shoot me. "Shoot me first, if you are going to commit suicide." I loved him that much. The ultimate sacrifice for lovers. Shakespeare wrote of love this great.

Boy, do I know how wrong that is. Now. I was 'fooling myself' about reality at the time.

A fifth grader was quoted in the newspaper the week I am writing this section of the book:

> *"Don't do things that will make you stupid."*

I did not recognize the signs, which I am including here because I absolutely do not want to see anyone else go through this kind of loss:

Increasing Substance Abuse	Withdrawing
Giving away possessions	Anger or Irritability
Isolating	Depressed Mood

I have the toe tag hanging over my desk as I write. My husband eventually did complete his suicide by carbon monoxide poisoning, just as I had aborted him from doing several times. The blue smoke in the garage was thick. It housed his national award-winning Pontiac GTO muscle car, and our newest silver big rig, a Suburban, the most prized of his seven cars. At the time, 'there was some little spark plug issue', his rationale for running the car with all the garage doors tightly shut. I believed his 'spark plug issue story' (naïve as I am about cars) repeatedly and 'rescued' him from inhaling too much carbon monoxide a number of times. I wasn't stupid, but I wanted so to deny there was suicidal intent in my marriage-vowed-to man. I would open the garage doors and cuss him out for not realizing how much carbon emission there was in his man cave escape/garage.

Then he added alcohol. As much as his father denies alcoholism or even a drinking problem in the family history, my husband's uncle, was alcoholic, testified by his daughter. Genetically, my spouse was predispositioned to addiction to drink, the Disease of Alcohol. You cannot develop physical immune genes to this disease, but you can live with it emotionally, if you have the right wisdom. God gives us challenges through illness and times of doubt. Alcohol and depression were his challenges, and mine, too as a wife.

I was the codependent to the love of my life. I discovered I had to change my thinking to survive my own suicide thoughts. That, my friends, is why I wrote you a book.

If you could fMRI my brain, you would see actual reverberations of color in my nodules which have altered to hues of activity in the good and joyful parts now, more so than ten years ago. This has not been done without great pains and massive growth in character rebuilding. Fortunately, it can be done in leaps and bounds! Welcome to my book.

The OTHER Serenity Prayer:

Please grant me the serenity to stop beating myself up for not doing things perfectly, the courage to forgive myself because I always try my best, and the wisdom to know that I am a good person with a kind heart.

Addiction: Something done as an automated response to a stimuli; a learned behavior that has become habitual.

This book is not about suicide, addiction, or death, but about recovery and loving life, and choosing. I just had to start there to explain my need to change me. Stay with me and you will not believe how I make you think. Your levels of wisdom will rise as miracles pop before your eyes. Just watch. It is gradual until you see it and it wows you. Just wait. Come, turn the page.

Scenario: It took almost six years, but finally I felt I was confident and established. I wish I could say something like, "The road has been long" or 'The path was very winding." and dismiss the agony. But in my case, it has been straight from one place to another, progressive, positive, ever learning with amends for the past, and only warm memories holding onto my heart now. Life is a tough lesson. You take the test first, fail, and then learn the lesson.

I have changed. I belong in the world, in all cliques and on all teams, in a restaurant alone. I no longer hate myself or shy away from anything. I meet ugliness with acceptance, obscure bullying with understanding, crime with interest, and allow others to just be; to just be in my way, change lanes directly in front of me, live their disadvantaged, homeless life, or sweet surroundings, to brag, show bias, hate, and condemn. It is no longer my job to make the world and each of the people around me better – that actually belongs to a Higher Power I found. The only thing I have changed is my head – the way I see and hear and listen and feel and act. No Reactions anymore.

Let me tell you how to pull serenity from your heart and soul and universe. I know how. Yay!

And it is nothing you have to do or add to your "to do" list. In fact, you will take away from your list...your list of time stealers, deadlines, and must haves.

We will rid you of woulds, shoulds, and coulds. You will omit the word "but" from your sentences and paragraphs. And instead of having to do everything, you will feel privileged to 'get to' do everything.

Sound like a happy place? It is. I have the secret, the key to world peace. Follow me.

Smith Wigglesworth, the world's greatest Evangelist, to the universal question, *"How can we have great faith?"* he would reply: *"Great faith is the product of great fights. Great testimonies are the outcome of great tests. Great triumphs can only come out of great trials."*

Not You Too?!

"Knowing yourself is the beginning of all wisdom." – Aristotle

Wisdom is this. You know a tomato is a fruit. Wisdom is not putting it in a fruit salad.

So many discoveries in my research about the brain, it is even thought that someday behavioral therapy or cognitive recovery may be moot points as we are more able to scientifically change our brain chemicals, but meanwhile…

> *Each day is a new beginning –*
> *Another chance*
> *To learn more about ourselves,*
> *To care more about others,*
> *To laugh more than we did,*
> *To accomplish more*
> *Than we thought we could,*
> *To be more than we were before.*
> *- Kathleen Cardinal*

I am going to mess with your formulation of thoughts. I intend to give you new things to think about and take your wisdom up a notch or five, in levels.

I realized that the visions that God had for me, were not what he saw me doing! I was a conundrum!

Many of you are in a place that is unsatisfactory. This is not where you wanted to be at this age or ever. It may be a place that is harming your psyche, your body, or your true self. I would like to say I am going to help you fulfill your dreams but you will do that yourself. I am your guide and we are starting now. I hope that you will be intensely alive after practicing the guidelines discussed.

Your younger self thought that you could be anything or anybody you want to be. Why not just really be who you are first, and then figure out the rest?

Me? I believe that God intended my life to be of high quality and joy filled. I expected I would be taught by the light, without my own reactionary behaviors injected on that incoming light! Oops.

Who interrupted it? Me. ME. ME. That's who! Millions of writers and philosophers discovered a need to rethink and learn before me. Like them, this book is about that. It is also about HOW!

Emancipate yourselves from mental slavery. None but ourselves can free our minds. − Bob Marley

I needed to be rebuilt, starting from ABC, addition and subtraction, bone development, you name it. This book will give some renewal and recovery to your mind. Nutrition and exercise come from my dedication and action to my body. Why not mental clarity from dedication and actionary thoughts to your mind?

Your brain is an organ made up of many physical parts. Your mind is made up of the activity you either are fed, or you choose to allow to bounce around in those parts.

I had a large void − it was the absence of enough knowledge, courage and wisdom to know the difference. It has taken me years to find the correct direction and practice 'better ways'. My life seemed to be in constant transitional thinking, adapting to stimuli, phasing in and out of dimensions, unsure whether to be God's child or an alcoholic's minion. See, alcoholics sell stuff we don't need. Like a porn store; they offer actions and words we don't need! There is a difference between a woman who pretends to take action in score of deference. I was there many days. I was not living the life I wanted or life I might have. Even my imagination was stymied and not fully developed, just functioning on the cusp of potential – an imposter in my own skin.

The manuscript I have pulled together will offer elevated hope along with methods of getting out of the doldrums which I had told myself was my life. I am proposing that we together, obliterate the self-imposed boundaries that keep us from good. Or, Hell, from just being normal!

Dr. Daniel Amen, author, offers sage advice: *"Get your brain right and your mind will follow."*

Also, God expresses through the written psalms: *"What greater benefit could there be than sharing wisdom and contributing to other souls' healing."* I like that so I decided to publish.

John Stuart Mill claimed that *"Women mostly, have been coaxed, cajoled, shoved, and squashed into a series of feminine contortions for so many centuries, that it now quite impossible to define their natural abilities and aspirations."*

That, that, was what had happened. I succumbed to negative limitations – freedom, I thought, but with my <u>own promulgated covenant of internal constraints.</u>

Dr. Alan Muskett, cardiac/plastic surgeon, (yes, that is right) quotes:

"Vanity, self-pity, resentment, and a victim mentality are all self-inflicted wounds that deprive us of the richness of experience."

A prayer I say for myself:

God, You are capable of all things,
The Prince of Peace, the Almighty Healer and Protector.
Spirit, please guide my thoughts, heart, and actions so my life is a testament to you.
Lord, grant me patience, selflessness, and peace.
Healer,
Cleanse me from the evil thoughts of selfishness that so easily creep into my mind.
Jesus, protect my heart, keep it pure and full of love and honor for my family.
Spirit,
Guide my decisions with your ultimate knowledge
and remind me that your way is best.
May I be an example of your love and forgiveness today and forever more.

Reader, I am going to suggest much to you. Your work with me (this book) will be the testament to your change and growth. I suggest you read that prayer out loud, even if you are a nonbeliever. It is just the first of many exercises I will use to persuade you to change up.

"Often, people attempt to live their lives backwards: They try to have more things, or more money, in order to do more of what they want so that they will be happier. The way it actually works is the reverse. You must first be who you really are, then, do what you need to do, in order to have what you want."

Margaret Young

Wasn't This On
Your Gift Registry?

Do you know what you value? Do you know what assets you have that you value? Write a list of assets that you want from others in order to associate with them.

Some of the assets you value in others:

Friendliness	Does not drink in excess	Likes music	Organized
Pleasant	Loves Family	Ability to care for self	Nice
Kind	Smart with money	Generosity	Strength
Loves nature	Loves children	Good with kids	Nice looking
Neat	Honest	Listens	Hygiene is good
Good family	Does not smoke	Healthy	Faces their emotion
Works out	Has a job	Enjoys movies	Good in bed
Acts freely	Generous	Likes to take walks	Likes to travel
Worships God	Patience		

More: _____ _____ _____

_____ _____ _____ _____

Once you finish the list of assets in others, add your own assets to this list, your sister's, your parents', your best friend's, a teacher's, others you admire. I suggest listing one hundred.

James Michener once said, *"If a man happens to find himself...he has a mansion which he can inhabit with dignity all the days of his life."*

Now take inventory of you. Which of these assets do you have 100%? 90%? Which ones are you 50% good at?

So I ask you, how can you expect your friends and relatives to have them all 100% of the time, if you can't fulfill that perfection? Expectations.

Those values are your worth. If they are few, you think little of yourself. If you answer 100% to all, your ego is waaaaay out of whack. If you are not honest and fair to ALL others, you fail at some of them.

If we have values and ACT in accordance with them, we become worth something to ourselves. And we won't take less in our worlds. We will live right and good.

Are you a precious child of God? He, He, gives you so much value already. Keep in honest check what you think of yourself.

If I am going to do something with my life that matters, then I need to start with a true heart.

Do you know that your characteristics affect your biological makeup? I will tell you a great deal about this as we go.

Get up tomorrow morning and do what is right. Get up Thursday morning and do what is right. Friday, do only what is right.

Never let your values leave by the wayside.

Isn't that simple? As they say, "Duh."

My assets were dwindling. I was losing my self-worth.

Riding on the cusp, the tail feathers of a man, of anyone, a spouse, a parent; is asking to be belittled, negated, demeaned, etc. It is worldwide and an epidemic of inferiority. I was reacting to someone else's feeling or mood, their opinion or perhaps, their priorities. I discovered it could be a rebellious teenager lashing out, a spouse angry and hostile from his day, or a baby's profuse crying, whose tailfeathers I acclimated to react to. My reactions were running my life. When feeling trapped or unhealthy or fearful, I had so many negative trains of thought that included bitterness and resentments, they tied my stomach in knots. Fear makes us into people we do not want to be.

I no longer have to cosign that which others dish out. I now get to remain loving and kind, regardless of their escalated behavior in my presence.

Someone who is demoralized feels hopeless. I was close. The world I knew and things I loved were feeling unreachable. My interests dissolved. I was not involved with hobbies; didn't care if I paid attention to news, personally devalued. It was getting rough for me to see my way to be social. I was devastated and grieving loss of a husband who had been wonderful.

To become ourselves:

List also some of the assets that a relationship must have:

Forgiveness	Compromising	Empathy	Support
Share yourself	Share feelings		Confidence in each other
Mutual interests	Reciprocity	Laughter	Give what you want to receive

So first, we each must learn what our own values are.

Let's get serious about what I said. List your assets:

I'll start you cause I know you did not do this on the previous page.

1. I'm a reader
2. I'm pretty nice

3. I'm loyal to friends
4. I'm fair minded
5. I'm open minded
6. I'm sweet
7.
8.

Come on, Man, I'm not going to write them all for you, but come up with forty assets you hold.

I'll throw out a few more to get you thinking about yours:

Patient   Your turn…
Smile a Lot
Happy   _____
Gracious   _____
Exciting   _____
Fun   _____
Good Friend   _____
Sexy   _____
Thankful   _____
Trustworthy   Okay, now add some assets of your
A Friend   friends or parents, or brother-in-
                           law, boss, etc.

Upbeat   Determined
Caring   Challenging
Devote   Humanitarian
Intentional   Considerate
Honest   Giving
Kind   Good Looking
Indulgent   Easy Going
Stable   Not Sharp Tongued

Brief

Blessed

Involved

Polite

Always Civil

_____

_____

_____

_____

_____

Now add valued characteristics
of people you know about,
stars, superheroes, ministers,
champions, etc.

Dedicated

Beautiful

Lives with Grace

Spiritual

Strong of Body

Wickedly Funny

Hot

Interesting

Smart

Polished

Elegant

Debonair

Suave

I will start you:

Trustworthy

Honesty

Never Swears

Easy to Laugh

Come on, add more characteristics:

_____

_____

Caring

Neat

Likes to bowl

Good cook

Always on time

Knows her history

Gorgeous brown eyes

Small feet

Understands art

Great skin

Driven

Courteous

Calm

Humorful

Laughs easy

Respects others

Thinks on her feet

Very giving

People person

Authentic

True

Genuine

Spontaneous

Morality	Giving
Goodness	Communitive
Kindness	Accepting of others
Oneness with God	Compassionate
Loves unconditionally	Good friends
Intuitive	Can be counted on
Loves to Play	Make the world better
Fun loving	Fair and square
Appreciates being loved	And then some
Open Minded	_____
Kind	_____
Considerate	_____
Thoughtful of others and then some	

Now my question is, what keeps you from holding all these assets you admire and value? We will help you find what keeps you from being your best self. First you have to be aware that you like these things about other people, and explore the things you like about yourself.

Who do you respect? Let's approach our search for our personal defects of character, by looking at good characteristics.

To do so, I look to others I respect and why I like them.

Be bluntly honest. Yes, I like shiny hair and nice pecs. Vanity about hygiene is admirable, yes?

Think of your brother, friends, ministers, the salon lady, Michelle Obama, Lucy, and your broker. What traits do they exude that you would like to own? Perhaps you admire that they can do or be something that you can never achieve like, a great public speaker, a talent that you wish you could hone, etc.

Do you strive to be the genuine article that God put you on earth to be? We are usually gripped by high school age, by God's existence; at least to the point of asking about characteristics to live in God's realm. We are testing out our moral, doctoral, and love personality facets. What rules our heart by then may be unceasing. Are we Christian? Do we practice narcissism? How are we fulfilling our hearts, souls, identity and behavior? Do we renew with God every day? Do we have principles?

A typical practice we all get into is desiring. Or judgement sorts our characteristics (another chapter). There is a newer psychological diagnosis, RCD: Rejection Centered People. It is either love or hate; light or dark; humble or hate filled. We condone or concede too much. Those are stern characteristics, each one. The only treatment is humility, not just in our conduct, but moreover in our thoughts.

If you were to write a time-warped letter to yourself as an adult from you as a child, I imagine it would go like this: (You fill in the blanks.)

Dear _____ (Fill in your name):

When you were little you were so loved. Big people saw you as beautiful. They imagined great things from you. As you grew to school age, you started to learn things. Every minute of every day was an adventure, exploration, new learning, eye opening, and fun, for the most part. You imagined you would grow up feeling just as you did as a child – loved, healthy, other people caring for you, full of experimentation, discovery, and with much inquisitiveness. You envisioned your bigger self as popular, learned, skilled, able, perhaps flying, seeing the world, trying all activities, honing skills, capable of anything, having your own children, marrying. Money, or lack of it, did not even enter the picture. (As we, you and me, did not know about the 'economy' then.)

I pictured you as happy, satisfied, useful, secure, loved, and nurtured, ever developing into a wonderful adult.

I predicted you would use your creativity, intelligence, handiness, be wise, and all knowing, and keep this secure feeling we had as a child.

I saw for you loving what you do, in a vocation, having perfect relationships with every priest, pauper, banker, nanny, teenager, God, and sailor. I never saw a day ahead that you were not financially secure. When I imagined you, it was in a warm home with no cares, food aplenty, and people who cherished one another around you; always healthy, active, and sharing.

I prayed for your happiness, your growth, your development, and your evolution to be everything it could.

That is what I wanted. What I seem to have gotten instead is (YOUR NAME HERE) grown up but not quite sophisticated in everything; a somewhat whiney and complaining person, in need of more.

I see an unhappy and insecure man/woman, unfulfilled in home life and relationships. I see an older person not honest with himself; and I see a cheater, fooling others, somewhat committing, maybe small, but still, most of the seven deadly sins; maybe even trying to control surroundings rather than looking to God, who really does have control of all of it. Wisdom has not come to you and perhaps never will. We, you and I, could die tomorrow without seeing the African sunset or carving in wood, or hiking the Appalachian trail. Where did you lose me? Do you know? Why do you live in so much fear?

Love,

Me

P.S. I will not accept repugnant behavior from you any more.

Self-Worth vs Ego

—————

Self Check:

When in self-pity, do you:

Wallow, cry out, pout, recognize feelings, accept, collapse, or attract attention from others? Work your thought process through here. Know yourself. Know your physical and physiological reactions to self-pity. Take this time to review your behavior and consider what could you do differently. Self-pity keeps me in the problem, not the solution.

ISM: I Sabotage Myself.

If I am caught up in self-pity or judgement or self-will – I am in malarkey! These hold no goodness or truth. If you are having a bad day, say so to yourself, start again and remember you have survived 100% of your previous bad days. You get about five minutes of self-pity after intense devastating news. It is a shock, most likely you are still standing, then take care of the emergencies toward safety and security, realize this is your life in truth in front of you. The challenge in front of you is to feel the feelings and stay sane. Be a shoulder for others. Acknowledge that this is a truth, and that this moment too, shall pass through your life. Then, begin solution.

Nelson Mandela once said:

> *"Our deepest fear is not that we are inadequate. Our deepest fear is that we are powerful beyond measure. It is our light, not our*

darkness, that most frightens us. You're playing 'small' does not serve the world. There is nothing enlightened about shrinking so that other people won't feel insecure around you. We are all meant to shine as children do. It's not just in some of us; it is in everyone. And as we let our own lights shine, we unconsciously give other people permission to do the same. As we are liberated from our own fear, our presence automatically liberates others."

Beyond My Wildest Dreams

Remember when you were little and stared up, finding shapes in the clouds? I am doing that again. On purpose. I am happy within my spiritual world. I've found it again. I've found my wildest dreams to be coming true. And it had nothing to do with my dream of living in New York designing windows for Macy's and traveling abroad till I was discovered and then famous for something; or became that well sought-after guru or actress. (Wildest hopes from my childhood.)

Practical elements are as prominent as theoretical ones. Our ideology can change if nurtured correctly.

My happiness and dreaming and hoping again, has to do with God. I want to live according to His guidelines in the 21st century, A.D. A lovely acronym that induces me to think: "M A G I C: Me Accepting that God is In Charge."

My father's alcoholism took him to his death. My brother's alcoholism contributed to his cancerous death. Another brother's alcoholism separated him from his young family of four children and a wonderful wife. My husband's alcoholism took him to his suicidal death.

Alcoholic father, extremely codependent mother. Am I a Twisted Sister?

And then there were eight kids caught in this family where we each thought we knew how to control and fix everybody else; not ourselves!

Yet, my family achieved great things. Dexterity to survive must have driven us. Our family of ten had a huge beautiful home. We sought higher learning which included doctors, nurses, a pharmacist, each excelling in their area. My alcoholic father was town Mayor, Fire Chief, a First Responder, active on the school board, a very talented welder and carpenter – building fire trucks, tankers, playground equipment, and was surrounded with friends.

We were a prestigious family. I grew into a prestigious, proud woman, built a beautiful home on a beautiful acreage overlooking a beautiful small lake, edging on a beautiful city park. My beautiful husband and I achieved and amassed awards, trophies, certificates, became board members, and fund raisers, and were surrounded by beautiful friends. Beautiful. My wonderful man, in my wonderful life, country club friends, in a new home we designed, all taken by alcohol. It began by upsetting our lives, relationships, friends, family, job security and took a huge psychological toll on both of us.

While addiction loomed over us, we each regressed into a life of hanging on. A cloud of tension often hung over all these parts of our lives. I lived hiding my innards, hiding the 'Hell' in my home, hiding domestic violence in the final years of my husband's alcoholism and depression. I hid my spirit, and suppressed my devotion to God. Hiding and pretending that all was well. I had yet to learn the fact that my family members were not alcoholics because of me! It is about a disease. Alcoholics act, and we around them, react. We want to do what a sick person can't see or do for themselves; felt forced, in fact, to react, forgetting our own health. We wait with tension to react. We strive for perfect obedience to an actively sick person to an end of insecurity, for me anyway. Their patterns result in us making negative patterns and the dynamics of the disease dominate and spiral around us. When we are in unmanageability, insanity looks like sanity to us. I was living in my own distorted thinking based on fear and in search of false security, and following the illusions I created. Owning fearfulness is such a waste, I now know! When our motive is fear, we cannot give love out. Remember that.

I remember wishing I could be in the witness protection program.

I want to honor the people that I loved but in order to tell you what aided in forming my reliance on a disease were those people I loved who:

Lost their license, over turned their truck, were arrested for peeing in public on a storefront, had their belongings strewn on the front lawn, put a cop in the hospital while resisting arrest, had affairs, physically fought with former friends and were a public nuisance. There was much more. Those are some highlights.

− I was humiliated and shamed. I reacted to their behaviors like they were my own actions.

I was still trying to gain control of my life when others about me were failing. Pretending normalcy became my thing. Superficial appearance to others was so important. I was fooling myself more than anyone else!

I was a manipulator. I thought I was wiser than God and I could change others − especially those in the throes of a disease. Yes, an illness. Could I cure the flu? Cancer? Alcoholism? Wake up, Girl, to your own reality!

"Notice! Notice, Girl! Your capability to change yourself is at an impasse. You are not completely available to adopt the edifices for living well. You are not even putting in the effort, deciding slothily that you do not have what it takes. You have succumbed to life forces not your own."

It takes energy to act like you 'can't do it'.

We all have hopes and wishes at the back of our brains which we never entertain as possible. Let's do a little life check-up. You already have gifts, passion, and values which give you a sense of purpose. Let's give a serious mind to our bucket lists, as if the items on it were promises to really do. That takes your purpose into hope!

Urgent message necessary at this time: We love the alcoholic. We hate the disease, the state of unthinking, that alcohol put the loved one in.

I learned now to meet the alcoholic where he is. If he is uproariously laughing, take joy in his laughter. If he is doing harm, stay safe, leave. You cannot do anything FOR him/her but give them a blanket in the front yard. Detach and rely on God to take care of that other human and keep yourself safe.

I had to learn and relearn that I was in life for myself, no matter how attached I thought I was to my parents, my husband, or a friend.

Letter from a Bad Ass Acting Alcoholic while sober, in a relationship:

Dear Person-that-I-love:

I know I display unacceptable behaviors while drinking. And I drink to be high. I get drunk. This disease is highly weird. I often don't realize I am drinking to be high. I am just hanging out with a drink in my hand and before I know it, I am slurring and stumbling. The disease turned me into a monster in front of you and others. I don't want to be that monster. My body demands that I get another drink. I don't decide to have a drink. The bar looks like the place I can find something – some comfort. And a good high from alcohol makes me forget any other responsibilities, my boss's scrutinizing eyes, your scowl when I am not home on time, the engine light that is on, and the fact that I am overweight. It looks pretty attractive to get drunk over and over and over.

Yes, it appears I have lost interest in the two of us, that I have lost interest or have the time for my mechanic hobby, lost time to paint the house, and have no energy or awake time to help you out with household chores.

In the morning, I feel ugly – I am not pleasant to you. I am sick to my stomach every morning. I do not have energy to apply to my job, and I doubt I am a very good driver with drowsy eyes. I don't know what my feelings could even be. They are buried under a foggy mind. You are seeking to draw me out, invest my emotions back into our relationship, while I am just hoping that the disease doesn't happen again today. Then it does. There is no intentional forgetfulness. The disease is insistent that I feed it. I have no feelings that are not fogged over with a cloud. I cannot see clearly enough to be sincere. My emotional self has left my personality, what is left of that!

I know I act badly toward you especially. I stupidly trust that you will always be there, like a mom, and pick up after me and clean up the vomit. I actually don't care if you do or don't; I just walk away, not having a thought that you are doing that for me. I could care less who cleans it up or if it gets cleaned up. I just want to nurse the alcoholism demands within my body. If I were in my right mind, I don't know why you could even love who I have become. I will myself to change things every day when I am not drinking, but my car will not drive past the bar. I purposefully go that way and there I am again. It is like it is a passenger telling me, "It's okay. You really want to do this, so go in there again."

I am so low, with no self-respect, that I can't imagine one thing that could change my path. It would be incredulous to believe that.

I don't want you to dislike me or fall out of love with me, but I cannot bring out the old me. Scientists tell us that I have burned out some cells in my brain, fried it. I think that is true. My wherewithal to be a good person just does not work. I doubt I am even an important partner to you anymore. I would not blame you for leaving our home and me. I am no longer treating you fairly – I can't! Alcohol calls to me. That little high I get when I first set out to slither into numbness, is the best thing that happens to me all day; I want more of it, so I will have another drink, I am chasing the demon who mostly alludes me, 'cept for that little period of high numbness.

In my head, You are the most important person I know. I respect that you don't want to live with a drunk. I no longer respect myself at all. I respect that you are trying to hold what is left of our relationship together. I know you are a good person who is trying to find your spouse again; with your manipulative gestures and encouraging words. You are working so hard for something I cannot find. I so enjoyed what we had and how we started out this marriage. It was fun and you are fantastic. The cycle of disappointing you and not living up to my own standards is so debilitating, I drink because of that. I drink for any excuse. Your efforts at stridently forcing the disease to go away are noticed, but I laugh at them because I already know the disease wins. I would love to be again the one you want someday. When the demon gets out of my car and off my shoulder, maybe I can recover. I am lost to it. There is no reason you should stay here during this. I will miss you but when I am sober, I am aware that I am messing up your life too.

Signed,
Your loved one, the drunk

Alcohol had weighed in as an eccentric zealot which in truth, never meant to alter my being, but as you read, I did it as a reaction to alcoholism in my family. I had scripted and honed my reactionary thinking around a disease that had nothing to do with me. It was inconsequential to who I have the potential to be in the skin I live in. I had allowed my own devastation. I had let someone else's alcoholism and depression insult my thinking, destroy my truths, accuse me falsely and punish my self-worth. I did that! I gave the disease that power. As a reaction to someone else and a disease. I am learning that I don't have to have a bad day just because someone I love is struggling. If I pause for a moment before focusing on someone else's bad mood, I may find that I have feelings of my own that deserve attention.

Forty-three percent of Americans (close to half of us) have been affected by the disease of alcohol, and eighty-three percent of American adults, suffer in silence, yet have been exposed to alcohol abuse in the family.

For every person addicted to alcohol or drugs, it is estimated that approximately another four, usually immediate family members, are directly affected.

Our history is a truth and we must reminisce only in truth, not in construing it or blaming it. It just happened that way for me, or you.

We now, get to learn boundaries, what is right, what is true, and what is in God's hands. We get to own up, redo, face fears with grace. I am now refusing to give way to alcohol's lead. Yay. I had a metamorphosis! And now I will never relinquish my serenity.

It is key to learn boundaries. Hopefully as you glean tactics for a better life from this book you will design appropriate boundaries to know you wear a hula hoop in space around you, and there ends others' influence and advice. People love to hear your experience, strength and hope, but not your troubles or attempts to control their lives. The boundary you establish through learning also keeps one from absorbing what others throw our way into then becoming our issues. Their anger, verbal insolence, or needy traits are not ours. Put the only door knob on your side of the door and stop letting others walk through on their time and step on us like a doormat. From volatile bosses to unfriendly store clerks, we are going to be exposed to insecurities that are not ours; we may think we must rescue or that we must appease all to peace, or that it is our responsibility to make others happy. Boundary. Choose to not engage. I had to start with the word "ABORT". I learned to abort from picking up shit others lay down at my feet, pardon my euphemism. I choose now to abort from reactions. I leave their condemning verbiage or severe looks, in their air, not my hula hoop. My boundaries are clear – appropriateness only. It is a sweet life when we take a look at what others dish out and do not react.

If we grew up where there was no repair, we might not know that we can.

I Want What I Want and I Want It Now

This is not a workbook but you are going to work a bit.

What do you want?

Your troubled spouse, child, etc. cannot be in your answer. What do YOU want?

Your life is about you. What you want. I had nearly perished in a sea of alcohol. When mature, we see our old drives to get what we thought we wanted were warped. I was using: nagging, manipulating, begging, judging others, crying, yelling, condemning, complaining, and demanding respect from the one I professed to love the most. The letter previous shows that addiction could not muster a correct response. Respect comes through able example, not from those vain attempts to snag it or show power. We do not need power to feel useful and happy. Goodness sake.

What do you want?

Do you want to be loved by all? To be distinguished? To be famous? Honored? Powerful? Dominate and rule? Have material possessions; pomp and circumstance; lots of money? Most of those are self-declared prisons and the methods of achieving those if only desired and not earned through hard work, are perilous moments each.

There are permanent satisfactions of living right which no heap of possessions can provide.

True ambition and work are the deep desire to live usefully and walk humbly under the grace of God. I find it is best to be in gratitude at all times for all that you have. There can be no wants within those beliefs.

I have a couple of quotes I refer to, to keep myself in check when the desire to have more and bigger and better haunts me.

> *It is preoccupation with possessions that prevents us from living nobly.* –Thoreau

(That phrase seems incongruent within itself unless you understand it.)

> *Any so-called material thing that you want is merely a symbol: you want it not for itself, but because it will contend your spirit for the moment.* –Mark Twain

> *An object in possession seldom retains the same charm that it had in pursuit.* –Pliny the Younger

> *Possessions are usually diminished by possession.* –Nietzsche

What do you want?

Did our distorted drives and self-constructed prisons and egos give us that fame or honor or respect? Or did we have to use the previous paragraph to feed our insecurities? What we need: food, clothing and shelter, are met. Am I right?

Is what you want the best for a good life or are you lying to yourself about that too?

We are sometimes so obsessed with having a collection, gathering new, upping the Joneses, owning more, or appearing rich, that we forget internal nobleness, where we are right with ourselves. Right with ourselves - that has nothing to do with anybody else or anything we gather. It is an internal peace of knowing contentedness. And it has more to do with our sharing our wealth than showing our wealth!

Malcom Muggeridge once said: *"The most terrible thing about materialism, even more terrible that its proneness to violence, is its boredom, from which sex, alcohol, drugs, all devices for putting out the accusing light of reason and suppressing the unrealizable aspirations of love, offer a prospect of deliverance."*

And Bob Dylan (You'd be surprised how much insight there is in his lyrics.)

"Money doesn't talk. It swears."

Love vs Self Hate

I had to get over my shame.

"Shame on you." I heard from my Mom, the Catholic nuns, the neighbor lady, and my Dad when I did something naughty. "You should be ashamed of yourself." was the other phrase condemning me to Hell since I was born. Why wouldn't my mind be twisted with shame and humiliation? My elders condemned me. (Oh, I absolutely know they 'did the best they could with what they had and knew at the time'. – You will read this quote again and again from me.)

Shame can be summed up as the sense that we have committed a violation of a societal norm. Because I did not learn the Guardian Angel prayer explicitly – I mumbled through that last part, I had shame. It took my worthiness down (another) peg. Of course, I felt sad that I failed. Another nick in the bed post of self-worthlessness. I am not a second-hand person, but I put myself down as though one!

Shame, guilt, and self-recrimination are not real things! Surprise. Yet, I owned them. I even learned from my elders to shame myself, instill guilt upon myself when I broke their intangible rules.

We may have been harshly criticized by others or lost perspective and become overly hard on ourselves. You may know the Psalms...Twenty-Seven states...*'he will not abandon me to the desires of my foes...I shall see the Lord's goodness in the land of the living.'* Sweet passages to listen to

Shame has been referred to as the mother of all emotions. That is an appropro application of a noun, 'mother'. It represents an authority figure whom we impenetrably believed and obeyed. Often shame (an emotional, self-inflicted feeling) is instilled in us. It is like it has its own energy and brain lobe. It doesn't; WE give it that power.

Docile [doc·ile] *adj.* Submissive. Ready to accept control or instruction. "The dog was very docile around children."

At this point, we lost our childlike view of goodness, freedoms, and self-worth. We have learned now to live by how others judge us. We have learned to withdraw from self-assurance and decision making on our own. We may begin to lie or cheat to have a winning outcome. Our actions now will be under a cloud. And it was falsely handed to us! It creates an environment where we want to conform to others, hide our little indiscretions from authority figures, manipulate, cope in life. SICK. This persona borders on a psychological diagnosis! I may have 'tried' really hard, but it was with outdated and useless attempts which I had not discerned as 'harmful' yet.

Many people fail to become what they were predestined to be. Most often, the reason is because they fear what people will think of them. How sad. Other people's values and judgements keep us from our potential. They are demented and cannot possibly know our truth. Again, how sad. It is sad that we even listen to this output. Rather, we each determine our destinies along with God. I would like to tell you to never listen when you encounter a nay-sayer. Earl Nightingale once said, *"We become what we think about."* Do not think about the negative lore of another's judgement. Your mind needs to be clear of negativity.

We will, in this book, be marrying our minds and our behaviors to principles of hope, intelligence, and kind behavior. I hope to assist you, a co-regulation of self, if you will. The promises of this blend, the psychology of it, will result in a life developed to full potential with happiness as an aside! First, we must introspectively look at what we have been experiencing in our reaction to stimuli, downtrodden ways that are not satisfying and secondarily we will look at deleting those habits from our conscious personalities by conditioning and reinforcement, and finally, refining all thoughts to positive moments in our ensuing years.

Try defining shame as you know it. Here are some words from Webster's:

Disgrace

Embarrassment

Mortification

Humiliation

Self-disgust

Cover Up of Wrong Doing

Rejected

Judged as Impure

Oh, Webster gives it a good twenty lines to explain the horrors of shame. Another is 'violated'. Let's go with that: If told, as a young and defenseless child, that we are rejected and should be mortified, we learn the horrible wash of feelings associated with isolation, anger and bitterness, cynicism, and condemnation of self.

When we learn to feel foolish, rejected, and blame ourselves for things others see as wrongful, it becomes part of our persona to experience s h a m e. Maybe to the point of disliking, even hating ourselves; to the point of lashing out at, anyone who could humiliate us - before they do - thus becoming violent or abusive ourselves!

I was so low, that I let a store clerk, a janitor, a child, visibly rattle my shame quotient and retreated into undeserved guilt and self-condemnation!

A healthy brain-set will put the correct perspective on SHAME if we know how to gain that healthy brain-set. Being sad should kick in the reminder to rather be around supportive and loving people, and reach out from sadness. Having shame because we acted poorly, maybe in anger or hurt, should help us realize that does not work and kick start our cognizance of overreaction. We all have a deeper core of sensibility – however sometimes we need to have exposure and mentoring by others to bring out the goodness or gain the intelligence.

That in itself is the damage done to our psyches. A notch in our brain has made us guilt ridden. Add up all the guilt-ridden occasions we get into as a kid, and we soon have a habitual self-instilled bad image of ourselves. Can we overcome all this humiliation before we become thriving adults? Can we become healthy thriving adults with this t-shirt with S H A M E written across it? Many of us end up wearing this and being more than humble in situations. We have learned well to take the blame. You know folks that overly say, "I'm sorry". The millennium babies may not be so ridiculed, however baby boomers still make up most of the population, so you do the math.

We are fledgling about trying to rise against our own humiliation and shame. Some of us go full boat and condemn others to try to make our self-worth viable. So, what are we left to do with our Sick Ego? Here are somethings some things I had not thought about but realize they were definitely a part of my make-up. Take a review and check off anything that resembles your behavior:

Guile
Guile [guile] n. Treacherous cunning; skillful deceit. Particular skill and cleverness in tricking or deceiving people. "Considerable guile was involved in the transaction."

Obtuse
Obtuse [ob·tuse] adj. 1. Lacking quickness of perception or intellect. 2. Characterized by a lack of intelligence or sensitivity. "An obtuse remark." 3. Not distinctly felt. "An obtuse pain."

Intrepid
Intrepid [in·trep·id] adj. 1. Resolutely courageous; fearless. Persistent in the pursuit of something. "A team of intrepid explorers."

Acrimonious
Acrimonious [ac·ri·mo·ni·ous] adj. 1. Bitter and sharp in language or tone; rancorous: "An acrimonious debate between the two candidates."

Demure
Demure [de·mure] adj. 1. Modest and reserved in manner or behavior. "Despite her demure appearance, she is an accomplished mountain climber."

Divisive
Divisive [di·vi·sive] adj. Creating dissension or discord; Causing disagreement or hostility within a group so that it is likely to split. "Divisive politics."

Pervasive
Pervasive [per·va·sive] adj. Having the quality or tendency to pervade or permeate. "The pervasive odor of garlic."

A few of us realize the mistake that has been made in our maturing growth. We are able to separate behavior from who we are. Like separating out alcoholism from the person who has the disease.

This is a truth I want you to remember: When dependent on alcohol, people forget they are a human being. And a codependent on the person who has alcoholism reacts to all the untruths spewed by the alcoholic. Gees!

Even Hitler knew he could do nothing without the cooperation and willing submission of Jews, and he seized the opportunity to rectify – in his mind - the Jewish problem.

The power, the glory, and the kingdom did not belong to Hitler, and does not belong to alcohol or the alcoholic. That was one of the first principles I had to learn to release myself from the burden of a falsely held dogma.

The tighter you squeeze, the less you have. –Thomas Merton

At this point, I would advise you to understand Humility and Humiliation.

Humiliate: v. debase, chasten, mortify, make a fool of, put to shame, dishonor, self-effacing, depress, conquer, make shamed, disgrace, embarrass

Humble: a. un-self-conscious, tolerant, unpresuming, manageable, free from hubris of pride, gentle, without arrogance, tame

You see Humiliate is a verb (action) behavior. Humble is an adjective applicable to conscious thought.

So do you want to behave in a manner that others judge?

Or do you want to contain your actions, and think it through with kindness and non-egotistically?

You decide.

Humbleness can protect us from escalated hurt, brought on by pride, ego, better-than-thou attitudes.

Humiliation takes on what others judge us to be. If we don't go where the thugs hang out, we won't become a thug or a victim. To be humble frees us from confronting other's behaviors when it is not our business, and keeps us from confronting other's egos - where biases form and attitudes deteriorate and negative thoughts linger like gators in a marsh; leaving plaque on our souls.

Who told you that you cannot go up to the lecturer or the priest or the doctor and ask them further about the topic? Who made you <u>that</u> humble? You are worthy of answers to questions. Gees.

This book is somewhat about taking control of your behavior in a better style - just one principle of many I am attempting to instill in you.

Remind yourself of your compassionate self. That alone makes our lives valuable. We are each and all human. Sometimes we forget that.

Can I Still Love or Am I Ruint?

———

Do you give love well? Or do we give an act of love stoically?

If we are selfish, we often are not giving healthy love. Ask yourself, in this relationship (and it could be any type of relationship) do I just coexist? Function? Wrong answer. And it may not be a fulfilling marriage or friendship for anyone.

Here is the most caring message I ever received. Can you fathom wishing this to your friends and family?

> *You came to mind,*
> *So I stopped to pray.*
> *I asked the Lord Jesus*
> *To make you a way.*
>
> *To give you His peace*
> *And His strengthening grace,*
> *To give you endurance*
> *While running this race.*
>
> *I asked Him to help*
> *When the path seems unclear,*
> *To bring assurance*
> *He'll always be near.*

To show you each promise
He's made will come true.
I'm praying, in all things
He'll carry you through.

Is my love sacrificially costly? Pure love shares without thinking. For believers, I ask you to give your thoughts to Jesus coming to Earth to show us and tell us of miracles, real hardship, devotion to a God, a way of doing life with great sacrifice, to share His knowledge of a loving devout spirit in His case, the love for God and mankind.

Many of us, myself included, lie to ourselves about how good we are in our relationships. Once I admitted to myself that I was relationship ignorant, even if I appeared on cue, felt I was in love, in vogue with trends, in a chi, or status quo, club member, community involved, family oriented, read all those magazine articles and church going, I didn't have a clue about correct one-on-one interaction.

My actions and feelings around any relationship are mine. I cannot change, cure what ails them, or control what *they* do. But I can change my part in the story.

I wonder if you are aware (can put a name on) all of your emotions. Some brains appear desensitized to emotions and feelings as if they did not occur. What a pity. I once had a boss who responded to his employees' personal needs as weaknesses of character and dismissed or demoted those displaying them! I am simply supplicating people like me to approach our emotion with eyes wide, as symptoms of our character; cognizant of the impeti of the circumstance leading to the emotion. Then, regulate the interaction of biobehavioral processes we do.

Among the realm of emotion, you will find these categories:

PROTECTIVE EMOTIONS:

FEAR   ANGER   PANIC   SADNESS   WEAK FEELINGS   SEEKING

CONNECTIVE EMOTIONS:

CARING CONNECTION   PLAYFUL CONNECTION   SEXUAL CONNECTION

I'd like to break this down for you into a more recognizable scenario of each:

Fear

Horrified	Uneasy	Tense (Body)	Nervous	Insecure
Cowardly	Terrified	Scared/Fearful	Anxious	Hiding
Cowering	Worried	Afraid	Threatened	Avoiding
Frightened	Fearful	Panicky	Shaky (Body)	Stiff or Rigid
Frozen (Body)	Timid	Intimidated		

Anger

Bothered	Irked	Critical	Mean	Annoyed
Bitter	Livid	Raging	Fed Up	Agitated
Outraged	Finger Giving	Frustrated	Irritated	Mad
Stern	Disgusted	Resentful	Furious	Seething

Panic

Flummoxed	Trapped	Perplexed	Anxious	No where to escape
Frozen	Paralyzed	Disbelief	Stunned	Lost
Unable to move	Closed in	Insecure	In shock	Desperate
Mixed up	Uncomfortable	Disoriented	Stuck	Helpless
Close to floor	Troubled	Faint like	Hysterical	Unsure

Sadness

Tearful	Miserable	Hurt	Awful	Terrible
Gloomy	Low	Harmed	Outside body	Crushed
Heartbroken	Lost	Unhappy	Hopeless	Devastated
Helpless	Down	Distressed	Depressed	No way up

Physical Weakness or Fatigue

Low energy	Worn out	Shaky	Body aches	Lifeless	Low activity
Emotionally Tired	Run down	Unable to fix	Lifeless	Suicidal	Unable to rise
Thirsty	Tired	Impotent	Exhausted	Vulnerable	Hungry
Overwhelmed	Sick	Uncaring	No desire	Helpless	Isolated
Headaches	Powerless	Frail	Stressed	Defenseless	Friendless
Discouraged	Sore	Ill	Fragile	Insecure	Alone

Now the Connective Emotions of care, play, and sexual sensing.

Play

Relaxed	Dreaming	Giggly	Happy	Glad
Contented	Light-Hearted	Silly	Cheery	Up lifted
Impulsive	Amused	Optimistic	Gleeful	Imaginative
Creative	Delighted	Comical	Jovial	Joking
Alive	Spontaneous	Delighted	Whimsical	Spirited
Elated	Ecstatic	Energized	Excited	Animated
Lively	Ready to go	Teasing	Playful	

Care

Helpful	Supportive	Secure	Tender	Touching	Empathetic
Attached	Connected	Attentive	Friendly	Considerate	Loving
Understanding	Jointed	Close feelings	Nurturing	Warmth	Fulfilling

Sexual

Warmth	Physical	Flirty	Touchy Feely	Affectionate
Tender	Aroused	Sexy	Turned on	Amorous
Love to be loved	Orgasmic	Desirous	Romantic	Cuddly
Frisky	Passionate	Desired	Stimulated	Hot passion

Why do we experience emotions? It would be a dull world without them, that is for sure. Fear alerts us to harm or threats. Joy propels us to seek activities and people that make us feel good. Love helps us to bond with others. Awe helps us to search to discover. Expression of these emotions depends on the behaviors we have seen and been taught, or inherited, up to now. Scientists believe we only have 27 emotions! Heck, Aristotle already counted more than a dozen in his day. They believe up to sixty percent, 60%, of our emotions are inherited! (From a Journal of Translational Psychiatry)

Can you check off three that you felt yesterday? Three today? We are going to learn a lot about having any of these feelings and acting on the positive; or our poor reactions to the negative.

A text book example of Reaction is the student who received some critical comments on a term paper, who sees the professor only as evil and hostile.

We will bolster you, if you will, up to meet feelings in the moment and walk through them appropriately without doing self harm or damage to others. You can learn ways to augment emotional presets. Look at the list again, what was common in your family home?

The feel good emotions above correlate directly with better mental health.

You, me, and the next guy all get to have our feelings. Fear is healthy to keep us aware of threats to ourselves. Joyful feelings propel us to be around people and places that make us feel happy. Awe helps us to feel gratitude and excitement and continue to explore. Love offers to us to know others better and connect. We GET to feel – it allows us to enjoy life and people, and watch out for ourselves. We add to these sensations from our life experiences so far, in the form of upbringing, influences of experience, our genetic locks, personality we form and social lifestyle. Expression and/or voicing feelings are behaviors we allow or bring forth from that package called our personal history. What we are going to talk about here is wisdom to tie all this together well before harming ourselves or others with words and actions. It requires adding more wisdom to acquire a filtered presentation with a more satisfactory outcome in love and connections and bonding and spiritual feeling. For many of us, feelings are subjective based on the above and involuntary actions, sometimes our subconscious bias or (I'm going to say it) lack of knowledge take us to places we cannot back out of (foot in mouth or hurting others or self-condemnation/self-degradation). Charles Darwin, of course, believed we have animal ancestry. With that thought, why wouldn't we use our lower reactionary thinking? It is natural to us. I am going to redirect all that for you, most memories are completely useless, let's prune those extraneous details. I promise you more time to think in the end.

It is automatic, inane, when we have a sensation; we react, demonstrate with an emotional output. When we feel an extrinsic impetus, we are not only experiencing that emotion, we are having frontal cortex reasoning activity in the form of physiological reaction, in less than a nanoblink!

The basis of this book is to enhance your thinking skills and create new neurons!

T H I N K.   Is what you are about to say or do:
True? Helpful? Inspiring? Necessary? Kind?

I love that young teens, especially, it seems, use an Emoji Board to express feelings. What a totally healthy prop to have. Ninety-two percent of teens, in fact, use emojis on social media.

Some of us have learned negativity quite well. From that, we view the world as more threatening when we are repeatedly abused or live in stress, or endure long term verbal putdowns and irrational responses.

A perfect example here is a formerly abused and abandoned boy grows into a man who fears abandonment by wives so much he leaves first when there is discourse - to control his situation. He fears he will lose loved ones again by them leaving. Emotion triggered by familiar stimuli.

I lived with belittlement and dismissal so much that I lost my self-worth. Environment can take a toll.

When you see someone in danger (terminal illness or suicidal) over a prolonged period, our own empathy can prolong our stress.

"Stress prevents us from being objective about our stress."

We react within milliseconds to the cued sensation by sprouting neurons rhythmically jiving around in our brains, with reactive behavior.

Fear is An Acronym for: 'False Evidence Appearing Real'

Are you in fear? As a babe you flinched when a door slammed. If you fell over, you cried. Some innate fears are instilled when very young. A fall disappointed a babe's desire to stand. Fear tells us that disappointment or danger may be quite near. The fear sensation has to run around in our thoughts for a millisecond to discern awareness and fight or flight. It is a sensation; where until we know the source of what is coming, we have a restless feeling.

Fear is a feeling, not a truth. Fear is only thoughts, nothing real. Reread those two sentences over.

Various psychotherapists disagree whether fear actually has three, four, up to eight phases: Perception, Vulnerability, Reasonable, Unreasonable, Imagination, Control, Anger, and Withdrawal. Watch for these to occur in yourself.

"My importance to the world is relatively small. On the other hand, my importance to myself is tremendous. I am all I have to work with, to play with, to suffer and to enjoy. It is not the eyes of others that I am wary of, but of my own. I do not intend to let myself down more than I can possibly help, and I find that the fewer illusions I have about myself or the world around me, the better company I am for myself." - Noel Coward

Fear happens.

o   Fear of structure holding me back
o   Fear of not measuring up
o   Fear of loss
o   Fear of success and the envy or jealousy created in others
o   Fear of criticism
o   Fear of not being able to say no
o   Fear of not being loved
o   Fear of making a mistake

Does my stomach quiver? Do I get a quick nausea, back off, avoid, pray, harm others, verbally condemn, take an action, don't take an action, muster strength? Work your thought process through here. Know yourself. Know your physical and physiological reactions to your fear. Take this time to review your deportment and consider what you could do differently. Fortunately, if we have had some resilience in our past, and support from friends or family, we got through many complex painful experiences still wanting to grow in our emotional health.

If I am in fear, I interfere.

An acronym I heard: I.C.E. (my personality can be icy!) Interfering, Controlling, and Escalating seems to fit what I do in fear.

Fear comes to us from being threatened. Our reaction is what we must acknowledge. *"Do not be afraid"* is in the Bible 365 times, once for each day of the year, offering to us to "Tap into the strength of Christ's power."

I am my own enemy in reaction.

Fear is one of the feeling responses with anger and love. Those are strong emotions. So is fear as powerful, in guiding our actions.

Helen Keller once offered: *"Avoiding danger is no safer in the long run than outright exposure. Life is either a daring adventure or nothing."*

If I say, "I can still do it, afraid." I can then do it.

Broken Thinker

———

Fugue like: a pathological state of altered consciousness in which an individual may act and wander around as though conscious, but his/her behavior is not directed by his/her completely normal personality and is not remembered after the fugue ends. Sometimes this is just their season to be a grudge monster.

Dr. Henry Cloud with Dr. John Townsend, in their book <u>Boundaries,</u> express:

> *It is sometimes easier to see in other people the very thing we would do well to change in ourselves.*

I love their writing. Questions they provoke us with:

> *Where are you watering someone else's yard while your own grass withers and dies?*
> *Where are you letting someone else water your yard?*

We are talking about **MYOB**. Often, it is easier to condemn the mess in someone else's garage while yours looks nearly as discombobulated. See, we accept what we do readily. But are we cognizant that we judge the same things in others as unacceptable?

Cognizance of previous insights is consolidated into my brain so that I continue to move forward. But I now move forward morally wiser, with this accrued self-awareness where I examine my thought before speaking, look at reality because it is truth, and reexamine my habits or what mother told me. Wouldn't you love every moment to be a moment of clear vision?

"Always aim at purifying your thoughts and everything will be well." – Mahatma Gandhi

What are you doing right now that is good?

I was 29 until I was 45, then 39 till I was 55, but now, at 61, I finally tell my age! Lying about my age was fun, until I realize that maybe I was also stuck at that age of emotional maturity!

Baby boomers are so happy to reach retirement age, so as to relax a bit from the churning, pressing responsibilities of children and jobs. Many however - look around you - decide that their skill set has been used up, they are too old to learn new things, and brains have reached maximum capacity. Hell, what am I saying? You do not have to be old to wear that attitude! Such a loss to society they are. I am afraid they are doomed to a rough ride out.

Nonwork time more likely should be the opportunity to rewire your brain. If your cerebral cortex goes into dormancy, no new connections allow a happier, more serene life to be absorbed. People who continue to engage in exercise grow greater neural connectivity than those who are sedentary.

Wisdom: putting together experience and a body of knowledge; accumulated learning with ability to discern inner qualities and relationship insight, good sense, and teachings of ancient sages. A friend saved my emotional life with a probing question. She asked how my control of my life was going. What an honest and shocking answer I had. I had lost the grown up my little girl wanted me to be.

We are constantly absorbing input. We have discussions and we process, digesting what has been offered. The larger your exposure to the world and its people, the bigger the offering. If you lived within a tribe or cult, the smaller your body of knowledge and choices. We add to reflect, analyze, challenge, expand, and refine our thinking until the day we die. All I am suggesting is that we do it in a manner that is progressive for us.

So I let God have me and all others whom I was trying to control. What a release to not have to worry about and plan everything in life. Wisdom came.

One must have willingness to say, "This is not going my way, I don't control it, God does." Where most fail, is in cognizance and owning that we are unhappy. 'This is my lot. My body is aging and sore. I have always..., blah, blah'. Reacting to others is not living our fulfillment. I was so overwhelmed by alcoholism that I lost my sense of how to be healthy in our relationship. I was accepting "blah" from myself. I was holding on to a relationship that had been important for many years, even though it was harming me NOW. I metaphorically compared it to a soldier sent out to fight a battle, who instead, hid. In every instance of the war, he hid, scared shitless. I get that.

I now choose to let God make decisions, take them off my shoulders, instead of trying to force issues in my life. I choose to take care of myself so I can fulfill what God led me to do, and what he created me for. See, God sent me down here as a Mercedes without an engine. I put all the action and thoughts in my life. When the focus on "poor me" left me, I began helping others in ways that He gave me; skills, talents, and knowledge. Sensations I had hidden from myself – giggling, fun, creativity, and prayer of childhood dreams came back. Side effects are happiness and fulfillment!

Realizing time in life is passing is the way to wisdom. You can't be 16 or 32 and know you are not headed in the right direction, unless you cognizantly sit in God's lap looking at yourself. You can go, "uh-oh" or cheerlead yourself on. Either way, your life will change for the better when you involve the Big Guy.

NEVER MAKE DECISIONS OR PURCHASE WHEN YOU ARE IN H A L T:

> Hungry
> Angry
> Lonely
> Tired

HALT.

Those basic physical needs must be covered before seeking wants. These needs take precedence over moral clarity or intellectual fulfilment. We blame street people for stealing things quite easily. Their moral clarity cannot be clear since their basic physiological needs are not met. We sometimes put our safety and security at risk because of being hungry, angry, lonely, tired. (Fine! I will just show you!) Mothers give through all of that. We cannot be the most thoughtful of others when we are any of the four. Think HALT. I must stop and take care of my basic physiological need before engaging anyone in conversation. An example here is "I must pee.", and then not going to do it!

When, when we are not feeling up to snuff: hungry, angry, lonely, tired, or sick (I like to call it instead, SHALT with an S for sick), we will behave poorly and our full self-actualization cannot present itself. (Example: Tattoos when drunk.)

See, many of us have grown comfortable with our logic and sensible nature. We get along. We plateau in a well-respected knowledge and perhaps relish in a title such as, teacher, speaker, chairman, boss, father, welder, baker, or whatever reference we or society has pinned on our lapel. That is not enough. Plateauing in lesser wisdom is not acceptable. (Two years old and under, are the only people who have not yet developed wisdom.) It emanates no essential forward motion.

wis·dom: the ability to make sensible decisions and judgments based on personal knowledge and experience: good sense shown in a way of thinking, judgment, or action: accumulated knowledge of life: insight, astuteness (Webster's); utilization or possession of well used principles.

Solomon said that the beginning of wisdom is fear or awe of God. We start to get wisdom by asking God to help us out of our fear.

What good is reading, learning, acquiring experience, if we do not examine it and plug it in to our associative side of the brain? Admit, 'Okay, so I made a mistake'. If you truly want to not harm others - grow up a little and then, never stop maturing in wisdom. Lackadaisical stupidity is so unappealing. Reading, seeing, listening is impermanent and is a short-term memory acquisition. Learning is as much about information as well as formation − of the thoughts processed with the information.

My Second Chapter

Depression can leave us empty; it seems our life is on hold. That is an untruth. Time and life are still happening and we simply are not mentally present. Moments of the will to live are being used dully and unfulfilled. Physiologically, our circuits are not automatically prompt. This thinking impairs our happy, with limiting thoughts on replay, less connectivity with others, anxiety, dysphoria and focus problems. It appears somewhat like white noise, a din or cloud sits overcast on our ability to move on. Do you want to help yourself?

Search for wisdom. Knowing that we are still able to function and be useful, we must put a foot out – one step before another. Then practice that again. Uncloud the truth.

I want to add a word – simply. Simply do not repeat this in the future. You will find this strangely good, but gaga to believe, but I have more time in my head now; and after much practice with amends, I use it progressively and positively for myself and others...that is, since I simply do not repeat mistakes in the future. Even if Ego and Self-Righteousness RSVP, I won't let them cloud my truthful thinking.

Open up your neurons and put the lesson in your brain. Since you were four or five years of age, your retrieval cue has been working; your prefrontal contextual cortex has been proven to adequately contribute to memory formation. With cognizance of emotion and thinking at the time of the lesson, memory grows. Repetition of goodness gets consolidated in your cerebral cortex. It is physiological, not just from the heart. So machoistic, biased critics stymie their own comfort with themselves, with continuous guilt and regret. And open, conscientious minds propel their inner vision to joy and ample time for everything. What a difference between the two. How we think accounts for the persona we deliver and fill our lives with. Everything is in its own time. It is that simple. It is a truth.

If we nourish guilt and regret with time and thought, it becomes a part of us - a guilty conscience. And the road that it leads to is unconscionable, filled with depression, regression, and distress, ruminations, and inappropriate actions when attempting to escape it.

So even if I apologize and make corrective measures, I must now act in a manner which I just learned from the lesson. My subconscious needs to hear the corrective measure and feel the emotion from both the mistake, and the personal growth toward being a better person, and then be a better person for thinking like that, and ad infinitum growth.

What are you doing right now that is good?

John 10:10 reveals what Jesus said, "*I have come that you may have life and life abundantly*" not, "that you may have life and worry, fret, sin, forget, and be lazy". Sometimes I forget what God would want me to do, like spiritual Alzheimer's. Right now, I am thinking of the Seven Deadly Sins, but that opens up a whole 'nother issue of ethical, religious, and legal mistakes.

So what are you doing in this moment? Is it good with God? Would your mother have wished this for you when she first looked down at your face? Could you tell someone else what you are doing? Will you? Many of us are in worthless movements, watching mindless TV, worrying, plugged into a game box, doing repetitive unhappy motions, overeating or controlling others' lives. Those are mistakes, People. Self-condemnation and stupidity are growing if you are whiling away the precious gift of the moments of your life without involving your mind.

At this point, I could say something in my essay that would negate all I have expressed, like, "Well, I am not perfect. I still make mistakes" - that would be a mistake. I am a work in progress. See that, that positive word 'progress' makes all the difference in the world. Cognizance of previous insights is consolidated into my brain so that I continue to move forward.

I realize that there are different facets to my synergy – my biologics, my psychological knowledge, social mores, and inherited traits.

Old Diagnostic and Statistical Manual diagnostic descriptions spoke to a 'chemical imbalance'. It is much deeper than that in that the construction of our brains actually changes. Chemical imbalance can happen while you are sitting there. Some circuitry of the chemical imbalance has effects that cause the neurotransmitters to function faulty. Therapy becomes essential. Hopefully you will see therapeutic principles in this book you can use. Simple activities can so assist depressive patients. I am leaving this up to the psychotherapists with a suggestion that if in depression, you seek help.

I take a second each time I note the time of day by looking at a clock saying, 'Thank you, God for this moment."

I do know that to be fully ready for diagnosticism, you must experience the signs and symptoms of a disorder for two solid weeks, so if you have passing thoughts but not recurrent, you are okay, Kid. More normal than you think. Depression however, is the single biggest mental health disorder. Don't deny those symptoms. Anxiety is the second. Often, we have no idea when or where our descent into the abyss of the depression or phobias began; and no idea how to get out. If you feel either; you are in a recovery stage and able to work through your affects through communication, to a fulfilled life, reducing symptoms to controllable – once you admit your cognizance. Give yourself a break before you self-diagnose or become a drama queen with your quirks.

Many folks wander around meaninglessly – no direction, seeming half-asleep even while doing things they see as important. We often chase the wrong things! (I could read books and listen to music all the time – but thankfully my butt gets tired.) You know these people. You see them everyday. My favorite is a room full of people not talking to each other; instead on their phones, some even texting the people across the room.

To get meaning in your life is to actively devote yourself to loving. Love yourself – who you are and who you show to the world. Then love others, your community in active ways, and devote yourself to spending time in something that gives you purpose and a meaningful life.

Just for your self-care check:

Symptoms of Depression

(Remember there are levels: Major Depression, Bipolar Depression, Post-Partum Depression (20% of new moms!), and Seasonal Depression and more)

Fatigue
Lack of emotion
Lack of energy
Sleeplessness or constant need to sleep
Appetite changes
Weight changes
Headaches
Sex drive lowers
Aches and pains
Irritation
Crying
Withdrawal
Sadness
Guilt
Anger
Anxiety
Mood changes
Hopelessness
Self-blame
Pessimism
Suppressed trauma
Memory and concentration difficulties
Suicidal thoughts

Then I will discuss Anxiety traits just a bit for your self-evaluation too:

Phobias
Social anxiety
General anxiety
Panic
Agoraphobia
Negative self-talk
Worry
Confusion

To be clear, phobias exacerbate fear into persistent, excessive and unrealistic mindsets. Irrational fear loses sight of the reality of a situation. Phobias severely avoid a trigger. I will tell you about that in a minute. Phobias include tremors, tics, palpitations of the heart, sweating and shortness of breath.

I was getting sicker in my co-depression and codependence. After my spouse's death, I swore I would never love a man again, or marry, never have another nemesis in my life. To the point, when I was liking my current male friend a lot, and perhaps falling for him, I went into tremors of extreme anxiety. I was worried about the extent anxiety had taken me. Was I now suffering from another diagnosis? Codependent, Depressive, Self-Condemnation, Anxiety Disordered Phobian. Trauma driven, we may lose our minds.

Children suppress trauma not knowing there is help. It is well known that persistent childhood trauma sets little people up to higher than 'normal' worry and negativity and emotional problems later. STOP and assess whenever there is self-harm and involve medical personnel for anyone involved in it.

The brain's Basal Ganglia are involved in learning, habit formation and repetitive behaviors. Overactive Basal Ganglia can cause some negative behaviors, and with long term anxiety, show to be participants in Parkinson's Disease, loss of facial expressions, and nail biting, tremors, risk aversion, and tics. This is serious folks.

One in five people experience panic attacks. Be mindful if the symptoms persist 10 days or more, they need addressing. There is credence to our behaviors.

"When we become afraid of a space, we often create a space to be afraid of." – David Bader

Elevators. Need I say more?

Just a little less than half of us needing treatment seek it! That is just wrong, people. Check in with yourself.

Self-harm in either of the above cases is often a coping mechanism. Men more than women use suicide as the fatal release sooner. One-fourth of suiciders have drug and alcohol diagnoses.

Am I Cognizant of the Meaning of Cognizant?

Am I cognizant of the meaning of and connotations of cognizant?

Better known as metacognition – thinking about thinking. Name four things your brain does.

Oh boy – I just opened a can of worms. Thoughts include:

Facts	Description	Recall	Judging
Values	Speech	Abilities	Symbols
Concepts	Matching	Rote	Syllabus
Estimates	Predicting	Rethinking	Analysis
Grasping	Synthesis	Examples	Operate
Pictorials	Attention	Production	Comparisons
Rules	Dimension	Designing	Judgement
Methods	Principles	Innovation	Contrasts
Signifying	Assumption	Discovery	Criticism
Creating	Inferencing	Separating	Contrast
Suggesting	Generate	Revisions	Involvement
Conclude	Supporting	Discussion	Decisions
Tasting	Smelling	Hearing	Intrinsics
Knowledge	Remembering	Defining	Worth
Naming	Identifying	Key Words	Solving
Learning	Understanding	Generalizing	Compare
Math!	Explanations	Verbalization	Outline
Meanings	Summarizing	Implications	Planning
Analysis	Translating	Application	Logic
Theories	Key Words	Evaluation	Combine
Familiar/Un	Paraphrasing	Consideration	Compile
Breakdowns	Demonstrate	Components	Compose

Recognizing	Differentiate	Distinguish	Devising
Organizing	Possibilities	New Ideas	Solving
Processing	Justification	Recommend	Selection
Envisioning	Sensitivity	Capabilities	Old Ideas

Please scan that again. I find this list very impressive! Your thought process is very impressive.

If I were a performer on a stage, and I thought I knew every aside, cue and next line or act I would need; I wouldn't need others or advice from them. I might jump toward the stage front erroneously, or fall back because I didn't heed or listen to the written cue, I fall with bruises, wounds, scars, and pokes from trying. Also, let others perform. They may also miss cues, forget direction, but they fall on their own. I get to support and clap or cry and feel. I can do that from a comfortable seat. We all make mistakes.

My rationality was given to me mostly by Mom and my peers in the seventies. HOLY SHIT, that's old material now, you know? I better realize that. The question is, do I know that I am functioning with a mind from the 70's?

That is not altogether a true statement because that was my former self. I now live for education, knowledge, and to then shake it all out with wisdom. But how many of those walking among us got stuck and never matured in some facet of self-growth? Stuck in:

THOSE CONTROLLERS - You cannot justify your resentment or bitterness. Ever. Mom said.

RESENTMENT with so and so, plus

REACTION to others, plus

RELATIONSHIP with a partner not good for either of us equals: ABSENCE OF CALM THINKING

Back to the beginning of this book, I asked him to shoot me. "Shoot me first, if you are going to commit suicide."

I discovered that I could not nourish or repair my mind with my own mind!

"She slapped me!" I would run, so righteously, crying to Mom, as my fourteen-month older sister, Yvonne, ran beside me, yelling, *"She slapped me first!"*

"That's enough, Kid.", my mother would say. And that was the end of the fight. Mom merited our full respect; she was fair, kind, loving, and tall! With those three words, my mother could control each orneriness of her eight children. When the words, *'That's enough'* were uttered, we knew to be quiet and quit, as nothing but peril was ahead...an escalation of a fight, a worse arm twisting by Yvonne, or maybe a time out from Mom.

So when Yvonne told me, *"That's enough, Kid."* at our then ages of 57 and 58, I realized I was in peril, and in my situation, in danger. What she meant was, *"You deserve to live free without the pain."* – a phrase used by Eva Kor, Romanian Jew and Nazi Auschwitz survivor. She knew terror and pain first hand.

Married over 30 years, I thought my marriage insurance (my wedding vows) guaranteed nursing home care and financial coverage throughout my life. My union to my husband was that bad, down to only basics, hanging on. At 57, I had remained in a one-sided love relationship to be guaranteed that someone took care of me in my old age. That was pretty sick thinking, I now know.

Severe depression followed my husband's heart attack seven years earlier – a common occurrence among cardiac patients. And later alcoholism reared its ugly addictive head; and brought with it suicide attempts, an affair, a new smoking habit, hospital stays, pernicious negativity, violating sex, arrests, and violence.

My days were often loveless – a routine of going to the office, cooking, cleaning; fearfully answering the calls regarding an ongoing affair my husband was having or the altercation he got into at his work, or just waiting for another fight at home leading to his threat to shoot himself. I would plead, beg, manipulate, and coddle him to act better and healthier. In front of friends, myself, his relatives, my spouse attempted to drink himself to death, play with his guns, explode our home with fire and gas, drive speedingly into an accident, and sometimes attempt to take my life with his.

Another Auschwitz quote from Eva Kor: "When *you walk into a crematorium that's still there, you see the scratch marks on the wall.*" What I experienced was psychological scratch marks on my wall of personality, wall of intelligence and sanity, scratch marks on my logic and sensibility – some I had put there, hell, most were self-created, and then I also allowed others to scratch me. I had seen the scratch marks she spoke of, the hooks for hanging people by the flesh, the concrete shower benches, the human stretching machine with its leather cuffs, the train cars and tracks into Auschwitz in person when I lived in Germany. I knew what Eva meant, but the heart, the heart is what is damaged most prevalently; we lose our lives inside. It is inconceivable that people can survive here. I had not gone through what Eva had but I had allowed myself to be condemned to a life dealt to me. And I had a choice, which Eva and millions of others did not. I had failed 'getting out' on my own accord. I was choosing to cope in another person's life.

My life became a void, an empty place that restricted my ability to think freely or breathe fully.

Another Nazi war camp survivor observed many others during his circumstance there, Viktor Frankl. His observant realization rendered that those who had a vision of more for their lives and a conviction impelling them toward fulfilling a legacy seemed to give them a principle toward surviving. People held onto their sense of contributing to society. I had not.

In my case, I was watching someone else also lose their life, slowly. His flat affect affected me. He didn't feel like talking. He spewed words of condemnation about my lifestyle. He didn't care about anything, including me. Depression was his own Auschwitz. He was clawing and losing. He felt worthless, lonely and miserable. This book is about recovering from my tag-along-with-a-depressed-alcoholic. I chose in those moments of his closed-off times to feel bad about my lot in life – my own depression – not able to recognize what I was doing to myself. I had no idea of the physical changes of depression and codepression, other than the visible. I dealt with what was visible, with my own claw marks. Meanwhile, with my alcoholic's inability to feel anything other than fractured and energy less and uninvolved, I told myself falsehoods about him, our relationship and dealt in cope only. I was waiting for his former self to come back. Ha, Ha, Ha, and Ha.

Manipulation, psychiatric visits, counselling for me and he, medication, threats, court orders, hospitalizations, kindness, care, and gentleness – nothing could change the demise of the neuropeptide brain chemicals, serotonin, dopamine, when alcohol was added. It hijacked the brain! The limbic system's components (hypothalamus, amygdala, and hippocampus) act as a system, that when combined with the properties of alcohol, are depressed and suppressed. Brain cells do not regenerate from this destructive combination. My husband's psychiatrist told us, he will never get better; and to me in private, that the meaningful part of his life is over. Physiologically, the ordinary interactive transmissions, especially the GABA neurotransmitter, were now inhibited and failing. My husband's psychiatrist told us as a couple, that my husband was killing himself with the combination of psychotropic meds and alcohol. Being apprised of that threat of fatality by his own hands, did nothing to alter the path he was on. I could do nothing to help. Many of you have been in this circumstance, with a terminal illness in a loved one. You grasp at any possible helper. A judge mandated that my husband attend a Twelve Step program, the court order also did nothing to get him away from the deadly course he was determined to follow.

Threats and attempts at my life intensified.

So, *"That's enough, Kid."* from my sister opened my eyes. That was a day that changed my life. It was my deceased mother's words repeated in my ear via Yvonne that gave me the courage to leave. The friend that drove me far away from home, with half of our savings bonds and savings account, my jewelry and two suitcases to Yvonne's home in another state, 1000 miles away, changed my life.

She asked me all the right questions about my reality:

Was I the cause of my husband trying to kill me?

Was I in danger of losing my life?

Had anything I had done, altered the path we were on the last seven years?

Did I still think I could change him and stop alcoholism?

And lastly, why would I want to think like that? I was void of happiness. Where was the "me" in my life?

Marriage vows had kept me there, I argued. For better or worse, in sickness and in health. That, and the ideal I had of promised nursing home care coverage. Can you imagine staying in a domestic abuse situation just for the security of nursing home coverage? What was I thinking? Have I stopped noticing what is going on with MYSELF?

I admitted my husband to a hospital, informed all his family, doctors, and the courts of his status. The day my friend drove me away from my geographically close family, my new house, a collection of thirty-plus years of wonderful assets, seven cars, and my personal belongings; my friend talked and I listened. There was another way of thinking; she said, I needed to face my reality, instead of living in the manipulation, death threats, wishing for different, and suffering. I had an emotional void I was denying. I was so far down in my lonesome pity party, that someone else had to open my eyes.

"The saddest thing I can imagine is to get used to luxury." –*Charlie Chaplin*

It was like she turned on a light in a tunnel. My focus had been on surviving in a place I allowed myself to be, rather than choosing better for me. I was living my husband's miserable life with him and ignoring me. I was willing to die, just because he was.

I was existing. No more. And that could have ended any minute.

I Can Call It A Near Death Experience If I Want To

Now I am hoping that my experience, developed strength and eventual hope will assist others in taking charge of their lives.

I have heard that Hell has three gates. They are 'lust, anger, and greed'. That should make you think! I know I am guilty of all three.

As an exercise in being more cognizant, I would like you to begin to 'name' your feelings. Expand your emotional vocabulary. What are you feeling in this present moment? Name it. Describe it in a few words. Accept that you are there in your body. This will reduce your brain's responsibility to REACT wrongly to a sensation; and open up the nodules that feed wisdom to respond appropriately.

Did you realize that those previous rationalizations you were reading about me, edged on the Seven Deadly Sins?

I was too proud to give up, I wanted financial security he afforded me to continue, I had a new home, I was too mad to see my lot in life was self-created.

Envy, greed, sloth, gluttony, pride, lust, and wrath.

"Earth provides enough to satisfy every man's need, but not every man's greed." –Mahatma Gandhi

Now, each day is a day that changes my life.

Cognizance that life is happening to us, is the first step. Reality of your current existence is the catalyst to change your own demise.

Secondly, knowledge that we can make life happen in a different manner with adjustments to our thinking, gives us license to live differently. Living in gratitude of all good things and carrying the attitude that life is to be enjoyed is a choice. To not live in gratitude is also a choice. A poor choice. Every day now, when I am challenged, I try to think of three things I am grateful for...maybe it is that: 1) I have a job, and 2) this boss coordinates our company with the public, and 3) I earn a wage here, (instead of thoughts of wanting to kill my boss).

I have children, who are full of voice and lilt, who add joy to life, who play, who challenge me to be a mom, instead of thinking they are loud and demanding.

I am grateful to be at the mechanics! They will repair my car, get me back on the road, have knowledge about what is wrong and how to fix it; instead of thinking, Damn, damn, damn. Bad things always happen to me.

Adding thankfulness to your day or minute is an amazing action. Try these: "I am thankful for my heart, the gift of being able to love, I am thankful for life, laughter, beauty, kindness, others, abilities, skills, talents." This lesson, this repetitious reminder of my goals; is acceptance of reality.

Thirdly, believe that living large includes more than you. My dot of a tiny mobile body on the globe can go on perpendicularly hanging on someone else's life or it can glow all by itself.

Check your reality. No more duplicity - lying to yourself about what is real. Honest inventory of personal assets and goodness we wanted for ourselves but failed to achieve, is a must. Put your grocery carts in the rack. Don't cheat clerks, or push your way in traffic. And think about the greater reason for your purpose. Aren't we all here for love and support? Receive and give it freely. Give freely to yourself first. If a mother on an airplane does not put her mask on first, there will be no chance to get one put on the baby. Then once you are taken care of, give it universally. That is living life large!

That change of thinking is the day that changed my life. That day is today. That day was yesterday. That day is tomorrow.

"To know what you prefer instead of humbly saying Amen to what the world tells you that you ought to prefer, is to have kept your soul alive." – Robert Louis Stevenson

Do I need to say, "That's enough, Kid" to you?

"I cannot <u>make</u> someone else's well-being more important to me than it is to them."
from <u>Discovering Choices</u>

Fear of Failure –
The Power of the Mind

Now that you know self-awareness is the place to start examining who you are, let's look at actions.

Fear is the most common paralyzer.

Promptly admit when you are in it. Or you will be left behind.

Yes, at first, we feel sick to our stomach. Fifty percent of fear of failure is due to worry about the future, sorrow, or fear.

Are you willing? Or do you have to pretend again that you are in control? Does my self-righteousness get in the way or bravery and accomplishment? I may look stupid either way, failing or being stubborn about thinking I am right.

See willingness is a process in itself. Are you willing to be better? Are you willing to change? Are you willing to grow? Are you willing to participate more positively? Are you willing to listen more? Are you willing to believe God will help? Are you willing to look at the mistakes you have made? Are you willing to realize times have morphed since you learned habits? Are you willing to let go of things and people who bring you down or put you down? Are you willing to receive a better clarity of your role in relationships? Are you willing to take on better actions? Willingness to change up is a complete step of the process on its own.

I often prayed to my God to give me the willingness to have courage. Give me the willingness to be nice. Help me have the willingness to be patient, or truthful, and a multitude of other things I was chicken to do.

Go back to that previous paragraph with all the questions and answer those questions!

God encourages success. God encourages care and peace and sanity. I must be aware of my needs, likes, and take care of self. How about thinking, I will survive?

What can you control?

Who you hang out with – Those whose company you choose to keep, your relationships.

How seriously you take life – Is everything you do worth it?

Your happiness – Your perspective in spite of your feelings at the moment.

How open-minded you are – Have you learned all there is to learn?

What you think about – You can control thoughts you save only; not all that are fed to you.

What you talk about – Our tongues can be tamed.

Your efforts – What you put in (you choose that) will impact what you get out.

How offendable you are – Being offended is your reaction, however, it is not a correct response.

What you believe – Look for truth only in what you research, hear or see.

Your promises – Keep them like gold.

How kind you are – No one else will be blamable for our level of kindness/lack of.

You. Those are under your control. Other people's thoughts are not yours and you cannot affix your thinking into their heads. Furthermore, it is really not your job to control others' thinking or doing. (Unless, of course, they are your little child or you are their only security.)

Often, I didn't want to act the way I did. Change is possible within me; focusing instead on a mentally and emotionally healthier me. I am able. Is my safe place just a way to say, "I don't want to try?" Do I want to live just coping and working to protect myself from others? Don't I want more?

Maybe I volunteer my own self-judgment? Do I assign that power to judge me onto others? Fear forms my life's sentences. Why not add faith? There I can anticipate and am able to meet my needs, demands and expectations of self-love.

The truths of life never go away. My actions and thoughts and attitudes are all I've got. If I react, I may never step on the stage of my own life.

Why am I not acting all grown up?

Fear keeps me from action.

Fear keeps me from getting out of bed.

Fear keeps me on my duff.

Deceit of self is one of the Seven Deadly Sins

Driving Down The Right Path

———

Just a fun little perception of self-test:

<u>Are You Driving Safely Down Your Own Path?</u>

How we drive in traffic is often an indicator of how we live. Read the questions all first, then reread each question and read analogy with it. Used to be, nobody drove well enough to suit me. The car ahead of me goes too slowly, and I am forced to get very close and push. I would swear at other drivers. In other words, through constant criticism and expectations of others, I act like a victim. We must alter our lives in order to alter our hearts.

Do I ever give the finger?

Do I give the finger…cuss under my breath or aloud?

Are these the manners I want from others when I error or sin?

Do I think other drivers are horrible drivers?

Do I judge and condemn others as horrible drivers??

If I am judging, shouldn't I thus be judged also, and condemned for my faults and defects and misnomers? Would I make it to Heaven or Hell if others were in judgment of that?

Do I refuse to let other stupid drivers get in front, or give up a lane when someone is off sided by a mistake they made?

Do I give up what I can for others, especially if their life has made them less fortunate?

Do I not want my mistakes forgiven? My misjudgments allowed? And my lack of knowledge to be accepted and allow me to learn from the past?

Do I feel the need to beat the other car to the light, destination, turn off?

Do I think of others' needs ahead of my own, with understanding of their urgency?

Am I really the most needy person in God's eyes today? Or do I have abundance? Don't I live in a sunshiny world with my basic simple needs well met?

Do I pass frequently?

Do I have an egotistical need to appear best, or be first or larger than others are in their lives?

After all, aren't I the king of kings? Oh, I do not think of myself that egotistically? Yet I think that pushing others back, breaking a speed law or breaking any rule of self-conduct only a little, is acceptable to others.

Am I in the fast lane on the interstate most of the time?

Do I feel I am righteous to not share what I have more of?

Am I truly enjoying the moment I am given for these 60 seconds or am I personally driven to mad house, the future, or stress at all times? What happened to serenity, enjoyment, thankfulness for the time we are of this world?

Do I run yellow lights?

Do I push the edge with little white lies?

Do I secretly seethe over others' faux paus, an illegal turn in, or being in the wrong lane and then pulling out in front of me?

Do I forget that God made us all? And that we each have rights.

Do I get in the wrong lane without thinking?

Do I lie, judge, or condemn? Or maybe steal? … just a little?

Do I not realize I am in the turn lane by mistake?

Do I expect from others what I do not give out?

Do I not realize I passed my turnoff?

Do I forget to pray?

Do I always use my turn signal when changing lanes?

Am I correct to think I am always right and others should just not be in my way?

Do I backseat drive? Do I tell another 'how to' drive, when to slow down, when to look out, etc.?

Am I controlling, even though I am not in control of another's 'steering wheel' in life?

Do I think that I know how they should lead their lives or their vehicles? Do I tell them without them asking?

Envy of the Envoy

Do I mentally race with the Denali, wish I had the little red convertible, want to beat the Mercedes to the valet?

Ask yourself this: If material items cost no money, what more would I have to have to exist?

Find that insightful?

Through The Night with
A Light from A Bulb

Ever discover you have been singing the lyrics to a song wrong? I was 'going to a jack-o-lantern' since the sixties when the words were, "Going to the chapel, and I'm..."

This chapter is about consciously getting the words and actions right in your mind.

This is a mindful act:

Breathe in.

Breathe in air for yourself.

Put hand deeply on chest to feel heart

Other hand on belly.

Feel the rise of belly

Feel the fall of belly

Feel your heart beat

Breathe in.

Count 5,4,3,2,1 as you breathe out.

Listen to life inside you.

You did that with great thought. That is cognizance. Cognizance of your physical being breathing.

Mindfulness is essential. Being cognizant of our thoughts is mind blowing. Changing how we think is liberating. Mindfulness of each moment interrupts anxiety, worry, and our perfectionism. Bring your sense back to what is, and what is now. Worry and lament are about another time of which we have no control.

> *"Those who dwell …among the beauties and mysteries of the Earth, are never alone or weary of life."* – Rachel Carson

These come from Chinese philosophy:

1. Think back over your last hour or how you spent time this week. Have you been running around needlessly or foolishly? Sit quietly and realize what you do.
2. Speak only to the good in others. That is a period at the end of that sentence. You may realize you have been talking too much and inadvertently or advertently harming others with your words.
3. Avoid too much involvement. Does it have your name on it? Are you wasting time on trivial matters that are not your business? Others need to learn to take care of self, fall, fail, pick themselves up.
4. Do you have your needs met? Then all the others are wants. Limit your desires and realize the joy of contentment.

Do not concern yourself over questions for which you do not know the resolution, illnesses that will not happen, mechanical breakdowns that you envision, spills that are going to happen anyway, harms that do not come. That is worry. Take it out of your brain. What a time waster, when you could have been happy and having fun in those moments of concentration instead. Sleep at night instead.

Many of my decisions have been based on reasoning that I have so far. Many were bad decisions and I will continue to do so until my wisdom is honed by lots more reasoning being fed to it.

A councilman in my home town shared with me that decisions are often made by following the creed of the guys in fellowships who wear the fezzes:

What is true?

What will benefit all?

What is fair?

What builds betterness?

Not a bad idea. Few of us are that altruistic. Our egos get in the way. We want what someone else has, we want more, we want it now. We don't want to have to do much work to have what we want.

See, we need to observe something several times before we recognize the value of it to us, good or bad!

Be aware of what you think about. Let's practice good thinking with the following:

What makes you smile?

Just because I can't leave a whole page blank, I'll start you off

1. Pandas
2. Staring at the center of a perfect blossom
3. A gentle hand on my shoulder

4. If you mention my home town
5. A baby's blushed cheek while sleeping
6. Hearing a giggle
7. Discovery of a rainbow
8. Good night's sleep
9. Seeing a loved one
10. Being pulled in to a hug
11. With a back pat or rub
12. Fresh washed hair
13.
14.

Past Bad Habits and Experiences are Bright Red God Gives Us A Green Light to the Future

———

I kept trying to fix what seemed wrong in my life. If something went wrong, I would try to fix everyone involved and the 'it' that caused the problem. I would condemn myself if I did it wrong; or I would tell the other people 'my way' to control their life. It was reactive and compulsive. How many different ways are there to make a baby eat? Insisting that my way is the only way is insane.

My habits were often reactive and compulsive and I constantly ruminated and searched to control the issue.

Many times, the issue did not have my name on it; nor was I outfitted with the principle, tool or knowledge to create a better circumstance. Habitually, I attacked it though. My mental powers were put to task on someone else's situation. NOT MY BUSINESS.

I had to disengage autopilot and learn to think again.

Or I simply could have accepted that what is, is. The truth is that something had already occurred. The truth. I can't fix history, but boy did I try, or attempt to skew how it came down by convincing you I knew better sometimes with hyperbole to back me up. (I hope you are laughing at this incongruent thought process.)

Our past has been nothing but self-will. That is all we knew. So we grew up and used the outdated tools in relationships. We must forage for ourselves as to what personality traits *we want!* Maybe you watched your parents fight a lot, your father drink, unhappiness to the tune of great sadness in one spouse or the other. Perhaps there was fun but then a change occurred in a parental figure's personality or a mental incapacity. See parents befall us. When adult, we must become our own high performing individual. The truth I guarantee is that life, technology, and relationships have changed greatly since your parents were in charge of you.

Play with your answers as a checkpoint:

Material Sins

Have you taken actions that may have affected an individual tangibly?
Have you overspent money?
Have you not fulfilled an agreement with someone?
How about a promise?
Have you been selfish to the point of stinginess?
Have you damaged another's property?
Do you lie on your income tax?
Have you overly attempted to gain love or acceptance with gifts?
Have you borrowed anything and not returned it? Money??

Spiritual Sins

Do you always show gratitude, even for little favors and niceties?
How about major favors and objects?
Do you daily show gratitude to God?
Do you show gratitude to those who help or assist you in life?

Do you owe thanks to someone?

Do you owe someone a pay it forward favor or encouragement to another?

Do you take care of your mental, emotional, health, need for learning, exercising and fun?

Do you pay attention to others with intentional listening skills?

Do you talk with God?

Do you do your part to keep your community neat, clean, and friendly and in good order?

Do you show your gratitude to family, especially to our parents?

Moral Sins

Are your behaviors with others moral and ethical?

Do you remember people's special days? Birthdays? Events?

Have you broken promises?

Are you selfish with your capabilities, money, and things?

Do you conduct yourself always in a fair manner?

Do you always set a good example for others? Children?

Are you kind?

Are your behaviors in good conduct?

Do you help others? Share your talents or skills?

Do you involve yourself in wrong doings?

Are you aware others need help?

Are you faithful? To spouse? Boss? Your God?

Do you lie?

Can you be trusted with another's property and 'dirty laundry'?

Do you spew ruthless, unkind, even mean words to anyone? This includes your spouse.

That all makes you think, doesn't it? My suggestion here would be to give yourself a percentage of how true you are in all these actions. Read this book and learn, and review the questions a year from now.

Visions of the Lord are inconceivable, ask five different people for their vision. The soul falls anew into ecstasy when we pray and/or contemplate happiness. God did not want our souls to be stricken with terror. Our sufferings seem all to be forgettable and amended with prayer to the Lord. We already have abundant mercy from him. Our hearts will mend, let our headsets also.

We are our only roadblocks, stubborn when we could be enjoying love and mercy.

Control – The Wreckage of My Past

"I was born to others' things."
Beverly Lewis in The Shunning

I thought I was the center of everyone's life. When I learned to let go of my exaggerated sense of responsibility, a whole new world of satisfied feelings and experiences began.

We get to control brushing our teeth as to when, speed, and how hard, etc. We start our day in control of how much cream we put in our coffee, whether we make our bed or not.

Or not? Actually, how much cream we put in our coffee is a conscious decision, or at one time it was, and now is our unconscious habit. Originally, it was a choice. Not a control. We were offered at one time: no cream, no coffee, which cup, what time we have coffee, where we have coffee, as choices. At one time they were new decisions, but not controlling issues. Whether you have coffee, whether it was ever grown or discovered brewable – those were under God's control. You see, He has got it. You don't.

Yet, we continue to think we control things. We continue to think we know sooooo much and have all the right knowledge to make best decisions, we believe that soooooooo much, that we inflict it on to others.

And before you know it, we not only influence them by suggestion, we advise, sometimes even, 'behest' others to follow OUR rules and directions.

Then we get worse...

Some (children, those under our leadership, spouses, students, relatives, friends) start to follow our orders, and THEN we have expectations. Expectations that they will do as we suggest or say, honor us!

> *"A man has made at least a start on discovering the meaning of human life when he plants shade trees under which he knows full well he will never sit."*
> – D. Elton Trueblood

I saw this poster and will repeat it here: When your grown children don't want to listen to you, stop talking. Life will teach them.

Who the hell are we again? Doctor of All? God? Oedipus?

So you want to change a habit...how much we eat, how much coffee we drink, the fact that we are ordering people around? We can consciously choose to break the habit, to eat less, to get out more, to plant a garden next year, to improve our knowledge. We can choose (choice again) as we are in self-regulation of our behavior. God only knows what is ahead. He offers us decisions and choices in our actions. And He wants only good choices. He likes when we do that. It usually means more peace and food for everyone else, when we choose good. When we have a sense that we should not do what we are about to, there is usually a reason. Is it good? Is it progressive? Is it helpful to others? Is it someone else's choice we are making for them? Uh oh. We have mirror neurons that cause similar feelings when we see another person in distress or harm. Example: The sight of a cut on a finger can elicit a moan from me and raise my stomach up to my rib cage. But can I heal that cut? It is not on my finger. We may have a strong urge to get involved and fix everyone else; or perhaps prevent our grown children from a fall. Life is going to happen to them. Thank goodness they are experiencing. Their lives are not mine.

When we sense we should not do it, take a look at the humanitarian need. Eating a piece of heavy chocolate cake, for instance. Is it good for anyone? Is not putting your Walmart cart back good for anyone? Is turning without signaling good for anyone? Is firing the first shot in a war good for anyone? Is it progressive? Is it helpful?

Impulsivity, routines, habits, 'we have always done it this way', are tenacious little maneuvers that are decisions. Wake up your conscious. Decide again what you are doing. And then be conscious in that moment.

In retrospect, our actions depend on thoughts and ideas we have historically accepted. Whether or not we do the intelligent thing depends on how hard we considered all our thoughts and ideas. How many times have we acted without a single spiritual element on our minds?

I love this statement heard in a Twelve Step meeting: *"You are only alone if you absolutely insist on it. God is here. He is not yesterday or tomorrow."*

One way to get full satisfaction from life is to live with God in that secret place of the spirit. You will have a feeling of being on the right road, and doing work that counts in the eternal order of things.

If you choose to worry, that is again, a choice, folks. Are you too busy concentrating on your own or a loved one's imaginary future? You are controlling what you do with your time. And this particular use of time has no value. No weight to humanness. No positive result. The desire to be somewhere other than where YOU CURRENTLY HAVE PUT YOURSELF, is paradoxically absurd. It is like going against a barometer that has declared the true air pressure. Moments that could have been serene and spent in Joy have instead, weighed you down, used up priceless endorphins, and perhaps over a long time, made you stressed and sick.

Over 40% of adults suffer from stress related health ailments. Close to 90% of all doctor visits are for those ailments! Stressful living is accountable for more than half of deaths (18-65 years of age), which includes: alcoholism related deaths, heart disease, lung ailments, accidents, suicide and cancers. Much of the above from "Contentment Magazine" on-line news source, headlined 'Stress Is a Leading Cause of Premature Deaths'

Anger is a healing energy. It stimulates action. Realize it is anger, absorb what it is conveying to your body. Calm yourself to truth only. Then decide based on truth, your response. Sometimes stepping away from the crazy or the stimulus is the only best decision. Let your true neuropathic ways work.

A quote from Alexander McCall Smith: *"Truthfulness in statements which cannot be avoided is the formal duty of an individual to everyone, however great may be the disadvantage accruing to himself or another."*

Lying is just wrong. There are no okay lies. Your friend's new car in putrid green 'should' get a thumbs up from a friend. So you lie to make them feel good and praise the car? Even 'good' lies are bad lies. You are pretending to yourself. It is hypocrisy. How far will you go to cover up: your feelings, hurting others, getting out of things, keeping everybody calm? It just explodes! Boom! How about, "I am excited you got a new car. Congratulations!" and just stop speaking there.

Oh, there are sick fucks out there who play with our emotions, scam us, demand from us, using anger, bring us in on their hoaxes and we find ourselves in interaction before we know it. When faced with a crazymaker, first identify them. Definition: someone harmful, a personality which will take you down, though sometimes more fun than a barrel of monkeys, they have sick ideas, they have corrupt distortions of rightfulness, they may harm you. They tend to expect you to do their ways; they discount your own reality and think of themselves only, they will waste your time, maybe your money, zap your energy and triangulate your life for their own ego or power. They may blame you for all they did. Distance yourself from these thieves of goodness.

Fright is not hidden. Nor is self-doubt. Repressed energy will manifest itself in somatic illness. Our mental health is tied, inextricably to physical health.

Control is only an illusion. Need to control resonates in not knowing what is coming. We will never know what is coming, so get over that control issue.

There is an illusion, only a phantom plan, that we need to be in control.

Write down 3 things that you have control over.

I have control over:

1.
2.
3.

Are those three things choices about behavior?

When I do school work. (No, that is a choice; and there are options out of it.)

My stomach gets tight and I go ahead and lie. (No, that is a choice.)

Behavior looks difficult. It is costing me a lot. It would be a shame if I spend my whole life in destruction of self.

Did you lose control? You never had it.

Stress is self-created. Don't manage stress. Prevent it. All behavior is learned, much of it mimicked by the age of eight.

Examine your own belief system, not others. You have no control over them.

I have an obligation to look at my own belief system but not to question yours.

Rather, enjoy when you wake up in the morning.

If I try to control you, I am in fear of something about you or me.

Let go of control and gain back your life.

We only believed we were in control.

People with high Emotional Intelligence (EI) behave and perform better with more satisfaction and contentment. This is what we are about in this book, increasing and growing levels of Emotional Intelligence. We need to start, however, with where you are. Until cognitive intelligence is achieved, one cannot jump up to change behaviors – you innocently are allowing up-to-now emotional knowledge and lore to enter your physiologics and control your behaviors. Many of us bumbling around in this stage of growth are doing harm to ourselves! And others. My book hopes to accomplish preparation for good relationships in society.

Here are your charges: (places where you can control your life)

What we think:

What comes at us is not our control, but how we process it in thoughts, we totally own.

Open-mindedness:

Open up to education in any form. Open up to two sides, three sides, of every story. Learn to listen well. Weigh the lore up against knowledge and wisdom. Seek more wisdom till you die. Seeing is not always believing.

"Like an ability or a muscle, hearing your inner wisdom is strengthened by doing it."
— Robbie Gass

Who our friends are:

> Set boundaries to keep you from negativity. State with clarity what you will/will not do in the space of being God's child. Sometimes, even interactions with relatives need to weighed. Choose up. Be cognizant of your own promises and moves toward closeness.

What comes out of our mouths

> Language can corrupt our thoughts. The limits of my vernacular are the limits of my world. One of the most important charges put to us. I am completely responsible for what I say and how I say it. You can have ALL the thoughts you want. But what you articulate orally should be well processed and good language skills used. Ask yourself, is this kind? Thoughtful? Insightful? Nice? Take control of your habitual vocabulary to change the quality of your life.

Our Effort at Life

> Ya, the energy and adrenaline that we apply is under our control. Efforts at hurting others or negative actions waste our time.

Here is a story of what I learned by being more cognizant of my personal history:

Two people died. Only one left this world. A single alcoholic suicide had taken two lives. But it ended only one's physical being on planet Earth. I was the other victim, stoically enduring pain — I had willingly killed my own spirit and spirituality. I made myself spiritually bankrupt.

With suicide, family members often experience stigma, shame, and self-blame which includes our own anxiety and stress actions, as well as depression.

For seven years, I lay virtually dying, growing sick with my husband's depression and alcoholism, allowing my promise of better or worse, sickness and health, rule. I may have been sicker than he, just in different ways.

"Read this, honey. It talks about your isolation from others."

"My counselor said to try exercise. Let's go for a walk. No? Okay, I'll just sit and watch shoot-em-up 'Cops' with you, while you drink.

"I made your favorite, cherry cream cheese pie. Oh, you have a beer. Okay."

"Let's go visit your favorite niece. No? Okay, I'll just sit and watch shoot-em-up 'Bad Boyz' with you while you drink."

"Hey, I'll go to the bar with you. Let's play pool. Oh, you'd rather play a game with her? Okay, Honey"

"You are drinking alone. Did you realize that you are drinking alone every night?"

"You are out here in the garage hiding your drinking. Want to watch 'Cops'?

I gave up on myself. I watched my demise. I designed it. I sat and watched while IT naively stupefied me.

When past bad habits are recognized and leave you for good, when the insight you are working on penetrates, one feels healthy, even eager, to know more. The sooner you realize you are in an unmanageable situation, the better. Realizing that is wisdom.

I often talk with my clients about plateaus of wisdom. It is so fun to realize when you have left the tier of thinking that you are doomed or a victim! Then a level of wanting to know more about our own habits and how we accrued this belief that past actions worked in the world, another phase of discovery happens. Then we search within and without, thinking about our words, idioms and beliefs mostly instilled, sometimes by inept folks (no offense to teachers but I have seen a myriad who lived on their egos because they knew the most about Science or Algebra, so we martyred them in our minds and boom: their egotism happened in us.) We search and we research and we look again into our past outcomes from our behavior. A level of wisdom. THEN, we begin to alter where we walk and how we talk and watch outcomes change for us. Bam, another level. And in fruition, we discover change has happened, our thoughts are purer and positive, worry has left us, joy is in our hearts. Level! That is this book in a nutshell, you can quit reading.

I heard from a friend that joy is like hand lotion. You can spread it wide. It feels good. It relieves little nuisances. And it gives you a good feeling.

One more message about "JOY": Tylenol blocks the chemicals that allow joy!

Ego is Deceptive

Has anyone ever cut you to the quick, causing you indignation? I've had a boss or two try that in my career.

Have you ever used manipulation or indignation of another person to get your way?

I was extremely self-righteous, to the point of lying to prove my point. I find that hilarious now. It probably wasn't then, especially to my victims. When self-righteousness (it can be mine or someone else's) dominates a conversation, someone is probably lying, and others are losing out on the truth. Two wrongs do not make a right.

Indignation, accusations, judgment, nagging, tears, hysteria, self-righteousness - are all weapons. (Review these in your next argument.) Those are bullets meant to harm. Fact based discussions need to be had with open acceptance from both parties.

I recently read a cartoon in the Washington Post about offending people. The word balloons above the characters alluded to being offended by another's words. The offender was labelled 'unintelligent" and the character who had been verbally insulted walked off in his own thoughts, not offended. What do you think about that thinking?

Initially in the program, I wanted freedom from my negative alcoholic's influence on M Y life. I still thought snappy nagging and begging would end the alcohol use if I did it well and long enough. I created my own emotional prison. Today, my life is more about my connectedness to God and serving my fellow man. I didn't create that change. God did. I just found the willingness to let Him. I, you, we want the best for a good life, don't we? Yet, our minds get stuck in defiance.

Killer weapon.

Defiance and unwillingness to change kill my desire to have a better life. They kill respect for one another. They increase guilt. And they destroy those that use the weapons, as well as their condemned unsuspecting victims.

I have to pray to not be self-righteous.

Let me broach with you the ACT of PRAYER. The action, getting down on one's knees, is humbling, and says, "I am vulnerable and I am asking for change of the current circumstance". It is just saying with a physical movement, that I know I am not in control of the universe. We are just a prayer away from help. I am one human on this earth. I acknowledge I am not Mr./Mrs. Universe in this moment. Thy will be done.

Philippians 4:6

"Do not fret or have anxiety about anything, but in every circumstance and in everything by prayer and petition, WITH THANKSGIVING, continue to make your wants known to God."

I pray to learn the way to see myself as a Child of God, bearing in my heart and mind the dignity and grace he has given every one of his creations, every one of his children.

Gravitas [grav·i·tas] *n.* Dignity, seriousness, or solemnity in manner

I would not treat anyone as harshly as I treated myself. I would never ask someone I loved to go without rest, never letting up or ask them to never be the one to have the fun. Why am I putting stops on my own happiness factor?

If someone else rules your destiny, you are both misguided.

Think about being on opposing teams (football, baseball, tennis doubles). One Team is the *EGOMANIACS,* and the other is *GOD'S TEAM.*

Take a look at the next page.

Let me give you a picture of the Yellow Flags of ego:

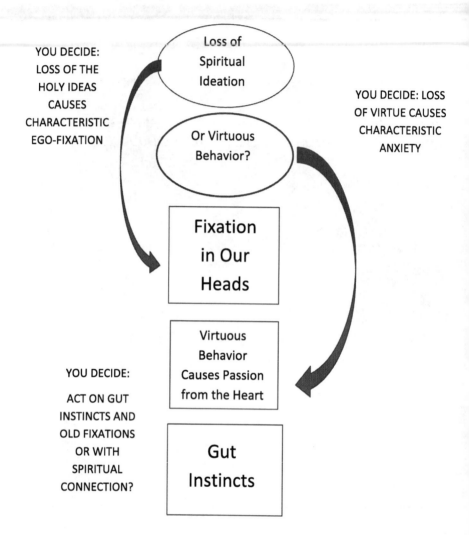

Pick ANY team on previous page. (Play one side for a minute or two, then switch teams.)

I hope this is crystal clear for you. Two teams cannot win. This is especially evident in marital discord.

Our EGOS manifest in our personal habits. Our ancestors taught us how to play the game of life. Our teachers exerted much effort, for the most part, to give us better rules for gaining points in intelligence in the game. Our friends may have been on both sides of the bleachers, supportive, or leading us to the world of crime. Our environment at home added ideas about aggressive maneuvers getting you ahead, or controlling you to stay in the lanes, and play a fair game.

Our heads intake all of this. We get fixated on what we know, THE KEY WORDS HERE ARE, what we know SO FAR! This seems an odd dilemma; however, there is a simple fix. Take all that we know and open our minds to change, listen and learn, evaluate our speech, and break bad habits. That's all.

Have you had a fair running start with all the rules applicable (INSTINCTS)? Have those before you and around you shown you what PASSION truly is and its potential?

Has a figurehead bullied you into submission with aggression, abuse, neglect BECAUSE OF THEIR OWN SELF-WILL: FIXATION OF SELFISHNESS IN THE HEAD WITH LIMITED VISION OR WISDOM – SELF-WILL RUN RIOT?

Where are you now? Do you know how to manipulate others? Are you traveling with God on your shoulder and passion in your heart? Do you know the fair-minded rules of life?

As Tim McGraw, country singer lauds:

> *"Hold the door, say please*
> *And thank you. Don't steal,*
> *Don't cheat, and don't lie.*
> *I know you got mountains*
> *To climb, but always stay*
> *Humble and kind."*

What you may have been precedently shown or taught will not fulfill your legacy unless you do all the laps around the field, know the plays by heart, and test your own skills to the limit. And practice, practice, practice only will change up your characteristics to win...to win friends, to win self-respect, to win confidence. Practice time and attention toward changing-up will get you the results. I don't have to earn love from others. When I am better, they will step out and reach for me, want to be around me.

There is more to you. There is a deepness in you, perhaps crying for a better life. There is a way. There is a way to stay in your current environment and have a better life. It is about discovering what is so deep in you, looking into portals untapped. And using our souls to direct our progress in positivity, simultaneously with new revelations our brains can design. Many changes will be called for, so subtle but pivotal to life. A year from now your experiences will be so satisfying, you will even forget that you HAD to make a change. The positive life you have made will take over your actions, your articulation, your thoughts. You will have practiced toward a win!

Let's rework your thinking system. A local life coach, Jane Smith, quotes:

> *"How wonderful to discover that two of our most common plagues, fatigue and apathy, can be resolved by intentionally developing our inner compass."*

I am going to air my dirty laundry so that you get the gist of how honest you also will have to be with yourself.

(Whew, this is hard, knowing thousands of people will know my worst sins.)

) Lied to my best friend when I was young, pretending I had a boyfriend and she didn't.

) Made covert purchases with 'our' money without telling my husband, hiding them in the trunk till he was not home.

) Engaged in petty shoplifting.

) Lied about my part in issues, since I was little ("I didn't do it.")

) Panic-ing about fearful things and reacting wrongfully.

) Defying my mother and disrespecting her, and others.

) Hating, yes, actual antipathy toward two of my bosses after they refuted my work.

) Fighting for my way, even though I knew I had wrong thinking or used subtle white lies to cover.

The first time I put these in writing, I realized my patterns of avoidance, accepting criticism, and my self-created pain brought on by using words to fight back and demands to gain undue respect. Accepting criticism is like looking at a fun-house mirror and believing that is how you look! I lived in groundlessness and accepted it as a reality. My choices back then were to feel powerless, live in denial, and react to pain and unpleasantness with my ego, and be obsessive. So obsessive in fact, I was a prisoner of stubborn! My vanity ruled me. It was my Achilles Heel. We are a product of our choices.

"There is something perverse about more than enough. When we have more, it is never enough. It is always somewhere out there, just out of reach. The more we acquire, the more elusive enough becomes." –Unknown

I did not know that a Higher Power could show me peace, laughter, serenity and happiness in spite of my thousands of thoughts. I found that I could rather do something that will nurture my mind, body and spirit. Do things honestly. I am not helpless. I am not ineffectual. Helplessness is a learned condition! I can treat myself and others with tenderness and love. I have a chance now to feel good about my honest and progressive actions. I now have regained my sense of curiosity, wonder, enthusiasm and delight – senses which many older people seem to give up on. I am now seeking a richer, more meaningful life. I take up risks, face fears, and make changes which make me available to reality.

Together, we will be looking in depth at our concepts, categorization, language, accidents, events, and traumas. We will discuss your previous understandings, decision making and social, emotional, and medical aspects of your personality. If we were to look at only your actions, or only your I.Q., we could not bridge the multitude of faceted relationship issues.

Cognition of these behaviors with adverbs and adjectives brought me wisdom. I recognized that I had a lot of fear. I lied, trying to make my fear go away, or disperse, because I skirted an unmanageable challenge. It never worked. My selfish ways were not open to all the learning that was offered. I have learned to now trust and surrender to my mistakes. The basics of horseback riding taught me to not insist on my way, or to continually repeat a demand or command or a lie, trying to change facts: the horse won't go. All my manipulation does not make honesty. I had a disease of perception: how I have been mentored with old styles, how I chose to live and form my habits. I used to think that I would be loved if I was (4 M's) Mothering, Monitoring, Measuring, or Managing others. Instead, now when I don't do those, I get to be calm and with God. Hmmm. I am aware and focused.

Most habits form in a quick repetitive action in, like a month, some only a week. How long we have been using them makes a huge difference in how long it takes to break bad ones. There is a process:

) 1. Do it again
) 2. Be cognizant (aware)
) 3. Pause to realize (Oh, not a healthy thing to do.)
) 4. Stop mid sentence or action of habit
) 5. Stop again mid sentence or action of habit
) 6. Catch yourself during the intent to do it again
) 7. Stop the intent, repeat next time it occurs to you
) 8. Stop having even the thought to do it

All the above becomes then an unconscious thought to abort the bad habit.

The most damaging words in the English language are, "It's always been done that way." – Grace Hopper

With good direction and mentoring anew, I let go of worry, resentment, judgement, killer thoughts, to never give the finger again, or go into the depths of worry and woe and pity for anyone, most importantly myself. What was my motive silhouetted behind those negative actions and thoughts? My ego has diminished and a new person has erupted with a cleanliness of spirit and desire to do nothing but the right thing in the days ahead.

List your shortcomings here: (Hey, I just showed you mine!)

)

)

)

)

)

)

The Many Coats We Wear

Straight Jacket – My hands are tied from participating in my life.

> I may be holding the strings to release in my own chattering teeth.
> I'm stuck here.

Hooded Coat – I am hiding my potential.

> I am ineffective, yet I try to control my world.

Rain Coat – I am fearful, protecting myself.

> Living defensively, fearfully, denying truth and reality.

Parka – Heavy Cover Up

> Based on ego, only warmth I get is inward selfish ego, and
> addictions in this clothe, wanting the best, biggest, most to cover
> up my indiscretions and shame.

Down Vest – Heavily but only partially covered

> Immature me, relying on others to look out for me, a point of
> codependency to pretend I am safe and warm.

Light Jacket – Expecting better days

Self-discovery done but not quite secure enough to step out without leaning back on old stinking habits.

Vest - Exposing myself bit by bit.

Learning to let go, a piece at a time.

Also Carry an Umbrella

For when shit really does fly.

Be certain that any coat you don has pockets.

I realized in my fifties that not everyone I love can stay in my life; not every beautiful place I have seen can be captured in essence through photography; not all lessons will be retained.

I must have pockets to make that possible.

My best friend in third grade is different than my junior high cheerleader group, from my high school clique and outreach, from my close roommates, from my boyfriends, aunts and uncles who have passed and it goes on.

I keep (virtual)pockets on every coat so that I may put the memory, the lesson, or the place in a loving pocket and not feel I have lost or left behind what makes up my life, only collected it. Are you wearing any of these cloaks?

Google Thyself

My sister has seven names registered through a court house, social security, etc. She was married twice, has had a nickname since birth, and then added a doctorate title. At any given situation or event, she can pull from this Straw Names list; the name and title she wishes or that is called for at the time. She can present herself as anonymous or titled.

Many of us use pseudo-personification through our lives without being registered. If I need to bow out of this tragedy or traumatic situation, my pseudonym mentally leaves the premises. If I am full of fear, I can wear the hat of a fear filled codependent, innocent, even inarticulate, unable to take care of me personally - an unproud moment, but nevertheless my reality. Or sometimes, I am proud of my achievement and want to assure you know who did this great feat - my full name and any rhetorical titles that precede it. Pride and covert actions, among the Seven Deadly Sins. Children as young as four, have awareness of moral transgressions and rule breaking.

If you Google yourself, what would the world be privy to? Every article written, business venture, blog, tweet, every product or book you ordered, and every team you chaired or played on.

Moreover, what would God see if He googled you? Has your Google self been living the way you want to? Are those titles and contributions worthwhile? Do you qualify for the list of WWJD? Is your pseudo persona acting on your behalf or are you reacting and less Googleable? Point of thought, huh?

Jesus has a plan for us, but he also gave us our own behavior – one of them is stubbornness.

He gave us self-worth simply because we were a being created by God. He has the only credentials to give us a great soul and life. Self-worth cannot be taken; although it can be given up. That gift of self-worth is not based on behavior, or work we do, or service we perform. We have learned to act. That promise does not include our behavior of re-action.

o   He offers us a balanced life and the methods to take care with ourselves.
o   He gave us the ability to choose.
o   He gave us the ability to step up to responsibility.
o   He gave us joy.
o   He gave us the ability to set up boundaries and not compromise our boundaries of goodness and hope.
o   He gave us the ability to help others in appropriate ways, to allow them to act independently.
o   He directs us to be free from compulsiveness, knowing that God only brings ultimate results.

What's your hope at this moment? What do you want to happen in your life?

Did you know it costs nothing to hope? It costs you everything if you do not have hope, or dream.

Ask yourself, why am I not fulfilling it? If it is truly yours to act within and obtain, then do a first step toward achievement. Right now. No, I don't mean put it up on a list. I mean, look up the cost of the trip, buy the materials, call the old man, register for a class, offer a small donation. Start.

I heard of a 91-year-old man with a bucket list. Make your bucket list your "bucket to-do list", not a dreamless check off list. That exercise makes you less fearful of the giant leap toward the life of your dreams.

Fear eats up hope. Lost hope kills spirit. Lack of spiritualism makes a curmudgeon. An irascible curmudgeon is not well liked and accomplishes little. Is that your legacy? Ha, ha! Get the lead out. If your teenage son sat on the couch as much as you did, would you have something to say to him?

The process of knowing our assets and our weak characteristics doesn't happen in one hour. It takes a lifetime. But guess what, that is what you have to obtain it in – your lifetime. That worked out well, don't you think? Begin.

If you take God's omnipotent gifts (your endowments) and add your actions, you have a good purpose for your life. Voila, a legacy. I'd like to know my legacy exists before I die, wouldn't you?

What are your special gifts? (Worksheet time again)

What do I already carry? Knowledge, wisdom, caring, kindness, prayer, respect for others, lots and lots of love, gratitude, grace, smiles, giggles and poise. I am also a little country, some culture, live in wonderment, and inquisitiveness, have a vision for art, a love of music, am a dancing soul, have a love of photography and the written word. I have cheerfulness much of the time, but I also carry a little lonesomeness for family and friends I have lost. I carry the love of God. I also have fear, terror, some panic, some shyness, but those are transitory feelings and I know with God, I won't carry any of them long. And Empathy. I carry a lot of that. I carry a little extra weight, love of mankind, secrets about love and sex, torment around some old habits that were judgmental and mean. Those are just a little salt and pepper that keep me humble; reminders necessary to keep me in line. Mostly I carry a heart full of hope and excitement for life. Wow. That is a list.

Your turn: (I need you to write a full paragraph here.)

Let's sum up this chapter in what you think Heaven or death, when you pass over, is going to be like. Write a letter to others about it.

Here's mine:

> *I've loved and will miss the people influencing my life but I will be consciously and unconsciously excited to be among all my past moments and friends and in oblivion to time or dimension that the Earth side of Heaven affords me.*
>
> *I'll probably miss the ocean, the rise and fall of our geographic horizon, the beauty I have shared with you on the Earth's plain, but I know the beauty of Heaven will outshine anything earthly.*
>
> *Yes, mostly I think I will miss the anticipation of the coming to the place I get to go; knowing I will be satiated in all Your glory.*

Deception - It's All Relative

I did not get the instruction book of life. I grew up a little faulty.

Do you lie? Do you pretend to like something you don't?

Guess what, if we lie to ourselves; in all likelihood, we, at the very least, tell little fibs, white lie, or deceive by omission to the rest of the world. Yup. Without knowing it. The extrication of the truth is too easy.

Think.

Thinking is opening our minds to our absolute maximum true potential, our possible genius.

Now go. Think. How will you expand your mind today?

Think about this - our parents and teachers hammered into us the things that were true back then. We carry them in our subconscious as derivatives of rules in life. Cold Hard Facts. Maybe we received parental admonition over some of their inalienable beliefs! Wake up that subliminal cortex – The planet Pluto is gone! Blue jeans can be worn to church. You can own a home with no money. History has made a whole bunch more pages since our parents 'knew all their formalities'.

Gloria Steinem said, *"So many of us are living the unlived lives of our mothers."*

Deception of self or others robs us of peace of mind. How could you have serenity when you have deceived someone, especially someone you claim to love – yourself? Deception and lies keep us from living a life as we had mentally designed. We are guarding and interpreting life as we think it. The belief of that is stilted; in scrupulous light, it is clearly incongruent.

You may talk about the "id". I call it inner voice of conscience and control. Our ids need improvement.

Way back in 1777, when sage men ruled, the definition of Moral Conscience was described as present at the heart of a person. It enjoins him at the appropriate moment to do good and to avoid evil. It judges particular choices, approving those that are good and denouncing those that are nefarious. It is a judgement of reason whereby the human person recognizes the moral quality of a concrete act that he is going to perform. By the judgement of his conscience, man perceives and recognizes the prescriptions of man's laws and divine law.

The question I propose is, "Do you always use your moral conscience?"

See, deep down, I believe most of us know right from wrong. When I run a red light, I have a tug of 'illegal' and risk of life. But I had no visible fine, traffic ticket, or accident, so it was alright, right? I was believing in my formed opinion that if no repercussions, go ahead, called "obedience to the unenforceable". Does a bear shit in the woods? Yes. Is a red light offense offensive? Yes.

I wrote this book because I personally need to mediate between my inner mindful world and the reality of life - how do I channel my instincts, my subliminal characteristic, my individual approach, my ego, my inhibitions in this crazy world? Someone told me I am a pioneer in my own psychoanalysis. However, I do know that without a good reservoir of experience and intelligence, I have done many approaches wrongly. There are so many dimensions to explore – I will try to walk you through the markers that make up your personal character, offer a method to change where some need an uptick; and create a method in your head that makes emotionally and spiritually healthy decisions for yourself. We are going to talk about what stimulates you into action or reaction and how to respond for the betterment of all around you. You will be the operant toward positive outcomes and influences.

I am going to walk you out of your life of deception and into purity of heart, peace of mind, and effect many other organs as you heal your own unmanageability. Your assignments will be to practice finding peace and embracing serenity in every moment of your life, regardless of a disgruntled business partner, an alcoholic spouse, a former felon, an inflamed, angry teen, and the rest of the little issues too; the driver in front of you. God already gave us the grace to accept serenity. You and God will be giving yourself a dispensation from sins you have nefariously, many times seemingly innocently, walked through.

Take a closer look at where we went wrong. Let's get our hearts back on track to be people who don't hurt inside and who don't harm others.

Why would I harm myself on purpose? Why would I lie to myself? Why would I want to be that way? Are my actions always in harmony with my heart? Do I deceive myself? Sometimes I can't believe my lying eyes!

If I lie in my own hula hoop – the visual sphere of orbit that is my business only – what then? What then am I doing to others? My family, best friend, a clerk or customer? As we become aware of our own deceptions, we will grow to see perpetrators all around us. The gest to not fall prey to cheating society and others who deceive, is hard. But the payoff is out of this world. The payoff connects us with the real universe, the one we want to see grow purer and cleanse our own minds of misnomers and rule breaking. We have to face and admit and disclaim poor corrosive habits.

Deception can be quite tricky. We justify and rationalize away all that we do; and many of the things that others do. Why of course, if my spouse wants to not tell the bank about their $200 mistake in our favor, I will go along. After all, the person I profess to love the most has made a rightful decision on our behalf. We deserve extra money however it comes. We have probably been shortchanged and cheated that amount before. And they charge us too much for services anyway. WRONG! You are both in the wrong.

Self-deception, plus rationalization, plus justification. There. We always want others to know the justification we feel for our negative actions or that others use. Just in case they have a swindler personality too.

I waxed so poetic when I would rationalize my opinion, with quite an artistic interpretation off the truth.

Now go back and count the lies in that paragraph. The outcome also includes that you and your spouse both cheat. Ouch, huh? Did you count lying by omission?

Much later in this book, you will find, that I am now devoted to cultivating how to tell the truth in a gentle, compassionate, and loving answer.

Try this on: I love to look pulled together, knowledgeable, self-assured, well spoken, wise, and emit the epitome of kindness.

Which of all that is truest? Any of it? I may 'love to appear' all that, but is any of that true of my character within? Am I fake?

Fake, fake, fake, and fake. But don't we want everyone to see us in a light of "doing well" and self-confident? Oh, you bet! What if we stopped bluffing? What if we came to the world and always asked questions to actually become wiser and well spoken? What if we stood back and let others shine in their moments, stopped interrupting with our more all-important topping anecdote about your topic? What if we accepted people and offered nothing but gratitude about being in their company and enjoying life here, now, in this moment? Gratitude = Grace and Attitude.

See, if I firmly hold my ideas with absolute consistency, even if lies; doesn't that make them true?!

Would you feel better about yourself, if you believed your lies? Hmmm...

Are we ourselves? Do you go along? Do you insist on your way? When you start to talk, do you want others to stop talking and listen? Do we need to be one of the first 10 in line or we become disgruntled and complaining? Someone has to be Number 11. Do we bully others? Do we demand? And then do we expect better from others?

You go to a fine restaurant, you expect a degree of taste. If told cost of food, you expect service, hot food, etc. You then judge the taste, service, delivery against that "name" or the higher cost of food. How much did you like it? Are you satiated with the amount and flavors? Your preferences, your perceptions and your expectations are then processed into your judgement of the restaurant. Expectations lead to disappointments. What if we considered each experience anew without expectation or judgement?

Further, I will remind you that your tongue has receptors, transductors, electrical impulses, taste cells that it sends by neurons to your vagus nerve in your frontal lobe, thalamus and temporal lobe. You are experiencing something like never before. That, my friends is where the brain is involved. Taste is a gatekeeper between a physical activity and the internal brain work. Do you get that both your physical organs and your responding thoughts were working coincidently?

That is psychophysical action with introspection, cognition, and self-observation at work. If you further add negativity or bad judgement of the restaurant, food, etc. you have engaged more brain chemicals, but not in a positive way. You are now thinking about thinking.

We have complex translators, gatekeepers, and neurons that thrash around in an orderly fashion toward thinking. Do we ever entertain rethinking? Do you specifically allow open flow or do you have strong biases that new thoughts can't break? Do you have expectations in every scenario of your life?

Here is a great example of our formation of bias by Malcolm Gladwell, a social theorist:

> *"The unthinking, unconscious mind makes snap judgments that can provide us with fairly accurate insight to help us read situations and assess danger levels...can also lead us to the downside of leaping to conclusions, such as racial and gender discrimination."*

Did you ever think that expectations of others lead to every single disappointment we have had? Hm...Who owns the disappointment and reacts inappropriately because of it? Yup, Me. Capital M. Expectations in my head are just ideas, not written rules. I needed to realize that my first reaction has always been dubious, maybe not healthy for me, or you! When I am feeling insecure, negativity has an open door to my mind. Not everything in my mind is reality. I thought I was born with this thinking and that is where I was to live. After much research, I realized my thoughts might stop at my hippocampus, failing to synap to the logical and knowledgeable parts of my brain. The hippocampus can cause personal catastrophies if listened to. They are like ASAP reactions from our bodies. They only recall and record all occurrences. Even one jump over and you will encounter the amygdala where we are told to run from snakes. Let those synapses work with a pause before speaking.

Rumination –
Let Go of Your History –
Detach from Opinions

All my knowledge. All my logic. All my sensical and practical thinking. All my research and reading. All my hiding. All my cooperative ways. All my pleading. All my threats. All my angry dialect. All my crying. All my pouting. All my crossed arms. All my pleasing. All my walking on egg shells. All my hugging. All his favorite recipes. All his favorite people. All my work for his parties. All our tries at new sexual excitement. All the attempts at self-treatment. All the Valium, Ambien, Xanax, Tylenol. All the somatic illnesses. All the extra work when he didn't do it. All. My all. Nothing worked.

There was still alcoholism; still misunderstanding and mistreatment, and still a suicide. I had completely lost my life, myself, our relationship, our life, and eventually his life.

Had I known others had rehearsed this trauma, had written this same story before me, I maybe could have saved two lives. As it is now, only I am saved, but experiencing more joy and spirituality than I remember since the freedom and security as a young child in my family home. What altered my path?

Altering how I lived could have saved two lives. I needed Al-Anon to do it. Altering how you live, could save more. Other attendees to the Al Anon meetings, offer patronage by saying, "By my living a different style and perhaps my influence, my alcoholic stepped into AA and saved himself from death by alcohol." Stepping into Al-Anon saved me. Remember that poster, "All I Ever Needed to Know, I Learned in Kindergarten"? Well, all I never needed to know as an adult, I learned in Al Anon. (Many people think Al-Anon is about the alcoholic. But no names are mentioned and we talk about me, not the him/her.) I have a new life. He had to love that I finally learned to get off his back! My new life is full of strength and spirit. My new life is full of deep camaraderie and close friendships with those who know me well. My new life influences everyone I encounter in a better way.

With a 93% stat of changing for the better in the Al Anon program, odds are good you will find answers there also. Another statistic that is stunning, 99% of folks who walk in the door never come back. Fear of losing their pride and status, mostly keep people from helping themselves. Fear, which is exactly what Al Anon diminishes in people.

Opening the really heavy door with the electric shock doorknob into the tv crew and audience (NOT!) of Al-Anoners is quite a first step for many. Actually, members usually welcome you with open arms and a handshake, "Sit anywhere."

I HAD TO CHANGE OR DIE.

I Am Neurotypical and
I Need Correction

The most terrible thing about materialism, even more terrible than its proneness to violence, is its boredom, from which sex, alcohol, drugs, all devices for putting out the accusing light of reason and suppressing the unrealizable aspirations of love, offer a prospect of deliverance. –Malcolm Muggeridge

We can get caught up in possessions, power, position, personality, and pleasure and neglect our relationship with God. We find then our lives are lacking purpose and feel empty.

Materialism is the only form of distraction from true bliss. –Doug Horton

Most of the luxuries and many of the so-called comforts of life are not only not indispensable, but positive hindrances to the elevation of mankind. –Thoreau

And/Or we deceive. We pretend we are better than we are. We lie. We take all that we can get away with. We superficially agree to dates and responsibilities we never intend fulfill.

We deceive ourselves and others. We hate ourselves more. We get worse, and sometimes, years, and years pass, where we continue to exacerbate the madness, the cycle of no love for self. We can spiral in a whirlpool downward and become so removed from the true happiness we wanted in life.

My behavior toward myself was unacceptable. My mental criticism of me created dislike and unworthiness.

Many of us seem to have inner critics, doubters, saboteurs, perfectionists, etc. all sitting on our shoulders, vigilant. They are tyrannical and work on our egos constantly. They go to work to protect our psyche from being wounded, telling us we will never be good enough, safe enough, satisfied or gain love and acceptance or safety, and a bent ego may strike out.

The twelve-step system has allowed me to let go of those critics, along with them went my ego and pridefulness. But I had to learn how to, and be willing to let them go, after realizing each one did me no good in my pursuit of happiness.

Step Seven in the program is simple – it is about asking God to help me be faithful to my values, to treat myself with love and respect. I no longer liked having negative thoughts about myself. I was damaging my own self-worth. I had secretly been blaming others for their cutting words. I had to first be aware I was doing both things; self-talk was harsh and I was believing others judged me harshly! Cognizance allowed pessimism to be ebbed to nil. What a cool result. I had clarity in who was creating my visceral feelings in relationships – me. It was a very valuable lesson. No one is omnisciently perfect – you or me. Heard that adage, "Let it begin with me"?

Our job is to love others without stopping to inquire whether or not they are worthy. – Thomas Merton

Prayer by Jay Gilbertson:

"Oh, Great Spirit, whose voice I hear in the wind and whose breath gives life to all – hear me. I ask for wisdom and strength, not to be superior to my brothers and sisters, but to be able to fight my greatest enemy – myself."

Carolyn Myss, five time best selling author by the New York Times in <u>Life Lessons</u> says:

> *"When you evaluate your health, you have to evaluate every organ in the body, but you have to start with the one that is most inflamed."*

That one can be *emotion!*

Dear Adult Me,

I don't like who you became and it looks as though you have lost any potential.

Signed, Little Me.

I bet if the truth be told, you have at some time in your life believed that you were so out of control, so far from your real self that you would make a great actor!

Do you pretend to have an image different than you really are?

Do you pretend to be rich?

Do you wear too much make up? Overspend on a clothing item you feel you deserve or would make you look successful?

Is your credit card balance out of bounds with your income?

Does your family refuse to speak to you?

Do you sit/eat/spend too much?

Have you lost motivation to use your talents?

Do you allow someone to rule you other than God?

Do you get to pick the restaurant, movie, etc. or always deflect responsibility to another?

Do you back off engagements you promised?

Do you neglect your very own values of righteousness, truthfulness, and fairness?

Do you have any self-esteem?

Have you defaulted your security to another?

Are you scared to death to tell the truth about how you feel inside?

Do you have any legacies to list?

Have you ever wanted to be in the witness protection program just so you could run away from your own tangled web?

Do you lie? Do you pretend to like something you don't?

Rosellen Brown wrote:

"When it comes time to do your own life, you either perpetuate your childhood or you stand on it and finally kick it out from under."

Where did my ideas come from?

Let the past be the past.

Are we qualified to force our will on others? We may know they need to change according to what we know, and we may have their answer, but is it up to us to force them by using the oral word? The only change anyone can make is through their own willingness and ability.

Older folks had their methods to survive which they passed on to us. Many formerly used modalities often serve no purpose today. We must adapt to today. It is up to us to redo things: rebuild, reorganize, restructure. Even a house as old as you needs remodeling. It is up to us to invent, try, and experiment - if you have the willingness, because you most likely do have the ability.

What defined me for years is that I thought in my dreams, that I could change the effect my personal history had on me, that by symbiosis, better things would shine through that history just by wishing them true. My former reactions, were the commentary I heard in my head. What use do I have for their (my ancestors) reasoning in the past?

The belief that my mind held, was that everybody lived under some trauma in every house. My mother said that we all have our troubles. I thought that the reasons for all that had happened to me wrongfully, would show up in lessons for life. Inevitably, many happenings in my family left me in fear and some abandonment, as all in the household were busy protecting themselves. I kept reactivating my old reactions. Our reactions in a ten-person household, comparably, were the same. (Yes, most all of us have been involved in some sort of treatment, service to others or program to heal.) See, living with an alcoholic had altered our upbringing and former exposures. I had unconsciously submitted myself to define my humanness based on sickness. And I kept doing it! To the point of disappointment in myself! I was inadequate and worthless, and kept the cycle going with my own created thoughts and images. Now I see the patterns. I was embarrassed all the time. I thought it was how my life cycle was to be. One of the first things I needed to do was identify where I was deficient – when did abandonment occur, for instance, arrive or what facet was I needing to look at that didn't get fed as a child or young person.

I always love when the airline employee asks me if I have anything given to me by a stranger. Hell, yes. Everything in my emotional and intellectual baggage is from others. I have been influenced by people who fear Communism, the Freedom Fighters, nuclear bombs, tomorrow, the revelations, etc. I just might have a bomb in my emotional baggage made of fear.

Close your eyes for a second. At what age/period of time did you feel most loved, felt respected, and knew you were cared about? Hone in.

What was okay about you? Design today around that same place. What was your purpose/vision then? What is your vision today? Whatever your answer, to do God's will, to be happy, live in peace, to love; let that be your mission statement. Will you create a quality life with that? (After a discussion once, someone asked me if my mission statement was just something I hung on the wall? Wow.)

God does not participate in evil; when people choose on their own, he lets them go.

I love this quick little prayer:

Dear Lord, help me to undo illusions from my mind and heart. I pray to live in the real world of love.

But wait, it isn't over. We have more to do than realize we still have potential to grow. We have to take actions.

"Much of our activity these days is nothing more than a cheap anesthetic to deaden the pain of an empty life." - Unknown

What are your terms that you will accept in life, compared to living the life in the throes of alcoholism or someone else's disease?

Secularly, alcoholism has distorted some truths for us. Do I live in profanity, in benevolent air? Is your creative dexterity stymied? Your desire to live a long life? Do you fight? Are you giving up to a more demanding force that someone else has laid out?

Who said that you cannot hang with teenagers when you are fifty?

Who said not to visit with felons because they are labelled bad people?

Who says? Who broke your thinker?

I learn the quickest when I hang with people not my age. I learn life lessons from all my elders; for they have been in many of my walks yet to happen. And I learn new lingo, how to use my phone, and get reminded of young love when I hang with teenagers. And I learn from toddlers that I need to learn, as I watch them discover life with their new ways. Hang out with everyone. Shun no class or age or religion. (And I want peace in the world, Bob. Signed, Miss America)

Worry, Worry, Worry
Marsha, Marsha, Marsha

———

Check out how you truthfully answer these questions:

Do you worry?

Do you have money problems?

Do you worry about someone else's problems?

Do you lie?

Do you cancel plans frequently"?

Do you make threats, "If you don't, I won't/I will…"?

Are you afraid to upset someone else?

Are you hurt or embarrassed by others?

Do you have anxiety and fear?

Do you feel you are failing?

Habits are Us

Why do we practice habits?

Amy Johnson, author of <u>The Little Book of Big Change</u>, says:

"Every habit (negative) starts as a well-meaning attempt to feel better in the moment... then we realize we are doing it again and realize it is creating angst...it is a method that has worked before but it is a personal failure."

Our basal ganglia in our brains might be the culprit. By repeating a particular behavior over and over for a long period, we learned the activity subconsciously! It takes very little brain power after that to do it over and over. And unfortunately, the patterned behavior maybe an irritating or undesirable habit. It takes a lifetime to unlearn these, unless you acquire the method to refocus contained somewhat in this book.

We've learned so far that what we have experienced and the people who influenced us, pretty much make up our styles of living. We know what we like and we are working on boundaries of things that are harmful in another chapter; we are headed for Heaven on Earth.

But, here comes the kicker: Is what you are doing and saying yours? And is it giving you happiness?

Or a habit? Or an influence? Or just what we know so far? Or someone else's forced opinion?

Do your answers to those questions suggest a need to refocus? Resolve now to be aware of when you are not thinking but rather, repeating others' tapes.

When you were younger, before some of the inventions that have been produced in your lifetime, no one had ever thought or invented those inventions. I'm older so my examples will put you into giggles but I never contextualized as a five-year-old person: computers, memory typewriters, a phone without a cord, backup cameras, a kiosk for coffee. I remember repeated and lengthy, on company time, business meetings discussing purchase of items that no longer exist.

So if you take that statement, you can guess that I was also imprisoned by some thoughts my authority figures put into my head. Best descriptive phrase my mother ever said to me to help understand this was: "I did the best I could with what I had at the time." She had no more to work with. No derogative to my mother, but she didn't know there would be so many changes in our two generations for her to be able to teach me futuristic knowledge.

Her habits and those of my educators, elders, ministers, camp counselors, nuns, etc. were based on what was known up to their time. You cannot make someone understand what they cannot foresee.

So 'those people' gave us their all. But it wasn't enough for our world today. It could not be. BUT YET, SOME OF US DRIVE AROUND WITH ONLY THOSE TOOLS OF OUR PARENTS. You've seen it; the cars in the yard in three generations. My 35 years with the Department of Social Services included three generations of criminal families! There are some cultures who wish to keep their traditions in-tact – children must follow the rules of the tribe, or hunt for their food, or buy Fords, cheer for the Packers. I mean habits get instilled in us.

Where then is there growth, unless we learn better? And get gooder, as my friend says?

Those controllers are all in your head. The committee. Brain cells. "All's I know is..." Habits.

Without stimulating activity in our first three years of life, low to mediocre brain development only, occurs. Three of four infants are less than stellar in that development. Wow. Habits and environment create us.

You do have a committee in your head. I will tell you about them.

From Dr. Anthony Komaroff, clinical investigator:

"Stage 1 of memory is about Acquisition.

When you learn new information, it takes the form of temporary pathways of nerve cell activity in the brain. (Short term memory)

Most of this quickly fades. The memories that endure are those that were encoded most completely in the first place – the information that you paid the closest attention to when you learned it. Memories that involve multiple senses as well as emotions are more likely to be retained.

You probably remember clearly what you were doing when you heard about the 9/11 terrorist attacks, for example. You probably remember who else was with you, where you were, the first picture you saw of the twin towers. That's because the emotional charge of learning that our country had been attacked caused you to store everything about that moment in your mental history.

But you probably have no idea what you were doing exactly 24 hours after you heard about the 9/11 attacks.

Stage 2: Consolidation. For short term memory to become long term memory, the initial neuronal pathways must be strengthened. When an event is emotionally charged it is more likely to become part of a long-term memory. Once a memory is established (consolidated), it is stored in areas of the cerebral cortex, where memory and perception are regulated. That is the large, domed outer layer of the brain. I say large, because this is where your brain can expand, increase surface area if fed the right input, healthy messages and correct snacks. You want to make this large by using your cognitive skills!

Stage 3: Retrieval. Memories are stored in the brain as unique patterns of nerve cell activation. When you are not thinking about a memory, the pattern is inactive. When you want to recall a memory, your brain must reactivate the pattern. How long this takes depends on how familiar you are with the information you're looking for." (end of Dr. Anthony Romaroff)

Just to scare you into taking heed; memory, problem solving and creativity shrink – think of it like the pronounced signs of little hearing loss, grey hair, a wrinkle. I know it is shocking to believe. I am being straightforward with you, if you are forty-ish, your memory quite likely is diminishing. Your frontal cortex is shrinking. This book is written with trueness of intent to work against that very shrinkage!

Three Types of Memory from Douglas Rehder, Doctor of Audiology:

Episodic Long Term (a childhood baseball game, Christmas at grandparents, last summer's vacation)

Semantic Long Term (Memory of things, ability to read, count, write, and recollect general knowledge)

Working Memory (Right now, what is worth paying attention to, categorizing into important or not)

Knowledge about the different types of memory and where in the brain they are housed, has come from research. I give great thanks to the two great minds just quoted.

So why do you care about what you just read? Because you are using your brain to get wiser. But in order to get wiser, you must think; in order for you to break a habit or change a pattern of what you are pulling forth and re-acting from, you must believe that your physiological make-up is capable of growth.

It is a real, maybe intangible, but recognizable biologic process. But what we funnel in, especially when other 'notes' (memories) are ingrained there, must be recognized as a replacement. Equals = a change in our thinking or breaking a habit. Willingness is a huge part of adapting new ways.

There really is great power in training in positive thinking. Once your synapses are metabolizing the right newer, progressive openness of thought, wisdom happens.

> *The pessimist complains about the wind.*
> *The optimist expects it to change.*
> *The realist adjusts our sails.*
> William Arthur Ward

If I lived with what my parents told me and only the knowledge from previous years I used to live in, I would not have new insights, progressive technology, or efficiency in my life. My problem is I still believe everything I think. So I have to upgrade my thinking. I nearly named this book, Passive Human Scrolling, as it seemed it was easier to do as I always had done.

Routines, outdated intuition, 'Mom said...', 'But Sister Philomena said I would go to hell'; librarians, and then of course, the stuff we make up with our opinions, fill up our judgement, social conscience, and rationale.

Sister Sue, Joe Blo, Aunt Edna, and Buddy each had different 'rulers' before in their lives that created in them different judgements and rationale. Okay, maybe Buddy was in Sister Philomena's class with you, but mostly, different stimuli created differing opinions from yours.

Now take the driver in the car next to you who swerves into your lane. He has stimuli. It might be of a completely different source than you imagine.

The court house clerk, the supplier, a shoe salesman, a homeless person, your CEO, especially coworkers, your best friend, your aunt, your broker, the neighbor. Their stimuli, their physiological genetic make-up, their 'rulers', the priests, their law professors, their mechanics, their books, influenced them to their way of thinking, AT THIS TIME in their education about life.

What makes you of superior opinion? Your ego. Period.

What makes you an exemplary researcher on that topic? Maybe books and on-line sites you found. More so than the up-to-then experienced forefather. What makes you feel one up? Your ego. Period. Drop that part of your psyche and just be happy you are learning.

Drop that need to be one up. Drop it like a hot potato. Willingness to learn opens you to upgrade yourself.

An ego only makes fools of us. We infer, we opine. We advise unrequested. We profess things we don't know. We tell others what to do, how to do it, and when we expect it. What makes you one up?

You still get to tell young'uns not to touch the stove, but beyond safety and security, your words and thoughts belong in your own hula-hoop.

I can tell a teenager not to pop his pimples, it leaves scars. I can tell off the guy who ran into my car. I can curse about the doctor who missed spotting my mother's cancer earlier. To what avail folks? My verbalization of those thoughts is lower intelligence speaking. Current reality is the only truth. Acceptance of such is wisdom. Let unswerving integrity be your watchword, stop for nothing less.

That in essence is the motive behind this book; not to tell you what to think but rather, to help you to know that there is a need, a necessity for you to think bigger.

High Ego Defense Mechanismistic people are extremists who are dangerous to themselves and others.

Pants on Fire

My mind repeats certain things even though they are not true! One is that I was unlovable. Another is that I might go to Hell for all the bad things I have already done. My internal and personal monologue was telling me that I might not achieve or make a legacy or live in God's grace.

If that set of personal philosophical beliefs hang around in your mind, what expectations do you think you might have? - A very low standard of living and expectations of yourself. Fact was, I didn't know differently! Growth, risk, stretching my potential, I thought, quit at about twenty-six years of age. These beliefs, these personal untenable truths you rehearse - I rehearsed - allowed for me very low self-esteem and personal worth.

The capability to take on challenges or meet obstacles was nearly defeated with placation and laziness. My efforts were always going to be fruitless. No one will listen to me. (- All stupid responses toward 'fulfillment'.)

It is a wonder anyone became my friend or for that matter, that I ever admitted to having any fun! The consequences I faced daily at my own demise were excruciating. Kicked myself in the head. Should have kicked myself in the butt! On top of that, I doubted anyone knew better how to help me. I didn't trust anyone to be smart enough. If I could not adopt intelligent ways just by aging, I doubted anyone else knew what they were doing either.

That was my impression. However, I had a viable life style going on in pretense. I had limited intelligence, but by God, I was going to let you know where your deficits were. I could chew on the poor salesclerk in a fast minute.

That is called arrogance. Combine those dementias.

The view I had for my future was dim. Believe it or not, I was glad I hooked up with a hardworking man. We were dull together but stable and wage earners. Therefore, I would have security into old age. Money and a man to help me use the walker and wipe my chin when I dribbled.

The shocking arrest of my husband while under the influence, alcoholism taking over our lives, and near death of myself, him and several others shook my mind enough that I went into fight or flea and a sort of relinquishment of my sanity. The program of Al-Anon stepped in via a GREAT friend. There was a Y in the road and I was given a choice. Some professionals label my previous state a fixed mindset of trouble. I had heard also of being stuck in grief, as a diagnosis. I was leaning on both those diagnoses.

I walked into the rooms of Al-Anon broken. I was so embarrassed and humiliated to be there. I had to admit I needed help. That alone was terrifying. Someone said if you change your thinking, you change your whole life. Someone said that we are all in denial of true circumstances. After meeting, she caught up with me and asked if I journaled. She suggested that I do and then see what patterns of negativity I was making for myself. Wait, this problem I have is because of my alcoholic, not me. She said, maybe I will find some places I am lying to myself and doing repetitive behavior, hoping for a different outcome. (Bully Al-Anoner.) Son of a gun, if she wasn't right on target about me. I was so in denial that these were my circumstances, I blamed the alcoholic for all of my defensive actions. I found I was doing whatever he said, drunk or sober. I was embarrassed to go to second and third meetings also. I had failed. I was so defensive I could not argue for my own place in humanity. I thought I did not deserve better, because of what an alcoholic had told me. Someone else's perspective on the same scenario played out in worldwide homes, was immediately noticed in those rooms! I had to ask myself, "What happened that made me believe my lies?"

I began to have personal epiphanies!

With a program in place, I could begin to grow up, mature, and put on big girl panties that I never knew existed for me before. I could change. I could eliminate some of my, now distinguishing themselves, personality traits that were unbecoming. I could add assets that help me to communicate better. I gave myself permission to be truthful and to pray again, and to focus on my likes and interests. It was like I became hungry for wisdom. The steps, one at a time, offered hope. A little bit of clarity came with each meeting. Daily morning readings afforded me the crutches I needed to step into the day. I started to believe that even I had potential.

Through my experience in the program, I have had the good fortune to already experience the removal of many defects or at least a chipping away of old habits that had clutched onto me in my depths of depression, unhappiness, judgement, resentment and all those other icks. I humbly learned that I am not the center of the universe and I ceased trying to play God by controlling methods. See there is a prize in working through the steps: relief of charades, defects and shortcomings. Wow.

What I discovered after my inventory is my illusions were greater than the reality. Fear of facing my defects (I blamed them on 'brain glitches') kept me at a standstill. Until I became willing to put pencil to paper, I was arresting my growth based on an intangible.

See, here is what happened when I allowed myself to engage in only good things in my life, when I talked with God about the gift of life each day, I became grateful for every moment.

When I humbly let go of stinking thinking
When I humbly let go of bad habits and preconceived notions

When I practiced these new tenets
When I read
When I worked with others who had gone before me
When I let go and let God

I read about a psychologist who knew about my codependent diagnosis. Others in meetings spoke of being stuck in their lives. Dweck wrote of children like me who choose to redo an easy puzzle, stay safe, and thinking that is a smart choice. Other unstymied children always chose the hard puzzle.

She quotes: "*I think intelligence is something you have to work for ... it isn't just given to you.... Most kids, if they're not sure of an answer, will not raise their hand to answer the question. But what I usually do is raise my hand, because if I'm wrong, then my mistake will be corrected. Or I will raise my hand and say, 'How would this be solved?' or 'I don't get this. Can you help me?' Just by doing that I'm increasing my intelligence.*"

In Al-Anon, I learned to ask. I am amazed by how rich that can make your intelligence. This proved to me that I could still learn. I was not going to be incessantly deficient.

Direct Quotes from Dweck that I can't say any better:

> "*But one of the most profound applications of this insight has to do not with business or education but with love. Dweck found that people exhibited the same dichotomy of dispositions in their personal relationships: Those with a fixed mindset believed their ideal mate would put them on a pedestal and make them feel like the epitome of perfect, like "the god of a one-person religion," whereas those with the growth mindset preferred a partner who would recognize their faults and lovingly help improve them, someone who would encourage them to learn new things and became a better person. The fixed mindset, it turns out, is at the root of many of our most toxic cultural myths about "true love." Dweck scops:*

"The growth mindset says all of these things can be developed. All — you, your partner, and the relationship — are capable of growth and change.

In the fixed mindset, the ideal is instant, perfect, and perpetual compatibility. Like it was meant to be. Like riding off into the sunset. Like "they lived happily ever after."

Perfect appearing people often are insecure or shy and anxiety filled...about being perfect!

One problem is that people with the fixed mindset expect everything good to happen automatically. It's not that the partners will work to help each other solve their problems or gain skills. It's that this will magically occur through their love, sort of the way it happened to Sleeping Beauty, whose coma was cured by her prince's kiss, or to Cinderella, whose miserable life was suddenly transformed by her prince."

Our culture has accepted two huge lies...the first is that if you disagree with someone, you must hate them. The second is that to love someone means you agree with everything they believe or do. Both are nonsense. You don't have to compromise convictions to be compassionate.

Dweck goes on to say:

"This also applies to the myth of mind-reading, where the fixed mindset believes that an ideal couple should be able to read each other's minds and finish each other's sentences. She cites a study that invited people to talk, vernacularly about their relationships:

Those with the fixed mindset felt threatened and hostile after talking about even minor discrepancies in how they and their partner saw their relationship. Even a minor discrepancy threatened their belief that they shared all of each other's views.

But most destructive of all relationship myths is the belief that if it requires work, something is terribly wrong and that any discrepancy of opinions or preferences is indicative of character flaws on behalf of one's partner."

And Dweck offers a reality check:

"Just as there are no great achievements without setbacks, there are no great relationships without conflicts and problems along the way.

When people with a fixed mindset talk about their conflicts, they assign blame. Sometimes they blame themselves, but often they blame their partner. And they assign blame to a trait — a character flaw.

But it doesn't end there. When people blame their partner's personality for the problem, they feel anger and disgust toward them.

And it barrels on: Since the problem manifests from fixed traits, it can't be solved. So once people with the fixed mindset see flaws in their partners, they become contemptuous of them and dissatisfied with the whole relationship.

Those with the growth mindset, on the other hand, can acknowledge their partners' imperfections, without assigning blame, and still feel that they have a fulfilling relationship. They see conflicts as problems of communication, not of personality or character. This dynamic holds true as much in romantic partnerships as in friendship and even in people's relationships with their parents. Dweck summarizes her findings:

When people embark on a relationship, they encounter a partner who is different from them, and they haven't learned how to deal with the differences. In a good relationship, people develop these skills and, as they do, both partners grow and the relationship deepens. But for this to happen, people need to feel they're on the same side... As an atmosphere of trust developed, they [become] vitally interested in each other's development.

What it all comes down to is that a mindset is an interpretative process that tells us what is going on around us. In the fixed mindset, that process is scored by an internal monologue of constant judging and evaluation, using every piece of information as evidence either for or against such assessments as whether you're a good person, whether your partner is selfish, or whether you are better than the person next to you. In a growth mindset, on the other hand, the internal monologue is not one of judgment but one of voracious appetite for learning, constantly seeking out the kind of input that you can metabolize into learning and constructive action."

Well said and very in-depth to our core thinking.

Good person, as they say in Britain, is an 'Upright Man/Woman'.

I had to fully know that it is WE that share in a relationship. I am not alone. We are each an individual in this promised relationship. And we are each fully capable to make good decisions and choices on our own, toward that good relationship. There is a clause: Provided that what we do individually does not hurt the other or the relationship. Sometimes that is a fine line, but we must remember that we are individuals first.

Are you still trying to get your partner to be all things to you? That's false thinking. You are lying to yourself about that possibility. True! Do you still want someone to do for you what you can't do for yourself in a relationship? Do you have expectations that someone else will support you financially? How about emotionally? To heal you from emotional wounds? What world are you from? Reread those. Are you an unperson? What pampered world did you walk out of? If you don't like who you are, change up. Get your own self-esteem. Yin and Yang are treats when they work out to be fifty-fifty.

You cannot love anyone (!) until you know how to be good and treat yourself with love. You need first to accept who you are, with the flaws you come with and the actions and behaviors you do. The only way a partner wants to be loved is with their flaws and the behaviors that they do. Learn to first be your own best friend and cheerleader. You have got to feel good about you, to give that same acceptance to another. And caretake with yourself. My goodness, if you are not able to care for yourself in good order, who wants you? We each are a made up of conditioned responses so far. Until we uptick to allow for a better self, we cannot fully be good, without pretension, to another.

Walking into a relationship, especially a committed marriage with the idea that you will not have to fully support yourself is grounds for divorce. Both parties will be unhappy at some point. Here's your job: Fully support yourself emotionally, mentally, spiritually, financially, physically and health wise. Isn't that what you expect from your 'other'?

It also goes without saying that we cannot depend on any other to fulfill our needs. The 'other' friend, relative or stranger cannot carry out our responsibilities. To take on others' jobs or responsibilities is to rob them of dignity and self-respect which could have been gained had we taken care of our own load. Not doing our share upsets the balance and allows disrespect, resentment and disappointment to sneak right in!

Well, here's how to be a respected individual with self-worth:

1. Stay within your own budget
2. Stop allowing abuse of self
3. Take care of the responsibilities listed above

Think of granting yourself with kindness at all times. Then what you have for others is the respect and kindness you give yourself. Start there.

Isn't that what you expect anyone else to do? Pretty clear. So that means, eat right, believe in your potential, relish in your own talents, pick up after yourself, make your bed, get some exercise in, have a reserve in the bank, read, listen, open your heart with empathy and to receive love. Apply the principles to your life that you know are right and just. My Momma always said, "You know better than to do that!" She was right.

A word here about limited empathy. Just as we crave acceptance of our own motivations or tendencies, we must offer patience and understanding, along with appreciation for our differences when communicating. That starts with perception of how others feel, how they think, and our interactions with them.

More can be learned, however, one must work at it and be exposed to mentors. Our mirroring neurons can be trained. Mirror Touch Synesthesia (MTS) happens in people whose empathy neurons are profoundly sensitive. Their brains can create emotions in themselves that others are having and they shudder or cry, or become physically ill. We have all seen cops and EMT's who throw up at an accident. Filtering what comes in, to a handleable notion helps build loving kindness and compassion meditation where we help relieve their stress or suffering. Learning to filter is arching your emotional intelligence. You can do this.

Fritjof Capra, physicist, ole "Frit", said of meditation:

> *"During periods of relaxation after concentrated intellectual activity,*
> *the intuitive mind seems to take over and can produce the sudden*
> *clarifying insights which give so much joy and delight."*

Whether you pray or not, the lines in this prayer are a great repetition of growth for all humanity:

> *'Lord, you know me better than I know myself that I am growing older*
> *and will someday be old. Keep me from the fatal habit of thinking I must*
> *say something on every subject and on every occasion. Release me from the*
> *craving to straighten out everybody's affairs. Make me thoughtful, but not*
> *moody. Helpful, but not bossy. With my vast store of wisdom, it seems a pity*
> *not to use it all, but You know, Lord, I want a few friends at the end.*
>
> *Keep my mind free from the endless recital of details; give me wings to get to the*
> *point. Seal my lips on my aches and pains. They are increasing, and love of*

rehearsing them is becoming sweeter as the years go by. I dare not ask for grace enough to enjoy the tales of others' pains, but help me to endure them with patience.

I dare not ask for improved memory, but for a growing humility and a lessening cocksureness when my memory seems to clash with the memories of others. Teach me the glorious lesson that occasionally, I may be mistaken.

Keep me reasonably sweet. I do not want to be a saint — some of them are so hard to live with. But a sour old person is one of the crowning works of the devil. Give me the ability to see good things in unexpected places, and talents in unexpected people. And give me, Lord, the grace to tell them so.

Selfie Video

Whose attitude is in your statements?

That's right. Yours.

If I only take care of my duties, my work, my hygiene, my desk, my messes, my trash, and what is within my hula hoop on this earth, I will know happiness. Let go of others' things.

I cannot control the world. It's true, try as I have. I couldn't control the him in my life. I couldn't control any him, any you, anybody. God's got it. Not me. As I try to control others, I am dissing your individualism, your personal growth and experience in this life. Outside of keeping you safe from harm with my words or deeds, I have NO RIGHT TO STEP IN your hula hoop. I cannot make another's life better, unless invited in. I need to ask myself, "Is this issue mine in any way?"

I was demanning my husband. Ouch. Nobody was left happy after I spoke out, not even me.

Example of a Fight: (Anybody want to act in this play?) Point a finger. Then shake it. Touch another person trying to convince them to your way. Swear at another. Get louder.

All sickening. Ever done it? Not me. I wouldn't. Well, okay, I did it 'back' at someone who yelled at me first. (Wanna call my Mom to see if that is true? I sure wish I could call her!)

So who does really control the future? Let me see, if I worry strong and hard enough, let me grimace my face and wish really hard, worry longer, play out all possible scenarios, THEN do I control it?

Hmmmm. No.

Does worrying or getting others to worry with me or get others to do something, make the future happen my way?

Hmmmmmmmmmmm. No.

Only God can make a tree. And your moments ahead. And the next one. And your child's next moment. And that person over there, his future moments.

Can you predict a single thing with accuracy? Only when you are blimey lucky on the bet.

Can you make another person happy? Mad? Sad? Glad? Mean? Drunk? Sick? Frustrated?

Another big fat <u>NO</u>. The other person behaves. It has nothing to do with me or my worrying, my desires, my wishes. They just get to be near me in my world and so I see how it plays out. If they are moody and cop a condescending attitude, did I give it to them? NO. NOR can I be the one to change their attitude. I cannot even soften the bottom for someone determinedly headed to their own demise.

I had to decide in my situation, that is just alcoholic behavior, not their un-inebriated behavior. That is just their point for now. That is just their current (under the influence) decision. Sometimes the hurtful semantics come from someone truculent, angry, sick or broken, not always drunk. My former alcoholic drinker friend was ranting the other day and I was able to love him in it. I asked, where did you get the paradigm that behavior like that, yelling, insisting, ranting, was okay to do with another human being? He stopped cold, and admitted that he learned it from his father beating on him while he was already down on the floor.

Where is My Hippo?

———

This could be a book by itself.

I like the word 'respond' much better than 'react'. React connotates action after something already took place. So, it is a real situation. It is a truth. How can I fight truth and reality? Furthermore, why would I fight truth and reality? It already is. Yet so many of us spend our entire days, our lives, fighting, arguing, impinging our opinions, wanting things our way, pushing our expectations onto others and then condemning that which is not done in accordance with my possibly falsified or outdated controller issued rule. Wow, that is a mouthful.

The anterior cingulate cortex of your brain involves power and self-control. And Introspective Cognition – that awareness of our actions and thoughts. This, my friend, is what I am asking you to use. Abort negative thoughts repeatedly to eventually change up your attitude about it. Soon you will find that you belong anywhere. You alone are in charge of achievement of your bucket list. You are no longer looking at ideas that others lay before you as urgent, debacles, tyranny of a disease. You are free, symbiotic with your feelings and charismatic.

First, we must be cognitive of what WE ARE doing and thinking. It is more innate to allow a quick perception to carry out a reaction. We have to learn to pause for the brain to engage.

That is known, in common parlance, as cognitive dissonance. Actions actually sneak by without sufficient intention. Sometimes after the sneak by, we take our reaction as a fact, our intentions were different – foot in mouth is a perfect example. I wonder if robotic arms controlled by brains ever unconsciously give the finger?

Machines cannot think, problem solve, or create. They can do repetitive tasks, yes. Only humans can be emotional and connect to other humans. This job cannot be replaced.

So if you want to be of higher intelligence, you must think better. That also implies letting go of unusable or negative knowledge, a retraining of controllers and rules thus far in our lives.

We think our thinking is effortless. Our brain is constructing our thoughts from a field of lobes that each hold lore, knowledge, vision, hearing, etc. We take in light waves, sound waves, atoms and molecules as stimulus and through a complex dance of neurons bombarding each other, we have a thought! It is called consciousness from qualia – the raw material of various types of stimuli. Different parts of the brain are responsible for one math problem, counting from one, and volume from another. See we don't consciously, to the eye or ear, know what is there, but our brain will get our body to acknowledge what "it" is in our environment. If one pathway fails (as we see predominantly in dementia, Alzheimer's, and Parkinson's diseases) agnosia occurs, which means that this qualia bounced off or back from a lobe or a pathway that was degenerating, unable to clearly bring it to consciousness for us. Wisdom involves use of all pathways. That is why we must never stop getting wiser.

Many of us, myself included, stop our education with higher influences after attending a paid-for-campus. Didn't you have one professor who was unkempt, rude to waitresses, or would not accept internet copying? Oh, of course we have life lessons like how to drive a boat and interact with an authority figure. But I am talking about changing one's opinion, upgrading the influx of truth, finding out about a higher power, understanding hurt feelings and intervening with suicide in depressed people. Too often we carry our lens only to look out. Those lessons are not in books or spewed from bearded old duffers.

Education, knowledge and facts are easily available. Some of us foolishly stop availing ourselves to facts and truth. It is wisdom that arises from maturity in age, experience, and interaction. Ever think about that? Knowledge and wisdom are definitely two different pieces of our mosaic brain working.

First, realizing that we are thinking and changing equal wisdom. But we must also have new stimulus. Open-mindedness avails great clarity about serenity. Realizing that our jaws are locked in frown is cognitive thinking. Knowing we carry a judgmental attitude is cognitive reasoning. People can no longer hear you once you make them appear wrong! Being aware that we can alter a recognized thought is amazing. Once we wise up and allow acceptance with a serene mind, we will be the ultimate we want to be.

Ergo, think about this: You repeatedly meditate, pray and get positive messages constantly. You receive peace and serenity at all times. That, my readers, is reward. It is labelled by neuroscientists as *'operant conditioning'*. The brain learns through a system of continuous rewards and punishments.

One of the strongest points I wish to make with this writing is that the myriad effects of your chosen input (positive and/or negative types) directly relate to your happiness! "Your chosen input" are the key conceptual words here.

And it has nothing to do with power, money or prestige. Gees! Think about that. We can be happy and present pleasantness, find our inner peace, be kind and generous, and love without power, money or prestige. What a concept, Miss America.

Do not think me mad. It is not to make money that I believe a Christian should live. The noblest thing a man can do is, just humbly to receive, and then go amongst others and give. —David Livingstone

Let's take inventory of a reaction to take it to an action step:

Think of a recent fight or argument. Say, an unpleasant encounter with a forceful sales person.

) What do you dislike about the situation?
) What part did the event or person play in your unhappiness?
) What part did you play?
) What made you feel uncomfortable, or unhappy within yourself?
) Why did <u>you choose</u> to feel that way?
) What fear surrounds the Reactionary feeling?
) What action might have changed your feeling?
) What step can you take to change yourself toward a better outcome?
) What are two options you can do in life for a better scenario of that same event?

Check my attitude, live with a good asset, do the right thing, stop worrying about it?

Do two steps in that direction.

Clive Wearing, extreme amnesiac, developed herpes which destroyed function of his hippocampus. Everything was new each day, all the time. He was fixated on just a couple of things: all apples and being clean. Does your mind get caught on something because of obsession, mixed up wiring, deficit of a chemical, or previous training? It is pretty simple. Yes. While Clive cannot change his thinking due to a physical disorder, WE can. Why don't we? Duh.

Our procedural memory (versus declarative memory) is learned, from watching, training, listening, reacting, etc. Let's strengthen it so that we have 'All the Facts, Maam'.

If our cerebrum does not get fully used to its capacity, it may under develop. The cerebrum fills up most of your skull. It is involved in remembering, problem solving, thinking, and feeling. It also controls movement. This immobilization, or underdevelopment can be changed once this happens but it will take time and application of facts and use. For instance, I had witnessed a client, an abused 14-year-old boy who was tiny in structure, body the size of a seven-year-old. He had been locked in a closet for much of his life. When authorities found him, his teeth were malformed, arms misshapen, and malnourishment had distorted his torso and legs. His brain, though invisible, had atrophied, rather than grown. His vocabulary was limited, he often grunted, and sun and touch seemed to disarm him.

My point for this writing is that his brain as well as other organs had now barely explicated, had little stimulus, and NO knowledge was fed to it. Unused portions of our brains will atrophy or lose sufficient chemicals if inactive. If we haven't nourished the truth, our intellect falls apart. If a quadrant of our learning brain has not been exercised, we may never have balance to function in a normal world.

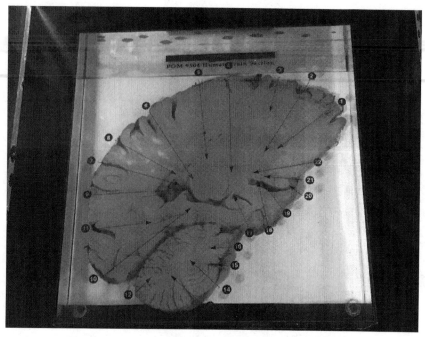

Transparency made of a cross cut slice of a cadaver's brain.

The above grey matter photo was displayed in the Bozeman, Montana, Science Museum, with all the various quadrants, nodules, lobes, and areas of the brain earmarked. There it was in grey and black, someone's post death photo. They were never cognizant it went to a wall in the museum and of course, every chunk, now dormant, dead, unstimulated, had at one time been doing the functions we are talking about here. This will happen too soon to each of us (not the displayed in a museum part). Emphasis here is to live each day to the fullest while your grey matter has some pink to it, okay?

Truth is A Choice

Do you lie? Are you lying about that?

Lying can also be the absence of exposing the truth.

Your imagination, hopefully, is always fired up. So, what is your motive to lie? Self-gain? That was usually mine.

I like to be right. I like to know the answer. I like to be on the good side. I like to consider myself smart. I like to be the best. I like to win. - All motives for lying.

I never want to appear dumb. I never want to be wrong. I never want you to think lowly of me. I like my ego intact, please. - All motives for justifying and rationalization.

The truth is that there is no peace in my taking your inventory.

Scents, smells, or odors comes in many colors. Note the huge differences and sameness in the flower photos. All qualify for God's given beauty.

Let me repeat that, what if NO OTHER PERSON EVER JUDGED ANOTHER? Oh.

"The conquest of the earth, which mostly means the taking it away from those who have a different complexion or slightly flatter noses than ourselves, is not a pretty thing when you look into it." - Joseph Conrad - <u>Heart of Darkness</u>

We are each different in our own beauty. I don't have to be right. I can easily say, *"I don't know." "I never went there or experienced that." "Tell me."* What heart-felt peace is found in those words.

Why would I have the right to measure your life? Your experiences? Your knowledge? Capabilities? Why would I have the right? What business is it of mine to judge you? Scrupulous judgement and criticism come directly from my need to be proud (a deadly sin). We get drunk on our own thoughts; when the truth is, God has the world, not me. It is not about what I do here. Let others be to their own illogic, learning from err.

What is the effect that either of these statements has on you? To practice, I suggest you pick a topic with a friend, the topic will be unknown to you but known well to the other, then reverse the conversation and try both ways. Let your ego fly and try to know more than Joe and then experience listening and learning with the rather pragmatic phrase, "Well, I don't know about that. I would like to listen to what you have to say." And don't go all 'a man hears what he wants to hear' on me. Listen. Watch their faces. Look them in the eye.

Reality is not near as painful or ugly as denial. In plain language, denial is resistance to the truth. When we lollygag in denial or resistance to life as a truth, we have wasted our time in maintaining bad feelings within. Why? Because we told ourselves this is the normal way to live. Bullpucky! We have created the ability to deceive ourselves and then believe it with rationalizations and slothful lazy thinking. It is almost like we go looking for loss!

The acceptance of what we pretended was 'normal' was extremely radical thinking! It constricted straight thinking! We were just avoiding the difficult. We learned to do that early if we came from alcoholic parents or family. We learned to be quiet when the alcoholic storm came through.

James 1:7,8 in King James version quotes: *"the double minded man is unstable in all his ways."* That is a loaded quote.

Others may wallow in this self-pity but we sure do not enjoy being around them. Negativity by others projected onto us comes in the form of anger, sometimes aggressively, depression, their own fears intensified by sharing with us. Pain. We don't need to grab their associated feelings. We need only to have compassion when they are lurking. For so many years I took on other people's backpack of troubles, NOT ONLY THAT but I tried to solve them FOR THEM. MYOB. This all triggers compassion in us of course, but not to the point of carrying worry, fear, depression, like them. Compulsion to do either (that's I-ther) is there. We have an option. Choice for the best outcome for our hearts is also there. Bring it to your conscious level. Fear is just a feeling, not a truth! The act of fearing is only thoughts, not real.

Who's happier and serene at each differing outcome?

Fear is one of the most profound reasons people want a partner. We turn to relationships to eliminate fears regarding security, finances, loneliness, self-esteem or sexual lack. And worry seems to be one of the most inherent characteristics of fear.

The honesty in this chapter about the truth is that, I get pissed off that people are not honest. Have I started with me and now carry remorse and revenge and self-hate? Deep. See Chapter on Self Hate.

Let's ask a question here. Do you or someone you know suffer from the following emotion pains?

> Negativity
> Irritation
> Impatience
> Depression
> Anger
> Unhappiness
> Fierce Actions

Bad Moods
Ambivalence
Resentment
Sullenness

Emotional pain are the key words here. Each adverb is resistance to joy. There must be some payoff in obtuse dull negative feelings for folks who choose to live in them. They are fixated on coping and then manipulating family and friends to believe them. (Unless, of course, there is a chemical mix up or brain damage physiologically.) Some people do choose this passage throughout their time on earth. Fathers teach sons. Home environments make people believe there is no other way. No other form of life is negative. Look at your dog, for goodness sake. I wish someone, when I was close to all those states of being, would have shaken me and said, "Quit! You are worth so much more." But it was not up to anyone else to realize my circumstances. And as well, our mere words will not change up anyone <u>we</u> yell at!

Hopefully, this book says: "Attention Low Feeler. Attention. This is not the way to live."

Find within what is making you "feel negative", be aware of it, face it, walk through it, take a first step. However, your very first step out is to find the truth of the "matter". Is it the fact that my attitude is stuck? Is my truth that I am in fear or feeling overwhelmingly stymied by my grief? Is my truth that I am reacting on one part of all my feelings: anger, sadness, judgement? So I discount the possibility of feelings of goodness? I know a widow today, who in her mind, is still wearing the black shroud like that of the 1800's widowed person. Something stuck in her historical training to do so, or forgetting that she has half of her life to live, I don't know, it is her story, but it is not her truth. She has constant pity parties. She may or may not be aware of her outward persona. I have seen her put on a frown because a camera was set to take her picture — she cannot let the world know she is doing anything other than suffering in 'poor me'. And she invites others, straining their empathy!

Rectitude (strict honesty of character); usually the phrase is moral rectitude, may be hard to live in if you are not honest with yourself first.

I hope that you look for all truths before you get a chance to go to Heaven and see the errors of human ways from that side. Cruising along can work easily. But a true heart, an ebulliently happy heart, a oneness with God, are the amazing truths. I would hate for you to be dead before you know that.

Check yourself:

- Are you clear in your purpose on earth? Do you do what inspires you? Or, are you confused or ambivalent about your daily or long-term direction in life?
- Do you have energy throughout and physical capacity during your day or are there things you'd like to do but can't because you tell yourself you are tired, ill, or not strong enough?
- Do you have satisfying relationships with others? Or, do you feel alone and isolated, unable to spend quality time with people you would like to?
- Are you constantly learning and gaining new perspectives or insight? Or, do you feel stagnated and slow?

What does a quality life look like to you? I have stood next to a terminally ill patient in a hospital bed while the docs talked with me about 'their' quality of life at this stage. Compared to that, what will be included in your legacy, starting with your daily activity? Will you have contributed? Will you have achieved? Will you have been satisfied? Will you have had quality in your prime existence; in your quality of life?

One of our forefather's in psychology, Abraham Maslow, declared self-actualization as the highest form of human experience. If you think about what self-actualization entails, you will find many of us are lacking in at least one aspect of self-actualization. Self-awareness is essential to know what you are capable of actualizing. Make sense? We are far beyond our narcissistic selves. We are aware of what we value, who we value, and what has no value in a much more meaningful way now.

Reality will be dished out accordingly by God and others. Our part, specifically my part, will be in acting on behalf of myself to the best of my capability; in relationships, in family life, in love, in contributions, in my connection with my God, ethics and morals. When, not if, I set a goal to be satisfied, achieve, spend quality time, and know love, I will be fulfilled. I will quit wasting thought-time with worry and regret. I will feel then that I have known God and done my best. I will have been generous. I will have contributed to society. How could you want anything other for your life? Or for another? There's my quality of life.

I discovered that I was trying to break from relationships many times. That's a truth I discovered in my self-awareness search. I would cancel dates, scheduled lunches, trips, only to always agree to go again sometime; knowing I would cancel that too. I was so full of fear. Fear that people won't like me, they will die and I will be abandoned again, I won't fulfill the friendship they were looking for, there will be responsibility in being a friend, I won't dress right for the culture, I'll snort if I laugh with them, I'll have bad breath and offend them or then my dirty laundry will be aired. Oh my gosh, I was afraid and insecure and so selfish.

The definition of responsibility is to be accountable in word and deed; having a sense of duty to fulfill tasks with reliability and dependability and commitment. If you are not doing all of that, sorry, but you are irresponsible!

So, I'd do the hateful thing of cancelling. And then I would feel guilty and desperate for a friend, or lover, or family. I had a penchant to act The Villain.

I was afraid others would take up my self-time; I would close off and move away so no one saw my fear. I so disregarded any moral character I had using fear of not measuring up to another person; afraid they would not like me, or that I would have to act on best behavior, and expose my true feelings about things; maybe they would know I didn't wash my hair today or had garlic last night and that would turn them away from me forever. I built walls so that others would not beat me to that. Pretty sick, huh?

When others tried to comfort me from my fears, I couldn't admit that it was my own weakness, and my own expectations that kept me from fulfillment. I would jump into that vast feeling of fear where breathing is restricted. I orchestrated every excuse so that I continued a failure and never had to live up to potential. There was responsibility there and I was not capable of such responsibility. Wow. That hurts to even admit again.

I lived in terror, uptight, listening hard, tiptoeing through our living room, never voicing my opinion. Lest the current alcoholic in my life be riled and cause me more terror. I believe I was the third generation to live in this manner. I was mentored well to be humble and fearful and quiet.

Al-Anon helped me to realize that I was the problem, that I had the defects listed above, irresponsibility, great fear, guilt, dread, overwhelmed, failure, insecurity, victim like, abandonment of plans, uptight, worrisome, and on and on my list of inherent defects goes. I labelled myself the petit bourgeois! I feared the thought of losing my tight control on things that were hurting me and others! Gees. Those darn components in the Twelve Step Program helped me to confront with ease and pain, that because of my suspicioned hurt, I was hurting others. When they are done in order, the steps offer a life that is better than anything we had before. They are more like Twelve Steps of Discovery.

Mark Twain – *Loyalty to petrified opinion never broke a chain or freed a human soul.*

Piero Farruca – *Eliminate something superfluous from your life. Break a habit. Do something that makes you feel insecure.*

And this next quote, of course, is from an Anonymous Person about the Twelve Steps:

"It was a journey of pain, laughs, tears, and hugs. I learned so much about myself. The more I grew, the more I realized that my recovery was not just about me, but also about others who are hurting and angry just like I had been. I find strength in spirituality and serenity. I allow others their dignity and grace to be who they are, my family has unified and holds each other up with love and respect."

Here are the Twelve Steps which Alcoholics Anonymous, Narcotics Anonymous, Al-Anon and Overeaters Anonymous are based on:

Step 1: We admitted we were powerless over alcohol—that our lives had become unmanageable.

Step 2: Came to believe that a Power greater than ourselves could restore us to sanity.

Step 3: Made a decision to turn our will and our lives over to the care of God *as we understood Him.*

Step 4: Made a searching and fearless moral inventory of ourselves.

Step 5: Admitted to God, to ourselves, and to another human being the exact nature of our wrongs.

Step 6: Were entirely ready to have God remove all these defects of character.

Step 7: Humbly asked Him to remove our shortcomings.

Step 8: Made a list of all persons we had harmed, and became willing to make amends to them all.

Step 9: Made direct amends to such people wherever possible, except when to do so would injure them or others.

Step 10: Continued to take personal inventory and when we were wrong promptly admitted it.

Step 11: Sought through prayer and meditation to improve our conscious contact with God, *as we understood Him*, praying only for knowledge of His will for us and the power to carry that out.

Step 12: Having had a spiritual awakening as the result of these Steps, we tried to carry this message to alcoholics, and to practice these principles in all our affairs.

So, I would like to give you a short interpretation of those twelve steps above:

Step 1:   I can't
Step 2:   He can!
Step 3:   I WILL let Him
Step 4:   Clean house
Step 5:   Trust God
Step 6:   Surrender
Step 7:   Attitude change
Step 8:   Prepare to end isolation
Step 9:   Amending actions
Step 10:   Basis for daily living
Step 11:   Peace of Mind
Step 12:   Joy of living through new actions

One more since I am on this subject:

Steps 1 – 3 are about giving up what doesn't work for you
Steps 4 – 6 are about owning up to your part

Steps 7 – 9 are about making up for damaging issues
Steps 10 – 12 are about keeping up the new and happier life

Bet you did not know there is more in the protocol of AA; Robert's Rules
if I may paraphrase:

One – Our common welfare should come first; personal recovery depends
upon A.A. unity.

Two – For our purpose there is but one ultimate authority – a loving God
as He may express Himself in our group conscience. Our leaders are
but trusted servants, they do not govern.

Three – The only requirement for A.A. membership is a desire to stop
drinking.

Four – Each group should be autonomous except in matters affecting other
groups, or A.A. as a whole.

Five – Each group has but one primary purpose – to carry its message to
the alcoholic who still suffers.

Six – An A.A. group ought never endorse, finance or lend the A.A. name
to any related facility or outside enterprise, lest problems of money,
property and prestige divert us from our primary purpose.

Seven – Every A.A. group ought to be fully self-supporting, declining
outside contributions.

Eight – Alcoholics Anonymous should remain forever nonprofessional, but
our service centers may employ special workers.

Nine – A.A., as such, ought never be organized, but we may create service
boards or committees directly responsible to those they serve.

Ten – Alcoholics Anonymous has no opinion on outside issues, hence the
A.A. name ought never be drawn into public controversy.

Eleven – Our public relations policy is based upon attraction rather than
promotion; we need always maintain personal anonymity at the level
of press, radio and films.

Twelve – Anonymity is the spiritual foundation of all our Traditions, ever
reminding us to place principles before personalities

The groups mentioned above also have Twelve Concepts and Warrantees they follow. This ain't no flim flam organization. These 'twelves' are <u>deadly</u> serious. Many people die from addictions if they cannot dedicate themselves to changing lifestyles. Life is not a pretending game.

Many, in fact I would bet most people, pshaw the followers of the program. "I don't need that."

Then, I also remember a priest speaking the summary of his sermon being, "all people should take a page from the twelve steps of the AA program and we would all get along in this world."

Working the steps with a Higher Power enables us to acknowledge much of our negative or repressed nature.

The fact that the programs have saved billions of folks from themselves and their demise should interest you. The world could seem so much lighter and nice and friendly if more of us drank from that fountain of wisdom. The number of 'users of the programs is beyond trillions.

Personally, I needed to listen to recovery mates' insights. I had many of the same issues in my life. I gained wisdom in the listening.

> *"You have to go beyond words and conceptualized ideas*
> *and just get into what you are, deeper and deeper.*
> *The first glimpse is not quite enough; you have to examine the*
> *details without judging, without using words and concepts.*
> *Opening to oneself fully is opening to the world."*
> - Chogyam Trungpa, Tibetan Meditation Master

Without wisdom, we decay.

You've got to Change Your Evil Ways, Baby

Let's address another common communication/friends/relationship breakdown.

Topic: Resentment and Willingness to give it AWAY.

Resentment is simple to understand. If I created a resentment in my head, I had made myself a victim. Isn't that silly of me? What on earth is there to gain by calling myself a victim?

Sadness, anger, resentment, attitude, poor behavior, bitterness, not liking people, obsession, lack of trust – they all make ME THE FOOL. I, I now own those irrelevant, sick self-created thoughts. I was allowing others to control my peace, serenity and stability.

Resentment is a "Number One" offender. It destroys us. Yet we practice it. It is a habitual pattern in thinking in our brain. But you can't take a pill or have surgery to remove that part. We can, however, take the Al Anon prescription: Study of the Twelve Steps. I was astounded at the wisdom in the program – it was like looking at people who had developed "Snoops" (internet all-knowing wisdom). They could run my thoughts past Snoops, discerning lies in speech or action of others.

Resentment is just a pattern - an old way of thinking.

And within resentment, we are RELIVING OLD HURTS. Why? Why would we want to?

And it bars the 'Sunlight from my Soul'.

Our old belief was that it was normal. Ha. Ha.

It is a mirror of our old thinking and there is some thought in me that I might even attract other people who think this resentful way. Do I want people like that as friends in my good, future life? So that goes to say that I don't like that trait!

Resentment is long held.

Resentment can eat away at the body and become its own disease... that we then behave accordingly based on a sickness.

It is imperative that we release the past.

It is imperative that we forgive everyone, ourselves included. Now I said, forgive. That does not mean that you must achieve reconciliation with everyone. Sometimes a boundary is necessary for protection and security. Smile and move along.

I forgive you for not being the way I wanted you to be! Repeat that, only this way now:

"I forgive myself for past errs of my ways."

It is loaded with truth. Take a risk, forgive others too. Tell yourself that you absolutely refuse to live without forgiveness. Declare yourself to be of full conscience.

Carl Richards, the Sketch Guy writer, tells this story.

Two traveling monks reached a town where there was a young woman waiting to step out of her sedan chair. The rains had made deep puddles and she couldn't step across without spoiling her silken robes. Her attendants were holding her packages, so they couldn't help her across the puddle.

The younger monk walked by. The older monk put her on his back, carried her across the water and put her down on the other side. She didn't thank the older monk; she just shoved him out of the way and departed.

After several hours, the younger monk said, "That woman back there was very selfish and rude!"

"I set the woman down hours ago," the older monk replied. "Why are you still carrying her?"

Decide to live not carrying emotional weight of 'stewing' in resentment, anger or frustration. Can you afford to carry all that? What could you set down this week and savor in the future, by not carrying that burden? It is extra peace for you!

Do we get angry when we have dusted our room in haste? No. Forgiveness is the same thing as dusting off our mental house. There is no need to get angry. Who experiences the mercurial temperament, correlated with the raised blood pressure and negative thinking? Me! Someone I talked with recently called it "soul plaque", similar to artery plaque. Maybe we need replacement thinking (a stent) with new channels, new blood flow. Only we can instill replacement thinking in our conscious selves! No one else has that power or capacity over us!

Why does this matter to you? The brain stem connects the brain to the spinal cord and controls automatic functions such as breathing, digestion, heart rate and blood pressure. Your brain is nourished by one of your body's richest networks of blood vessels. When you are thinking hard, your brain may use up to 50 percent of the fuel and oxygen each day.

Get this, a blind member of our group once said, "My negative thinking can get to be too much for me!" That message sunk in, because of his blindness. Here I was fully capacitated and having a 'poor me' attitude! Who the hell am I to be upset with my lot in life?

We tend to believe that the world operates as we perceive it. What if I told you that we have errors of perception!?

We just need to get on the task of forgiving that dust happens and clean up the past thoughts. Why would we dig into yesterday's garbage to make our dinner meal tonight??

Yesterday's mental garbage, the mental trash thoughts, resentment, anger, criticism, etc., can be tossed out and not picked back up.

Why do we want to limit our beliefs or clog our fresh thinking with old ick or bad habits? We now have mental clarity and time 'up there' to think progress/positive action. We can remake a situation by just stopping to clean this up in present time.

In a moment's time we can go back to our old mental garbage and keep doing what harms and hurts us. That is called prediction error. Those behavior errors are not associated with rewards we want. By changing the context of our input ratio to good thoughts and actions, we 'blow our own minds'.

"Can a nation organized and governed such as ours endure? That is the real question. Have we the nerve and the will? Can we carry through in an age where we will witness not only new break-throughs in weapons of destruction but also a race for mastery of the sky and the rain, the ocean and the tides, the far side of space and inside of men's minds." John F. Kennedy, in a Speech on Going to the Moon

Take the opportunity to sit back. Imagine a small stage in front of you. Imagine the person that you resent most on that stage. It could be past or present, living or dead. See them clearly in your mind, visualize good things happening to this person. Things that would be meaningful to them. See them smiling and happy. Hold this image a few minutes and then let it fade away.

As they leave the stage, put yourself up there in the essence of only good things happening to you. See yourself willing and happy. Ponder that - the abundance of the universe available to you. The same abundance is available to my resented person. Truth. They are no one better or worse than us; just another traveler of God's planet. And I have been wasting thoughts on history which can't be undone. And those thoughts are negative!

We delayed our own emotional and mental prosperity by being resentful or jealous, especially if someone had more than me (old thinking). We no longer will criticize the way they live, or spend their money. It is NOT MY BUSINESS!

Each person is under the law of their own consciousness. I have a lot to do to take care of just my own thoughts.

It doesn't matter where it starts, it has started. It has rooted itself. Till altered. Biases, judgement, jealousy, wants and needs, fairness or un, having vs not having, knowing or feeling dumb, condemnation, degrading, negating, disdainfully berating, superficiality, egocentricism, lying, coveting, envy, greed, laziness, they are all traits we visited. Do these sound familiar? Judgement usually originates in the mirror – our lack of beauty, our insecurities in ourselves.

Reduce the complexity of life by eliminating the needless wants of life, and the labors of life reduce themselves. —Edwin Way Teale

The seven deadly sins:

Sloth

Jealousy

Envy

Greed

Pride

Gluttony

Lust

It is all there. Subconsciously or consciously, we have learned of these lessons in life. We have been exposed. Unless, of course, you were locked in a closet - which is a whole 'nother set of hatreds.

Were you (past tense) engaged with any of the following?

Torment	Lust	Murder	Wrath	Agony	Envy	Ire
Impurity	Hypocrisy	Adultery	Drunkenness	Hatred	Spiritual Sloth	
Lack of empathy		Deceit	Selfishness	Slander Lies		
Blasphemy	Avarice	Falsehoods	Sociopathy	Greed		

These are all terrible things for your penetrated soul to carry. Perpetual remorse gets you no change. The suffocating, even the smell of these is putrid, until we realize what making amends for our sins can really mean. Can you fathom recovery? I am told that breaking habits and creating better novel ways into new habits happens at a rate of one month improvement equaling one year of habit.

What we, or any child does with the exposure to the above is his 'doing the best we can with what I know'.

So changing the force of nature, so far in our lives, is the best answer.

That's easy, then. Right? Ha.

Do you remember your first 'leap and bound' in life? Maybe it was going out for football? Cub scouts? Joining the army? First job? Going to camp? First apartment?

Y o u h a d t o a l t e r y o u r l i f e s t y l e. And someone (an adult most likely) showed you how, emulated for you the style in which you would learn.

Were they a good role model, or did they also inform you of their biases, their sins? Or were you set out to learn through the school of hard knocks?

We are influenced into action on our own accord. We also learn from REacting on our own accord. Either could be good or bad. Security and safety reactions could be good or bad. Could lead us to pleasant or diabolically devilish behaviors. We learned it all on our own. We must be on guard for the temptation to be prideful. "Lead us not into temptation…"

And then we set out to do life.

Whoa. Hold the phone. Isn't anyone going to check on the children to make sure they only picked up on the good guidance, the 'right' lessons.

The answer is no.

There is no checkpoint, gateway, SAT test for goodness. What is going to happen to a child has happened. No changing history and no more prevention done by a parental figure. It is what it is.

And today, this one or that one, is bullying. Knowingly or unconsciously acting and reacting 'to what they know'.

This equation sometimes results in: Bullying to the death of another. Racial bias. One-up-man-ship.

Wake up, America. This is wrong.

Step up. Raise your consciousness. Gees, we are all capable of learning to be good. When did the dumb gene get stuck? Early Greeks actually believed their gods controlled their behavior; reminding me of schizophrenia where your psyche has two or more personalities. I have a second voice – it criticizes me.

And it is a level of consciousness that we can work on. You and I. Not just me. Hello, out there, did you hear me? N o t j u s t m e!

All people are teachable. All have exposure to life. Each person is able to think for themselves. No one wants to stay dumb. Goodness comes in all forms. Mentoring and showing are a path in life. We all want better for ourselves and others. Everyone gets the same 24 hours each day to do life.

Those are a given.

So why not turn on the switch to change?

Notice the phrases: want to, have better, always learning?

So rather than bullying led by jealousy, comparison, conceit, envy, pride, etc., why not take care with ourselves and leave others alone to do the same? The first sentence is full of sins of the flesh, not of higher spiritual or intellectual quality at all.

When did the headset to reach out and kill somebody enter a young person's mind?

Their consciousness must be changed. And you are just the person to do it, by mentoring good in all your ways.

What Do You Want Most?

What does Sara want? What does Nathan want? What does a baby want, a grandparent, a Vice President, a mine worker, you? What do you want?

I am guessing, as you walk about your daily routine and function, you would like more than anything, to be loved and allowed to be (supported) the best that you can. Am I right? Am I right about this? Guess what! That is what I want too! Nathan too! Stella! Sara! A whole world of people wanting to be secure and happy. Hm.

God doesn't call the qualified, He qualifies those who are called! Don't believe everything you think!

Getting love by theft, envy, jealousy, bullying, cheating, lying, taking, pushing, shoving, etc. ain't gonna happen. OUCH. You will not gain loving and supportive friends through those maneuvers.

I love this argument which takes place in many a household. "I saw you looking at Dora's cleavage. Don't deny it." Him: "What? I never looked at her boobs. You are so jealous."

So after this discussion, how are both parties feeling? Attacked. Mean. Displeased with their spouse. They were each accused.

They did not gain or show love in this discourse. See, it comes down to each and every word that comes out of our mouths. Don't you want to show love in every instance of your existence, especially to your spouse!?

Don't you want to feel loved and supported in every conversation? We set up our own failures.

We must collectively alter the minds of others to feel we are grateful for their existence too, that we value our own selves, that we all have a greater purpose on the planet. Mentoring is our only method. Example for others. Give grace and peace to others. And it cannot be at the cost of another, warring nations, nor bullying children.

To wrap it up neatly, we each are responsible not only to love ourselves, and a greater being who is in charge of all others, but to then pass it on - to teach and mentor and example.

"I want world peace, Bob." (Said by many a Miss America candidate in the 70's.) Sounds like a high and mighty endeavor. But no, people, it is not that difficult. Like the multitude of Tupperware/Pampered Chef parties, we can exhibit our wares: gratitude and love and support and spread it out. Others will like the feel, the security of it, and enjoy what it does for their life style. Thus, they will want to share the news with more.

Do you see where this is going?

Can you change your consciousness to this level? Or are you stuck in dumb?

My guess is that the majority of the folks reading this already actively pursue and practice 'all of the above'. Then it is our job, even more so, to expand the learning of the others by example of the way we live our lives.

Did I force you to be nicer? Did I put it down in a rule book you MUST read? Did I threaten you to follow instructions or else? Am I "bullying" you into submission?

Sway. Persuade. Example. Show the way. No advice giving. Mentor. Suggest, only with nice attached. You are not so much the 'instructor', you are the example of better living. Got it? Maybe you can write your own book!

So what do we do about the schools? Take your mentoring and suggestions to your children, grandchildren. Use kindness only, while at home. And while out. It will eventually show its colors in more of us.

Skits. Seriously. Role play. Try it on. Have 'nice' days. Example equality and fairness. Not once in a while. Get back to the core of each person who wants to be loved and supported. You don't have to be liked or hated. You have to be loved. So does Laura. So does Kevin. So does Jody who has epilepsy. Colored or uncolored skin. A divinity unlike mine. No matter. It does not matter. They get to be them. I get to be me. Get it?

Actually do random acts of kindness all day. Whew. It is acting out of the ordinary for most of us. What is the ordinary for you anyway? All about self? Ego? Pride? Oops, I hear those 7 deadly sins creeping back in. Deadly. Sins. Bullying. And you thought you were as saint-like as they come.

We all want to appear better. Better, stronger, more likable, prettier, smarter, blah, blah, and blah, than the next person.

When I think I am smarter or more special than all *those* other people, it is called "terminal uniqueness". We end up killing relationships because we think we will be saved by someone other than ourselves. A fed wolf is a pet. Are we feeding our codependency to the point where, if the other was taken away, we would rant and rage to get our way? It is also called self-flaguation. Well, I call it "enteric fermentation"!

Heard of 'Stockholm Syndrome'? It is described as where hostages begin to express loyalty to their captors (cults). When they are rescued, sometimes the victim desires to remain with the captor and serve them. Battered women and children sometimes experience this with their abusers. We must make a conscious decision about how much to give to another person, being mindful of another's needs.

Many times, in the romance of a relationship, the infatuation wears off. You see each other on the bathroom stool, sick and vomiting, over involved in friendships or hobbies, or just going off in directions that are not joint ventures. It often happens in the first few years of marriages and we sit there wondering, was this relationship a mistake?

King of the mountain is a game. As long as we have most needs met - let's remember here that those are Food, Clothing, and Shelter, as long as we have those n e e d s met, that is enough. Wanting more, lusting, driven to gain more money than the other guy, have the better car, blah, push or put others down in that process is hurtful. Do you like yourself after inflicting your brag onto another? I do not get to hurt people. Wow, let's put that on your tombstone: "Here lies Steve. He won. He got to hurt people. He is the king of the mountain. And he is now dead. No better than others."

Treat others well. Let them be themselves. Treat them how we want to be treated. Speak and respond with them. Do not control them. Listen. Put no pressures on them. Never make them feel bad. Offer trust.

Do you remember having to save for the hoola hoop, for your down payment for your first home, having a car that would run, or excited to get canned peaches without cheap brand pits in them?

Do you remember a parent telling you some basic rules for life - 'doing the best they could with what they knew at the time'?

> *"The purpose of life is to live it, to taste experience to the utmost, to reach out eagerly and without fear for newer and richer experience."*

Breaking Habits

What if you planned to:

"Sing your death song, and die like a hero going home." (Tecumseh)

Did you obey your parents? Teachers? Grandparents? The Librarian? The neighbor?

All the collective wisdom of our forefathers and foreneighbors gave us only a foundation to build from for ourselves. Think of them as 8-millimeter movies, dated.

Social determinant includes social status, gender, education or lack of, jobs, where we live, our culture, among others. Our grandparents had a place in society, our parents had a place, in my case, and we have a third generation of progress we live in.

Not to dis them, but what our forefathers taught us was already a generation old. Maybe two or three if they were instructing us according to their youthful life then and teaching us recurring lessons of what their grandparents taught them. Our beliefs may be as old as Cicero.

But why wouldn't we believe that our ideas are our norm?

Children are fluid to a point. We know that their ideas and opinions will be formed and reformed in the ever-changing patterns of relationships and events. Let's give them a better chance at better. At the very least, mentor them in imitation.

We have adopted the belief that if we work hard and long to learn to do things better and faster, we will be able to do it all. This adage usually leads to shame or guilt that we cannot do it all. If you get really efficient and organized, you will have control of your life; maybe, the peace you have been searching for. – False! We think we can win with shortcuts or cheating ways – not so much!

We fell victim, as if what grandpa says is written in stone in our minds. We stand by grandpa's stereotypical and aged dialectical words rigidly, while the truth is that we are capable of altering our perspective. Maybe we attached wrongful truth to hearsay. Knowing the truth, and accepting the truth of it today, can be a seismic change to a positive life.

There is error in those who reason by precedents drawn from antiquity. Their reasoning stopped with their generation, not the one we live in. Many of these practices which prevailed in our conscience are currently contrary opinions! We, the people, seem to know half of history and then get confused. We have no other information to guide us until we have more experience or teaching. We have yet to have faced all our moral dilemmas and human experiences, today's aesthetics. The remote past is inadequate for the distinct emersion into the future.

We fell in stride with their opinions and limited knowledge of *their* time. I did not want to be weird and shunned, naughty and punished or conspicuous, God forbid, or conspicuous and prideful together. Shame and judgement ruled us. Some of us were abused for stepping out of our parents' and others' thinking. We learned to react. I am so sorry that any of us had to learn that way. Reactionary living is such a sad life. Those reactions became my truths, my habitual actions, suddenly seeming timeless, predictable solutions to all things, including negative forces. How do I know? I did it. I did it for a long, long time.

Everything I did, how I acted, responses, thoughts, all controlled by people two, maybe three generations passed. They had just invented plastic; they remembered how to live in the depression, those earlier kin had strong prejudices, civil wars, back of busses thinking, closet gays, discreet abortions, illness, baths only on Saturday, no cream rinse, stresses, dark ages.

And that, my friend, is what I built my habits and habitual decisions, and rationalizations on, based on the strong forces that all adults were right. Quite frankly, I didn't even KNOW me!

I love to read Steven Covey. From <u>First Things First</u>, he lists a First Generation, Second Generation and Third Generation and their 'ways' of life. The changes have emerged, from grinding-their-own-grain-for-bread era, to our Generation Z, if you think about it. Each had a method of being and doing in life, different from their children, and then their grandchildren, etc.

To quote Steven Covey in 1994, based on three generations only

"First Generation is based on reminders. It's 'go with the flow' but try to keep track of things you want to do with your time. – write the report, attend the meeting, fix the car, clean out the garage... Characterized by simple notes and checklists...Without an empowering sense of lifetime vision and goal setting...first things for (this generation) are essentially whatever happens to be in front of them.

Second generation is one of planning and preparation. It's characterized by calendars and appointment books. It's efficiency, personal responsibility and achievement in goal setting, planning ahead, and scheduling future activities and events...(believing) preparation increases efficiency and effectiveness...performance and results…Other people become interruptions or distractions and keep them from sticking to their schedule and carrying out their plans.

(I fail this because of my lack of follow through. I insulate myself and do not allow anyone else to stymie my actions. I got psyched up, as Covey says, trying to get somewhere - achieve something - when I didn't realize it was the wrong place.)

Third generation's approach is 'planning, prioritizing and controlling…You've probably spent some time clarifying your values and priorities. You've asked yourself, 'What do I want?' You've set long-medium-and short-range goals to obtain these values… planners and organizers…Third generation people have some serious flaws – not in intent but in unintended results created by incomplete paradigms and vital missing elements…or mindsets."

Steven Covey's take on this back then is one great example of generational differences in how we live. Those paragraphs only surmise our exposure to time management. Time management, if you will, is our perspective on life and events. Think about how colonial life had no time for emotional conversations. Spend a moment reflecting on the invention of appliances changing the amount of time spent on bread baking, for one. Later, mothers had time for jobs outside the home – they got exposed to more societal and cultural mores. New generations alter life styles, communication methods, and interactions between people. Our mental processes have altered maybe three times by the time we are forty years of age. I am saying to you, that one must change their thinking to keep up with the times and sometimes, to save our lives, to enable us to live in the new and better times here and now.

With influence from our forefathers, their judgement of others became mine. They "formed" my early thinking. Big Girl Panties require thinking for myself. Change how you think and change the outcome of your life. Deciding anything before was led by old school. Are we still in the 1950's?

No. The 1960's? No. 1970's? No. We are not in that century even! Put on your responsibility-for-my-thinking panties. We want to have our way but we don't even know 'our way.' We know old material and our brain waves still act on those memories put there. You can replace every single cell with an open and kind mind. Wow. What a gift! Do so now.

My challenge to you here, again, is:

What do you want?

Is it based on an old style of living – what your parents told you to go for?

Is it a clear and fair, valuable, achievable goal?

Are you getting what you want?

Do you have the right attitude and behaviors to have the goal?

Do you have the right vision of the end result?

Have you reached appropriately, without harm, for what you want?

Do you know how to reach for what you want?

Do you have the willingness, energy, and commitment it takes?

Do you still want it, or did your parents want it, or did society tell you it is important for you?

It's all new substance to learn but your brain can achieve it with the right tools.

And boy, does it have tools! What we want to implant in the brain are didactic principles. The neurons and reactors consolidate their decisions

>f, we have thinking. Just to help you to pause when you have input
> amygdala, let me lay out what is busy while you notice life.

Chemical signals are transmitted into correct channels as soon as we are struck with a thought in the amygdala and hippocampus, be it fear or pleasure; the chemicals react. That input goes to the basal ganglia, our switchboard. From there, it strikes up the band (nodes)as necessary. According to which chemical and which channels, we either react impulsively or act respondingly.

These will be no test, be assured.

Those channels include:

> Ventral Pallidum: Pleasure center
> Substantia Negra: Motor planning and learning
> Subthalamic Nucleus: Increases impulsive behavior, seeks rewards
> Globus Pallidus: Regulation of voluntary movement

See why I ask you to take a pause to think? Lots going on up there.

To further my plea, the basal ganglia plays a very important part in the brain. If messed with by disease or genetics, individuals display impulsive disorders, OCD, ADD, Parkinson's, and the like.

So have you derived that to CHANGE, one must decide that the style we are currently living, is not the path to happiness?

Second question, who can give you the key? Those ancestors? Apparently not. At least, I hope that is your summarization.

The life ahead of you depends on no one else. Of course, your journey through life began with others teaching you how to walk it, but it is your journey and will be different than all those before you and after you.

That is probably one of the most important takeaways from this book.

We relied on parents, we relied on teachers, we reacted to teachings and folks and events. But none of that is now. We rely on only ourselves. As many of us age, we go from relying on our origins (family, foster family, institutions in some cases, friends) to relying on a spouse or an addiction.

Way cool, huh? With an addiction or a sugar daddy or even relying on the government, I don't have to grow up. I just get to grow old, sick or complaining, most likely. That is not a way of life. I have seen 3 generations of poverty, 3 generations of juvenile delinquents, 3 generations of active bias. What kind of wholesomeness or love is in that family!? What kind of happy, joy and freedom are they each experiencing?

We had attended Old School of Thinking. We have a need for a Ph.D. in new ways of thinking in today's world.

Proof:

Neuroplasticity, also known as neural plasticity, or brain plasticity, is the ability of neural networks in the brain to change through growth and reorganization. These changes range from individual neuron pathways making new connections, to systematic adjustments like cortical remapping. Examples of neuroplasticity include circuit and network changes that result from learning a new ability, environmental influences, practice, and psychological stress.

So by now you have realized that habits need to be broken to change our neural pathways. Most essentially, habits in thinking have to be broken to have a better life. Then, of course, just like learning the alphabet or numbers, we must practice and repeat and check ourselves. Practice new ways, especially in thinking. Of course, we may forget the order of P-Q-R-S, punctuate in error or do addition wrong, and forget thoughts of judging or our rudeness, etc. occasionally – mental challenges happen. But keeping on the path of changing up, we can't go too far off course. Practice.

And here is a beginning:

List who you are resentful of. Whoa. Hold the phone. That's just mean. You are telling me to have more positive thoughts and then you ask me to think of the people who have hurt me? Really?

Really. If you are going to grow up, let's learn about ourselves, our habitual reactions, our part in our life, our part in all relationships, our past thinking and judgement, including people who have hurt or harmed me, according to me.

The exercise of bringing up old hurts is a most enlightening experience; when we see it through new eyes – with our new open mind to wisdom.

Okay, so Joey pulled my hair at recess. My boss yelled at me unfairly. Santos speaks Spanish in my presence with his friends, when he knows I don't understand it. My husband hits me. Crazy drivers, have they ever passed a driver's exam? More major things, like, God tore my wonderful son from my family. I lost my job. Cancer. Prejudice. Theft. Loss. Maybe our anger is toward God or someone in particular over these events.

People have lied to me. People have played roughly with me and hurt my pride. People don't tell me they love me. People have bad habits around me.

I guess I do have resentments. I have been hurt and harmed in so many ways. Let's take a look at each that I can think of today...

Start by listing the person, event, agency, etc. that hurt you. Along with that, let's just list the cause of my pain, as well.

Take a day or week to list these.

I am resentful at:

Joey – who pushed me on the slide
The Boss – numerous slights and reprimands
Spouse – similar to above with lack of loving ways
God – not leading me away from hurt or harm
Myself for being chicken, ashamed, bullying my way, cheating, lying, hiding, passive

Next week:

List beside the name or event, just what was bothered or harmed. What had 'they' done?

For instance, most likely in my cases, it was my ego, my self-esteem, sometimes my financial security, or emotional security, that I felt had been stepped on. At times, people berated my accomplishments or my physique. What a terrible injustice they performed. Yes, my pride was often hurt and I was sexually hurt in a couple of relationships. I felt myself shrink in value. The list of what about me was damaged can be mulitudinal; the same emotion or ambition stepped on repeatedly by other names on the list.

Discouragement can paralyze us; almost make it impossible to move forward. It steals our confidence and throws us into a downward spiral. Watch athletes who miss the shot; their faces tell of loss, ruin, and discouragement; very hard to refocus on winning.

If you want self-esteem, you need to take esteemable actions.

Take a week to think about what you have entered on your list. Those painful moments in life are out on paper. The very thought that I can list why I carry grudges, is an exercise that I have never done. Cathartic in a way - a list of the bad in my life. The list of people who have hurt me includes my name, where I disappointed myself, where I felt incomplete or lacking and failing to behave in a Christian manner.

Add to this list as you want. In fact, add to it as you go through the rest of your life.

Someday, not long down the calendar, you will know how to "do" this list in your head and it will walk you toward wisdom about yourself and your thinking.

This can be like a double-edged sword feeling. If you/we have not accepted personal responsibility for our part (our feelings or reactions), we thus have low self-esteem. Do you complain, quit, get angry a lot, blame, act pessimistic or irresponsible, and act fearfully? Most likely, you have low self-esteem and doing all those ugly things does nothing to raise your worth. Turns out I have much broader issues to address also.

Next week:

Behind each event or person whom you felt harmed you, write in a phrase or few words, the course I/We/You of my action that ensued during that uncomfortable action or that person or activity or event.

For instance, we were headed for disaster. Examples: I thought I was going to lose my job. I was being judged unfairly and I build a resentment immediately. 'I was planning how to hurt that counselor after they took my son into foster care.' 'We were going nowhere – her nasty words ended that friendship!' Those kinds of 'Where was this headed?" evaluations.

Perhaps somewhere in there, God will help you to notice that those things and those 'people' were just temporary, a passing part of your life. Most likely, they or that event, are not a part of today or tomorrow for you, right?

I would bet you have formed a decision that you could not have done what they did to you. You have your morals, after all. And they were stepping all over them. Good thing you held on to them. So far.

We are not done with this first list. Take the wrong done to you and look at your part in it.

Oh, yah. If you were hurt, Kiddo, you had a part, even if only a 'reaction'. You own that. You own that you RE-acted to the harm.

Were you selfish in your thinking?
Were you dishonest about the ordeal?
Were you fair-minded about their part?
Were you aware of their side of the fence?
Were you frightened of an outcome?
Were you to blame?

Create an image in your mind where you and the other person are restored to friends. See their value.

We own every feeling we feel. Our emotion is inside us, not externally controlled by the boss or the bully. No one appointed them stewardship of my brain or heart, not even God. My thinking was self-designed with perhaps my parents' old style of judgement of others, caught in my brain. Perhaps Sister Augustus told you hair pulling makes Joey a naughty person.

Print the next page for your own worksheet.

People I am angry at or resented:	Resentment with them:	What harm I feel was done to me. What has this affected? i.e., Personal security endangered? Self-Esteem lowered? Ambition stepped on? Relationship ruined? Monetary security threatened? Pride hurt? Sex life injured?	Their part:	My part:	Why I had a part: Selfish? Self-Righteous? Self-Seeking? Frightened? Dishonest? Indignant? Lazy? Scared? Insecure? All the above?	My fears: Not being accepted? Being thought of poorly? Not being smart enough? Aggressive people? Intim dating people? Paranoia? Anxiety? Being alone? Frail? Illness? Sounding stupid? Others' anger at me? Other fears?
Me						
Spouse						
Mom or Dad						
God						
Boss						
Justin						
Michael						

Mom Said: 'Stop Acting Like That!'

Take a look at how you are acting right now.

Our brains are not born with a perfect filter to our mouths. Each reaction is not carefully plotted.

Application of knowledge generates opposition to our reactionary state, our habits. Practical application of wisdom leads to less:

Assumptions

Poorly stated phrases

Saying Yes when inappropriate

Unnecessary actions

Hurtful Actions and Words

Obsessive actions

Emotional responses

Poor body language

Untruthful statements

Loss of faith

Personal faux paus

Self-criticism

Unethical activity

Unlawful activity

Unfulfilled commitments

Fear based actions

Self-condemnation

Feeling bad

False representation

Poor judgement

Rationalization

Failure

Having ridiculous expectations

False beliefs

Lack of gratitude

Giving Up

After filling out the previous form; next you must pray for each person who made you feel harmed or scared. Yes, for the person who harmed you. Yes, you must orate words that allow them to just be: in your past life; in their own life; or, hurting/not hurting others. That's easy to agree to, don't you think?

I am not asking you to believe in my God.

Did you create the universe? Did President Washington create the earth? Did your grandfather plant all our trees? Something has the universe in their power, not you.

There has got to be a seed in your head that, even if, for you it is the Big Bang; its 'out there' and has control of the air and sea and rotation of the earth. Go with that.

Here goes your prayer; something like:

'Dear God: Give Joey better behavior.

Dear Higher Power: Help me to be willing to not interact with Joey in my life space.

Dear Mother Nature: Let me not allow myself to be bothered by Joey again.

Here's the kicker. You have got to pray for the people on your list every day for 7 days. If you miss your connection to a higher power in those 7 days, there is a penalty. For your penance, you must pray for a month – 30 days – for that person that caused you harm.

My guess is that something amazing will happen in your thinking. Just wait.

If your prayer worked right, you came up with your part in the development of action. No one else CAN FORCE an action by you. We had a part in this harm. Even if it was only that we decided to take on the pain and cry. That was our Reaction. Pain is God's megaphone. And the mind that got me into the pain CANNOT get me out of it without change.

New concept to your thought process, huh?

Other people get to just live among us. We have no control over what they know, say or do. The only control we have is what we say, think or do. Let's clean up our act. I guarantee when you take the inventory part of how you acted and why you acted in that manner, you will discover your humanness and perhaps a reason why you acted appropriately or inappropriately and why you let another person, event, or think take over your reasonable life. Those thoughts then, are the cemented habits we PUT in our previous frame of mind.

Then, then I realize I HAVE BEEN REACTING insanely.

The moment I realized that my reactions of being hurt were MINE only, AND furthermore, I am in control of the negative thoughts I planted as a result of my defects. My defects are now black and white. I get to concentrate.

Here is an ACTION I then realized I could do instead. Thank you, God, for putting Joeys in my life. I learn things I do not want to do to others by watching him lash out at me. Thank you for the sniping details my boss said about my work. I learned that style of work is not his expectation. Things fall into the real perspective that they should be in. My tears, my reactions, my anger toward others is not their doing. They are challenges to make me a better me; a force laid out for me to find a solution to. Do you know a stronger way to learn life lessons? You burn the eggs, you don't put the burner on high next time.

If I were to meet God, I would blush and be all gushy as I have so much to say to Him. He has heard it all from me before, but I know I would be so excited that I would be dancing and jumping gymnastics around and probably pee my pants!

I'd be repeating "Thank you, thank you Lord." loudly and saying every word of gratitude in my vocabulary and, and, in foreign tongue, 'graci, merci, danke'.

And I would be searching over His shoulder. I would want to see my parents, my husband, all my grand and great parents, my friends, famous people, listen to their voices and feel their essence as I did on Earth. How happy I would be to see those I miss because they left this world called Earth too. I'm pretty sure I will end up in Heaven. Old hurts will be wiped away. You can do that while on Earth.

It would probably be too late for God to tell me what I did wrong or right so that part would be nice, unless He is sending me back. I want to ask Him about that part too.

I would want to know about why Muslims and Christians, etc. can't get along overseas and the truth about abortions and where is the planet headed, weather wise, war wise and all that.

Do You Want Friends?

One of our most common denominators is to want to be loved. If we are truly looking at our part in our own lives – we are looking at our reactions and responses to others – and how we act, talk, go, feel.

I want to be aware of each of those things so that I can do them well. If I want to move around in society, I am going to have to change up some of those things I do among people. I cannot always be selfish and demand my way. I need to understand that each person around me has needs they are acting on also.

Doesn't contributing to the <u>common</u> good just divert me from my personal progress? No. It is an intricate part of association with others and things - your responsibility in being human.

After finally learning to *focus on my own default actions and thoughts,* wouldn't helping <u>others</u> distract me from the goal of self-growth?

How many have experienced these selfish thoughts?

When meeting new people, courage and friendship naturally occur as we listen.

We let go of our controlling minds and listen with intention to know others and gain in camaraderie.

Something adjunct happens, we start gaining clarity, and become cognizant of the vastness of our emotions. We begin to notice the gifts that come our way, the gifts of joy, truth, and life with more laughter, through interacting with more people.

We watch others who have contentment, friends, and love. We want it and we want more and we want it now! We experience maturity, no longer feeling battered, we begin even to yield hope to others, to welcome everyone to our lives (because they are already there) with learned love and comforting words. Fulfillment and wonder and risk-taking become within our capacity. We are surprised at ourselves and our newfound capability to grow. First, I had to learn to push my security out of its comfort zone.

The be-all and end-all of life should not be to get rich, but to enrich the world.
– B. C. Forbes

We acknowledge that we have made progress on our own, but with the help of many others and through the guidance of a Higher Power. With the help of many others. See the pattern I am talking about?

Remember, we at one time, were each in various stages of desperation, confusion, distrust or terrified. If we open our minds, we will no longer be terrified, we will discover we are free to delight in life.

In helping others, we drop any pretense that 'I *am alone' in my journey.*

A humanitarian task is not, being asked, as a nonswimmer, to jump in the water to save someone. After a short time in the program, we are beginning swimmers here, we have progressed, we have learned, and we are qualified to assist others, or the lesser-experienced who is drowning in their desperation, confusion, and distrust.

Wait, how did we get our own selves from there to here? <u>With the help of others.</u> See the cycle? Others helping others? See the common thread?

When it comes to reaching out to others, what might hold you back? Answer this for yourself, then read on.

People don't like to be put upon
Fear of
Poor reader
Severely codependent
Fear tells me, 'no'
Shyness
I don't know how
That's for other people
I am done serving others
I get nervous
I'm incapable
I have too much anxiety
I don't need more stress
I don't know enough

My next question has to do with "In giving, we receive…"

What are some rewards that come to us when we give to others?

Teachers are not in it to get rich. Every day, EVERY single day – they have rewards seeing little people have lightbulb moments. Demonstrating to another 'how to' is beautiful for both parties.

Tested and true humanitarian ways.

I never thought I could be a humanitarian type. I never thought I would give enough to others that God might smile down on what I am doing. I FEEL THAT NOW.

Before, I never thought my life was working well enough to tell others that I knew something about living right. Now, I have small steps and giant leaps to use as examples for them to follow to better living; not by demanding or controlling them, but by mentoring.

I NOW KNOW that what I have learned has given me great gains in relationships. And in a community that is larger than myself.

As the pastor said this last Sunday: *"Love everyone with truth of heart."* What a great gift to yourself.

I gained the fact that when I talk only in truth with positivity and progress in mind, people want to know me. No one came to my constant "poor me" pity parties; not sure God even RSVPed.

Communication Starts with Me

Emotional issues. It's complicated.

Just think. Now think about thinking.

Here are a few questions to get you thinking about thinking:

1. In say, 300,000 B.C., when the only function for caveman was to forage food during his day, and there were no names assigned to any body, when a man died, did anyone experience sad?
2. Furthermore, in 3200 B.C., when man thought of someone else or recalled them talking, it was labelled as more of a hallucination, perhaps a voice from a god.
3. If your hands receive an unknown item behind a curtain, and your left brain turns off, can you orate the name of the item?

These make you think about thinking.

It is almost like learning a second dialectical method or another language. Think about how your brain mechanisms connect to themselves, all those lobes holding hands and channeling pieces of thoughts.

We are going to make you think about your thoughts, acquire more knowledge, and 'act' in behaviors which resurge in friendships.

Master bifurcating: Using two branches; forking off. What if you gained full control of what you do and say?

This is what is meant by using only 10% of our brain at any one time. There are three pounds of brain with one hundred billion cells in your noggin. Why not engage all of them?

Wouldn't life be in better shape? That means you would also control the output of your mouth and not be mean! Just as your exercise and nutrition contribute to the medulla which controls circulation and respiration, your knowledge and intelligence need to be fed many hours a week.

So here's the question:

If you don't like the negativity that is in the harbor of your first portal; if you don't like the sway your historical self is putting on something or someone, if you are not happy with your own thoughts, HOW THE HELL COULD ANYONE ELSE like everything that you spew?

Hey.

We all know inveterate crepe hangers; those folks with pernicious personalities. Are they your first choice to go out for coffee? No, we often set a boundary to not be around them. If we dislike being near them, why do we entertain some of their same habits?

Let's first communicate with self. If you turn all thinking habits to good and nice and positive, wow, you will be loved. It takes review in the thought process to transcend only moral consideration, even for self.

So Yogans tout meditation, Christians encourage oneness with your Lord, and Gurus encourage seeing within self.

You don't have to dig that deep. I am just asking that you umbrella your thinking with pausal time for synapses. This is strong awareness of self-actions and self-talk. What you do in private does count. Remove cheap cuss words not from just your speech, but from your working oral language;

and furthermore, from the vocabulary bank in your head. Cognizance of what you say or do goes to the depth of how much you love yourself or not! And let's face it, if you don't like yourself, HOW THE HELL COULD ANYONE ELSE?

So now let's get to quality communication. Start with being aware of your thinking, changing up thoughts to a higher level of intelligence, and then putting that forth to others. It is referred to as do-it-yourself behavioral therapy. It is one of the key elements between the clinical practices and cognitive neuroscience. We can bridge that on our own, with practice. This book is about jumpstarting, tapping into the neurons with new voices.

"Left brain" and "right brain" differ in function. In most people, the language area is chiefly on the left. Right now, please tap the left side of your head. Say, "Come on team, let's jumpstart."

Let's go. Here's how:

Clean out the mind.

Clear out the mind of oldies that gain nothing and /or do no one any good.

We must consciously stop the cacophony, turn off the 'have to's', take a first step toward inner stillness.

Shut yourself in what you now declare your meditation-and-reading space.

Meditation, as you know can happen by chance. On a long drive, you find you are mentally visiting places in your mind. It might be as simple as reviewing the grocery list (as you drive), listening to music (as you drive) planning a meeting (as you follow all traffic rules), or designing the new bathroom shelves you will put in. We all do these things already.

So plan to meditate. Aha. See it is simple. Plan to THINK about the beauty of the ocean last time you stared out at waves and white caps; or calming reflections of the sun. Not hard, in fact, quite enjoyable, right? That is 'thinking about thinking'.

What if I told you that only the educated can meditate? That is somewhat true. Biologists and quantum physicists convey, there is a certain level of development of the mind that is open to the suggestion of meditation. What if I told you that you do it all the time? Practice meditation that is. Practice is a key word. Believing that it works is mind over matter. Meditation happens when you put your face in a clean towel after showering – nothing else is present. Meditation happens when you scrub your head with shampoo. Nothing else is happening to you. Practice those moments with complete abandonment. Practice. Go outside and just listen. Find your favorite place on your porch or a park or backyard. Just listen…for different bird songs, ape them, guess how far away they may be, listen for a train, far away traffic or animal calls, just listen. Meditation comes over us. We just need to change what we concentrate on. Concentrate on the vibrations of the moment. Sense is a verb.

Plan other clearings of mind. These are also easy:

Sit by a lake

Go for a walk in a new area, the woods if possible.

Pack a lunch for yourself in the park.

Drive to a great vantage point for a sunrise or sunset.

Listen for nature, ignoring other manmade sounds.

Buy a musical instrument, be a gleeman. A drum is easy and beat it, establish your rhythm, or spell out your name in sound.

Drumming therapy is so, well, therapeutic! Teaching drumming therapy, I have noted the exact time on someone's face and shoulders when they gave themselves over. There is a calm presence, a stare like no other, when the heart beat rhythm is one with them.

Assignment:

If you were a color, what would you pick?

I'd pick green - nature, the leaves and grass in contrast to or foreground to a deeply blue sky. You can't see a forest for the (green) trees.

Teal, celery green, camo green, lime green, seafoam green, moss green, sage green, avocado green, green apple green. Most of those descriptors are based on growing things. See why I like green?

This is an exercise in enacting your imagination. Give yourself the freedom to be you.

What's your color? Describe ways you see it.

Let your thoughts just flow. Act out the feelings. Dance. Breathe. Or sit calmly. Acknowledge the peace that comes over you. This is very important to balance your life with relaxation, as day to day challenges do otherwise.

Permission to be: Mom used to give us permission to have a cookie, to go outside, to go to our friends. We needed permission. If you have ever worked for an autocratarian, no doubt, some of 'do what Mom says' is still instilled. I believed that everyone older than me, knew better than I, what I should do.

GIVE YOURSELF back permission to do anything. Make sure it is the next best and right thing to do, however!

Start easy. Give yourself permission to take a coffee break. Take a break whenever you need it. Breathe, visualize, get water, move your muscles, stand on your tiptoes, lift the shoulders, bounce in place. You don't have to go far or leave the task you are on, but take a break. Feel how good that change of focus can be? Allow others to do their breaks as they need to. Give yourself the freedom to do. It is revolutionary.

Your cerebellum sits at the back of your head, under the cerebrum. It controls coordination and balance. The repetitions of a mantra, the beat of a drum calm this portion into schematics with the heart. That is also a break.

Dr. Daniel Tranel, Professor of Neurology at the University of Iowa, recently verified the authenticity of the research stating that the basal ganglia and cerebellum are the two organs in the brain which allow music to become indelibly embedded in the brain, never to be removed or erased during the remaining years of a person's lifetime. This may be the first time in the history of music and medicine that an announcement of this magnitude is released. Just in the past two years, we have discovered that Alzheimer's patients may not know their children's face, but they can sing every word to a song learned in childhood.

I hope you have a pet. Within the heart of a pet God put the desire to purely be by your side. I hope you behold them as well. They virtually love us and love to be with us and watch our activity. They live to smell our human scent, our breath. They cherish us for who we are, period. Sit in the glory of those astonishing and sweet thoughts and deep breathe.

Really listen to yourself – notice where you veer off to conscious thoughts of work, office, chores, tasks, jobs, yard work. Listen here! If you can't, during this one chance at life, take time for yourself, when are you gonna be better? Never.

See this is probable. You may be thinking, it is not even possible. Why would you immediately default to Negative Nellie thinking? The change up is in the 'seeing meditation as probably happening'. Wow. New courage, huh? I ask you to try to just be willing. You might just ace this with practice! Whoever would have said to you: 'Don't be so brave.' (I am laughing as I write that.) "Stop taking good opportunities.", "Live in fear", or "Think only about the worst that could happen all the time." No one said that, ever to you!

"Courage is always with me." - Me

I will share my mantras that get me through. These were nouveau to me and I had to repeat them and do it wrong, then repeat, repeat. But now they stick and they come up as my first thought:

'If not now, when?'
'Why wouldn't it be okay?'
'Am I living the life my Mom would have hoped for me as a child?'

I bring up these mental billboards when I am faced with stress, problems, both tangible and inanimate that scare me. It is natural for me to think in this manner now. You can switch that up for yourself. People will like you better. Huh! Go figure.

See this difference you will make in yourself by taking a few new routes with your reasoning and processing, will fill your life with more goodness. What do you have to lose?

Courage is already yours. You only have to own it.

When you have graduated to this level of wisdom, this stage of positive thought and a new tranquility that you readily engage, you will be worthy of friendship by unbelievably nice and good people. I guarantee it or the price of the book will be returned. You put out good, you get good back.

Involve your body when you listen to another person. Turn into them. Put both ears on their voice, your mind on their meaning and your eyes in their eyes. You are paying them homage for talking with you. It is gratifying communication for both. We all know folks who do nothing in conversation but think of their next contribution to it. Doing that takes away from truly listening. It is a precious moment when someone listens to me. I want to give out that same value. Silence and absorption of messages are so crucial.

Instead of: "I'm not going with you." How about, "Thank you for asking. Shoot, I have an engagement at that time. I'm sorry." (Your engagement could even be to relax!) You both leave the conversation with understanding.

Or, "Unfortunately, I can't make it. I'm sorry."

Or, "Thank you for that opportunity. Homelife comes first today."

Or "I'm torn - I made another obligation. Guess I better do what I promised. I'm sorry."

Don't leave feeling rejected. Leave knowing your sincerity. Be up front and honest as you can be, always being kind in the 'say so'.

Or "Haven't been home all week. I need to make my family know I love them too. I'm sorry."

Be good with asking. Demanding folks and louder people might get attention, but they often leave a derisive note to the exchange of communication.

Honesty works best here too. "I lost my sense of direction. Which way to United Airlines? with a smile, takes you much farther than, "Where in the hell is Gate 9!" People do not want to approach you because of a sensed anger.

One of many prayers for friendship:

> Lord, You know better than I know myself that I am growing older and will someday be old. Keep me from the fatal habit of thinking I must say something on every subject and on every occasion. Release me from the craving to straighten out everybody's affairs. Make me thoughtful, but not moody. Helpful, but not bossy. With my vast store of wisdom, it seems a pity not to use it all, but You know, Lord, I want a few friends at the end.

> Keep my mind free from the endless recital of details; give me wings to get to the point. Seal my lips on my aches and pains. They are increasing, and love of rehearsing them is becoming sweeter as the years go by. I dare not ask for grace enough to enjoy the tales of others' pains, but help me to endure them with patience.

> I dare not ask for improved memory, but for a growing humility and a lessening cocksureness when my memory seems to clash with the memories of others. Teach me the glorious lesson that occasionally, I may be mistaken.

> Keep me reasonably sweet. I do not want to be a saint - some of them are so hard to live with. But a sour old person is one of the crowning works of the devil. Give me the ability to see good things in unexpected places, and talents in unexpected people. And give me, Lord, the grace to tell them so.

> Cathartic Amen

Obsessed with Obsession

If you don't 'get why' you don't laugh enough in life, read this chapter.

You say, 'If I had a little more, I should be very satisfied.' You make a mistake. If you are not content with what you have, you would not be satisfied if it were doubled. –Charles Haddon Spurgeon

Why do I let a mental obsession possess my life, time, and mind; and become my god?!

Like, "Why do I feel miserable? And then I mentally list the reasons. Talk about obsessive! Whenever I think, 'why is this happening to me?' or 'why is this happening now?' I am wasting precious 'mind' time I could spend in solution. Gees. Conversations in the mirror are not helpful. Life usually is not fun when I stay and listen to my own created crap. There are so many things wrong with that harmful self-talk sentence. Gees. I do not know the reason why. Hee, Hee. Talk to the only one who wants my talk – God. Self-thinking without spirituality or connection to God *paralyzes me!* Do just one progressive, positive thing, like dusting one room, checking the air in your tires, call a new insurance agent. Investigate a religious sect you have no ideas about. Smell flowers. Read Genesis. Understand politics. Choose a ball team to root for. Change up your thinking away from obsessive thoughts once you recognize you are doing so. Some obvious compulsions include: getting stuck in my thinking about being obsessive, stuck in thoughts of pain and hurt, addictive behavior, constant worry, road rage, arguing, not letting go of pain or hurt or grief, inflexibility. It seems impossible for people to switch their concentration. Only you can recognize you are in it and abort it. Quit being in an unuseful rut. You first have to tell yourself, "I chose to live this way, and I don't have to. I want fruitful progress."

Today, we have an opportunity to stop the self-destruction. Today we can counter stinking thinking. We are learning how.

Why do I think that going over something in my mind is going to make me sane? Ha! It will take time for the old self to heal our wounds, after we realize we are made up of them. Self-confidence will come, just as a good free throw – with practice.

I am funny. Hang with me. I will amuse you eventually. Humor used to get me attention and out of a few debacles. Many of us disguise our true selves and pains behind our use of humor. I hid behind my humorous actions. I manipulated to get my way, got the focus off a serious topic. I learned to pretend…even pretend I was intelligent or witty. I wanted to be in with the in-crowd or invisible at times, and I pretended I was, with my bourgeois affect. Because reality for me was painful. I believed I was painfully shy, unattractive, selfish, and manipulative, and thought I was wryly funny.

Zechariah 4:6 "Not by my might, nor by power, but by My Spirit, Sayeth the Lord"

(Not mine, but Thine is the Glory and the Kingdom, and the Power)

I was self-destructive.

Do not gloss over the paragraphs below, saying to yourself, "I've read these a hundred times." Truth be told, you read them before and have glanced over them a hundred times. Abe Lincoln is quoted. Happiness is found within, and encouragement to lighten up and think smarter are persuasively put. Read these for 101 times.

Borrowed from anonymous of Alcoholics Anonymous:

Just for today, I will try to live through this day only, and not tackle all my problems at once. I can do something for twelve hours that would appall me if I felt that I had to keep it up for a lifetime.

Just for today, I will be happy. This assumes to be true what Abraham Lincoln said, that "Most folks are as happy as they make up their minds to be."

Just for today, I will adjust myself to what is, and not try to adjust everything to my own desires. I will take my "luck" as it comes, and fit myself into it.

Just for today, I will try to strengthen my mind. I will study. I will learn something useful. I will not be a mental loafer. I will read something that requires effort, thought and concentration.

Just for today, I will exercise my should in three ways: I will do somebody a good turn and not get found out if anybody knows of it, it will not count. I will do at least two things I don't want to do – just for exercise. I will not show anyone that my feelings are hurt; they may be hurt, but today I will not show it.

Just for today, I will be agreeable. I will look as well as I can, dress becomingly, keep my voice low, be courteous, criticize not one bit. I won't find fault with anything, nor try to improve or regulate anybody but myself.

Just for today I will be a program, I may not follow it exactly, but I will have it. I will save myself from two pests: hurry and indecision.

Just for today I will have a quiet half hour all by myself and relax. During this half hour, sometime, I will try to get a better perspective of my life.

Just for today I will be unafraid. Especially I will not be afraid to enjoy what is beautiful and to believe that as I give to the world, so the world will give to me.

I live near this scene now; only one and a half hours to be enmeshed in this! I chose to live here.

And of course, I want to include here the Prayer for Today:

Lord, make me an instrument of Thy peace. Where there is hatred, let me sow love; where there is injury, pardon; where there is doubt, faith; where there is despair, hope; where there is darkness, light; and where there is sadness, joy.

Read it again. Mean it. Plan to live in goodness as much as you possibly can!

Change My Heart, O Lord

I love this cloudy picture. Scary that this was taken on a curvy mountain road, but it represents just what I have control of – my immediate surroundings. God has anything beyond. Only I can make my immediate surroundings comfortable.

O Divine Master, grant that I may not so much seek to be consoled, as to console; to be understood as to understand; to be loved, as to love; for it is in giving that we receive; it is in pardoning that we are pardoned, and it is in dying that we are born to eternal life.

If thoughts were weighed on a scale for righteousness or not, which end of yours is heavy?

Life is not about waiting for the storm to pass; it's about learning to dance in the rain.

Unharden and embolden yourself. Jesus would want it.

From Mark, 12:30, then the Corinthians:

> *Our minds and thoughts are important reflections of the image of God.*
> *We are to take captive every thought to make it obedient to Christ.*

A key word for me is Pull. When I feel I am pulled toward a side in a tough decision, it is usually the easiest and pressure of NOW, direction that I go. That is called COMPULSION. My key word here is com PULL sion. When I realize that I am being PULLed, I stop. Can I let go of the entire mess? Is my name on the happening? Does worry bring any good to the scene? Have I submerged myself already? Has worry EVER made anything better? Am I playing God with a decisive force without knowing the odds or stats or outcomes? Does this even need me to put time, energy, or hope into?

'Let go and let God' has a LOT of power.

Worry is an over exaggerated sense of responsibility that is not even mine. I had spent most of fifty some years worrying. I wasted so much time pacing, calling, snooping, wondering, questioning, telling others of my worry, actually blaming and chastising another person for making me worry, etc. – all at the cost of sanity cells, losing friends, living with destructive thinking.

Make an extra effort to know what you are doing negatively and counter it. Start your reentry into the good life by thinking of five good things. Whenever I use a cuss word, for me it is "shit" or "damn", my second thought is what good things are about me in this moment right now; such as, "I own a good hammer. I am building something good for myself. I still have all my thumbs. Thank you, God, for the nice heated building I am carpentering in and being of full mind to move my thumb before landing on the nail." Seriously, I do this, and seriously, I mean it. See, "the mind grows by what it feeds on" (Josiah g. Holland). If I repeatedly use the word fuck in my vocabulary, soon everything will be fucking bad. (Excuse my French, but I wanted to get the point across.) I cannot surround myself with bad words or thoughts and think that I will be happy. I am doomed to think I am doomed. Be succinct.

Our body registers 'worry'. Can you sense that? Scan yourself, reviewing your tense places. Take a deep breath. Change where your eyes are staring. Pause.

When do we need to reach out the most? Exercise the most? Call friends? Expand our minds? That's right, when we are feeling down. Another incongruency within our minds: how we think when we are abused, derided, berated, rejected, or negated. And of course, I blamed my husband, like a perpetrator, because he was predacious, aggressive, and controlling. And I succumbed. It's like being on the back of a bicycle built for two with no one driving. So is there some enjoyment in submitting your joy to one person who can't give it to you? I may have been suffering from Demoralization Syndrome, but no one diagnosed me with such at the time. If I could 'blame someone else', that justified my retaliation or rectification.

Lacking in self-esteem or a sense of self-worth, does nothing for the goodness within us. Does that answer your question as to why some archetypal people live in Snickertyville? It is a level of wisdom and a 'higher thinking' to know yourself; to cognitively stop your words before they hurt, to deny bad thoughts, judgements, rationalization. It must be performed in the frontal lobes, intelligently. Do you say, 'Duh!' to yourself when you err? That's the kind of thinking I am talking about here. Where you not only think "duh" but you actually abort the thought before you spew out a misnomer, a bias, a cutting quip. It takes habitual clean and clear thinking with progressive and positive thoughts. And to pay attention to clipping your own hedge, not others'.

Sue Monk Kidd writes in Firstlight:

> *"I begin to observe myself in the presence of others, friends and strangers alike, and I'm surprised by the level of my availability. I watch my restless heart, the mercurial way my mind sweeps from one thing to another, the way my ego holds forth, keeping me abreast of my own expectations, wants, and preoccupations, criticizing, comparing, competing, imposing view. I realize that I can be with someone, but on a deeper level, I'm not available to them at all. I have attention deficit of the soul."*

So, you have been you for twenty, thirty, perhaps fifty years. You have lived with your habits, thinking, and reactions for that long! Wow! That will take a bit of time to re-habituate; to shift, change up your knowledge and abort ugly thoughts (some of us actually forecast a picture ourselves being rejected when 'our loved one' gets home, like a child waiting for punishment) and actions. It is not just habits from parents and friends, but poetic, literary, historic, prophetic, and other forms of discourse that formed your current canons about life.

The difference between you now and the curmudgeon you later in life, is now. Upgrade your processing mechanisms. Don't offices bring in a new piece of technology when available? The old Xenon 10 is sitting by the dumpster in the alley. They know when to change for the better. So why would we stay with ideas created in 1976, 1959, or 2001? We formulated those decision skills and factoids in our head by watching our mentors (parents, teachers, ministers, sages, staunch in-laws) perhaps ten, fifteen or forty years ago. So let's just say that what we have seen, heard, smelled, touched, and been instructed or were deprived of, is who you are perceivably now. How on earth could the old stinking thinking still be applicable to our current age? Do you drive a Model A? No. Do you dry your clothes on a line outside? No.

With all the thoughts, knowledge and rote I had, I could not think my way out of discomfort – that feeling of unmanageability, off balance. Sometimes

I thought and thought autogenetically and ended up with only a migraine! I realized through research, a great deal of reading, and from listening to others that I was so busy putting out fires and mulling over my sad life, that I had no time left to do what I knew would make a difference. How sad is that? Then, I had guilt over what I was not doing, and found I was not enjoying what I was doing. I was missing moments where I could have been absorbed in the ascent, of loving relationships, of joyful times, creativity and fun. I had chosen disengagement. Automatic flow without direction in my brain is useless, parallel to a broken assembly line. It is, rather, important to use this organ, emphasizing cellular health.

Who are you? Are you so busy with daily life happening that you forget who you really are, apart from duties and tasks? What if you fully lived the moments you are in the tasks with joy, embracing the fact that you 'get to do' more today. You are still on the planet, and this is your CHOICE as to where you are and your decorum and thinking in this one moment of the one thousand minutes you are awake today.

Rote is repetition of something to be learned. In this case, it can also refer to things already learned. We are going to switch your rote learning. Just as the cones in our eyes see, using the vision lobe and have a memory bank to refer to for what we think we saw, so does a habit. We think it should be this way. Until we open our mental eyes to the experience anew, we will see things as we always saw them before. We need to shake up our rote bank from schematics and look for ways that are incongruent with what we have always known to be true to us.

We have had logarithms radiating wave lengths and tones of color. We have stored memories of old tapes. We will forever operate under that modus until our mental experience is enhanced by more outside and new views. Just as our acoustic perception is picked up in the cochlea, our thoughts must go to the part of the brain that aligns our thought formation.

I knew then that I needed stimulus, new knowledge, helpful guidance outside myself. The first step in the Twelve Steps of Alcoholics Anonymous includes admitting unmanageability of our lives. The second step sparks the idea that I can restore my own sanity. Both so powerful.

Psychologist Martin Seligman speaks of three P's that stunt our recovery:

1. Personalization – the belief that we are at fault
2. Pervasiveness – the belief that an event will affect all areas of our life
3. Permanence – the belief that the aftershocks of the event will last forever.

I suffered from all.

Do you still 'type' on a Corolla? Do you have to know the metric system by heart or will your cellphone convert? We have to upgrade or we are left behind not only unintelligent, but stupid about the ways of the world and the ways of interaction with the world.

Grow up to glow. My desire to grow and glow was outweighed by my overfocus on changing someone else's life. It was my life that needed the uptick all along. I was dealing with my own ineptitude!

"Grow little glow worm, glimmer, glimmer"

When did you stop growing? It is a continuous process till we hit the dirt, drink the bottom of the well, blow this pop stand. Spiritual leaders coined the phrase "invincible ignorance" for those who cannot grow because of a life situation. You are not that. You can no longer plead ignorance. You are reading that excuse is no longer allowed.

So as you are maturing, growing, learning, open up your heart and mind. We all know curmudgeons who walk or 'recline' on this planet and as they age; their opinionated, biased, complaining selves are all that is left for us to encounter.

Gosh, don't be that. Grow in physique, mind and heart your entire life.

What are you doing that matters most?

And speak the truth. Make good choices. "Let truth arise!" as my one pal says. Instead of advice and opinions, give experience, strength and hope.

"The years go by; time will change and even reverse many of your present opinions. Refrain therefore awhile from setting yourself up as a judge of the highest matters. – Plato

That's it. That is all there is to a good life. The secret is out.

That means:

Speak to your own bad habits. Be cognizant that a minute is passing by – your one chance at this one. Look for sound folks to be in your circle. Don't live in 'heartsick'. Your heart is not truly broken – address the issues that make it heavy. Who would you be if we were metaphysical only? Speak to worthiness with the best love you can muster. Demonstrate your humanity. Who is styming it from the world, but you?

Commit to the wellbeing of yourself and others. We often have a nebulous, intangible humanitarian dream of who we will be when we are rich; how giving we will be THEN. Then is now. Hello. Knock, knock.

Is hope an emotion? Or a developed attitude about something? Hope triggers lobe loads with happy chemicals. Hope lessens pain. Hope in attitude or emotion is a defined passion for better. Hope to be better. Hope to feel good. Hope to get past this bad event. Hope to have better physical strength – for ourselves and others. Hope to forget this mess we are in currently. Hope for a brighter future. When we hear about hope, we actually calm down and actually see more clearly, and release our tension.

Hope is a smooth operator.

What dominates our consciousness and dictates our actions is what we ultimately value. It masters us. And ultimately, we become its slave. When hoping for money or possessions become our ultimate value or drive, we will have no time or energy for the type of security that God provides. If we seek God first, the anxious quest for more material security will not be as all important as it once was.

> *Thousands upon thousands are yearly brought into a state of real poverty by their great anxiety not to be thought of as poor.* —Robert Mallett

Ask yourself, what do you value most in life? I believe we want to look at how we spent our money to know that answer. Television ads are a prime contributor to what we value. They show happiness in a marriage when a new car solves the problems of transportation for kids. Our culture teaches us to buy and wear makeup in that search for beauty and perfection. Decades ago, the churches were the centers of culture, a meeting place. Today, only twenty percent of the population attend. What do you value? Are you inclined to act in a manner that enhances that life?

A reminder I read daily:

"What loving action can I take today? Maybe I will make some time for nothing more practical than simple pleasure – a movie, a good book, or a breath of fresh air. Or perhaps I'll deal with paper work that I've been setting aside. I can now make commitment to eat well and to get the rest I need, or make amends for something that's been on my mind. A simple gesture can be the beginning of a lifelong habit of self-love."

The book, <u>A Spiritual Path to Higher Creativity,</u> written for artist
some great ideas for positive lives. I have somewhat paraphrased the ideas
all attributed to their spark, because I love their premise:

1. Affirmative reading every day. Find written materials that focus
   on attitudinal shifts that uptick. See yourself in more positive
   settings.

2. What five activities will take up your only chance at these next
   24 hours? Will time be spent in ignoring your needs? Will you
   go where you want to go? Do you plan to enjoy each of the five
   encounters?

3. Make a written list of 100 things you have not yet done but want to
   experience in your lifetime. Pin this on your chest. – Well, pin this
   where you and others will see it. Use this as a map of your life –
   'Oh the places you will go' (Dr. Seuss). Give yourself permission to
   explore how to accomplish this life you would like.

4. In that list, include two for this week's schedule.

5. Write your own affirmations. I like to include assets. You will find
   a multitude of good substance you allude!

6. Write assets you appreciate in others. Do two exercises toward an
   asset you would like to have now. I said, make the effort toward an
   asset you would like to adapt.

7. At the end of each day, review in your head, what strides and joy
   you have had because of your efforts. Have gratitude that you are a
   living, breathing human being who is taking this one great chance
   at your fulfilled moments.

You will find others want to be around you, that you are not falsely living
others' demands and lives, you will be fulfilled, you will live in gratitude
and quite possibly, you will get bigger and last longer.

> *"The words that lighten the soul are more precious than jewels."*
> Hazrat Inayat Khan

Judgement – I Cannot Believe there were 6.3 Million Sperm there and You Made It!

Did you ever think that everyone is doing their best? No, we lie in disdain and pomposity of their failures ACCORDING to us. Judgement.

We don't get to do that. They may be lazy, in our judgement. We no longer get to say or think that. Instead, my interior monologue goes, "That is all they know to do at this time, or perhaps, that was exampled to them in their upbringing or they lacked a great environment to grow up in, they have a medical issue, a mental insecurity or disruption in maturity". <u>IT IS NOT FOR ME TO JUDGE.</u> They get to just be. I visit the other side of my self-inflicted limited vision.

So I have questioned authorities, "How come you do not pay attention to me or my needs?"

I questioned my mother, "Why didn't you do more for me?"

I have no right. Why didn't we learn more about Science in grade school? Why do I have such a time now with spelling, accounting, etc.? Why are the tax forms so complicated? I have no right to blame anyone but myself because I can always upgrade my knowledge. That is up to me, not a former teacher or boss or parent!

Obsessively reviewing everyone's ethics focuses my attention where it does not belong and keeps me too busy blaming, to have any serenity in my mind or soul. What a waste of my time.

I just quiver now when I think of the time I challenged my mother with why didn't she finance sending all eight of us through college. Am I kidding? She was doing the best she could. I was so wrong about challenging her or thinking that I knew something that SHE SHOULD have done.

I do not know what other people should do. I might have expectations, but I have no right to judge them or change them. Whew. That is hard to take when I have so many cascading wishes and desires and changes I want for them! Mind my own business and do better at my own business.

We even condemn ourselves. 'We should have done more... We could have... We would... If only'. Yeah, see? We have expectations for ourselves and we even let ourselves down sometimes. How on earth do I dare judge someone else? They are doing the best they can with what they know at the time. And in God's eyes, everything is happening just as it should. Some lessons we just don't know yet. More to be revealed.

Twig, a Native American, once wrote for the "Warrior" about mirrors:

"I see myself in everyone
But I find myself in you.
All things in everyone I admire
I now see admirably in me.
All things in everyone I dislike –
I now see, are, unlikeable in me.
Every strength, and every weakness
I always see in others.
I see now in this mirror
Looking back at me."

There is another side to judging someone else to be lazy...answer these TRUTHFULLY:

Which would you rather do:

Wait an hour before having ice cream	Give in to sight of carton or DQ sign
Watch all of Monday night tv	Watch fav show / Do activity part of evening
Physical therapy prescribe (d) exercises	Sit in chair
Read healthy book, grow and learn	Read love story, sci-fic only
Delay the hard task or chore	Do a first step toward task
Look at dirty dishes and think tomorrow	Take care of them after meal
Make your bed	Believe you will be back soon, so why?

Your own limbic system may be working against you. Maybe you do have a slight headache or feel too tired. Maybe.

Is it true, or are you leaning on an excuse to allow you to procrastinate? We tend to go for the fun versus work. Why not!!? Obligations, promises, and safety and security are your determining factors. Run a truth check on whatever you are putting aside for the fun. Will you fail the class? Is getting drunk really a relief from facing the boss or will the repercussions still be there and you will feel sick later anyway?

We go for the less distressing, of course. We like easy and quick fixes, and achievements rather than tedium. So, what just happened? In the last chapter, you called someone lazy. You chose your judgement of another who puts aside obligations for more fun, as a slothful immature person.

Perfect true story in my life. My live-in boyfriend loved his hobbies, spending much in the way of tech support to have fun. Came time for a couple of routine payments, contract on a vehicle and water bill, he didn't quite have the amounts. I judged him as too lazy to make enough money, irresponsible, poor at money management, and making poor choices. Yet, every night I watch tv and eat ice cream, my poor choices.

We must speak truthfully, sometimes 'talk to ourselves' about a poor habit or a slothful way. It is too easy to rationalize away the challenge or responsibility. Others do it. I do it. Admit it, you do it.

Hopefully seeing yourself in the mirror will abate the quick summation of what we see in others. There are legitimate reasons to delay work, but those, those are truly rare!

Sensation - Al

————

How do you feel at this moment?

How did you feel before bed last night?

How did you feel last time you got in an argument?

How did you feel after your last kiss?

Lists of feelings have been used in cognitive therapy to identify the sensation behind cognitive distortions. Often revelations from below are exemplary for assertiveness training to identify feelings during communication.

Try to find your sensations:

Anger

angry	exasperated	resentment
agitated	frustrated	resentful
aggravated	furious	stubborn
annoyed	hateful	touchy
bitter	hostile	outraged
bothered	impatient	pessimistic
contemptuous	irritated	prejudiced
disappointed	jealous	provoked
disgusted	mean	vindictive
enraged	mischievous	violent

Contentment/Esteem

affectionate	friendly	safe
accepted	full	satisfied
appreciated	fulfilled	secure
beautiful	genuine	self-reliant
brave	generous	sexy
calm	grateful	sincere
capable	hopeful	special
caring	humorous	strong
centered	hysterical	supported
cherished	innocent	supportive
comfortable	involved	sympathetic
compassionate	lovable	tender
competent	loved	thankful
connected	loving	trusting
confident	loyal	understanding
content	open	understood
courageous	optimistic	unique
creative	passionate	valuable
curious	peaceful	warm
desirable	playful	witty
easy	proud	worthwhile
engaged	relaxed	youthful
exhilarated	relieved	validated, valued
forgiving	respected	

Fear

afraid	apprehensive	desperate
alarmed	bashful	doubtful
anxious	concerned	fearful

frantic	panicky	threatened
helpless	paralyzed	uneasy
horrified	paranoid	uptight
insecure	scared	vulnerable
nervous	set-up	worried
no follow-through	suspicious	wishy-washy
overwhelmed	terrified	

Happiness

alive	great	silly
amused	happy	excited
cheerful	joyful	playful
delighted	loved	proud
eager	love-struck	thrilled
glad	pleased	wonderful
good	satisfied	

Isolation

alone	left-out	rejected
apathetic	lonely	repelled
bored	lost	repulsed
ignored	pushed-away	torn
isolated	pushed-out	unappreciated
jealous	quiet	

Sadness

defeated	hopeless	rejected
dejected	hurt	remorseful
depressed	melancholy	sorry
despairing	miserable	unfulfilled
devastated	muddled	
discouraged	numb	

Shame

ashamed	humiliated	resigned
awkward	inadequate	rigid
bewildered	incompetent	restrained
blamed	indecisive	scattered
closed	ineffective	self-conscious
cold	inhibited	shy
conflicted	insecure	stupid
confused	judgmental	suspicious
cut-off	needy	unattractive
defeated	negated	unsure
deprived	phony	useless
dependent	preoccupied	victimized
embarrassed	pressured	worn out
foolish	puzzled	
guilty	remorseful	

Somatic (Physical Feelings)

back pain	head ache	sluggish
breathless	heart racing	stiff
energized	nausea	tired
foggy	neck pain	worn-out
gastrointestinal	old	
discomfort	sleepy	

Wow. I believe I have experienced every one of these! How about you?

Anger is A Disposition You Chose

If you find you are constantly feeling resentful or angry, be concerned about yourself in that relationship. That is inappropriate in close or living-together partners. It may be you that emits the dis-ease in the relationship. I found that I consistently did the same thing in my early relationships with friends and that I was still doing the same behaviors as an adult. Should you have told me that it was me? Do not avoid having serious discussions with folks, children, spouses, mates, friends. If the relationship is worth putting out love, then it is worth frank discussion. I am stating here right now, your relationship will fail if you are not honest with every nuance and facet of your being. In sexual contact, your moles, one smaller breast or testicle and gray hair and crooked front tooth are exposed. Overcoming the cold fear of exposure in that manner is so relieving; and extremely loving and caring. Why not then, be honest in every aspect of your walks of life? It is also relieving, extremely loving and caring. My spouse knows my fears, my moles, my bad breath, of my one short toe, my failures, my famous person crush, and all my cues. It is wonderfully comfortable to be with someone who has address to each of your flaws and ways and accepts you. The honesty I am giving him is what he wanted all along from a partner in his search.

Truth keeps us from mistakes in relationships. Truth allows for acceptance. Truth never hurts with intent. Truth gives no cause for resentment or envy or judgement. My opinions are not truth.

I create resentment often when I am angry. It is powerful. I get to have rage wash through me, or self-righteousness qualms, or fear, for a tiny bit, *but only in my mind,* not out my mouth. Till I realize my blood pressure went up, that it was me eliciting the cuss words, my ugly side and revulsion to others, I cannot change. It can happen with emotional disgust, sadness, surprise and inequity. Equity is not equality. Those are all my reactions to trials of life. Mine, even though I thought it was YOU who pissed me off. I get to experience animosity, bitterness, indignation, irritation, dissatisfaction, disgruntledness, discomfort, acrimony, bad feelings, hard feelings, rancor, judgements, ill will, grudges, friction, spite, dislike, venomness feelings, peevishness - all that. That sentence started with 'I get to experience'. *Only in my mind.* Where do I really wanna be? In gratitude with goodwill or, in division, disharmony and discord? A choice. Mine. Wow.

Rage has its own colors. Your body really gets a poor going over when angry:

Pupils dilate	Hearing sharpens	You sense an enemy
Breathing quickens	More oxygen gets into blood	Heart rate quickens
Body temperature rises	You perspire in response	Body gets ready for a fight
Muscles tense for action	Digestion slows	Blood goes to brain and muscles
Endorphins get used up	Stomach gets upset	We clench our jaws
Teeth grind	Forgetfulness happens	Teariness happens
Headaches	Dizziness occurs	Swallowing quickens
Dry mouth occurs	Aggressive feelings awash	Hormones trigger anxiety
Blood glucose drops	Immunity weakens	Risk of disease upticks

What do you do when you are angry?

Do I get quiet, rage, grit my teeth, jowls tic, leer, raise a fist, pace, breathe fast, eat, accept, hold resentment, keep score? Work your thought process through here. Know yourself. Know your physical and physiological knee-jerk reactions to anger. Take this time to review your behavior and consider what could you do differently. Own your behavior and part in every setting.

You are twice as likely to have a heart attack because of the rapid heart rate, even within two hours post being ticked off. See where counting to ten under your breath can allow the brain to recall these dangers to yourself when YOU have anger with someone else.

Acting on hate is like taking rat poison and expecting someone else to die by feeling MY pain.

A beautiful wash came over me when I gave myself permission to cease my hostility toward anyone, even someone who threatened to kill me.

Wasting Time and Space in My Head

Wish I had a shredder in my head. One that would take out unnecessary thinking like, worrying, controlling others, the anger gene, bad attitude, and anxiety.

Worrying is so useless.

Self-talk, pacing, experiencing anxiety around worry is sick in itself. Do I excite others unnecessarily, complain, fear my lack of control, fear the future which is at this moment not reality, then do I lament?

Anxiety and depression overlap. Docs say if you feel excessive anxiety for over six months, you get the 'Anxiety' diagnosis. But often, by six months' time, people become depressed about their constant anxiety and worry! They trigger each other, anxiety and depression.

Work your thought process through here. Know yourself. Know your physical and psychological reactions to worrying. Take this time to review your behavior and consider what could you do differently.

Your basal ganglia are in the brain and vertebra. They are cells in your body which react and respond according to other lobal input. They are most active when anxiety befalls you. If you think you are not affected by fear and the unknown and events, you are wrong! The ganglia are ganging up to offer feeling and movements (sobbing or trembling) you may not want to experience. 'The gang' affects formation of habits, pleasure or ecstasy (seeking resolution of fear with overdrinking or drugs or sex). Anxiety can gang up and do weird things my friends (tongue tied or faint, lead to Parkinson's Disease, and decrease the dopamine production you so desperately need.) Since you know how to calm anxiety by now, it is best to meet it at the door and avoid running down the street naked or punching someone out. It is on your plate to be aware. Fear annihilates hope.

Anxiety CAN BE HELPFUL in that we realize we need to overcome a trouble, solve a dilemma, or take care of business. Anxiety used properly says, "Let's meet that and take care of that." Rise up to the challenge presenting itself. Wow. That is a different take from cowering or getting an ulcer, huh?

Prolonged anxiety will, there is no doubt; will sicken you. Therapies and sought-out help, sometimes medication, to get you started on a better path can tremendously counter the reactionary anxiety issues which we erroneously think are real. We all know people, maybe family, who overreact. They may persuade us to worry with them. Correct response to the 'feelings' of anxiety are your only choice. We have internal resilience; why do we not rely on that more? We have developed instead, a fixed mindset which is made up of fast-food-like facts, habitual go-tos: grandpa's provincial 1940 advice, Dad's alcoholic mentoring, insecurity from abandonment, your teacher's inept knowledge, poor advice, and/or wrongful acts.

Recall the way that information and memory are processed – it's how we organize our memories to fit in with what we know. (Which is markedly limited by immaturity, exposure, and lack of experience.) We have confirmed biases, firmly held religious tenets, familial tendencies. Since we own our own memories, we then rely on them to be true. Un-uh! We have been influenced, and absorbed much of our lore, profoundly. We have to question these things. Do we know all the universal truths about mankind? No. Open thy mind. Not everyone loves cats. What happens when we hear contrary evidence to what we think we know?

I'ma Blamin' Ma Family

A demonstration of instinctive naivety follows:

Dad beats mom. Then it is okay with me to hit Sara. Dad beats me. Then it is okay with me to beat littler people. The neighbor screeches at my sister for stepping on a tulip. Then it is okay to scream, taunt, pester another for walking in front of my bike path. It festers, it grows. We watched and learned negativity.

Maybe no one talked to you at home. You never knew what bipolar personality might come out of the bedroom - so many facets of personal behaviors. Bias was founded in our house as easy as not liking coconut flavor. "What? You don't like coconut? You are missing out on the best thing in life." We learned judgement – assignment of adjectives. Maybe you are something I have been influenced to hate.

Maybe you didn't have much food. It was cold every night at your house and you fought for blankets, rugs, and towels to cover yourselves. You learn to fight for basic needs. Therefore, you were going to steal others' belongings. Don't talk, don't trust, don't feel, became our motto.

And I had judged the above person as a thief.

There is not always a reason. It just happens out of 'I did the best I could with what I knew at the time.'

Privileged kids are a whole nother ballgame, but seem to be bullies for a different stack of reasons, mostly based at the same core - not enough love and care or from constant demonstration by their elders of 'warring' for more of the riches.

"I have the perfect party dress." "No, you don't, I have one from Bloomingdales. "My mother got mine on line - on line, did you hear? She is smarter technologically than your mother."

Always in competition for better or thieving our way to more, while tossing others aside. It happened and we were mentored these patterns.

My crazy was obvious. I asked my mirror if I was, and the lips in the reflection said it was just my actions that were untethered, not my whole body.

I had been lusting after other people's experiences and attitudes or mockingly hating them for their mental freedom. Little did I understand that the hate was either taught to me or learned by people watching. So many beliefs were shoved down my throat that I had stopped believing in myself. I had innately given away my embedded personal freedoms, the ability to feel things and then let them through into actions or words. Others lived in AWE of goodness. I was silenced and stymied by coping with a disease, not EVEN MY OWN inherent disease! I actually found myself revering the paroxysm of emotional outbursts as power. Insanity of a sort. The tantrum I expressed as a grown woman is now so embarrassing. I had misplaced my ability to make my own choices and when I did, it was not based on goodness. I had replaced it with a fixation and silence around alcoholism. By symbiosis, I was not present in my own preservation.

Like a tornado, alcoholism often brings along additional societal or familial problems, including verbal, physical, and sexual abuse, illness, debt, prison, infidelity, and even death and the vulnerabilities around each of those. Some of these problems seem embarrassing to the family; but yet we don't talk about them. And then that abashed shame became our excuse to hate ourselves. We create our own trap.

List what you have been exposed to that led to detrimental times in your past.

Society saw my action, actually they saw my irrational-appearing-decisions. I imagined that they shunned me or exonerated my likeness to them maybe. I appeared to be functioning. So, what was lacking in our home and in my life that made me appear crazy? In answer, it was that my own gentle compassionate heart had been taken over by fear and conflict.

I found that I didn't know often why I was doing what I was doing. A twelve-step program was introduced to me. I started questioning my morals, my decisions, and where I found myself in life – living in cope.

No wonder every decision that befell me was as big as purchasing a car: when, how much, which, what will the purchase do to me, my bank account, my life? Gees.

Where would I find my ultimate security? From a man? Another person? Was my dad coming back from the dead to support his 50-year-old kids? Anxiety and panic were easy to come by, worry was easy. I felt I had to be a codependent or I would die.

Where was my financial security going to come from?

A revelation came to me. Believing the Lord looks on us from Heaven above, why would I follow any one else?

Where was my emotional security?

Could I rely on God to provide either?

Acceptance that there is no financial security or another person to carry me through emotions, always got my heart anxiously palpitating, like the feeling your throat is clogged and your stomach rises up.

Will others care for me when I am sick? Or do the paper work when I need to go to a care center?

Have I built my house of branches, not locating my own tree?

Many of the answers to my unknowns were within me. I had to learn how to accept life on life's terms. I needed to act on my own behalf. I had to plan for my old age. I needed to realize what is of value to me. I needed to support myself, find my own food, be able to withstand traumatic events on my own. That is scary until you are comfortable in your own skin; until you find ways to handle things. Hopefully this book will give you lots of strength, trust in yourself, and self-worth to deal with all those what ifs.

One definition that comes to mind when I talk about big-girl panties is intrinsic.

"We are men of intrinsic value, who can strike our fortunes out of ourselves, whose worth is independent of accidents in life or revolutions in government: we have heads to get money, and hearts to spend it."

- George Farquhar, Irish dramatist.

Neuter Your Neurons You Moron

Much of my formed opinion was only my non-professional hypothesis. (I hope you are laughing with me.)

Mind Benders:

Fatigue. Lack of sleep. Task Oriented. Teenagers. Elder care. Driven. Suppressive. Obsessive. Controlling. Problem focused. Trying to impress. Judgmental. Disagreements. Willpower. Resistance. Money.

ICK!

Just saying those words depletes my reserve energy. Are we born with any of that? So, one must ask oneself, where did I pick up all that "stuff" and why did I decide to carry it? Again, I must tell you that each one of those mind controllers are ONLY in YOUR head. A simple acknowledgement of the chaos immediately diminishes it. I can step back outside of the madness and watch it wash away or scatter.

I have allowed chaos to take ahold of my feelings and thoughts. I lived in a Reactionary world. I felt powerless. I hurt others. I could justify my actions in a flash. When I saw happiness, my first Reaction was jealousy and envy. I had pity parties and no one came. I was powerless. Envy is one of the Seven Deadly Sins and guarantees us perpetual insatiation and dissatisfaction.

The best passage in that last paragraph is the admission that I was powerless. I had let the chaos over rule my sanity. So much so, that it had infringed sin upon my actions. In some people, to admit to powerlessness is to realize letting go is a relief. In some cases, it leaves us empty. Perfect! That gives us an open place to begin healing. What started as poor thinking has controlled my actions. Maybe my thinking stinks or my controllers were broken.

I finally realized that my thinking was stale, habitual, and old fashioned. I was set in some of my ways, and I believe, often that I was the only right thinker in conversations; and/or I became superficially self-righteous because I didn't know any more than I knew. Just saying that out loud makes me shudder to think I am talking about me!

Confession:

I think I can fix others
I most of the time, forget about God
I gossip and repeat others' vengefulness
I put people down
I am judgmental
I think I am better than you
I think my decisions are best for everyone
I think I know YOUR answer
I allow others to berate, negate, deride, upbraid, reprove and deprecate, reproach and demean me
I have a mousey persona
I embellish stories for drama
I have a lack of knowledge
I seduce men to flirt, I rely on that for self-worth
I treat my family poorly, without love, disrespectfully
I am content being stuck in my minimal wisdom
I ignore my talents

I don't allow others to just be, because I KNOW HOW TO FIX them
   AND their PROBLEMS.

I blame others

I have high expectations for others

I carry resentment

I have shortcomings

I need men for my self-worth

I walked out of Walmart with something they didn't catch

I am an impatient listener

I interrupt

I am extremely indecisive

I do not exercise

I think I am smart

I lack confidence

I don't put gratitude in writing ever

I am a shopaholic

I could go on and on.

Let's read that this way.

EACH one of those mind controllers is only in your head.

Each ONE of those mind controllers

Each one of THOSE mind controllers

Each one of those MIND controllers

Each one of those mind CONTROLLERS

Each one of those mind controllers ARE ONLY

Each one of those mind controllers are only IN YOUR

Each one of those mind controllers are only in your HEAD

Ouch. That means, I am controlling what I think about.

Word assignment for the week: Each time we say "I have to", change it. Abort the sentence midstream. Stop talking. Say, "I get to" … get up early, drive my child to soccer, finish the report, see my boss. Afterall, you only have one chance at this life. These moments are GOING AWAY. So if one looks at them as PART OF MY LIFE THAT WILL never happen again, it takes on a changed meaning.

I get to see my child in the morning, spend a few minutes one on one, I know how to and am capable of driving a car, I am able bodied and youthful. I have a smiling child who loves to play ball. He is learning to socialize and be active. I get to drive my child to soccer. Gratitude exudes.

I get to write the report. I have enough intelligence to pull the research together. I am capable. I am a thinker. I earn my own way in life. I earn money to keep me going. I participate in an agency that needs my contribution. I get to finish the report.

Are you getting it? So this week, ABORT your 'I have to's'. Replace them with "I get to".

See, my thinker was broken. God, as I <u>imagined</u> did not accept me as I was. I would never be in Heaven. I would never be sensational here on Earth. I rationalized with impunity, that I knew everything, no matter how old I was, I relied on what I knew, and by gosh, I'm pretty intelligent. I've had college learnin', school of life, school of hard knocks, my parents were extremely intelligent and incented us to be driven.

We were agrarian people. We knew about the universe and how land and animals reproduced. City kids didn't have that advantage. You see, I could 'rationalize' everything to my advantage with this thinker of mine. I made up the part about city kids.

And my theory about God as a punishing god, was affirmed by my priest's sermon every week, the nuns every summer, and my parents, and the commandments.

To think that some people didn't believe in God was outlandish to me. They just said that to get my goat, I *rationalize*d. Those people in the 'other' churches, just had not found their way to the right church - mine, yet.

God was a limiting force, I *rationalize*d. If I did all the big no-no's, I would go to hell. If I continued to just fight with my brothers and sister, I would still make it to Purgatory, I *rationalized*.

Yes, God was my *self-created limiting* force where I did not allow my self-creating ability to always choose the right path. I had confession to rely on and be cleansed with just three Our Fathers and four Hail Mary's, I rationalized. I continued to act according to my (unknown to me) limited view.

I now know that God has given me a chance at a much fuller life and I am taking it now, instead of wallowing in my rationalization and self-justification of old.

At the very least, folks, I am asking you to look into Christianity. Nonbelievers are missing a general knowledge piece of the world's thinkers.

Your suffering is done. You are safe. You are saved. God is comforting you. Jesus is faithful to us in that. We can know our blessings. He will see to your holiness. That is what God wants for us. He will rush in with blessings anytime.

Wow. Now knowing that, all you have to do is glide through life.

Now you can take care of everything without the need to experience affliction or discomfort, unshaken.

Didn't that make your life simpler?

Yet we DENY ourselves to allow Him in.

Euphoria is even possible when we let Him in.

We are so self-oriented. It is a learned behavior. Spiritual immaturity is a learned trait.

Jesus walks with us. Today and tomorrow. Think about twins who always feel they are together even separated in their daily activities. That essence of spirit they feel, can be ours with God. Just lean into it. Recognize the beautiful centerpiece of our lives.

And if you have lived a few adults' years or have sinned, we begin to doubt that salvation is meant for us. Ha Ha Ha and Ha Ha. You are already redeemed. Oh my gosh. Is that true? WHY oh why do we deny it with all our mighty strength? Why do we want to believe that we are already dirty, trashed, and unsalvageable? Those 'sins' of ours are so bad. Ha Ha Ha and Ha. Who put that notion in your head? You? Then, YOU can take that notion out.

The suffering you have already done is your sanctification. Society HAS in our pasts, told us what we should have/want, geared us to be selfish. What if they no longer ruled us? Oh my gosh. What if I, from this moment on, lived in a manner that was pure? Who is stopping me? ME! Receive the goodness of God again and then again. Today and tomorrow.

It is internal. It is warmth. It is peace. It is pleasant. It is pure. It is unselfish. It is good. It is full.

It is a waste of ourselves thinking about sin. We could have that last paragraph full of wonder all the time.

Why would I Suppress God's Gifts to Me?

Ask yourself these questions:

Do you have:

- An exaggerated sense of responsibility for the actions of others
- A tendency to confuse love and pity with a tendency to love people you can pity and rescue
- A tendency to do more than your share, all of the time
- A tendency to become hurt when people don't recognize your efforts
- An unhealthy dependence on relationships; holding on to a relationship to avoid feeling abandoned
- An extreme need for approval and recognition
- A sense of guilt when you assert yourself
- A compelling need to control others
- A lack of trust in yourself and others
- Fear of being abandoned or alone in this world
- Difficulty identifying feelings
- Rigidity
- Difficulty adjusting to change
- Problems with intimacy
- Problems with boundaries
- Chronic anger

- Lying tendencies
- Dishonest tendencies
- Poor communications
- Difficulty making decisions

Do you:

- Mask feelings
- Appear ingenuine
- Think in as-ifs
- Plan and plot
- Live in fear
- Withhold love
- Envy others
- Criticize others
- Tend to be perfectionistic
- Overly conform to others
- Love conditionally only
- Deny feelings
- Hold anger
- Hold resentment
- Become passive
- Avoid fun
- Rationalize
- Pretend to be strong
- Distrust
- Avoid nurture of yourself
- Feel separated from others
- Act unconsciously

Your existence may be counting too much on others to take up your spot in the world. Yup, this is the time of your life to put on the big girl panties/

boxers. It is too late to repair your past, but by God, let's change-up your future relationships so that you are mature enough for your age. Gees.

How dare I condemn thee? Well, I come to this notion quite naturally. You see, I was all of those things. But did I want to admit that I answered yes to many of the questions? Absolutely not. That is how dishonest and capable of lying I was – I lied to myself! Yes, I lied to myself more than to anyone else. Silence of lying, even by omission, was so much a natural part of my family that I was left clueless and silent much of the time. Deceit was automatic – hide your feelings. Pretend insouciance. I am so ashamed of how much I betrayed myself. And I must tell you that the tape looped over and over in my head. I said, I am very capable, I am very smart, but I don't want to be responsible for myself. Let me lean on: my parent, my husband, my bosses, I will work in support and services my whole career; let me watch how you do it first, let me see what works first before I step up, let others donate what is needed. I was a passive visual learner by default. Looking back, I was almost useless in society. To look back at who I was and know that I now could step up to take responsibility for myself, my doings, my earnings, my decisions, my friendships, was like looking down Alice's rabbit hole. Life was opaque – I was just here for others to move along. My actions then were purely functional – enough to get me by.

What a farce! Why on earth would God create me, a beautiful human being with so many capabilities if he wanted me to be a mouse, an unassertive, reactive, distrusting, guilt ridden, yet dictatorial controller in my limited stupidity? Having guilt made me feel even more guilty! That is not what He wants! God is my screen door between controlling everybody's everything and letting it go. When I finally realized through mental growth, I realized I did not want to live a minute more in humiliation. A humiliation brought on by my habitual, rote stinking thinking.

> *"Life is a spell so exquisite that everything conspires*
> *to break it." –* Emily Dickinson

To bring this home, a wise friend offered:

Write a letter to the King of your true being, telling him of yourself. Tell him to welcome you because…..

Dear King of Best Living:

Enter into your kingdom _____*your name here*_____ *and welcome him/her.*

Because:

He/She loves to… (i.e., see the good in people, help others, give generously, take care with herself and others)

Allow her to walk with… (grace and levity in serenity and peace of mind)

Give her/him… (love and warmth and surround them with your goodness)

Give her time, give her resources, help her to keep her strength to do works that will enhance all the living she can encounter while on this earth.

Walk with her.

Do this in the name of your kingdom.

So we just revealed that perhaps you have not done what you set out to.

Perhaps we are not the adult we thought we could be, or grow up into, or achieve the things we had imagined.

The question for me was; did I stymy myself? Did I conform to life; to others; to a spouse, to a dictatorial boss, did I lose me to the service and satisfaction of others?

I had given myself up, my dreams, my hopes, and wishful thinking, while being the kindest person you ever met – the giver, the do gooder, the do for others in hopes that they would love me for my dutiful promise to give care, and take care, and take on, and do as told. I loved hard, as they say. I knew how to find a place for myself… find an ego stronger than mine and get under them and do as I BELIEVE they would like me to do.

Sometimes relationships collapse because one cannot carry the other person's load as it is dealt to them. Young people often do not yet know their direction in life and so during the growing up phase, they grow into a person you no longer want to be with. Careful how you fill your void of wanting to be loved.

I got stepped on. Ever feel that way? The pious nun in summer school, the priest in the confessional, and my mother had told me to always, always be the humble one; put everyone ahead of me, and serve. That, that, my friends, is the staircase to Heaven as I believed it to be. Doing for others. I set myself up to be subservient to any and all. After all, the promise of Heaven was in the offing. Wasn't it?

And then to further humiliate me, a penance was administered, which in my child's mind, was never going to make up for the bad things I had already done. I condemned myself to Hell. I was disassembling my own self-worth, bit by bit.

I was sabotaging myself by looking for your approval of who I am. You were my self-esteem. And if you didn't deliver praise and approval or compliments, I had no worth. I felt I had many broken pieces. How sick is that?

About in my 20's I believed that I was not well liked, nor was I well loved, other than by my core family members, because, well, they had to. And I was not as happy, or carefree as many others around me. Strange to feel that I didn't believe I belonged in MY OWN WORLD.

I hadn't learned better than that. I had learned that I must serve harder and more, to be loved, striving to be the best at just that, taking care of others to the nth degree. There, that would mark my place on the cloud ride to Heaven.

Sorry to be so strong, but WHAT THE HELL WAS I DOING WITH A WHOLE LIFETIME ON EARTH, TRYING TO DO NOTHING BUT PUT MYSELF BELOW OTHERS AND SERVE THEM? That was good, I thought because I also <u>thought</u> I knew everybody else's needs. How could I?

I forgot, actually, I was forgoing, my own living – acting in a manner of pretense that I thought was my destiny, ever growing stronger in mind and body.

In my late 20's and 30's I started having attention seeking illnesses. Oh, they were very real to me and the doctors I sought. And they required medication and many expensive tests, and trips to Mayo Clinic, and attention being paid to me. Not a good kind of attention, but kindness and pity came my way. I pitied myself. I thought, this is how broken my thinker was. I thought that ingratiating myself so much that I was wearing myself out physically, would get God's attention and he would take me up to Heaven early, instead of waiting for old age. Because so far, I had taken care of others and been subservient.

I didn't like myself though.

That letter we wrote to the King of a better land – my letter – was full of sadness and regret ABOUT MY OWN LACK OF CAPABILITY TO GROW. I was putting myself down. And consequently, so did the people around me. If I was a measly care taker, I would not go first in line, I did not deserve a birthday party, I am not pretty enough to be married, I am not smart enough to be a manager or run a business. My husband once told me I didn't sing very well, so there went that hope. My sister said I married beneath me, a hillbilly. I believed her. My painting abilities, supported strongly by a high school art teacher, were laughed at as useless by my spouse. But I took vows, and those were binding and legal. I was stuck. I used to find an excuse not to ever be team captain or chairman, or teach, doubting my abilities. To lead, I believed, would be to demonstrate that you believe you are self-important. That possibility dissipated in my humble shy thinking. Since I could not do it, I justified it with 'those people' being braggadocious. That was long before now. Once I decided to share nothing but truthful facts, why not tell them? So I wrote you a book to read.

In my research, I find many disingenuous egotists display pride, prowess, and aggression. Here is what my mind says to them:

"If you think you have wisdom, you have to do the wise thing."

Often, I observe that they do not have all the wisdom. *"I am thankful for all those difficult people in my life, they have shown me exactly who I do not want to be."* (Kushandwizdom).

Today, I love the challenge of being a leader, instructor, chair, or coffee maker. I am human and I can take on responsibilities because I am capable and have potential and worth; not because I am a servant or braggadocious.

It is within My Power to Make Everything Better

Much can be learned in referring to any well-known Personality Inventory test. Some health professionals have tossed this aside, but I personally still find its worth full of self-awareness and a baseline understanding. It is definitely worth your look-see. Many folks ask their best friends or spouses (hopefully the same person!) to take it also.

Awareness is always a choice. In the process of searching for on line personality testing, I suggest you try several as these have been proven extremely in discovering defaults in your own methods of socializing and your own mental health. Being aware of, not only that you have choices, but making a good choice using a value you have developed. A perfect example can be found in which stocks you purchase yourself. Yes! That fine decision making which you value monetarily.

One facet revealed to me was that I was dependent on my spouse for particular chores and tasks, which I, I was the one who wanted them done, not him!

I also found out some of my outstanding and/or too strong common behaviors.

If we didn't learn correct values on the way to this age, we are immature. Much of the values you hold on to come from growing up and environment. Environment here includes your home and community.

It would be best if we make a life study of our core values. They change as we become wiser. Always act with adventure and knowledge seeking.

Basically, I am asking you: Have you always been the way you are? Have you change(d) your values and assets in adulthood? Perhaps one or two defects are lodged in your way of thinking? Pay attention to what you do and things you do not do. Why do you do/not them?

The tests I mentioned above help you to find your strengths and weaknesses. What were they at a younger age? Have you nurtured yourself to be the way you are, or learned by exposure to saying 'a little wrong is okay'? Where you hang, who you have hung with, the stimuli from them, whether good or bad, has cemented in your "It's okay." cranial decision maker. That is your personality trait now. Is it good? Were you enriched? Your development – or lack of – creates how you journey through life.

The enrichment or demise of personal development is our own journey, no one else's.

This is strictly for SELF STUDY and cognizance of action/reaction to life, because I want cognizance of actions and thoughts to be your new middle name.

Which do you most normally do:

Create fun	_____	or	Turn to others for fun	_____
Act first	_____	or	Think first	_____
Get inspired by others	_____	or	Ideas come from contemplation	_____
Open your mind	_____		Pause and doubt	_____
Need others to stimulate	_____		Spend time alone creating	_____
Have interactions with many others	_____		Prefer one on one	_____
Focus on task at hand	_____		Look for alternate way to do	_____
Use step by step process	_____		Multitask during project	_____
React to moments	_____		Plan	_____
Act immediately	_____		Contemplate Action	_____
Stick with common sense	_____		Create new ideas	_____
Dislike Stress	_____		Finish close to deadlines	_____
Dislike to Guess	_____		Like to guess	_____
Remember in Detail	_____		Remember the Essence	_____
Are you Logical?	_____		Do you sense feelings?	_____
Schedule and plan?	_____		Prefer flexibility?	_____
Understand that people will conflict	_____		Need harmony at most costs	_____
Do you judge people?	_____		Embrace differences?	_____
Judge on facts?	_____		Think about impact on others?	_____
Are you objective?	_____		Need opinions to base yours on?	_____
Follow standards?	_____		Look for New Ways?	_____
Appreciate that there are 2 sides?	_____		Admit your mistakes?	_____
Refrain from interrupting?	_____		Accept responsibility for your words?	_____
Stop talking?	_____		Use kind body language?	_____
Support decisions?	_____		Presume goodwill?	_____
Look for areas to agree?	_____		Come back to discussions calm?	_____
Are you honest with yourself	_____		Show interest?	_____
Keep your voice pleasant?	_____		Discuss, nonattacking?	_____
Holding a resentment?	_____		Acknowledge ideas?	_____
Avoid confrontation?	_____		Avoid dominance?	_____
Use spiritual principles?	_____		Accept personalities?	_____
Think about different outcomes?	_____		Realize what you don't know?	_____

There are many tests and since I am not a clinician certified to give assessment tests, I cannot in any way analyze or present them verbatim. Please request testing through a licensed clinician for more understanding of yourself and others, if you have serious doubts about your sanity.

However, many such tests are available on line for you to test yourself and then review your results and probable outcomes! Do it for fun. In many tests, you may find you are a crossover or have strengths in a couple of categories. I recommend strengthening your own brain's muscles by figuring you out yourself.

Including:

The Enneagram which identifies nine personality types:

1. The Perfectionist/Reformer: Conscientious, Ethical Hardworking, Striving, Fear Imbalance / Gut Instinct: Teachers, advocates for change

> Type 1's are honest, dedicated, self-disciplined, responsible, and ethical when at their best and living in healthy levels. When 1's are in unhealthy levels, stressed, or not at their best they can be critical, rigid, perfectionistic, judgmental, resentful, and inflexible, fear being wrong.

2. The Giver/Helper: Empathetic, Sincere, Warm Hearted, Want to Belong, Fear Being Alone / Heart, Feelings and give unconditional love.

> Type 2's are selfless, warm, friendly, generous, intuitive, self-sacrificing, and giving when at their best and living in healthy levels. When 2's are in unhealthy levels, stressed, or not at their best they can be prideful, martyr-ish, insecure,

possessive, flattering, people pleasing, and demanding, fear being unloved or unwanted.

3. The Achiever: Seek Validation, Self-Assured, Charming, High Standards, Role Models, Authentic, Fear Being Insignificant

> Type 3's are confident, efficient, energetic, hard-working, and optimistic when at their best and living in healthy levels. When 3's are in unhealthy levels, stressed, or not at their best they can be inauthentic, workaholics, self-promoting, impatient, status conscious, validation needy, and vain, fear not being admired.

4. The Individualist: Quirky, Self-Aware, Sensitive, Passionate, Authentic, Lack Identity and Emotionally Honest

> Type 4's are authentic, highly creative, expressive, introspective, and compassionate when at their best and living in healthy levels. When 4's are in unhealthy levels, stressed, or not at their best they can be moody, stubborn, temperamental, withdrawn, and depressed.

5. The Observer: Alert, Insightful, Curious

> Type 5's are observant, objective, insightful, independent, and calm when at their best and living in healthy levels. When 5's are in unhealthy levels, stressed, or not at their best they can be withdrawing, can become detached, high strung, intense, arrogant, cynical, indifferent, and distant, fear being incapable

6. The Loyalist: Skeptical, Trustworthy, Committed, Need Support and Security

> Type 6's are loyal, witty, committed, prepared, responsible, hard working, self-reliant, trouble-shooters, and supportive when at their best and living in healthy levels. When 6's are in unhealthy levels, stressed, or not at their best they can be anxious, rigid, defensive, evasive, paranoid, pessimistic, and hyper-vigilant.

> *Note about 6's: 6's have two ways of dealing with their fears. They can be more on the phobic side (this is the more stereotypical 6) but some 6's will push against their fears and be counterphobic. Counterphobic 6's still have the same desires, fears, wounding message, etc. but they react to it slightly differently.

7. The Enthusiast: Extroverted and Content, Seek Adventure, Fear Being Deprived and Optimistic, Appreciative, Joyous, and Satisfied

> Type 7's are adventurous, imaginative, enthusiastic, spontaneous, and positive when at their best and living in healthy levels. When 7's are in unhealthy levels, stressed, or not at their best they can be unfocused, scattered, over extended, superficial, restless, impulsive, escapist, and self-absorbed; biggest fear is being trapped emotionally.

8. The Challenger: Self Confident, Strong and Assertive, Need to Prove Themselves, Decisive, Can Be Intimidating

> Type 8's are protective, resourceful, straight-talking, magnanimous, energetic, decisive, loyal, resilient, and direct when at their best and living in healthy levels. When

8's are in unhealthy levels, stressed, or not at their best they can be insensitive, manipulative, controlling, intimidation, rebellious, and confrontational; they hate to be controlled and fear being harmed.

9. The Peacemaker: Easy Going, Oversimplify, Need Stability, Fear Loss, Accepting and Trusting

> Type 9's are amiable, open-minded, optimistic, nonjudgmental, supportive, and peaceful when at their best and living in healthy levels. When 9's are in unhealthy levels, stressed, or not at their best they can be conflict avoidant, indecisive, unassertive, passive-aggressive, stubborn, and insecure; they fear separation and conflict or the loss of conflict.

> (I think I have the characteristics of all of the above!)

Clifton Strengths

Clifton Strengths discusses top strengths in order of intensity and focuses on finding talents and sets aside weaknesses. These offer advanced insights into the thousands of thoughts we collect.

Some similar questions are on a previous page. These are just a few I have enjoyed reviewing, however, there are hundreds of personality tests. Take a look at a magazine.

Some folks totally subscribe to their horoscope or color definition or where they fell in the family line up (middle child, eldest, etc.). Any or all of the common observation tests are great. The most important is self-examination to know your make up.

I also want to mention here another book very sensitive to your senses! It discusses HOW you relate to people. It is very good for understanding yourself and your partner in relationships and during arguments! 5 Love Languages by Gary Chapman has been published in six editions and holds much value in societal's neo norms; supported and purported also by Oprah Winfrey. Chapman tells us that each person has two love languages, a primary and a secondary. There are many ways of expressing love. They offer:

1. Words of affirmation
2. Quality time
3. Receiving gifts
4. Acts of service
5. Physical touch

Even monkeys are born with an underlying need for the comfort of contact.

Chapman discusses actions to take to contribute to the above five ways of expressing love and he extends actions to omit or avoid if you would like a satisfying and comfortable relationship. Worth a look see.

I Want What I Want When I Want It.

———

I can see me as a pouty little kid saying the above, actually!

You already have all you need. Do you have capability to see existentially, the colors in sunrays, pristine fresh dew? Do you have the capability to have indescribable bliss, to marvel at nature, to smile at a child, and give love? Yet we choose to identify with suffering, to react to pressures that force our consciousness to withdraw from serene feelings. You already have serenity. You just can't feel it because your mind is making so much noise. What is keeping you from bliss today? Cognizance is our number one filter allowing us to clear out fear and unhappiness. Happiness has three basic components: Pleasure, Engagement, and Meaning. Allow those to be more present in your life. Gees!

Jesus was pretty clear that the thing that really poisons us are those negative words and actions that fly out of our own hearts. (Reference the Ten Commandments)

The more pulled together, self-aware, the more we live our truths, the better human we are. We can then take that good human being out to the world and attract the kind of people we want to be with and live with.

Someone to Love (Me)

Explanations and arguments are two different things. Arguments are usually accompanied with detrimental words and sentences that are not applicable to the real reason for the argument!

Arguments may include many of the following:

Rhetorical flourishes	Asides	Digs and Disses	Tangents
Innuendoes	Propaganda	Exaggerations	Fallacies
Hyperbole	False theories	Persuasive insistence	Yelling
Attempts at jokes	You always	Insults	Embarrassment
Persuasions	Lies to look better	Omissions of truth	Anger
Uncontrolled emotions	Assumptions	Physical intimidation	Abuse

STOP THIS.

One has to sort through the hurled insults and references to insecurities and attempts at humor. It does not enhance the solutions for the discord. Often anger is substituted for good reasoning. Loudness is often substituted for good reasoning and lack of knowledge of the topic, or the love of aggressively winning an argument.

Perhaps when we can't get our view across to someone, it is time to consider whether the point even has validity.

Some folks are prone to elucidate, throwing their knowledge at another in a harmful, downputting attempt. This escalates the circumstances.

some time in arguments with all of the above. My old judgement dismiss the words of someone who spat when they lectured, or their circumstances (father in hospital) made them late. I had no good leg to stand on in those judgmental arguments.

Read that again.

And yet, this person or these people whom I argued with the hardest, were often the people I claimed to love the most. How about you?

A 'good' argument can only be about explaining truths to each other. Premises, viewpoints, myths, beliefs, convictions, and ideas cannot be part of a good argument. Proof surrogate works but only if you cite your source. Be ready to do so if you are going to spew.

The most important lesson I learned in self-aware cognizance was that I often spewed OPINIONS, ADVICE AND SUGGESTIONS like they were candy I thought you needed. I would give all of them to you without one tiny bit of request for any one of them. No solicitation on your part.

Until someone told me to check myself on these.

The sooner you learn this, to tell only the truths and commitments, the sooner you will be surrounded by people who love to be with you. Think about that – Do you want to hang with someone who uses 'possible lies' to communicate, or someone who has researched and has facts to present to add to your life? Do you want to listen to someone who expresses mostly their 'maybe ideas' or, their truths?

"To the wrong person you will never have any worth; to the right person, you mean everything."

It's about which of these feelings you have with another.

But even more so, it is about what you put out there for another as a whole human.

Do you start a conversation with any of these?

"You always…"

"You should…"

"If only you would…"

Who is it that you are responsible for again? Why are you saying to another person, "You…", when we are only responsible for 'me'.

So telling others:

what they should do,

what could fix them,

what would make MY life easier if they…,

…Is not my business!

When my voice is using those words, aren't I imposing MY values, MY expectations, and MY way upon others?

SIMPLE CHANGE:

Your challenge this week is to pay attention to every time you use the words:

SHOULD   WOULD   COULD

And eliminate them from your language.

Others may choose to do as I say in fear of me, all the while building a resentment toward me, and be thinking of revenge toward me.

Ick. No one is left happy again.

•

So, I add this trick to my list of values:

If they are not responsible to take care of what I value, and I feel like I am telling them to do so all the time, do I want to be around them? Do they want to be around me? (That's like 3 questions to ask yourself.)

Do the dishes. Who wants the dishes done? Who wants the dishes done now? Yup. I need to do the dishes, if it is myself that wants them done now (unless an assigned chore, of course). Who wants the stool lid down? I do. I am responsible. (Although, that is a basic consideration all boys should know, but girls are very capable.) It is that basic. If you want the trash taken out, who wants it taken out now? Who is then responsible? Who wants a better life? Who is then responsible? Who needs a special milk in the household? Go get it.

Who expects the house to be picked up? I do. Who expects that laundry will be done timely? I do. Who likes the bathroom sink clean? I do. And hopefully as I mentor these better habits, others follow. However, if I am the lazy one with expectations, I deserve to live with messes.

Unconditionally

(It might be fun to show this chapter to a teenager.)

Integrating yourself into a relationship has a purpose. Until we know intricately, WHY we want to be in ANY relationship, we should not be out there looking. Yup.

Do you want intense love?

Physical companionship?

Someone to listen?

Devotion to you?

Control of another's happiness in love?

Someone to care about you?

If any of the above are true in your case, you are *lying* to yourself! Those are not reasons to be in a relationship! This will end in grief and horrible jealousy and blame. You will ask yourself how did the rest of my life disappear?... Doing those very things, unless you take charge of your own doing and show your loved one how YOU do those things. Hopefully, whomever we pick is fully capacitated in love to know how to love also, then together your(you) have the Mutual Admiration Society.

First, you, me or that promising love-interest should be intensely alive with life. Love is a part of life, no question of its presence. Your capability to love must be a given, no question.

A relationship exists because each party wants meaningful conversation, mindful availability, undivided consciousness, and presence. You arrive at the same care and companionship for each other. Sharing is mutual in its amount.

And as Sue Monk Kidd spoke in <u>Firstlight,</u> *"Do it the way Mary sat at the feet of Jesus – with an undivided heart."*

Neither of you overwhelm the other. Neither of you depend on the other. You each feel whole when together or alone. Of course, there are many moments when you will support, even 'pick one another up'; but those must be temporary or one becomes a drain on the other's livelihood. I am not applying this, of course, if there are major health issues.

Divorce rate is at 50% consistently and constantly. Other than obvious reasons to each person in a marriage, the four key problems that lead to divorce are these:

1. Criticism
2. Defensiveness
3. Contempt
4. Stonewalling

If you already practice these or see these in someone you are promising yourself to, run, don't walk away from the relationship now. Marriage intensifies feelings – whatever they are. It does not make questionable morals better. Too often the wedding is the best thing about a marriage!

When we are satisfied with our own lives, we have something to present as a whole person, not a wannabee half couple. It is very easy to be addicted to a fun person, a sexual person, an active go getter, someone who realms in things we are not. His/her proportion to a partnership must be equal coming in the door. Bring your best self and if you do not like yourself, let's go for an uptick so you gain the necessary self-worth. Assets which he/she has, will not lightly dust upon you as an extension of them, like a snow fall and make you stick together. As old as this adage is, it still holds true: '*You cannot change someone after you are married.*' And probably will not change yourself if you are adored, followed, and treated royally; but rather become tired of the lazy nincompoop that latched onto your star.

He is no fool who gives what he cannot keep to gain what he cannot lose.
– Jim Elliot

I would love to know that before you test the dating waters, you are self-fulfilled. You go in knowing that a fight is a discussion, there will be resolution, no one leaves; in fact, you will be glad the topic came to light so that you can each face truths. Lying to ourselves about the person we thought we married and having expectations of them being different, is so unreal.

The end of a love relationship is not the end. You know it, if you have been there. We grieve. We might be angry at ourselves or the relationship 'spouse'. We are lonely, missing the companionship that was present. Loneliness is more dangerous than cigarettes. We have no one to tell our intimacies to now; no shared empathy. Daily patterns are altered. Many times, it was only romance: shared indulgence of senses. Along with what is referred to as break-up, or heartbreak, there is a feeling of disenchantment with 'love'. *I gave out love and it was spurned or abused.* Unconsciously, we all want to feel love and experience the hormonal high from giving love in our own ways. Disattachment is painful to our emotional self on a very high level. Some folks love those feelings so much, they have many short relationships and sexual encounters, searching for romance again; lying, musing, to themselves about what their heart life needs. There are actual cravings caused by dopamine uptick and dopamine drain. It is real. Oxytocin has been quite active and it stops when the feel good is gone. It is up to us to realize this and resolve to become whole and good again, alone, first.

Intense romantic love which takes over the brain, releases a slosh amount of dopamine! So, love!

The gift of love is irrevocable. Give it and receive it gracefully.

You have been reading how you maybe formed your beliefs, isms, and knowledge to this point in your life. What if...what if that other person you have your eyes on, has not matured in two or three facets of personality and psyche, like you? Sometimes we have to let people go who are not healthy for us. Usually our parents or a mentor (older person) sees clearly that our 'pick' is not mature in the ways to enhance a relationship. Sometimes they tell us and we do not want to hear it because we are stuck in the flirt and infatuation game – which is extremely fun, don't get me wrong, but seriously gonna be harmful to our own fulfillment in life, in my opinion.

That is not only possible, it is an absolute! No two minds are exposed to the same up bringing, history teacher, or path in life. What if, what if, you made allowance for that other person you have your eyes on, to adapt to some of your lore, events, etc. as you are going to do for them? Now you see how clearly 'acceptance' is an adaptation 'to' a successful friendship, marriage, or acquaintance. You are growing into wholesome and a good person whom people want to join in fun and friendship.

For we each have our interpersonal psychotherapies. Never alike, rarely close!

As you mature about your own actions and fend to be a self-satisfied, wiser person, tell your friends that you have changed. If questioned about your better attitudes and ideas and personality, ask them to not hold on to what you have been, have expectations of the old you to get drunk, maybe break a few laws, take a bad risk, or cuss and swear a lot, etc.

Many happy, surprising, good events release a nice hit of dopamine, many when we are loving others. The thing is, we must keep dopamine coming, by staying in the positive light of life.

Neuroscience can now tell us that three brain regions are involved. I know, I know, you don't even want to know this when your 'heart is broken'. It is the emotional heart that we think is broken. But truthfully, all feelings and emotions synergistically transmit back and forth and up and down in the organ of the brain. Cholesterol content in the blood stream changes as does cortisol to feed our immune system. So be nice to your outgoing partner too. Do not destroy their brain chemicals.

Solomon, the wisest man, once wrote: *"For as a man thinks in his heart, so he is."*

The relationship spouse is only a trigger for _our_ feelings. (Say that out loud.) We invested all the feelings we gave out. We made that decision to give. Unfortunately, especially in teen years, as in an immature-in-emotion person, the ability to understand the above cannot yet be grasped. Our ability to be empathetic will be limited if our parental guidance was. We stop learning about empathy in adolescence. So the surface feelings or routine touch, talk, and hanging out felt so good when we finally did receive it from a teen partner, teens want it to continue, even when it is so wrong for them. That desire is so powerful, people stay when they are in harm or with someone who is not going to be committed to them ever, because of their same immaturity.

Concept love is vast and involves so much. When great grandma repudiates the anachronism, "My darling, you are so young to marry" … when a parent says, "He is not for you. He is never going anywhere. He does not believe as you do about God" …they have insight that teens don't own, yet. My senior art teacher took me outside the classroom to tell me something private. She wanted me to know that she did not approve of my choice of boyfriend. She told me I had places to go with my good grades and artwork. She said my boyfriend was a farmer, a man of the land, and he did not have the cultural visions ahead that I had. I was mad at her for twenty years for interfering. And then our marriage dissolved for most of those same reasons - well, with a lot more spice added.

My advice which was greatly influenced by Dr. Helen Fisher in an interview, is to have some relationship social-psychological experience. To live at least twenty years before choosing a partner. To listen to others who show interest in who you are with and what they say.

Some things need to match between promised partners *in lasting love*:

- spirit and zest for life (excitement and activity)
- morals (law abiding, rule following, respect for authority)
- gratitude shown to others
- spirituality (a universe bigger than you, honor of nature, expression of kinship)
- empathy (in sorrows and capability to express it)
- the principal of value (in gratitude for what we have and not out of bounds spending)
- analytical (rationalizing and reasoning close to yours)
- explorative (desire for future, children, dedication to skill or talent)
- creativity (honor for each other's mind and choice of career or involvement)
- religion (at the very least, acknowledge each other's choice of higher power)
- ability to use personal strengths and pursue dreams

I suggest we step back and evaluate in our minds, how close 'he' correlates with 'she' phenomenas. A tendency is when one or two interests totally line up, we assume we are locked in love and the rest will find its way. "*Uh-oh*", is all I have to say.

Here are a few assets/lack of assets most new lovers don't even consider, over their surging hormonal and adrenaline levels, to evaluate for compatibility:

Testosterone levels

Gestures

Negotiation skills

Risk taking

Curiosity

Compassion (care, sensitivity with others)

Expression/Quietness

Energy levels

Flexibility

Decisive/Not

Holistic/Not

Environmentally friendly as you

Use of voice and tone range

Trustworthiness

Skill set (engineering, mechanical, medical, music capabilities)

Traditional or conventional

Messy outside the marriage means messy inside

Theoretical vs concrete thinking

Calmness level

Important in the above evaluation is to know your own levels before engaging in the evaluation of the relationship! See, this is where maturity of mind or good mental health with open eyes, enters. Because the centers in your brain which deal with each of those are already formed for life! Unlatch your shutters. If Mr./Miss So and So does not synchronize, you will at some point, have a surfeit of differences to adapt to, in each other. Did you ever 'hate' your brother or sister, mom or dad? Yup. We are talking about being in the same house with people for years under a natural commitment! Same thing. Sharing a bathroom and kitchen are real telltale signs about compatibility.

And it is not about your feelings. It is rather about what drives those feelings that come from damage or exposure that make up your psyche. The brain is the center for emotions, as well as logic, wisdom and insight. It is smart. IF, I said, IF, the serotonin, dopamine, testosterone and estrogen have had normal contributories (parents, mentors, teachers, envines) your physiologics might be receptive to consummate harmony. Stress reduces serotonin. No one is that normal. We each have had some stimuli or synapsis break that is biologic, not on a feeling level, that our personality traits reacted to and formed, say an opinion or bias or a no-no, a value, or a lack of something in us. What we are bringing to the table and what the other's biology is bringing to the table must be looked at! Period. Divorce is at a 50% level. You have a 50-50 chance after all that research. Wow.

But wait, there is more. Just as we cannot define a soul, we cannot take our heart out and examine it on a lab table. (Well, we can, but not in the love aspect.) We could not possibly know what cellularly is happening between the heart and brain in love. We talked about social-physiologic, but not psychophysiologics. Your health is totally susceptible to how you love and are loved. How we think, behave, and feel is conducted by the science of our bodies. Whether we feel relaxed, appreciated and compassionate in love, coheres to brain power. (Review the Feelings List.) Your magnetics and rhythms' spectral patterns establish themselves automatically. I will go so far as to think and say that if the first list of compatibility does not coincide between two people, the body will conform when forced into a relationship, most likely, not propitiously. "We did this to ourselves." Is often said after an unhappiness occurs. Nuf said.

"Our society is starving for intimacy. We fall in the trap of thinking that sex satisfies the hunger." – Ronnie Nsubuga

It is the acceptance, closeness and romanticism that makes a true sexual encounter part of love.

See, I just love lust…testosterone drives us through self-will to want sex (and not always with just the one person we hold dear). Lust is sinful. It is self-will run riot if not in a committed and loving relationship. Our dopamine derives from lust, then fuels energy cells (oxytocin and vasopressin) to even nonromantic sex. We think we were driven there in the search for love. Actually, the 'car' you were driving was a dangerous heap of energy cells. Of course, we want to bond and love, that is our emotional health speaking. I believe, folks just crave sexual action for the orgasmic mental/physical stimulation and calmness it gives us in our uncalm moments of our walk-about in life. Some take a sexual encounter as security of physical needs and closeness. A minute attraction (lacy nylons, shiny black hair, a beard, blue eyes, apparent confidence) will be approached for the lure (flirtation) to the end result (orgasm). And sometimes in that lustful encounter, commonalities bond people, humanness abounds and a new relationship forms. We are sometimes misguided when we seek the promise of another orgasm in the future.

Intentional affairs are an attempt at playing childish games with a deadly serious human dilemma. You intend to hurt someone you love. That is one of your truths.

And we expect our immature adolescent children to abstain when their brain suggests strongly otherwise. Most teens and adults just go ahead with their hormonal surges. If not controlled, it will run riot. They have not yet had 'experience' to know about hurt and harm left in their wakes.

Lust throws our reins up in the air and we seek self-satiation. Actually, with the right person, love is present and the security makes the time we spend in the sexual encounter securely beyond pleasant - better.

Kenny Rogers and Dolly Pardon explained it well: *"You do something to me that I can't explain."*

Deception of self. Lost marriages. Lost families. Sometimes sinful. Hurtful to others. Leads to worthlessness. Misdirected. Affairs. Broken hearts.

That describes sexual affairs, but life emits so many more deceptional lures. Sometimes we stay in them for a long time, precipitously unknowing.

I had been misdirected by folks that had been through the depression, women who had been hurt deeply by their men but stayed in the marriage, the Catholic teachings of the 50's and 60's, society's placement of women in a servile position - not money maker of the home. I was influenced by old rules, old upbringing, the ways of the time, and society's old morals. A child sees adult rules, social etiquette, egos, morals, and bad habits. Those observed "rules for living" found a place in one of my cerebral cortexes and lived there for almost ever! As a preteen, I believed and professed, and condemned others for wearing blue jeans outside of the home. Think about how prudish, shy, intimidated, and fearful I was in other aspects of my life if rules like that lived in my head.

Misdirection, dis-ease, forfeiture of self, low self-esteem resulted, to name just a few, were listed in my characteristics. I did not like myself. I was ready to die. I wasn't depressed. I just didn't think I had enough energy, life, or intellect to grow into fulfillment. To change would require risk taking and actions on my part.

So instead of looking for methods to grow, I hated myself more. What a vicious cycle. No self-esteem – no wherewithal to develop – no good personality – alone – no way to break from it – more hate. Hate of self leads to less self-esteem, sometimes acting out when our subconscious wants us to break from the hatred we have. We might abuse drugs or alcohol, or look to small lifts of serotonin from shopping or rare wins at gambling. Hoarding, abusing self, or perhaps, letting the opposite sex use us, give us that short and slight good feeling and then we crash again with more self-hatred for having abused drugs, money, or ourselves. We falsely use acquisition of material goods, which false claims and billboards proclaim, to bring fulfillment.

A Sense of Possibility — How We Learned and Unlearned

As a child, what was your dream? What did you want to be when you grew up?

What do you think God could have done differently to get you there?

What do you think you could have done differently to get you there?

The difference between God doing it and us doing it is…us! We behave. His job was to provide us with us.

If we choose to live in 'bad' or stronghold the fact that "something has happened to us" instead of ACTING ON OUR OWN BEHALF, we don't create our own lives. We are living in the shadow and rules of someone else, or even rules we imposed on ourselves.

In Mark 4:24, and translated by author and orator, Dr. Joyce Meyer, Jesus tells us *"The measure of thought and study you give to the truth you hear will be the measure of virtue and knowledge that comes back to you."* I love this idea.

Whose rules do you get to live by? Do you create your own rules and, consequently, your own limitations; shutting your mind out to new thoughts? What is something that you tell yourself you must do that is against your gut? What is something you tell yourself that you must do because someone else inflicted the "must" on you?

> *What a miserable thing life is: you're living in clover, only the clover isn't good enough. –* Bertolt Brecht

Here are some sentences with "musts" in them.

Finish your plate. Have dinner ready every night at six p.m. Carry out your marriage vows till you die. You must attend their funeral. You have to rise at seven every day. These are not laws or commandments.

Let's set out to create new rules for ourselves. It takes examination of not only every action we do, good or bad, but every thought we have, good or bad. It is really hard to think about thoughts, as they seem embedded and concreted in. Not true. Using our neuro science now, we can write a new canon.

I am writing this book because I have come from your house…. different people at a different address, but your home atmospheric scenario.

Today, I am living large, living the dream, and can speak up for myself because I have self-worth. I didn't when I was back in "my" house which was just like your house. I allowed others to take away my self-worth by telling me I was wrong in their opinion, or they had a better way to do MY thing. I gave it, my worthiness, away.

I am sharing my story and offering suggestions to help you get back on the course of your own dream and what you can be in your only chance at life.

Days after my back was permanently injured due to being thrown against the corner of a wooden water bed frame, I lost my five-month-old fetus, turned out, my only chance at a baby.

I was so much under the control of someone else's rules. At that time, it was okay with me. I had no self-worth, esteem, goals, or where-with-all. After seeing the abuse the possible-father could inflict, there was no way I would bring a child into his life. I only knew from my familial background to follow a leader in authority – those select elitists I gave all credence to, leading me astray sometimes!

It was okay with me that I lost that baby. Pretty shocking, huh? But after all that I had been through I did not want to bring a baby into the world with a dad who threw people around and screamed at them. I didn't like even who I was. Why would I want to bring a baby into what I saw as a sour world, filled with bitter people and angry wars?

After 37 years of being negated, deflated, degraded, insulted, demeaned, disrespected, ignored, and berated, forbidden, belittled, I didn't think that I knew how to do a thing on my own, or right. Mind you, I CHOSE to succumb to those taunts! I felt inundated with smallness and accusations of being less. I failed to believe I was a quality person! I had been picking up what people had been putting down about me! I was disrespecting myself by taking on a negative label another person gave out. And I was sick of listening to my own complaints. Reacting to anger had led me to my own defensive anger and inappropriate yelling out harmful semantics. So unproductive for a relationship. Anger dwells inside the heart unless allowed to leave.

Self Check:

What do you personally do when feeling angry?

Get quiet, grit your teeth, do your jowls tic, do you leer, raise a fist, pace, breathe fast, hold resentment and keep score? Take a second to review your behavior in physical and psychological reactions.

I had no worth and I was scared for myself to even be in the world! I was my own greatest inhibitor and did not even know it. So I acted out in other inappropriate ways without my own censorship. Now, currently, I refuse to *receive* condemnation! I am now cognizant to those useless ways.

I knew I could not undo all the harm my strong desire to be 'loved' and laissez-faire attitude had caused to others.

Anything sound familiar from the page above?

No self-worth?

Being belittled?

Didn't think I could make it on my own?

Ignored and disrespected?

Dissed – Insulted to my face and in front of others

Negated – To be told no, denied something, to be made ineffective

Deflated – Cause the lessening of, move to a lower level

Insulted – Shown disrespect when talked to

BUT HOW I REACTED AND BEHAVED WAS MY OWN. (Say it with me now…)

I have come to own what is mine in any relationship and leave alone what is not mine.

Write this down: R E A C T. Now cross out the R E. That is the difference between then and now in my life.

Act. Take an action. Take the right action. Do the next right behavior that is healthy and safe and legal.

That is action, not reaction.

Leave no harm or hurt behind you EVER regardless of what the other person is doing. THEY are not in your control. Who is in MY control? Who is in YOUR control? Me, myself, and I. My recommendations come from living deep and dark pain.

And in whose life can we make changes?

If each party knew what the other should do truly and controlled them, do you think there would be no wars, except for egotistical ogres? This works from spat-size to war-size differences. We each need to consider another with moral seriousness, no bad manners or bad attitudes.

Your ectoplasm, endorphins and enzymes, must conjoin together with the appropriate syntax to create the mind-altering complexity for our physiological chemistry to salute the serotonin, dopamine, levels to thrust forth elan and happiness.

So, if you wanna be happy for the rest of your life, read the previous paragraph. It will save your life. Nurture your whole body.

If that doesn't influence you to take care of your mind and heart, what will?

Here are some life lessons. I am not going to mince words. Sager, wiser folks than I have pulled these suggestions together. I am only aping what data has been inserted into my head by others. Ever think about that much? We are what a parent, a mentor, a good friend, a minister, a librarian or a store clerk or sales manager offered to us at some time in our life.

go near the fire." "Don't bounce the basketball in the living room."
both ways." - All habitually repeated sage advice. Yet where did
the rule come from? Accidents/mistakes by our parents? Give us a little
slack. I'm seven. I have a basketball. It is raining. I don't know how delicate
porcelain is. I must learn.

So here it comes, the sage advice.

1. Do unto.

Ever been caught in the wrong lane and you don't see anyone coming, so
you go ahead with the traffic maneuver that makes your trip efficient and
convenient? (Just say yes, because you know you did it.) Well, that might
be all that Pa Jones is doing also. In my head, I say, "Oops, didn't see ya.
Oh, well, no bumps or dents. We're good. Just go on about your day. I
saved three minutes off my commute." While Pa Jones is going, "That Son
of a Bitch just pulled out in front of me. Get a clue, buddy before you kill
someone." and he has a gesture for me just under the dash.

There is no number two because "do unto" is the primary advice only.

Perspective. Insight. Feelings. Faith. Attitude. Love and support for
others. – Do unto.

It has to do with doing unto yourself first. Once you learn that you are
to be loved and supported – and sometimes that means unlearning what
insensitive parents offered you, life goes so much smoother. If you, if I,
take care with me; hygienically, socially, pleasantly, graciously, generously,
lovingly; won't I be more understanding of what the other guy wants? Hmm.

First, let's practice smile. Give yourself a 5 second smile. Now smile with
teeth. (1,2,3,4,5) Make it into a grin. Pretend you have a dimple. Hold it to
a count of ten. Smirk with humor five seconds. Add a glint. Pretend one
of God's beautiful creatures, a deer, just hopped a fence before your eyes.

There, smile like that. Lower your shoulders. Loosen your neck. Smile because you have life. Smile like you appreciate the warmth of where you are. Go ahead, take a minute and reread the paragraph.

That's being good to yourself.

The pleasantries of life never go away. One more time, pleasantries are here to stay. Why wouldn't it be okay to take them in? Your day will present to you, each of these, I guarantee: tension, nervousness, worry, anxiety, planning, fear, foreboding, dread and obsession. Tonight, check yourself. Did you experience any one of these? Your warranty of happiness expired when you go to that dark side. Did you rather choose the tension, nervousness, etc.?

Deemphasis therapy (focusing away) is needed ASAP.

Who grabbed onto tension and worry? Okay, You. Where do you feel it? Neck? Shoulders? Posture sagging? Where's your jaw?

Self Check:

While worrying do you pace, excite others, back off, complain, lament, cry, fear? Take a second to know your own physical and psychological reactions.

Oh, that's a whole nuther paragraph: Take a look around you at how people carry their lower jaw. There are the grumps which usually involve a lip look; or the too much sun or antisomething nose crunch expression. TMJ of negativity happens. Slack jaw or gumming of false teeth wearers gets habitual. Teenagers refuse to pretend to smile – stuck jaw. It happens to them. Concentrating office workers have a forward bottom chin. Bus drivers are sucking in one cheek inside. Truck drivers a blank stare. It is innocuous. We 'go into' a stare unconsciously. The jaw sets.

Thinking about that? See what I mean? A conscious choice – a higher level of thinking – knowledge that we are alive and visible and share the world can take us into a face ready to smile from a set jaw. Lift those eye level cheeks and pull the nostrils to your ears. There, a conscious smile. Did it hurt? Did it feel good?

Do unto (blah, blah) as I would have them do unto me. So, if I do unto me first with a face lifted to a smile, what have I done? Well, two things: Released some happiness endorphins, lightened my outlook, and I'll bet your posture is better. Plus, you've already read something helpful.

So attitude comes into play: Worry, anxiety, nervousness, tension and planful fear or over-focus happen. Practice a five second smile right here.

Let's take nervousness, worry, planning, and focus to task here. Are they happening right now? Must you be nervous? Must you worry? Must you be overly focused to lead others? Well, the answer is no. What, in reality, do you have in your hands? What is real? What is just in your head? Yeah, Baby! All of it is just in **YOUR** head.

"Why wouldn't my kid do the right thing? He should know better."

"Why doesn't the coworker use my system? It would make his/her work more efficient."

"If I could get a little more money pulled together, I could have dot, dot, dot."

Would. Should. Could. Your assignment for the week is to count how many times you use the words 'would', 'should', or 'could' in your sentences. In fact, this time keep two tallies. One for others, aware of their usage. I know I mentioned this previously. I am recounting the depth this deception can have on us and others.

Those three get us in trouble. "I should" means I probably won't, or I can't, or "Not in this year". "You should" usually involves a point, visible or not and is unsolicited, unproven, opinion/advice. 'I would' means "I actually won't" for some reason. And "I could" has no intent of doing something whatsoever. I discovered I was spreading this manure all over.

So eliminate those from your vocabulary. Secondarily, do not count on others to fulfill should-would-could false promises. Dispose yourself of them entirely!

You've got a smile and now know how to eliminate false promises to yourself.

You are beginning to 'do unto yourself' quite well.

Let's go for serenity. I know it is also early in the book but we'll try.

What is serenity to you? Floating on the back of the illusive butterfly in the meadow? Riding a magic carpet of a cloud? Where do you go when you enter chantifical meditation? Does putting your nose to a full blossomed rose do it for you? Now, watching a couple of two-year olds communicate makes me forget all other purposes of the moment. A vacuous blue grey tinted space of nothingness? Do you need drugs, illegal or otherwise to get you to pretend serenity and peace?

A child usually has it. Remember staring at dust particles in Grandmom's sun light beams? Remember the feeling of cool grass beneath your whole body as you rolled your body down a hill? What were you thinking of when on a swing? As you snow ski? Maybe deep-sea dive? Nothing. That's right, nothing else. Yay.

Children have it for a while. Pageant contenders want it. Yoga instructors exert themselves physically hard to take themselves there. And warring nations pretend they are gonna get it. Peace. Calmness. Serenity. Quiet. A melting of physique into mentalhood. Wow.

So make up your mind, what does the word serenity conjure for you? When was the last time you think you achieved it?

Unruffled. Fair. Tranquil. Unclouded. Calm. Completely motionless. Undisturbed. Not agitated. In complete oneness with the universe. Composed. Absence of motion. Freedom from storm. Evenness of emotion. That is about all Webster and American Heritage has got.

Where is your attitude right this moment? Do you have the opposite of those attitudes listed above right now?

Are you ruffled? Thinking unfair or unjust ideation? Are you moving? Is your thinking a bit agitated or bothered? Are you letting others or other things control your psyche? The opposite of serenity! You are exasperated (it). The only thing between complete calmness or complete chaos or anything in between is...your choice, your allowance of it to be in or on your mind.

Who owns that 'feeling' you carry? Who has added those negative torturous twists to your thoughts? Act differently than you feel, even in fear. Make a good choice.

It's funny what my humanness can come up with. It's what the committee in my head put on the board today: Impatience, worry, hate, anger, justification, rationalization, rudeness, revenge, self-will, fear, obsession. All made up. Apparently, my mind's lens has blinders. Falsehoods take up space in my head. It's a fluctuating perception, logic and illogic, and it is saturated with fear. Most of those verbs say you are not grateful for what you have. Such negative thoughts you are allowing to waste your head time. Tsk. Tsk.

So I consider fear a weakness. The opposite of that statement is that wisdom eschews fear. Fear is far more comprehensive than the adrenaline it produces. Rock takes scissors. Knowledge is wisdom. Truth is wisdom. Break from the oldest of thoughts otherwise.

We get a mammogram or prostate exam as necessary, even see the dentist on a schedule, yet do you do a life checkup? Do you review your hopes and dreams and rate if you are in line to gain? If we are not about progress and positivity, we are in fear and lost. Who wants to live with that person?

Who made the decision to worry? Who is shoulding, woulding, and coulding themself to death?

That, my friend, creates an attitude…a crunched face, a smirky grin, a tense jaw.

Are you getting it now?

I will tell you how to eliminate the 'don't wants' from your life and add a few new habitual smiles in the following chapters…

…while you learn to 'do unto yourself and others' with peace, love or support, and smiles.

Another rule: Do not repeat yourself…ever. Do not repeat yourself ever. Do not repeat yourself ever. Wasn't that annoying? See? Chances are, people heard you, or maybe they didn't, but how childlike to beat YOUR question, opinion, expectations, in the conversation, over and over. Goodness, have some respect for yourself. If others do not pick up what you are putting down, move along to where you are wanted and listened to and respected. Give up on those others. There are probably other reasons to leave some former friends behind. You can ask for them to not interrupt while you are speaking. You can ask that they also respect your time to speak. Maybe they were just not the right audience and it is up to me to find a correct place to discuss my issue.

Think about it. Do you repeat yourself in an argument? In a conversation with a teen? When you want things your way? When your expectations are not met?

"You always do this." "You forgot to carry out the trash." "You didn't clean your room." "You never come straight home." "Get in here now."

Do YOU repeat these kinds of things?

Try this with a friend, "I wanted you to wear green today. I told you to wear green today. Didn't I tell you to wear green? Why didn't you wear the green?"

ISN'T THAT RIDICULOUS? How demanding for me to dictate and repeat what she is to do! It's crazy to try and control another adult. Actually, how dare you. By our own command we are pushing to get things done every day – in our way – and do not realize the damage we leave in our wake.

Yet, those words come out of our mouths:

"I told you to get home earlier. I wanted you here earlier. You really screwed the evening up not being here when I told you to."

"I told you not to drive the car in this weather." "I asked you to clean up the kitchen." "Don't wear that blue shirt with those pants." "The kitchen needs painting and you are going to have to do it."

Is that controlling? Yah. You have taken away dignity and deprived the person of all freedom of choice. Sometimes we deprive the husband of their manhood when we take away their choices. I am guilty of all of that. I unwisely ASSUMED that those responsibilities should have been somebody else's. Each of us has a right and the obligation to make our own decisions. It is character-destroying to usurp that right.

Besides, if people do not listen to you or respect you, why on earth would you want to continue to hang with them?

Whose attitude is in the statements that you say? Simply say things once. You are trying to control a situation when you repeat. You only get to take care of you. Others will eat when they get there. Others will or will not take out the trash in their time, not yours. IF IT IS you that is bothered by the trash, or a messy room, or the fact that no one is on time for dinner, IT IS YOU! That is YOUR expectation. Who made you the boss of any other adult? Marriage vows actually screw us up. We both promised to obey. Hmmm, what if one of us just plain does not know how to lead the other correctly and is rather incorrigible ourselves? Instead, we can ask ahead, would 6 work for dinner for you? Can you take care of your assigned task by 5:00 p.m. today? I would like to see that happen before I make more trash when I cook for all of us. We can make our own lives run smoothly by stepping up to take care of our needs ourselves and by discussing the elephant in the room. Some folks run from discussing painful things, then personal stress happens within them. My family for instance, practiced what remains unacknowledged does not actually exist.

If you take care of your duties, *your* work, *your* hygiene, *your* desk, your messes, your trash, and what is within a hula hoop distance around you on this earth, you will be happier. Let go of others' things. What also happens is that the others in your home whom you have chosen to be with, will notice your methods of care taking. You just mentored a great way to live with peace. When you foster within yourself, a better way to live, your sphere of influence will respond to the new you. Where you play, share in the community, where you participate in sports, your memberships, the hair salon, vendors, health agencies you visit, all of your relationships will change to a more amenable exchange in conversations. You will leave no one in the weeds!

This stuff works.

It took almost 6 years, but finally I felt established. I wish I could say something like, "The road has been long" or 'The path was very winding." But in my case, it has been straight from one place to another, progressive, positive, ever learning with amends for the past, and only warm memories holding onto my heart. My life started getting better immediately when I admitted it was unmanageable. It took me years to say that, however.

I have changed. I belong anywhere in the world, in all cliques, in a restaurant alone. I no longer hate myself or shy away from anything. I meet ugliness with laughter, crime with interest, and allow others to just be in their own freedom; to just be in my way, change lanes directly in front of me, live their homeless life, brag, hate, and condemn. It is no longer my job to make the world and the people around me better. I will only do all that I can in my hula hoop. Sometimes cleaning the ditch along the airport mess is in my hula hoop because it bothers me! I work with the Alzheimer's Association as a Volunteer because my heart hurts thinking the constituents with Alzheimer's may not be treated humanely. The only thing I have changed is my eyes – the way I see and hear and listen and feel and act. No reactions anymore. I belong anywhere. And people have said they did not want me to leave their side. What a sweet feeling.

Let me tell you how to pull serenity from your heart and soul and universe. I know how. Yay!

Two more hints:

1. Omit the word "But" from your sentences and paragraphs.
2. And instead of 'having' to do everything, you will feel privileged to 'get to' do everything. Say that out loud now about a chore ahead of you today. *"I am healthy enough and strong enough to carry that trash out. Lucky me. I get to."*

Sound like a happy place? It is. I have the secret, the key to world peace. Follow me.

Thinking Straight

Let's apply that thinking we now know we are capable of doing.

Someone said that Alcoholics Anonymous is a mutual admiration society for people at the bottom.

I think everyone bottoms-out, but maybe just not yet. Step 1 in the Twelve Step programs is to 'Admit I was powerless over alcohol."

God has hovered in my 'former' life, but I didn't talk to him much. I reacted to life. I allowed others' lives to run mine. I was a second-class person, by my own hand. Afterall, I was the daughter of an alcoholic and a victim of abuse. Shame. Shame. Shame hovered over me. Self-inflicted. We now know how to counter this thinking.

If this was not a necessary societal intervention, why are there 63,000 Anonymous meetings a week in one-hundred and thirty-two countries of the globe! One-hundred and seventeen meetings are held each week in my city of 120,000 population!

Someone in the Alcoholics Anonymous program who I greatly admire gave me a virtual hula hoop. My business was all that I was in charge of. My business only. My attitude was the only one I could ever change. News to me at that time. Great wisdom to have.

Within my hula hoop laid only MY thoughts, attitudes, actions, no longer REactions. I could alter what I did within that space only. New concept to me, folks! So I started acting in that manner...stopped judging you, stopped judging the alcoholic, I obliterated the error of telling everyone that my way was the best way. The biggest thing I learned (and am still learning every day!) is to ACT and get rid of the RE. The hula hoop only holds my actions, not others' reactions. That hula hoop gave me a lot of mental time. That gave me the use of pause. Someone in the program told me that I could not change future, no matter how much time I devoted to worry; nor could I change the past, no matter how much time I lamented or was ashamed. I CAN change my interpretation of the past. Future and past were no longer in the hula hoop. Wow. What a freedom. Who gave me the right to live differently? A God of my understanding. I know that now.

Step 2: Came to believe that there was a power greater than myself. Wow.

Steps 3 through 11 led me to evaluate what I do.

> What actions I take.
> How I decide on things.
> When to pray.
> The right thing to do.
> The attitude I have.

I wouldn't know these things unless I had come in to the program when I did – vulnerable, ashamed, beaten in spirit, lonely even with friends, and having frequent pity parties. I guess I had to have a place to rise from.

I wouldn't know these new things unless someone handed me the books, shared and explained the steps and traditions, unless someone did their 12th step on me! I offer this during these pages, because these programs are great guidance to make a change.

This is a program which gives me miracles, where I suddenly engage and get in the pulse that reality is now.

We refused, prior to program involvement, to see and admit to creating our own demise. Heavens, no! Not me. We learn in the program that denial of veracity, blaming others, and rationalizing our way of thinking and behavior are deficits in our character that we can now obliterate! Many of us find that our available goodness was all used up, by failingly putting effort into 'protecting' the damaged and ill alcoholic.

Ism has transference properties. Alcohol takes homes, you, and all those who care, into a black hole with no ladder out – unless you realize there are steps. The program addresses each step in a chronologic manner which we can understand.

Do I just let go of the alcoholic? You have to decide for you. Do I take rigorous action for God, myself, and all humanity, or do I reactionally, follow the lead of an alcohol diseased and possessed person? Hm. Decide now. When things go wrong, I know now, it is best to not go with them.

We must see clearly alcoholism for the disease, disability and disfigurement that it is, love the person in possession of that crutch or taken to their bed, the person dependent on a substance THROUGH their disease BUT NOT TO THE POINT OF PERSONAL BANKRUPTCY, LOSS OF SELF OR LOSS OF SECURITY OF MIND. When danger and insecurity show themselves to you, run and seek help. Now use what you have learned.

Alcohol when it is drank, adds fuel to an already burning fire annihilating moments of beauty and warmth around it. And it causes scarring, end of life, and possibly everlasting pain and loss. Count those days as gone, now that you are more learned.

Alcohol has conviction. It has the pretense of false power, based on nothing but inane buzzing in the head. You will know how to abort those thoughts. Stick with me.

Alcohol takes one away from the reality, be it the height of the curb or strength of a man. Yet WE gave it credence and based our decisions on its activity. Who was the crazy one here?

Alcohol beats up people physiologically through killing cells; physically through abuse of family, and psychologically takes victims. Now, hopefully if you will work the worksheets and heed some instructional suggestions, you can see alcoholism as the lunatic it is.

As do Christian Scientist followers, however, is it their choice to forfeit medical procedures and cures. BASED ON WHAT IS IN OUR HEADS UP TO NOW, we yielded willingly our own logics choosing frenzied insane living around an alcoholic. It is also known as 'losing our minds'. We gave OUR power of authority to alcohol as the deity within the body of our loved one. We see the difference in where our trust and faith now lies.

I wouldn't know these things unless each meeting other members shared their like experiences and feelings...unless a sponsor re-read the literature and slogans till I understood them. I had to practice a lot and I still continue to practice the steps, especially through 3 – 11, until I morphed into someone I could love.

I wouldn't know these things unless God helped my heart and my hand. When we close meetings with the Lord's prayer, if you stand next to me, you will hear me recite it with great feeling, and proper-due reverence in my enunciation. After all, God has opened my mind, opened my heart, and given me supportive and loving friends. I need to thank him loudly. I treasure his divineness. To know God, I get to hurt a little over my past behaviors so that I know to reach out to Him.

For THINE is the kingdom I get to live in, THINE is the power, not mine, and THINE is the glory I give thanks for being surrounded by. Amen.

My Creator,
I am now willing that you should have all of me,
good and bad.
I pray that you now remove from me
every single defect of character which stands in the way
of my usefulness to you and my fellows.
Grant me strength, as I go out from here,
to do your bidding.
Amen

Unacceptable Behavior

"Every time you don't follow your inner guidance, you feel a loss of energy, loss of power, a sense of spiritual deadness." – Shakti Gawain

I was soooooooooooo selfish. And yet, my pretense was that I am showing love and acting out what I believe others may want. - Like I knew?? But you better believe if there is one bite left on my ice cream cone, my husband is not getting it. Whimsical example? I often choose the easiest way for ME. I am lazy in my giving. I now consider that a spiritual sin. I was lazy in my service to the community, 100% improved now. Me-time overrides many requests for help or camaraderie.

A few years ago, a friend thought his son was going to suicide on a Sunday morning. Dad was distraught, with no way to turn. All I did was go stand in the apartment complex lobby with him and suggested that the police come do a 'domestic check'. We, Dad nor I, will ever forget that moment that I just stood with him. The outcome could have gone either way. I will never forget that 'I gave' love. This is one way the program introduced me to selflessness.

Another me story, my first date with my now fiancé, included telling him the story of the severe depression of my deceased husband, and how I stayed with him through all the suicide attempts, making hospital trips and psychiatrist visits and sacrificing time, my emotion, my work, events, suffering along beside him in this painful passage. First date, mind you, and this beautiful young man said, "I knew you could LOVE long and hard." after your story. "I knew you were a keeper." At the time, the love and sacrifice were innate. And to think that God is even greater than what he puts in our hearts.

Let us not love in just word or talk, but in deed and in truth.

Our own hearts can also condemn us. To have hate in our minds or hearts is suicide of attitude and happiness, self-condemnation of our capability to love. If you were to watch a video of yourself today, are you as happy as you want to be?

From the practice of change, I found what all of us are looking for:

> "...a good life that is growing and expanding, with ever widening horizons and an ever-greater circle of friends and acquaintances and an ever-greater opportunity for usefulness."

A life better than we had before? Now, who doesn't want that?!?!

Step Ten is actually about tattling on yourself! Step Ten is about uncovering, discovering, and discarding. I asked myself if my name was on the old problems I made up. I found I needed to make amends where my quiddities/defects of character threw out emotional grenades. It was like I had a mental appellation of who I was when I was fake or untrue; a vicarious self that was a liar, cheat, etc., but not the real me inside. Rescind and recant – it's possible. You know, I found amends were very necessary due to my former actions in fear and judgement, or rationalization of my actions.

Someone told me that it was unacceptable to always run away. The word 'unacceptable' sure has a lot of clout. Well, it hit home. Me? Guilty of Unacceptable Behavior? I will not have that! Yet, I had been so easy to call it in other people. LOL.

I learned to give a sincere apology, but not just that; I could now giv promise of changing, and never committing that act of harm to anyone again. And then live with the promise consistently. At first, Al Anon let me be just willing to change. The unbelievable reward, I said unbelievable reward, that transpires is that one can renew a relationship, repair old memories with new closeness, and receive acceptance – maybe never forgiveness for the sin, however, accepted for a more mature person with wiser insight. There is a respect of self in doing the act of amends. Deep amends, digging deep into my 'hatreds' was essential. I needed to get it out of me so that I never plant hatred in my psyche again. I asked God at this point to 'get it out', as I came out of the dark. Hatred only costs me brain cells which could be used in a much healthier way. Life is simple, but not easy. I had been beaten up emotionally (not an easy recovery). I want to have inner peace. It's that simple. I like serendipitous states. I look forward to the 'wonderful after', after I have done the right action.

Lend an ear. E mpathy A ffirm R espect

Want to bring it home? Grow balls. Sign up for Big League Thinkers. Toy with the feeling of belonging to Mensa. Let's go farther than short term memory's 'acquisition' of facts. Let's grow into a new plateau of insight and perception, as a matter of fact. It is possible whether you are 6, 20 or 92.

James Joyce once wrote: *"A man's errors are his portals of discovery."* Be cognizant of your moment. Right now, what are you doing? What is your portal entertaining? Where are you sitting/standing? What does the chair/floor look like? Who is near you? What do you smell? What do you feel, really feel (the fizz, the question mark in your mind) when you make a mistake? What did you see, hear, feel when you made the amend? Be aware of your moment. Be aware of your surroundings while you are having this experience of a second in time. Think of this brief picture as being the last time you will see it – embellish your scene with your feelings. That is being cognizant; cognizant of your life. If at this moment you are in a mistake, acknowledge it. The first picture you conjure up when you think of this mistake tomorrow, next week, or ten years from now, will remind you of the awfulness inside when you made the mistake. Only if you made the corrections. But cognizance of making it and admission come first, then corrections. It all works together if you have the courage to change. Then plug in how to file it in consolidated learning for further reference.

I am a better person for my being cognizant of my previous ways, admitting to my mistakes and promising to correct the errors of my ways. Wow. That felt good. Read it again. I have the freedom to exchange covert activity, self-blame for positive thinking and feeling good...when I make the change; when I cross over from my mental static of, 'stuck in stupid'.

Swami Sivananda said: *"Do not brood over your past mistakes and failures as this will only fill your mind with grief, regret and depression. Do not repeat them in the future."*

Fear is in my head. I make it up based on false information usually. I needed to rather find solution/response/ and strength. When I took an inventory of the times I felt fearful, I found my response was usually to run, procrastinate, and berate myself for inaction! Faith and trusting in God are the opposite actions to fear.

Most people are prone to embrace uncertainty. Fear comes easier than solution. We take in the fear in hopes someone will rescue us or take care of the situation. When stumbling into fear, focus instead on the process toward the better reward. Solve. Look for solution. Take a first step out. Do something!

I did not like myself when I was in fear. Now, I step out, ask a question, take a risk, and I do life and I like myself. Fear really kept me in a cage. Only nonproduction comes from fear. I found I was often just circling the issues.

Some common signs of fear (Remember, we choose to have these feelings! And they are in your head only!):

Obsessiveness	Weariful
Belittling others	Pitiful
Time binds we create	Attention seeking
Consumption	Stressed
Negative actions	Feeling a loss
Negative thoughts	Life being full of buts
Insane actions	Feeling Uncontrollable
Depression	Some Physical issues
Self-victimizing	Guilt
Reactive negative behaviors	Scared
Pity Parties	Feeling alone
Anxiety	Wrongdoings
Paralyza-tion	Criticizing self
Feeling threatened	

We adopted those ways! The above list can be immobilizing and debilitating to us. And all those sensations we are experiencing are MADE UP! Who wants to think like that? Those self- adopted thoughts held me hostage. I was hurting myself by clinging to them.

Today is your fulcrum, the pivotal day to change it. Think, what can I do to make this right? Anything I can do to fix this predicament? Be uncritical of self or others and change behavior. Make a permanent decision to unplug from negativity. Can you do that, promise yourself?

Even outstanding Olympians and musicians and country leaders have fear. And here are the most common featured fears:

Fear of decision making.

What if it is the wrong decision? What if there is something I don't know? I can't tell the future.

Fear of Failure

You will fail at something. Know that. We are in this life to learn how and it doesn't always happen with the first or tenth time we try.

Fear of Missing Your Goal

We work hard and we want it to matter. I devoted a career keeping statistics for years and suddenly over one broken law, (no, not mine.) the agency closed its doors. My 'goal' all those years was for naught. I would have never learned excellent book keeping. Perfection is not attainable, but if we chase a goal, we will achieve excellence along the way.

Fear of Speaking or Being the Authority

Combines the above fears. We can only share what we have learned and what we have succeeded in and truth. People *do* need to know how we did it. We are an authority on our own lives. Share when asked by others to encourage their hope.

Fear of Criticism

Especially if you have been abused in the past or put down or labelled or shunned or have been belittled and demeaned, this fear lives in our attics. It is a common sense of go-to fear. When we find confidence and compassion, people will criticize (it is a given) but we know what is right and the truth. We can only listen to critics, without reaction. If you gave someone Heaven, they would probably say they are not ready yet. Critics are alive and unwell around us, full of condescension which we may choose to absorb or take a pass on.

Speaking with confidence uses these practices:

1. Share ideas only if they are truths
2. Share thoughts on improving systems or processes
3. Present your ideas and thoughts as statements, not questions to ponder.
4. Own your words by having facts behind them
5. Speak up, engage the others
6. Speak affirmations
7. Choose words wisely, not offending
8. Say less, appearance of rambling or repeating
9. Organize not just notes, but thoughts in sequence before speaking
10. Dismiss idea of aggression or force

School of hard knocks, but a school of education, nevertheless.

Have you heard of the Imposter Syndrome? It is described as "persistent inability to believe that one's success is deserved or has been legitimately achieved as a result of one's own efforts or skills." We simply don't believe in ourselves. Some doubt about our capabilities is 'normal'. We don't believe that where we are is a result of our doing. Who did it then?!

So, do you think you are worthwhile? Oh my gosh. Is that even a question? Whose mind are you borrowing to think with? Whose hands are those you are using? Is there not success in getting out of bed, tying your shoes, thinking and planning reasonable thoughts? We are each beyond worthwhile! We are worth something to every surrounding thing, person, and purpose. Why else are we standing in this spot of dirt on earth? Gees. Wish you could see how many people want to come to your funeral while alive.

True Confessions: Trick or True

_____

Here is what I found:

I was chasing an illness in another person.

Others do not need to change because I think so.

I have a voice. I can say: "That feels unfair."

I have permission to let things go.

History is never going to be different.

Whatever I judgmentally label in their life as unacceptable, I do not have to fall prey to.

It is very easy for me to default into being obsessed with others' problems and how they affect my moments of life. Gotta watch that one myself. I can create my own rumination and atrocity, imagining I am in another's mind! LOL

One thought prevailed – I needed to detach with love and care. First, I had to stop obsessing. This is a fine line. I was accepting their condonement of me, and making that my personal defeat. Then, wallowed in my inability to live up to their (sometimes wrongful) standards. I actually was bored with thinking about my own situation. Finally, God said to me through a friend, HER/HIS ACTIONS are not that significant in my life. Let HER/HIM go. I am not helping myself or others. Why did I continue to hurt myself, is a question I still carry in life. I have been told I have a limited perspective of this relationship. It stems from tradition and 'what my mom would have wanted'. I was obsessing, thus giving away my power to be. I have no more obligations to that person and it is a new freedom.

I try not to live harboring those thoughts. I was focusing on a better future with that person, when there may not be. I still believed I have control of an outcome with my best actions. Now, I know I cannot change another person. I hold only my own blueprint, not his or hers. This thinking sometimes steals from me my capability to relish in the moment. How tragic. Since then, I have surrendered them to God after praying for a week solid.

The above is a common perspective in codependent relationships between spouses. I had so many scenarios of improving something or someone that was none of my business. If only I had applied all the time dedicated to those unfulfilled expectations to create my own better life. I love waking up and saying to myself, "God, what would you have me do today?

I find that if I live in this moment, with awareness, almost mesmerizing focus on here and now, I am secure. I can make it the best moment with full attention, willingness to be here, and a loving attitude. That is all I have to do. Great gratitudes that I get to know, afford me the security I need.

God does tell me over and over, that I do not need to hold onto thoughts and actions that continue to bring pain into my life! I will get there. I am gaining in understanding.

Al-Anon axioms help. They tell me repeatedly, I cannot change anything but me, my attitudes, my actions and my thoughts. It starts with me. Another principle which applies is that it may take a lifetime to have wisdom to change the things I can, and know the difference of what is mine to control and what is not!

Simply, I have value because I breathe the breath of humanit

Hopefully you will laugh at the jokes below because you nov
after realizing the errors of your own ways:

How many codependents does it take to change a lightbulb?

> Just one, she keeps flipping the light switch repeating to herself,
> "This time it will come back."

How can you tell you are at an Al-Anon meeting?

> Someone spills their coffee and everyone gets up to clean it up.

You MIGHT be Codependent if...

… when you correspond with people in jail because you could relate to
  being guilty.

…when you starve at an all-you-can-eat buffet because your partner can't
  find something to eat.

… when it is your birthday party and you go out of your way to see if
  everyone is enjoying themselves.

… when you have been stranded on a deserted island for a week. You
  finally are rescued. You call home and the first thing you say is, "How
  have you guys been?"

…when your favorite childhood game was "SORRY".

…when you have 200 channels to pick from but you hand the remote to
  your partner.

…when you are from a warm climate yet you live in a place with a
  freezing winter because your partner has got this weird fixation with
  snowmobiling or ice fishing.

…when you train intensely for the Boston marathon and on the day of the
  event you don't run it because your partner is having a moment.

...when your guy has been arrested and charged with killing. Many people want this guy dead. You are upset (that) that these people just don't see what you see in him.

...when you apologize to your therapist for "talking too much" yet you are paying him/her for the privilege of

...when you die, someone else's life flashes in front of your eyes.

Risky for me, but I am going to print for you, parts from my ten-year anniversary testimony in the Al-Anon program, in hopes you see where my fMRi (Functional Magnetic Resonance Imaging) where blood flow is highlighted in colors) has color changes signifying improvement:

"I have chosen my ten full years anniversary in the program to talk about the changes I know about myself now, which I did not think possible ten years ago. To me, my involvement in the program has changed all my thinking.

In Step 1, my admission that I was thinking wrongly and living in my head only, in a 'poor me' state. I walked in to a meeting crying and walked out sobbing, realizing some of my truth. It was as if those people could see into my thoughts! You had lived like I was living!

Take Step 2: Maybe, just maybe, I could draw enough conviction that God has power over you, me and everyone and the trees, and my alcoholics, and others, and all happenings in our lives. I personally started on a spiritual quest to sort out what could be my Higher Power, talking with ministers, joining church groups, etc., to get closer to a meaning for Higher Power that I could rely on. The program had only suggested that I believe. I took an ACTION.

Step 3: All the folks talking in meetings, helped me to see how silly I was acting. I was cavorting around doing inconsequential activities and avoiding responsibility through my erroneous thoughts.

Improve My Human Condition

Work with me here. Take your own inventory.

Think of a situational communication in your past where you felt some one was petulant or irritable or mean to you, i.e., a boss put you down, a playmate bullied you, an uncle abused you, someone took financial advantage of your family, someone used their acrimoniously bitter tongue, you fought with your spouse. Ya, that one, that argument. Put it to the test below.

RESENTMENTS

I am Resentful at: (Name)	The Cause or Reason:	What was Affected? Where did I Feel Hurt?							This was Our Course:	Prayer:	The Exact Nature of My Wrongs Where was I:					What Could I Have Done Differently?
		SELF ESTEEM	PERSONAL RELATIONSHIPS	MATERIAL SECURITY	EMOTIONAL SECURITY	SEXUAL RELATIONSHIPS	AMBITIONS OR I HAD MY OWN WAY	PRIDE	Realize at once that the people who have wronged you are spiritually sick... That they like yourself, are sick too. Can I now see what it was like in their shoes – with their fears, insecurities, and background experiences. Could I have done to someone what they did to me?	Ask God to help you show them the same tolerance, and pity that they would cheerfully grant a sick friend. This is a sick person, how can I be helpful to him? God save me from being angry. Thy will be done.	SELFISH	DISHONEST	SELF SEEKING	FRIGHTENED	WHERE WAS I TO BLAME	

My Brother Did It - Blame

I want to start this chapter with the opposite of what it will tell you later.

Not to get us off the hook, but we do have a blind spot – scientifically proven in that our optic nerve looks forward and it can't see fine detail. The cones and rods are built as they are built and that is it. So we do not know any more than what is in front of us, right? I do not want you to blame others for anything we cannot perceive with truth. Until proven, actions appear as we know – so far.

The above paragraph should explain to you partially, why we blame. We have a blind spot that can't know more until we turn, whether we turn our heads to know more, or turn our minds open to more knowledge. Until we do that, we ARE going to have misquotes, misinstruction, lack of wisdom, and missing information. That is what this book is about; learning more that you don't already know. This chapter is about falsely assigning blame on others and things and happenstance because we do not 'look inward or look around'.

Too often, I get so caught up in me and wrapped in my own concerns. God still loved me, but my ego had turned Him off. My own old rules were primary in my thinking. I needed to add my new strategies for thinking better; and God to my every minute. However, God comes to me in mercy any time. A practice that has finally settled in my heart and mind is that I am cognizantly aware of compulsive 'busyness' or 'tension' or 'worry', of those silly mind-altering thoughts that lead to reactions. Thank goodness,

I have now learned to *humble my heart,* and open it up for God to set things right. Priority on this earth, at least for me, is to dwell gratefully in God's mercy; to believe that in everything, this too will pass. Que sera sera.

Earthquakes and floods and famine happen. Fires and hurricanes ruin lives and property. For the brief time that folks are involved or near or effected by these tragedies, it is horrific. People also experience first communions, wedding planning, victories, awards, 4.0, loves, and homeruns. For a brief time, the folks that are involved or near or affected by these wonderful things experience great joy and a time of happiness.

"This too shall pass" does not get enough banner time. No matter how permanently fixed we are in our lives, we *do know*, every moment will pass; every moment of pain, every moment of loss, redolent feelings, light heartedness, joy, celebration, grief, shared feelings, mourning, love – all will pass on through. We cannot capture time. We can only embrace each moment and live it to its fullest, and move on. When we let all these pass through, painful or poisonous or passionate secrets, then, they became only expressions of our experienced vitality. The sooner we accept that it is a past moment, the sooner we can have serenity about the moments and about times of our lives. We begin to live on the *solution* side.

It is so easy to point the finger at another thing or person. Sometimes we even mentally rationalize that we can separate our fingers or mouths from OUR responsibility for something. *"I don't know, Mom, my hand just did it."* *"Tom made me do it."*

Listen to this conundrum:

> *Whenever we blame something or someone for our*
> *own problem, we give them/that power.*
> *(Well, and lose our own sense of capability and responsibility.)*
> *We did it to ourselves! Own our part.*

We have a part in the blaming situation. We REACTED: we fought, we should have, we could have, even the thinking that he should have, or we have withdrawn from responsibility. Then we add guilt to our thinking. Sometimes we go farther by hating ourselves, or being negative to others, or guilt builds into despair. Whoa.

Before reacting, ask yourself what is the *absolute* truth (their's and mine) in the situation. Am I at fault? Do I know enough to be in this situation? Did I act in a reactionary function before using all my knowledge? What is a positive outcome here? Choose the positive direction. Essence of color in scans of brains during a reactionary period versus happy status, actually varies!

See, I have this problem with feelings getting in the way of truth. We must learn to tell facts from feelings that I/you have solidified, albeit, as 'right'. My old way of thinking is almost DNA-like, so innate. I am learning not to give reality to troubles that may never be. I have held on to habits that could have been calamities and I used a lot of energy holding on.

I had a bit of doing the same things over and over repeatedly, and I would expect that I would have the results I desired some day... the same over and over again, expecting different. Hm...

Our lives had been punctuated with good times, caring moments, love, laughter and good crazies. We worship those kinds of moments. They pass. Within a family unit with a disease, addiction, or mental illness, we wear a constant raincoat/shroud/shield. For when an afflicted person with a disease added nectar that pushed the disease between us – sometimes radically loud as if a bus drove into the living room and left diesel odor, splashed mud, made tire tracks, and holes in the wall; we basically reacted rather than responded.

Keep reading. I will grant you a masters/PH. D in Perfect Human Development once you release control of God's job back to Him, critique your own thinking, and examine your own history with different eyes. Then we set out with more intellect and wisdom. Yahoo.

"Any fool can defend his mistakes – and most fools do – but it gives one a feeling of nobility to admit one's mistakes. By fighting, you never get enough, but by yielding, you get more than you expected." – Lawrence G. Lovasik

Or blame mom and dad, it could always be their fault.

We can preserve our past, only to reference it as we would a resource, a history book or dictionary, that led to the Industrial Age facts, a breakthrough in Science, a War, or alphabetical order. See, our bodies will never lose our physical "epigenetic changes' or predispositions, but our personalities may learn better! Our personal history is fundamental only - there to look at and through, but we are no more in that war or Einstein's days or high school. What it WAS is no longer. It is ancient and a relic. Mimes in my head are not fossilized – no longer demanding me to continue to 'react to'.

"I didn't start it" many of us told our Moms.

So if we are not the guilty party in war, who is? Oh, the other ones. The ones with prejudice, great greed, and huge fear. I am sorry they feel that way; feel fear themselves.

Yup. I said it. F e a r.

We all travel with fear. That is why love and support are so important.

To cease and ease the fear in others.

I am judging you first, therefore, you cannot say that I am inadequate before I condemn your name first.

I am stronger, I will overtake you in the race. Where the fuck is the race? Who set it up? Furthermore, who cares about your race? That selfish little rat bastard named you? Is your lawn greener, do you chide your friend for his bad haircut, the neighbor for cutting his lawn angularly? Do you post script, 'I was only kidding about the baldness part'? Do you tell the off-color jokes when it is 'safe'? Does your car have to be cleaner? Does the money in your pocket make you feel best? The winner today? Do you leave your cart in the parking lot? Do you skip church sometimes, well most of the time, ok, so I go to weddings and funerals?

What is happening in our heads? We even project blame there, talking about a 'committee', not owning our own control of our thoughts. What is happening in our heads is the absence of love and support of others. We are talking to ourselves in our ineffectual old ways, our gimmie attitudes, make sure I have it first, I get my share; that Leonard put gas in the lawn mower when he brought it back. Or I will have to give him an invoice in my head and track what he 'owes' me.

'Paybacks are hell' is a favorite phrase that presents no charm, evokes no love or support.

What you do with your time had better be just about you. We better be presenting our best, truest self when we are with others.

Most of us don't know our true selves. We can't let that core goodness seep into our head. We are busy with scorekeeping, gaining, and want. Busy is a four-letter word. When someone says to you, they are too busy, are you offended?

Goodness. The goodness part. It is within you. It is in your common sense, logic, heart, your soul, your mind, your brain, your shoulders and stomach. You know the feeling – when something is done right - When we give - When we succeed in a surprise birthday party - When our child speaks with kindness to the next child – I taught him that.

When we mentor good, when we act on our goodness part, when we A C T rather than react, we feel good. The goodness washes away ick. It trumps ick. We are grateful. YeOeoeoew. What a feeling! Uh Oh. Pretty soon we are gooder. And those around us are shocked but feel it. They watch. Hey, it is working for him. I want that. What is he doing? - I want that feeling.

Voila! Mentoring works. So I am offering to you that if you try these steps, the suggestions offered in this book, that you may have a really good life where others want to be around you.

The natural talents within us and the passion we develop for something we love to do, too often are left untapped – BY US.

We devote more time to our shortcomings than to our strengths. If you are not a CPA but want to do your own taxes, you must learn some CPA/IRS knowledge to work it. If you want to be a better friend, you have to work it. People who have a 'natural' talent for something, yes are blessed. But the majority, 95% of us were not born with a Mensa brain or as a savant. Habits must be well rehearsed to be habits. So, if you have bad habits, it is going to also take a while to break them.

Picture two different doors in front of you. One is marked, "Same Old" and the other is marked "God's Way" or "New and Different" – which do you want to open?

Behind the New and Different door you will find a beautiful room which has not been entered before and you will never live through again. And it is vibrating with new and different possibilities. A room, where you feel the awareness of God, an inner stillness every moment, with cherished seconds, minutes, and hours.

Behind the Same Old door lies the experience of mistreatment, abuse, victim headset with anger and resentment or reactions to life – a miserable destiny, where life is only as good as I think it can be.

The *desires* of the world constantly pursue me.

Let's break this down. A talent is a natural way of thinking and feeling or behaving; an inclination to hone a natural interest.

Investment is time spent practicing or developing skills and collecting more knowledge about an interest.

Strength allows us to be as close as we can get to consistently performing nearly perfect, based on investment, time, and interest.

A habit is a repetitive manner or behavior.

You do the deductive reasoning of the above.

> A good behavior, or bad behavior, given time,
> investment and interest will grow strong.

I AM GUESSING YOU are reading this book because you want to like yourself, be more, accept others on their terms, have a GREAT relationship with everyone, and feel at peace with your life. This means we must partner with many strategies to find the best mentoring or leadership in the areas where we are lacking.

Acknowledge A Higher Diety

If your butt is squeezing up about now, yes, I am going to write about spirituality. To bathe in the sweetness of life, our minds must be open to all knowledge, beliefs and opinions, even speculations. Your neighbor might be possibly another Einstein, take it in, read everything you have time to, watch educational media, travel, take every opportunity. One thing I tried first was to attend every church in town. If hundreds of people were making a Sunday morning effort with and without family, I wanted to understand the drive, the force behind each person, if that which was being presented could open up my mind.

What I found was sickening – people 'go to' church for prestige, people go to church to socialize, lonely people go to be with others, rich people go because it looks good in several ways, mainly an obituary or a political run. Parents go to church with young ones to give them a look at a tradition and to understand the religious ways. Out on a limb here, but my guess is less than 20% of attendees could tell you the sermon's lesson last Sunday, and since I am making percentages up, I would guess that only 20% practice truth, and their actions are always nice to others. Let me say, there is value in the place (church) in the socializing there or just sitting in a pew contemplating. But maybe not being put to use at maximum intake.

A minister revealed to me that they distrusted some of their trustees and felt a presence of many uneasy parishioners each Sunday as they left his service.

What else I discovered was that ministers vary soooooooooooooooooo widely. My priest (since I am Catholic by family) tells basketball and football scores each Sunday. Some pastors basically just read the Bible to us, do not interpret. Many cannot find or were not gifted with the key to sing. Some cough in their hands before passing out communion. And if there is enough money, there will be a light show and band on a stage.

Now, all that aside, I am left with choices, but much more informed choices, knowledge of methods of worship, methods of interpreting Jesus or Buddha's, or a guru's orations. None of this necessarily has to do with spirituality!

Something, someone, a higher power, mother nature, universal power, etc. has their finger on the karma of our destiny.

Or if you want, agnostically, science just occurs as it will. The thing is, how would you form a just and fair idea of our people and our world if you did not explore possibilities.

Open up your mind. Understand why people do what they do. More pressing - understand why you do what you do. Church can be rote, family tradition or intensively a reminder to live a life of fairness and goodness. And if you add spirituality, a connection to a god, all the more wonderful for fulfilling your destiny. Simply, learn more.

Spirituality is a great base for good attitude in the rest of the walk around life we do. If exposure to last Sunday's hour at church is the most you can get as a reminder to be a good person, that is important. It is our attitude that makes or breaks each day, each moment, each occurrence, each encounter, each relationship. And even sitting in contemplation for an hour is good.

Rarely does good attitude abound just because you worship.

Life May Pass You By If You Do Not Live It Fully

People have flat tires, late nights, a close death, a sore tooth, money problems, you can name the ill will of the day. A pragmatic communicator knows these are things which have resolution and will pass. All excitements pass. All of them. Alacrity is momentary. All things can be healed or you die and then all tangible things have been fixed for you. Period.

What about the curmudgeon who lives to be sheltered? Well, a psychologist friend, early in my adulthood, made the bold statement that 99% of the population of the world needed a psychotropic drug, maybe theirs's just hasn't been discovered yet. More truthfully, curmudgeons self-learned to be such.

So much of life's mishaps and inappropriate actions are just metabolized failure. Not always a choice, so don't go blaming individuals.

Nerds choose their path. Grumps opt to put out ick. Serious intellects choose their facial expression, disarming as it may be. Staying in a negative or non-progressive attitude is their decision, consciously or unconsciously. Perhaps one's upbringing showed them no other way. Perhaps they were never exposed to that one hour on Sunday to think differently. It's probable their world was pretty rough to struggle through. Dark and baffling diseases or envines may have steered their course.

I want to take a moment to mention that the vision God has of us is different from what he sees currently. Hang on to those words. I can be better. I am learning about my own negativity in the forecast of aborting it!

Here are some questions to help us abort thinking:

Do I need this challenge?

What am I spending my energy doing?

What is my intention?

Have I given up on myself?

Am I being affected by other's resentments?

Is this a wrongful attachment?

Who was I then? They still expect that. Step away.

What is my fear here?

So listening to yourself is the first step to betterment. A mind that created the problem cannot solve the problem; it is the same mind with those same limited thoughts. I do not have my own best advice. LOL. Are you still rehearsing the reactions you did ten years ago? Let go of that. Let is an action verb. Rejection and blame of myself has no purpose. Move on. Wasted thinking. Do guilt and fear have gains? N period, O period. When you go back in the past, you go alone. God is about changing up. Pity and remorse are yours, not for God. Detach yourself from pernicious negativity. Step away and view yourself, shut up while you think. Listen, share, and accept what is.

Instead of detaching from reality, live up, give up, own up, speak up and grow up. Own your own worth.

Whenever my honesty or purity is in danger, I abort. I do not get to decide who gets condemned. I only look at reality and apply my honesty and trust. I will not give up my intimacy with God. It is unconditional. A quote repeated by an Al Anon friend so I can not tell the origin: "Keep your head Heavenly and your feet on the ground with your fellow travelers."

The crux is education. Many choose to educate themselves and open their minds to ever enlarging principles to follow. When exposure is limited or minds shut at any level or age, trouble often belies the human. Can you name even seven of your principles in life? Do you even have principles? No offense meant, as my 'principles' were pretty screwed up, I feel I can challenge another person with the same question put to me.

One principle I know that I profess is to:

"Maintain productive function and strength to enable care and love to self and other of God's peoples so that we all live with peace and happiness with our God."

Why name seven? In my repertoire, I have adapted about 11 great ones. Books, theorists, psychologists will parade usually seven to ten principles for life or graduation or for living with Christ. It is a matter of the direction you want to gain the most from. Here are a few common principles presented in those books and theories:

1. Always and Forever Gain, Become, Reach, Do
2. Avoid Negativity
3. Give More Than You Take, Help Others
4. Spend Your Time Aware of Each Moment
5. Create Your Own Road
6. Be Accepting of Random
7. Move in the Direction You Are Present In

Studies have shown that seven is about as many categories we can effectively mentally handle. Maybe four will be described as first most in your day and require your attention. Tomorrow, there will be two others of the seven which you are in mind to follow in another process. They are interrelated in your mind, keeping all of them active for complete fulfillment, but at a case-by-case decision. Each should be toward building your capacity to love and progress. Then you can ask, "Am I living an effective quality life and making a positive difference?"

The good news, is that we always have potential for growth. Opportunity is almost inevitably there. Fear often interferes. (That is a huge chapter up and coming. Stay tuned.) Fear of being disappointed in yourself and others is real. It keeps us ineffective.

Just recently, a client with whom I talk, mentioned a new boss said to her, "I guess you are too new here to know how to do things. If you don't know some things, maybe you were not right for this hire." Instead of speaking up for herself, she quivered into her self-doubt. 'Boss' had attritioned up from business manager, with no people skills. The truth here, my client was fully trained, had much experience, was loved by her clients, had renewed her license just a month before. Her first reaction was that he was right. See how we treat ourselves!? A simple ask I offered was, "What is the truth?" We rehearsed 10 sentences to use in response to his accusal. They are now laugh-together friends because she responded to him with care and concern for his place of concern at the agency, and how fitting she was for her clients.; it was just too bad that in her training, there was neglect to show her his particular demand.

Here Come The Judge

Let me preface this very carefully, I am not authorized to analyze or use the testing below. I give full credence to doctors of science who research greatly to discover the pieces and parts of our personality styles and I refer you to read others' books, take their tests and allow the interpretations that are done by doctors of psychology and psychiatry. There are on line tests available at this time of this writing that will help you more succinctly. But I find few better ways to discover your personal modes within a relationship than to perform one of these tests. It reveals to you and others, the personality style we have adopted and grown over our life time so far.

Cognitive Style Inventory©
most recent revision 12/12/06 - *Ross Reinhold, INTJ*
www.PersonalityPathways.com

To short cut what I feel was revealed in the test, I ask this question: Did I learn to be this way or was I born to be this way?

The tests go on to talk about brain development and personality evolution in your life time, starting with being born into a set of values and actions, to developing through maturing, our own values and actions. Are we set in them or are we still changeable? Puberty is mentioned as a core personality development age. Taking their well-researched test discovers innate abilities and our cultivated ideation. I refer you to this test for a very revealing self-assessment. I suggest you tackle this with a partner or team member, after you take it alone. Amazing results teach us who we have become and a compatibility scale.

To further encourage your participation in this full-scale exam, let me ask:

Do you pause when action is needed, or dive in?

Do you use GPS readout, look for a landmark, or
listen to directions to get to a place in town?

Any two people, any two people will answer those differently. I referred to three learning styles. Yet we interact daily using our innate response, expecting others to 'get us' or answer us in a manner we understand. Any two people will act differently.

These questions already demonstrate the differences in people. Put me in a car headed to an unknown address in a large city, with someone of the 'other' thinking and there will be a conversation and perhaps negative discourse because of DIFFERENCE in our expectations. No one is wrong. We each have gone to our default mechanism - all that we know to do. How we respond or react is based on our wisdom in relationships SO FAR!

Let's improve our wisdom. Going to our learned (so far) defaults is not demonstrating wisdom of character.

Do you react with natural responses on an automatic pilot rote manner? The common sense that you use is limited in structure. Our common sense is time sensitive. If you are three years of age, seven, twenty-one, forty-two, your common sense is based on YOUR exposure to the elements SO FAR. To base all your decisions on SO FAR KNOWLEDGE is dumb.

We must learn to learn, continue to take risks, ask questions, explore possibilities, develop potential. Tell me, why would you NOT want to do that!! If I functioned by intuition so far vs cultivating open-mindedness to all aspects of life and beyond, I will have completely limited outcomes! And most likely, I will not ever be fulfilled by my existence on earth; with no legacy or letter of recommendation from God. Living subjectively (within my mind as opposed to external stimuli) leads to feeling chaffed, sadness, disappointment, vengeful thoughts, judgmental mentality, and irrationalization. You choose. Stay where you are or learn better habits continually? Make it a quest to understand everything to upgrade the thoughts you have. Make comparisons based on what you know so far, and live in the insecure illusion you created, or know the truth? Feel relevant and have integrity and confidence, or use lesser judgement and rationalization to get by with things? The best way to have a good future is to create it. When you check off the to do's that have been managing and controlling what you do, will you be done and happy and content with yourself? Doing things faster does not get them done right. Following a list like this leaves no room for flexibility or spontaneity, that time when you enjoy the moment and thus enjoy your life as it goes moment by moment.

If there is one thread of judgment, denigration, or criticism in what you say, people stop hearing you – they shut you out.

Oh, we can find comfort of a sort in repetition till the recliner wears out or we have permanent sciatica. At that time, we are in crisis of our own design. Do you get what I am putting down?

It would be like having a land line in a wireless culture. We would be ill equipped to deal with reality, guessing.

I know I am a dichotomy. Some feelings are shortcomings. Some characteristics are great; and some, are not attributes. I don't fool myself anymore.

Based on my own experience and other testing modalities I have come across, I have created a cheater's guide to personality traits' exposure.

Your intuitive check list:

I am talkative

I find fault with others

I do a thorough job

I am depressed

I create new ideas

I am original in my thinking

I am reserved

I am helpful

I am unselfish

I am relaxed

I can be careless

I handle stress well

I am curious

I am full of energy

I start quarrels

I am a reliable person

I have a good imagination

I am a deep thinking

I get nervous easily

I do things efficiently

I am considerate

I am kind

I generally trust

I generate enthusiasm

I forgive easily

I tend to be disorganized

I tend to be quiet

I am inventive

I am stable

I am inventive

I am assertive

I am emotionally unreachable

I preserver till the task is finished

I am very emotional

I tend to be lazy

I cry easily

I can be cold

I can be aloof

I worry a lot

I am outgoing

I am sociable

I am moody

I finish tasks

I am moody

I remain calm in tension

I prefer routine work

I am sometimes rude

I value artistic expression

I am shy

I am inhibited

I follow through with plans

I like to reflect

I like to play with ideas

I have few artistic interests

I am sophisticated in art

I am sophisticated about music

I am a sophisticated reader

I am easily distracted

I like to cooperate with others

I need others to like me

I am politically liberal

Insanity Runs In My Jeans

———

I would like to take a poll at a recovery meeting, grief group, judges' chambers, etc. I wonder how many people there really understand Shakespeare, our renowned, revered master of language and thought. The language of thought – the overview and cognizance that some neurons went to a lot of work to put out an idea or paragraph from our mouth. Well, the answer is, less than 1%. See Shakespeare, as well as few others of us, was a dreamer and realism orator. His genius lay in his thinker. He could discern reality from denial, reality from dreams, reality in truth and discourse in it.

The confusion he left in his staid, lies within our thinkers! We are lazy processors. (stuck in Windows 1.0 perhaps?) First, Shakespeare's language confuses. Second, we don't need more confusion, we react. Third, we do not, when required to read Shakespeare, deeply comprehend his meanings. Thus, we may shun or never study the truth in his writings or garner the messages, because we cannot overlook our nuances in language and we have limited, default settings about reconciling what we don't know.

Compare this to our mental process to say, alcoholism in a partner: We are confused by the behaviors of someone we want to know and love intricately for their value and goodness. Their personality now leaves us spinning. Their conversation to us is bemusing and flummoxing. There are neurobiologics associated with the disease that have not been completely discovered. Second, we can't live in their activities, or their demands on the relationship. We react in fear. Third we cannot comprehend what seems to be happening and we shun, deny, or fight or flee from the part of the alcoholic we don't understand. In this case, we are begging Shakespeare to speak my lingo; searching for our loved one who is consumed by a different way of abiding with a different set of values now. We cannot beg Shakespeare to be or not to be the writer that he is. We cannot manipulate cancer to get out of our loved one's body. Coping with the words we understand about Shakespeare's works is only going to lead to despair. Why do we codependents usually choose to go inward, shunning more knowledge, explanations of our feelings and fears, toying with other ways or thinking? Do Shakespeare's writings and our literature professor scare us into sublimation? Sometimes. Does the disease of alcohol or cancer or mental illness scare us into sublimation? We end up in fear and just doing enough in the marriage or class to 'get by', settling for a "C" or "D" in our lives.

Let's just check if you have codependent tendencies for kicks, shall we?

You:

- o Assume responsibility for others feelings and behaviors?
- o Feel guilty about others' feelings and behaviors.
- o Have difficulty identifying what you are feeling.
- o Are afraid of your own anger, yet sometimes erupt in rage.
- o Worry about how others may respond to your feelings, opinions, and behavior.
- o Have difficulty making decisions.
- o Are afraid of being hurt and/or rejected by others.
- o Minimize, alter or deny how you truly feel.
- o Are very sensitive to how others are feeling and feel the same.
- o Are afraid to express differing opinions or feelings.
- o Value others opinions and feelings more than your own.
- o Embarrassed to receive recognition and praise, or gifts.

o Judge everything you think, say, or do harshly as never 'good enough'.

o Are a perfectionist.

o Are extremely loyal, remaining in harmful situations too long.

o Do not ask others to meet your needs or desires.

o Do not perceive yourself as lovable and worthwhile.

o Compromise your own values and integrity to avoid rejection or others' anger.

Codependency is defined as an addiction to people, behaviors, and things. If you fit the beliefs and conditions above, you are trying to control people's individual feelings and all things and events on the outside of your hula hoop. This drive has been central to every part of your reason for being. It is all a fallacy to the truth!

I am not a scientist, but if I could, I would explore PET scans and Cerebral Spinal Fluid to see if there are any biomarkers for a Pre-Codependent Personality! Imagine if we could drill into the brain and tweak that nodule that contains self-doubt, victim stance, or worry. There are 100 billion neurons going around in the forest of your brain. We have a stigma and it is terribly frightening. I would bet an fMRI would make up a new color to express the areas of my brain defective with codependency.

So the question is unanswerable. How do we fix the alcoholic? I personally cannot fix any other person. Nor can you! Surprise. People do not need to hear from me about their individual addiction. There are far more learned masters to speak to each addiction. I do know codependency well and will only tread there.

The oblique thought, that objectless actions 'alcohol and drug users' ('t)he Chronically Inebriated' according to our local PD) make, with their often pivotal or sloppy drunken loving is often temporary insanity. That WE, the undrunk try to make sense of it or live around, within or with these behaviors is even more INSANE. The sooner we realize we have been drawn in to a disease, the sooner we can become sane. The draw, the mind bend is those of self-proclaimed obligatory rules which when combined with alcohol consumption are deadly. We are likely blinded by love or our own temporary insanity.

Alcoholic acts are often shameful, humiliating, senseless and sad. Yet many family members or close friends, choose eyes half shut, to take on that humiliation and shame. It IS NOT EVEN HAPPENING TO THEM. Marriage vows and blood relation do not make us forced to be the victim here!

When I am humiliated, I cannot abate my talking. I used to make up excuses, rationalize and apologize repeatedly for my behavior. OR I took the defensive that no one understands me or bully others out of my way for my reasoning to stand alone! Defensiveness is a well learned habit! It is a reaction, not a response.

We are a separate child of God, adult and intelligent and everything. If all the other kids play in the mud puddle, do we naively dive in with our new Easter clothes? Adults should know better. Or be aware that they choose stupid. As Shakespeare left us with choices, to believe, to be or not to be, questions, deep thoughts; alcohol is baffling and cunning; sneaky, insidious, and harmful. Eyes wide open and brain fully engaged is the only way we can understand and survive. No matter who spews the discomfort and confusion - an age-old writer or our spouse or daughter in a disease - it is I, who must seek wisdom and sanity for myself.

The life and times of a currently addicted personality are unalterable, try as we may. That is a fact. Their inhibitions are taken by the drug, and their whims or fancies rule their world, or as much as is physically left of them tries. Remember, all people, drunks included, have limited knowledge. Want to know the IQ of an alcoholic? Watch him drunk.

Strangely, and I do mean strangely, those of us around when the throes of a drunk's whims and fancy get active, act accordingly. I want to scream as I write this. I also want to laugh at the ridiculousness of this revelation. We endure, we succumb, we pout, we demonstrate self-will of opposition - all reactions are futile in changing what already is the reality of the impetus of the moment. The concession we are left with, nothing that inevitably happened with the other person was predictable, intended, or nurturing. We have joined the insanity of it all by reacting.

The answer is in the Serenity Prayer. Wish God would jump right to granting me the wisdom so I could know the difference.

Some choose to stay in this distrustful life. Then wonder why they feel insecure, limited and trapped. Ha. Reread those two sentences.

Owing our existence to a spouse, a financial provider, the sole proprietor of income, will warp our very sense of self-worth. Reread that one.

Okay now read this: When the sober for a few hours drunk realizes we are dependent on their activities, they might reject us, as weak and feeble, unable to thrive. Who wants a leech at their side? Who wants a dysfunctional person in their tail wind? Yet there is love. They may have the same problem we have or listen to this, they may feel sorry for you, even want you to step away from their chaos to save yourself.

Now, given the above, who might take the first action? What is the outsider's view on this situation? What if you love both of them?

So go back to the beginning of the second paragraph which states, "owing our existence to a spouse". Do you see anything wrongful about that statement? We may have already put our worship and adoration into the wrong entity - a person on earth we happened to fall in love with. Worship and adoration belong with only one entity. That is where we got mixed up.

We may need to examine what love actually means to us. We have distorted the concept with our needy selves.

Let's say arguing with a drunk (the fight part of fight or flee) has failed us and manipulation and coping aren't working out either.

The parts of the brain responsible for short-term memory, concentration or rational thinking actually go on a hiatus when your focus is on saving yourself from hurt and harm.

If we are toying with the flee part of fight or flee, we have ideals, even plans should the drunk exacerbate his foils into a traumatic experience.

> In possession of phone numbers for a local U-Haul
> Squirreled money or separate account
> Mental directions to the motel on the Interstate where he
> would not look
> A trusted friend to call on top five
> A private list of what we will pack / take

So I gather, you are in possession of some rational calculations - enough to know when insanity doesn't work for you anymore.

For many the above is extremely terrorizing: on your own, where income, companionship, a dinner partner, sex, will be void. The thoughts of a life like that stymy many folks. No, I choose drunk and disorderly conduct of my loved one over a perceived aloneness. Oh, so sick we are. So unwise we are.

For some, the terror and scare lie in the fact that, though the alcoholic knows they are hard to live with, they want to possess routine marriage and devotion. They will come searching and offer the runaway anything. Usually promising anything - impossible things. "I will get drinking under control. I won't hit you anymore. Fill in your blank: _____. Come live in my uncontrollable insanity again and again."

Gosh, I wish I could just tell some women, "You realize you are living devoid of the truth, don't you? A relationship such as you describe is intellectually disabling and robbing both of you of the ability to thrive."

Secrets

What AA, NA, etc. add is the spontaneity of gratitude. So if you want to live in gratitude, you first have to figure out:

Gratitude for what?
Gratitude to who?

That right there is your answer.

With a step system, one evolves into gaining personal assets to be grateful for. With the steps, one realizes that control of life's happenings is not in our possession. Surprise. And that only a higher power knows what is going on, why or when. Ours is no longer to rue the past or fret the future - it is not in our hand of cards. The Dealer, one God, holds the deck. Give it up, or 'Let go and let God' as is often orated.

With the program, we realize we are sans some potential attributes. Perhaps we have given up or give up on acquirable assets. Surprise again! Principles within the program hone us back in on what is rightly obtainable, legal, progressive, and positive in nature. Oh My Gosh, we might find serenity of mind living with those assets.

From Proverbs 10:24-25

When the storms of life come, the wicked are whirled away, but the Godly have a lasting foundation.

Of course, it only follows that perhaps we are holding on to wrongful shortcomings. Moi? The nun who told me to Fear God! My mother's warning that all men wanted one thing. So I designed my looks to attract them to my 'one thing'. The teacher who chastised classmates who were actually from broken or impoverished homes. I promised in junior high to never divorce, hell or high water. My country club 'friends' who had expectations. The clique who had a non-written set of obligations. THESE are some of the contributors to my broken default thinker and my being shipwrecked on land.

So this leads me to talk with you about secrets. WE have deceived ourselves into thinking the values portrayed by others are valuable. So much so, that if a drunken slob lives in our house, we begin to see that as our routine, our only recourse is to now value that lower existence. If I looove them, I will overlook my values, reset my thinking to a lower form.

All our secrets like that and more that are embarrassing behaviors must be looked at. Every lost hope, shame and rejection need to be brought to mind, at the very least, to ourselves, honestly. Sharing them with one other safe person – a counselor, a priest, a sponsor in a program, calling a hot line. Tell them what you need to do and then spill it. We have been so afraid to move forward - because what we consider our 'dirty laundry' is buried deeply, creating a stopgap in our movement to positivity. Heck, I aired mine in this book to thousands. Once we let go of horrors that we have been harboring, we begin to walk in fresh air and find newness in life again. It is like reclaiming our purity of childhood. It is a release like no other.

Deception is now not only allowable, but becomes a practice. We deceive ourselves. We set up pretenses for others. We get good at it. Inveterately, we believe in our own lies.

Meanwhile, we start to think, well if I am this way, so are the multitudes. Judgement and rationalization become part of our vocabulary and core in our thinking. Out of judgement and rationalization come vengefulness, hatred, jealousy, greed. Sickness is overtaking us, sometimes straight into prison or a psychiatric diagnosis. (I believe we are all Borderline Something in the DSM, Diagnostic and Statistical Manual, once referred to as a bloated catalog of what's wrong with people. Tee Hee.)

We are evolving into the Seven Deadly Sins Realm. Well, borderline maybe. AND to top it off, we accept this devious behavior from others. So we stay in sickness, unsatisfied, unhappy, and without peace of mind. Path involving our many malignations is easy. Here ya go:

1. Prelude (your personal history, envines, and who you hang with)
2. Contemplation of addiction, wrong doing, evil
3. Determination and preparation to be one of life's rats
4. Action toward self-demise
5. Maintenance (Manipulation, Money, Actions, Hurt, whatever it takes to stay here)
6. Death and Destruction are your only courses here.

Voila! Your life is condemned. 'The debil has your soul'. You believe you are naughty, bad, big and ugly.

Guess what…

Recovery starts at the bottom. You are in the right place!

The Seven Deadly Sins, just for reference:

1. Pride - A sense of one's own proper dignity or value; self-respect. Arrogant or disdainful conduct or treatment; haughtiness. An excessively high opinion of oneself; conceit. Its spiritual opposite is humility. Seeing ourselves as we are and not comparing ourselves to others is humility.
2. Greed - An excessive desire to acquire or possess more than what one needs or deserves, especially with respect to material wealth.

Its spiritual opposite is generosity. Generosity means letting others get the credit or praise. It is giving without having expectations of the other person.

3. Envy - A feeling of discontent and resentment aroused by and in conjunction with a desire for the possessions or qualities of another. Its spiritual opposite is love. Love actively seeks the good of others for their own sake.

4. Anger or Wrath - A strong feeling of displeasure, hostility or impatience with the faults of others. Its spiritual opposite is kindness or goodwill. Kindness means taking the tender approach, with patience and compassion.

5. Lust - An overwhelming desire or craving, the self-destructive drive for pleasure out of proportion to its worth. This is what we often call "obsession." Its spiritual opposite is self-control or moderation. Self-control and self-misery prevent pleasure from killing the soul by suffocation. Blessed are those that are moderate.

6. Gluttony - Excess in eating, drinking, entertainment and other legitimate goods, and even the company of others. Its spiritual opposites are faith and temperance. Temperance accepts the natural limits of pleasures and preserves natural balance. Faith is trust that all that I need will be supplied.

7. Sloth – a repulsion of work or exertion; laziness; indolence. When we live a life stuck in our Lower Self, our defects of character combine to deaden our spiritual senses. We grow slow to respond to God and eventually drift into a spiritual slumber. Its spiritual opposite is Zeal. Zeal is the energetic response of the heart to God's commands.

Psych vs Psyche

————

So, you know that accumbens and dopamine and lymbics synopt in your brain, of course; well now you do.

Or not.

Let's take a minute to sit quietly and 'try' to synopt only good chemicals through that lymbic system.

Go.

How did that go for you? What I am saying is that some things misfire, some chemicals are not there because of our Ethnic origin! (That's true!) Some chemicals have withered in their function due to our style of living or environment. One client I worked with had been 'raised' (ha!) in a closet. Ten years old! His dopamine will never come to full maturity. Oh my. (Watch the movie "Malcom" if you get a chance.)

So, Substance Abuse Disorders have a good chance in many of us. I don't know when you will read this book, but an available stat from 2014 to 2019, Substance Abuse Disorders have increased 400 percent in those five years.

The tease is available. I won't even talk about marketing's expert tools and subliminal messages. Word of mouth contributes most to this abomination. Ninety percent, 90%, of SA disorders are not treated. Makes you want to watch who you walk next to, doesn't it?

Let me just ask you this: Last headache, did you take the recommended dosage? Have you fudged the time to take a pain med for yourself or anyone else suffering aches and pains? Have you demanded a physician find 'something' to alleviate the suffering?

Hm. We love to feel better. Sometimes at any lengths. Sometimes for our emotional health as well as physical.

My sister-in-law just informed me that she tells her chiropractor to try it again. Gees, I thought when the doctor says "get up from the table" that was ALL you could get for your money this time. I only need to 'ask'?

Hang nearer to the people you admire for their courage, the talents, those who act with courage, who appear without fear regarding any topic or action, step up when challenged with your own questions.

Who told you to suppress your inner self? Who told you that you could not do something? Maybe, if I dare, someone told you that you will not amount to much. Oh. That's why you fail.

Oh, grow up. Others' negative voices in your head do not belong there. This is horrible, I know, but I like to use the word 'abort' in my head. It conjures up such a bloody, sick and wrong, damaging connotation, that it stops my thinker. When I am listening to Grandmother's adage, "Mechanical things are for men." I have to say "abort" and put on my big girl panties and open the hood and check my own oil. I need to detach from my love for grandmother's, at the time, limited conceptions. I cannot live in grandmother's fear. I do romanticize my past presumed traits; however, my memory has some judgement and bias set forth unintentionally. How many times do you live with others' fears? How much do you hold on to outdated fears? Fight fear like the plague.

My now deceased husband used to tell me 'not to use my singing voice with anyone outside the house, not even with him'. Well, just like that, the person I gave the most clout and honor and promises to, just judged me and I suppressed, not just my singing, but my inner song.

Since leaving him, I discovered I have a fair voice. I can sing in church. I have a voice that I can put in a choir. I can enjoy the radio loud and sing at the top of my lungs in the car and participate in carols. I had to 'abort' his message and thrive again.

Thrive again…See, I believe I could diagnose myself with Mild Cognitive Impairment (Don't tell my last therapist.) as I fail to always see clearly what I am doing to myself or others. The switch to tell me when to not speak was turned off. I was a blurter, unaware of what I left in my wake. Many times, the harm was to myself, simply because I was not cognitive of my action and reactions to people.

How many things have you shriveled within you due to others' preachings or opinions and conjectures?

"Don't do that." Have you heard that? How about:

You will never measure up.

You have a disability…You have dyslexia.

Don't go there. You are not qualified.

You will never behave.

You can't do that.

You will never get it right.

You did it wrong. Give it here. I'll fix it.

You will never learn.

Bullying and name calling by uninformed others fall in this list.

Or, perhaps, you were beaten to submission to another's way of thinking, to their opinion about how life should go in their world? Did you hear that? 'Their opinion… their world'? Sometimes it can be a simple fix, just don't pick up the crap they lay down.

"If I am to be insulted, I must first value your opinion!" - Anon

See how the words, 'abort that thought' can work in my head? That was someone else's broken thinker living in my thinker. Sometimes in a thirty-seven-year marriage, you just don't sing. How sad that I did not realize I could make my own decision to sing!

That's introspection. Inspection of your intros.

Above are the things that ring in our heads that others may have put on us. Here are some negative self-talk phrases we subliminally tell ourselves: (I am enumerating them so that you have an idea of the amount of discourse you do to yourself!)

1. Everyone will hate me
2. I will hurt my friends and family
3. I might go crazy or off balance
4. I am gonna be sick and die soon
5. Others might abandon me
6. I can't spell very well
7. I don't have good enough ideas
8. I will upset someone if I say this or that
9. I am going to end up alone with no one to care for me

10. I might find out I am gay or dyslexic or biased
11. I might look like a fool
12. I think all anger is at me
13. I will never have any real money
14. I might not be good at sex
15. I might become an alcoholic
16. My spouse is going to leave me
17. I don't feel I deserve success
18. I am not good enough
19. It's too late for me to improve
20. I'm too tired to do what others can do
21. I've been too promiscuous
22. I was born into an unhappy family
23. I am always going to not have enough
24. I am doomed, I am the one

I would like to counter all those horrible lies we entertain with a quote by Louise Bogan:

"I cannot believe the inscrutable universe turns on an axis of suffering; surely the strange beauty of the world must somewhere rest on pure joy."

Where did you get the gall to decide that you were not enough and deny yourself beauty and joy of the world?

There is a thinker deeper than your thinker that knows you are a miracle of life. Some lack of chemical reactions went sideways for a while and you only need think more of yourself and be true to your whole, beautiful heart and soul to come out of the funky skunky stinking thinking. No one, not even you, can unmake the good in you that God has created.

Seeing within, changes one's outer myopic vision. I am a miracle – I'm just in the process stage.

So, our waves are like neuro behavioral impulses but, in the thoughts of your mind. The frequencies of thought are present at any particular moment, even when we are asleep and we are relaxed. Our brainwaves can be 'stressed' or can be recognized as a daydream, or meditative, or creative.

Our minds focus, create and concentrate on any passing brain wave. That focus dominates our minds and forms a thought. Our attributes and accumulated assets in our brain, such as education, personal stories, our past fears, our intelligence, other people's warnings - ALL of that leads us in our daily doings, our professions, and our hobbies. The buildup of attributes increases our productivity and enhances our life experience. We produce from there, to actions (production). After all, if hunger urges, tiredness felt, and sneezes came when they want, then wouldn't our ESP behaviors be true? Doubtful, especially if they cause hurt or harm.

Then IF we shape our minds with unquenchable learning, I mean knowledgeable, higher thinking self I n t r o s p e c t I o n, can we focus, refocus, on the bliss and happiness, peace or serenity that is grabbable. WE MUST learn to use the higher self. Left alone, our minds tend to have a bias toward negativity.

Some of us work so hard to meditate, not realizing that it is the absence of work that will take us there. Relaxed, or Delta waves can only be realized here. Some psychologists actually suggest fidget-spinners, stress balls or the like.

When you focus on a hobby or your work, there is a predominance of Alpha waves jumping around in your brain to energize and enhance your experience. You can even experience them when daydreaming. Delta waves operate when you are in a deep sleep or state of unconsciousness. Deep meditation is true bliss, full relaxation. Beta waves are you at normal, paying attention to the world.

The coolest part is that these generate electrical impulses (state of mind) which can be seen measured now through colors pulsing on an electroencephalogram.

That means, falling asleep on your problems may create nightmares and insomnia. Rather, you want to find your restorative Delta waves wafting in.

It is a state of absence of thought.

Humble Pie

Do you believe that your Mom and Dad gave you true humility and unconditional love and perfect justice? No one of this earth has achieved this; but I would like to think many parents excelled in these. Divine love? True agaping humility? Again and again, we shall need to return to that unflattering point of departure from our rote – humility.

Try unconditional positive regard. This human tendency keeps us from negativity and undesirable behaviors. Mothers and Fathers model as best they can for us to learn understanding and acceptance. Children are vulnerable and willing. Exposure to appropriateness or lack of causes permanent confusion. The ability to know embarrassment, shame, and humility have a healthy side. Once confident with self-esteem, the theories say we can grow. These challenges keep us curious and involved, allow opportunities to learn from experience. See, the practices of parents are very important in modeling. These development phases allow a sense of self.

My friend was taking a medicine that when she had to go, she HAD to pee. Three other friends and I stood watching her find her way to the, not-labelled-restrooms. She actually crossed her legs, turned to us and put her hands up. From where we were, we could see the huge RESTROOM sign high above her head, but the doorway could as well have been the kitchen, no label down near the door. She completely peed through her panties and down her legs into her shoes (the medicine, remember). We laughed ourselves silly. Not really because of what happened to our friend, but what could have been anyone. Underneath our feigned indifference, is the truth of what just happened. No choice for her but to pee right there. Her possibility of making it to the restroom was lost. She was humiliated, but not so much so that she couldn't clean it up herself, wash her and her undies in the bathroom when she finally saw the restroom door, and came out laughing harder than we. Picture this: Huge restroom sign and 48-year-old woman peeing in front of the door. She had a sense of self. She wore her humiliation like a truth. She accepted what had happened and what was left to do that day – spend the day with four friends who would begin to giggle every time one would think of it. A sense of self and humility even in the face of unflattering personal embarrassment. Find your peace of mind, in spite of yourself.

Example: You receive a compliment. You think, 'I did do/say/wear that well.' Ego has stepped up. I have had some practice, I am now at a place where I KNOW the point of that comment is that another person has qualities of friendship, kindness, respect for others, and appreciates people. That is where the good has occurred – in the words coming from the other person. I can bluster inside with good kudos raining down all over my heart, but my head must not swell. Instead, I realize the goodness of the complimentor.

Because children see fantasy and magic, they believe that everyone else is here for them. And when something goes awry in a child's life, the child screams and then sometimes gets the blame for screaming. Even for abuse and punishment given to them. They are, after all, the center of their world. This can actually get locked into, and stay in an older person's thinking! These sorts generally begin to hide their bad behaviors or lie. Their shame-based life is ineffectual for them. Validation by a cherishing mother and father and approval within their worlds can make or break an upcoming teen and adult. Few people come close to that perfect blend needed to nourish perfect children. Thus, they end up craving approval and crying to get their way.

I believe that only God has that sort of grace and acceptance. Thank goodness He is there. People on earth will always be in the human maturation process.

Sorry Mom, Dad, Grandma, Teachers, Nuns, etc. in my life.

By age 5, I was sure I had collected enough sins to give up on seeing St. Peter at the Gate. Fear of the wrath of God was instilled.

THAT took a lot to get over. I don't think I fully recovered until my forties. Seriously.

Not that I was punished a lot. I wasn't. I didn't need to be because my mind was full of shame. Good enough punishment. Shame was built into my childhood development. Whoa! Ergo, I lived in fear. I was headed to the fires of Hell, damnation, and tormented with those beliefs for YEARS! Any authority figure, dictator, our presidents, priests - all of those smarter, bigger, stronger, than me were better than I. I on the other hand was reduced to a pawn struggling along until I die and go straight on down, no purgatory vacation. My mind attenuated all that was good which I had done. Furthermore, I continued to add to my list of wrong-doings, I was gonna see the fires sooner and hotter or something. All because I took candy from my brother's shelf and snake twisted my sister's arm, oh, and lied about whether I 'did it' or not to my mom.

So I gave up my control to an authoritarian, good bad, or ugly. That made me an even greater victim. I looked for friends that were in the same boat. I joined grade B activities, never going to be the winner, the one to lead. I was condemned and guilty and full of shame.

Actually, one of my mother's favorite cuss-outs included, "Shame on you!"

Being the baby of eight kids didn't help. I never had a decision to make on my behalf: I ate what was left, sat on anyone's lap, never earning my own chair, took the hand-me-downs and liked it, and lived and failed under the expectations that my elders held. My voice was the last and least mature. Even just being little was my downfall. Everyone knew what was prognostically right for me, not me.

I was denied creativity, imagination, freedom to choose, desires, and feelings.

Who did that leave? I interpreted everything as 'happening to me', and lacked initiative, individuality. I was numb or naïve to normal.

Therefore, I expected God or maybe a husband, sister, others to rescue me and tell me what to do. My expectations of myself were very limited. I knew I had to be as good as I knew how, to earn a spot (house, wifehood, sibling status) in life. I learned to pretend. I learned to please everyone else, not myself. I learned to avoid turmoil. I learned to demand my needs. I learned to repute self-worth with arrogance and judgement.

Most of that is pretty ugly in a human being. There was too much to risk if I didn't bow down and obey or please others.

Bordering on overuse of medications and alcohol, I subjugated myself to self-justifying, lying, grief ridden, and infallibly EGOTISTICALLY selfish.

True friends had to like my inadequacies to even get close to me. I feared so that my shame and guilt and hell-bent ways were going to be headlines in the local paper. Believe you me, I towed the line as close as I could with covert and passive actions to everyone else's likes.

Rooted, wouldn't you say? Try overcoming that as an adult.

These are not laws; they are sins.

Sins against:

> Works of the flesh
> Immorality
> Impurity
> Lust
> Idolatry
> Sorcery
> Hatred
> Rivalry
> Jealousy
> Fury
> Selfishness
> Dissension
> Envy
> Drinking alcohol
> Orgies

These are choices of the human spirit.

Do you live in that list somewhat?   All the time?   Occasionally?

These are choices of the human spirit also:

> Love
> Joy
> Peace
> Patience
> Kindness
> Generosity
> Gentleness
> Faithfulness
> Self-Control

Wow. What if you expected God and his works in your every moment? Who said you can't?

Slow down your busy-ness. Lean into the wind. Feel your heartbeat. Use a gift of breath. Look for God's hand. Listen. Feel stillness. Ask for grace. Ask through prayer.

Or drudge through life.

Choice.

My resistance was more of a problem than the situation. 'Poor me.' came easier in my mind's discourse.

Today I start my recovery from that. I choose serene. I choose to become myself. Become a real person, not the object of Society. To learn a new process for living. Get my brain working correctly.

Your day goes the way the corners of your mouth turn.

Can we accurately judge people or situations by only the little that we know? But do we? Oh ya.

Here's a thought: Simon Baron-Cohen, psychologist long involved in autism research, touts that women and men have a brain type: Women are more geared toward empathizing and demonstrating greater sympathy and sensitivity toward others; and male brains tend more toward building and understanding systems and structures, and organizing things. Further, he states that seventeen percent of men have an empathizing brain and seventeen percent of women have a systemizing brain.

I want to tell you that in my personal analysis, men more strongly desire positive results through adopting my approaches; and have greater insight into understanding and interacting with people. It seems that personality cognition and changes seem easier to grasp for male brains.

Above are two judgements rationalized by data. Do I have a right to say that I will change your life? No, I can only state my experience of good and bad, strength by gaining wisdom and knowledge and practice, and lastly, my hope for all of us!

Choice

Ancestrally, family is second after God creating Man. We know it. It is a bit of Philosophy 101.

We choose to follow the rules, laws, and commandments set before us or not. We take oaths, we take wedding vows, put names on birth certificates, have a governmental straw man, and have a Social Security Number. Then maybe, we add living in the home of someone with disease or addiction. Maybe we were forced to forgo other possible choices. We believe our tie to 'them' is somewhat by law. Weeelll, not so true. If your story were someone else's, how long could you listen without shouting 'Enough!' – Something has to change for the betterment of all here. To become suicidal and insane due to our own promises to a diseased/alcoholic spouse, parent, caregiver, friend, house mother, etc. will take us down with them. I know, I begged my alcohol stupored husband to kill me first. That, that was carrying a vow, oath, promise too far. See it?

Did you know you can push an alcoholic with your own behaviors? You can push them too far with demands to change. You can love them so much they lose track of you as a separate human being and kill you as well as themselves. Your expectations and chastising words can make them hate themselves more.

Your story will evolve and unfold in its own way. I only hope that my experiences elicit from you thoughtfulness.

We had this idea that we could have a *grand* past, then we get to an age where we discover it wasn't and I am still in it. We kind of lived to change the future and would rationalize copingly that 'this is fine', denying our possibilities. My greatest fear was that I would never be happy again. Instead, I felt that the debilitating anguish was my next way of life.

Here are some great coping skills if you like to live in just 'cope':

) Nights of wondering where he/she is
) Fear of car/plane/motorcycle accidents
) Imagining a lifeless body on a gurney
) Homicides
) Abandonment
) Constant worry
) Trying again to rationalize with an altered mind
) Trying to add reason to 'their' lives
) All the other thoughts we make up in our heads
) The untruthful worries that will never happen
) False beliefs run amok
) Talking to God only when we want something
) Fill in your fear here

All of the above is not a well lived life. I had created false beliefs. I had given up the calmness that could have greeted the child, the drunk, or the mental health in normal circumstances, issued to a loved one at the door.

Alcohol took over my control as well as the drinker's. It is self-contained and all powerful. It is irrational and insane but holds onto the victimness till treatment, hospitalization, prison or death occurs. That is our neo truth, self-created.

Being falsely trained to deal with alcoholism, to shrink and succumb, we bumbled along till another alcoholic rigidity of false laws/demands gave us a structure to lean on – be it a house made of straw (mortgage) full of platitudes, pity, self-denigration, and unreasonable reasoning.

Disease or addiction are stronger than my self-determination. It has no limits than to win. It will take down a seventeen-year-old student as easily as a sixty-year-old CEO. It radiates to all those near, first as fun, then hellfire. Learned codependents easily succumb, because they used to love the person who evolved into the alcoholic. Addictive personalities easily succumb to the disease. Persuasion often wins. Children get abused. You cannot change the path of disease or addiction. That is up to the person with the issue. You cannot change its past.

I would like to offer a list of Addictive Personality traits. This can be used for addiction to gambling, drugs, food, alcohol, and as codependents.

o   Primarily focuses on the addiction, prominence of object/person
o   Object/person absorbs almost all attention available
o   Dismisses other sensations
o   Sets up a predictability – when and how
o   Seems to reliably be available
o   Gives very temporary release to stressors
o   Exacerbates life's problems
o   Decreases functionality / Self-destructive
o   Dissolves friendships
o   Can use up all money
o   Can use up all time
o   Gives false sense of power and control over nothing of value
o   Gives false sense of security to the addictive person
o   Is an artificial crutch of self-worth
o   Gives a sense of intimate ownership

For Your Penance, Say Three Our Fathers...

"I was wrong." Say it out loud with me: "I was wrong." There is kind of a fizz happening in my throat and jowl right now, my brain immediately puts up a fearful question mark, and my mouth gets momentarily dry. It seems like it is hard to spit out in audible syllables. "I was wrong." Just three words. If I hear someone else say it, I have a similar bodily reaction happening empathetically.

"I was wrong." It is emotional to admit: I deviated from my own principles. I told an untruth or stretched the truth. I acted or reacted poorly. I shirked my responsibility. I have to own up to something done in a poor manner. I have to say to someone else that my head didn't opt correctly, most likely with full knowledge and intent. What I did affected you in a negative manner. I was wrong. I apologize. - All require emotional embodiment.

No justifications. No rationalization. I apologize. I was wrong. I have learned the error of my way.

It is critical if we have put down or harassed someone, that we amend for the verbiage. Tell them you want to make an amend and apologize for your words. Ask for forgiveness. Ask. (Accept that there may never be an answer.) And promise that you will be more caring toward them. It is simple. The heavy ball goes to their court.

Perhaps the other - against whom you have made the blunder - can forgive and say so. But neither of us likely forgets the moment of the negative act I performed. A black mark has been made. I condemn myself for it, and then, on top of that, I rebuke myself on the fact that I have also hurt you in my action, non-action, or reaction. And then, I can spank my lack of intelligence, feel stupid, detest being embarrassed, and condemn my ego. See the cycle? If not amended for, I continue suffering inside.

The fact that I get to apologize to you, though, has great power. I get to admit, instead of beating myself up in the covert activity, I honestly know and furthermore, in essence tell you - I am not perfect - I slip - my mouth speaks before my head thinks - I react instead of thinking. Instead of internal, forever-to-live-with self-condemnation, I told you, "I am sorry for my mistake." I spoke also to myself. There, there was an error. A mistake. I have retracted as best I can, I have made amends, and I am paying it forward in a better version. I learned and will not harm in this manner again. I might need to tell you some of those things, too.

The most important letter in a p o l o g I z e is the 'I' part. I apologize.

Mis·take by the dictionary, calls it an error in action, calculation, opinion, or judgment caused by poor reasoning, carelessness, insufficient knowledge.

While a fact, I cannot rationalize, blame or justify away the error. I ascribed to that negative decision, when I carried out the offending act. Referencing that definition may be playing a victim of an alter ego, whom we all know is still 'me'. "It was careless thinking." or "My judgment caused poor reasoning." as Webster suggests. My least favorite is, "The committee in my head must have made that decision."

Never use these statements again:

"I couldn't help myself."
"S/He made me do it."

"I didn't know."

"But if I…"

"Well, I just wanted to say…"

"All I was saying is…"

"All I wanted to tell you was…""

"It's just that…"

These are also selfish and involve blaming, getting me-off-the-hook statements that resemble excuses. And reiterate what I believed. Using these statements is 'not listening'. I used them as caution tape, excusing me from having to do what is ordered or necessary. Hang up the phone, People. Your boss just stopped listening when he heard you begin the excuse.

If the intent is not only to quit making mistakes that you must apologize for, but to change your algorithms so as not to be in this maelstrom again, one must grow conscious balls. You may have sung along to, "Change Our Hearts, Lord". The level of skyward I feel in those words is far from my usual hauteur selfishness, pride, and neediness. I sing that one loudly.

Yes, I said balls. Many of us must truncate the thinking we now do, in exchange for new higher thinking. It is a conscious action to break from lazy. Your automatic recall is not working properly. One is never too old to continue to grow up.

To develop from the uncivilized errors of your way, requires a great deal more than one thinks. Normally, I hang on to just a snippet of justification. "Well, if he hadn't been listening, I wouldn't have hurt his feelings. "Ha! LOFL (You all know what LOL is, so just add the idiom.) My Self-Righteousness and Ego walk into every room I enter and leave with me. They are hard to break down. A civilized man or woman knows, or learns how to leave them at home. Let's learn.

Only after I become cognizant of the Egoist Thoughts that travel with me, am I able to put my ego and self-righteousness on a shelf. When they speak, I almost always make a mistake! A minister friend recently suggested that every time I think about myself, try thinking about God tenfold, as my mind is so prone to wander. As it is, I fall short every time I try to fix somebody's else's situation. Their preservation is up to God. And consequentially, their relationship with Him is up to them, not me by force.

Atonement. Forgiveness collapses time.

Did you ever run into a dear old friend, one whom you had had a slight disagreement and then never healed but had to go on with your lives? The friend whom you held in esteem but somehow, lost track of in time and there he or she was, with that dynamic smile that moved your soul. You forget the disagreement or what it was and you embrace what goodness you had shared.

I was blustering about being harmed. A wise friend asked, "Who is carrying dis-ease because of a resentment?" "Well, me!" I replied. The questions continued, "Who is carrying the hurt? Who feels pain around this? Who is developing a resentment? Whose shoulders is all this grief on? Who has angst and want revenge or to penalize someone? Whose blood pressure may go up?" All, in my head only. This is a tough one; walk away, let go and let God, look to your inner peace. Do you like to carry inner resentment or bitterness? It is like we are pouring acid on ourselves. Forgive them. How did I get so self-righteous and powerful that revenge and punishment is mine to deal out? Exercise, rather compassion and empathy. Pray for the person. Forgiveness of others is actually a gift to me in that, I quit suffering from their slur. The warmth of the sun changes all things.

Think of someone you hold a resentment against. Resentment and the word 'against' are so unhealthy. Why entertain either in your head? You have made yourself the long term victim by carrying the revenge. Good morning! That is not healthy. Again, who has an altered attitude and negative thinking still ongoing? Realize that it does you no good and it comes to no good.

Value love. Never stomp on it.

Make Every Day One Percent Better – Optimize Start with: 'Get Out of Bed!'

'Acceptance of things we cannot change' is so hard. First, we must discern that things are out of our hula hoop and leave them alone when they do not have our name on them.

Move along, as we cannot change our past, for instance. Mourn it, if we must, but rehearsing the awful things that have happened to us over and over is ridiculous. Pain and confusion are a part of life. Difficulties are a part of life and the road to betterment may be circuitous. Move on and keep moving. We can pause, pray, and proceed. That's it then. Is there something you have not allowed yourself to bring forth or grieve or forgive? It is suggested in Al-Anon, you give it one last thinking session, examine it from the point of view that YOU had a part in the experience, and then give it up. Give it to God, write it in a note to put in the refrigerator freezing compartment, or whatever you need to do, but DO NOT stay stuck on a happening of another time. It is not today's reality.

Do you have resentments left over from the past? That, right there, is poisoning your own thinking stream. Your brain is the one focusing perversely on enmity and revenge, no one else is wasting their precious brain cells on your doings; why are you? CHOOSE to accept your sadnesses and mishaps and embrace today's moment. Our healing is based on this.

Who wants to think in terms of overwhelming fear, obsessiveness? Pitiful, paralyzed, worriful, incapacitated, like we are losing, fretful anticipation, anxiety? All those are useless to good health. I can easily say now that I don't go there often, but all these thoughts and feelings are huge and can make us insane – they did me. We choose to adapt those into our thoughts or not. Choose. Advice was given to me and I will pass it on…Take a moment and walk through the sensation of fear, fret, etc. Then be done with it. Start today over again any minute of it. Look for solution for yourself. Afterall, you are the only one you are in control of. You are on your own. Mama is not here. God has your back and will create a new tomorrow for you. It is up to me how I handle my choices. It might surprise you but one of the first people that you make amends to in the program is yourself.

Does your ego lead you? You know there is a Power Greater than you, don't you? Even if it is just mother nature. How fervently you see yourself and act in those manners will ruin you.

Dear Jean,

I am now changing how I think. I have new insights and have stopped judging and rationalizing life away. I am so sorry for keeping you inept, shy, and acting as a victim.

I now see the errors in your actions and physical behaviors, especially in relationships. I apologize for losing friends for you, yelling, and swearing and acting in a manipulative manner. Those lies I told yourself about things and actions and feelings are much clearer now and I vow to not do them again. I am so sorry that I sucked you into them and hurt your heart, along with some other people you wanted to be friends with, and show love to.

My promise now is to clear my head to open it for more prayer and positive thinking, in all that I do.

Love, Jean

There is freedom when we stop controlling others. The first experience I had with letting someone else fail, even though in my opinion, I could have said for them to think differently, I let them learn their own lesson. Sometimes, they fall flat – but, by golly, they learned. That last sentence is to be used only for good. Some folks are so stuck and opinioned, (I know because I was one of those for years.) that there is no talking to them of different measures. See, the thing is, I cannot control what others do or their outcomes beyond offering safety and security for them. There is a freedom in our heads when we do not interfere and let life's lessons happen for others. Grant others the dignity to learn freely.

Write those whom you have interfered with or manipulated or lied to their own letter. Write it. What you do with it after is up to you. Begin with your commitment to be a different person, an apology for specific actions or words you have done, no generalizations or excuse making in this letter, and end with a promise not to do those kinds of behaviors again.

My husband needed a letter from me. He died before I knew how to write it. I realized I could separate the person I had loved from the monster of a disease that was acting within him, too late. I still wrote it and put it in a garbage can at the cemetery. The action of mailing it, calling someone to amend in person, etc., strengthens our commitment to ourselves to be the better version of ourselves in all our affairs.

You can love an active alcoholic only so far. When their actions are killing them, we cannot die with them. Our strange kind of love in that headset is also killing us. I tried over and over to soften the 'bottom' that my alcoholic was headed into. His psychiatrist had said, he is killing his brain cells, many tranceptors are dead, at the last appointment. He advised my husband to quit adding alcohol to depression. It did no good.

Substance abuse is powerful and cunning.

Check in with Yourself

Ask yourself tonight:

"How did I love today?"

Live only to progress in love and knowledge.

Let go and let God…give it up…give it up…That's right, now let go… ease out of it…things are not all under your control…go on, now, give…it…up. There, there, that's better.

Why wouldn't it be okay?

How important is it anyway?

Try these words when someone hurts/talks naughty to you: "You don't get to say that."

Is it within YOUR hula-hoop? Is it theirs, not yours?

Pray about it/him/her for seven days in a row.

Have you seen the cloud formations today?

Watch for lavender in the sky…it will be time to pray.

10 Minutes…that's all He asks of your day…ten minutes of prayer… beat the average!

This too shall pass. Tomorrow, will this matter? Next week/year will this same thing be a big deal? Will it be a deal at all?

God called. He wanted to see if you are okay. Call him back when you get a minute, will you?

Where Did You Go On Your Last Mental Vacation?

I come just as I am. It took me a long time to belong here in that manner. I was ashamed, belittled, demoted, self-condemning, etc. until I had help (Al Anon) to take a look at what had become. Once I was cognizant that I embodied all that I had been exposed to and exposed myself to, before now, I realized there could be some changes, some headway to belong anywhere I was. I now have a right to be. To be next to you. To be the leader. To be a follower. To sit, stand, stoop, roller skate or pray anywhere I am.

I belong.

A list of some traits to being a good person living well among others:

1. Be active
2. Be on time
3. Occasionally, volunteer
4. Wait well with patience
5. Help others, anyone, anywhere if you can
6. Offer only truths
7. Offer only facts
8. Improve something everyday
9. Focus on current moment
10. Accept others where they are
11. Read

12. Do not interrupt
13. Show interest in others
14. Accept all points of view
15. Create boundaries to negativity
16. Compel, urge and show strength of righteousness duties
17. No gossip or criticism crosses your lips
18. Support others in word and deed
19. Focus on solutions, not problems
20. End worrying
21. Do not give advice unless sought
22. Share well with others
23. Seek virtue
24. Do what is honorable
25. Live with grace
26. Do your responsibilities

At Purgatory's Door

I was halfway through my Twelve Steps when I had a wild dream of trying to get to my mother's home again and attempting to organize parts of my life in to perfect containment so I could call on and lean on each facet if I needed it again. I was on a track with boots attached that led me in a perfect direction but all my thoughts kept pulling me off to the side to take care of one more thing, and box it up. Mom told me that being at home was not going to do me any good and to not come back home. The track took off in to blue sky in the end and it was a glorious place.

This dream seemed a milestone in my changes. It was amazing that this dream came on the end of many, many, many dreams of trying to organize my friends and possessions and events into rooms, crates, drawers. train cars, boxes, and bags. Two full years of organizing my former relations into where they could now be in my second chapter of life. I had a new life of discovery and truth and this dream proved that I was transitioning from those old beliefs and old thinking, mother's outdated advice, nun's chastisement, my husband's belittlement – I had to 'walk through' the discernment of what would do me good and what had taken my psyche 'down'. It is like 'Whack-a-Mole" to take down your old emotional system.

It was cleansing. I hope that your dreams allow you to find patterns of thinking that no longer do you any good. We have to learn whether to stay in old logic or find our way in today's reality. There is only one choice there. It was so cathartic. I hope that you are bothered by your dreams during your transitionary period so that you too, can realize change is inevitable.

Take the trip! I was about to accept the old as times passed, and go forward, appreciating each new moment; and I had affirmation from above.

Logically, I knew I had to detach from old decisions I made about who, when, and where. My life is now mine to make better choices. No headgear or tracks will guide it except the goodness I put there NOW. I can concentrate my energy. It was a relief to let go and know I am a child of God. It is a release when you give back to God what is only His matter. The freakish control I had tried to have was so silly. My time and serenity are too precious to waste living in the future or lamenting about past pain and poor choices.

Wouldn't You Like to Have Caller IQ?

Your brain has so much power. Are you using much of it? Are you listening? What are you hearing? Are you reading at the same time? Are you seeing while doing both? Are you engaging touch? I am a Type A, plus I am creating. Meanwhile I am engaging tactile function. The processes all work together. Aren't we a fantastically powered machine?

We believe we love with our hearts. That's a cool concept and it makes for a wonderful Valentine's Day as an icon. I know that the brain is actually the first organ securely enlisted in love. So much responsibility of our bodies relies on the brain's power. (Eat your Wheaties.) Those three pounds of organ inaugurate abundant and profuse duties of our psyche and actions: loving, creating, behaving, learning, activities, strategizing, awareness, the list goes on.

I want to goad your compassion next.

Those prefrontal lobes: the cortex, involve forethought, judgment, planning, impulse, empathy, sympathy, focus, and awareness of mistakes. Daniel G. Amen, M.D., author of <u>Change Your Brain Change Your Life,</u> calls that part the executive branch.

If you have encountered someone with brain damage ever, I want you to reread that last paragraph. My mother's glioblastoma affected all those.

Think about a person you know functioning without those roles active. You may see or experience:

Hyperactivity	Procrastination	Short Attention	Disorganization
Misperceptions	Poor Judgement	Short Term Memory	
Anxiety	Inability to Access Emotion	Decrease in thinking speed	
Traffic violations!	Not listening	Careless mistakes	

Just under the executive branch sit the cerebral cortex or emotion and limbic systems. Expressing love would be impossible with damage or lack of ability to use this cortex. If you have been around in the clinical/medical world at all, I would guess you viewed or experienced someone unable to engage with emotion. Sad to see, but also impossible for the person to rally parts which do not work. Can you imagine one day without loving, without amplitudes of love, even simple bonding? Sexuality? Motivation? Snuggles? Pleasure? I shiver at the thought.

This is all so complex and in ninety percent of us, runs smoothly from one cortex to the next to form each and every movement or thought. If you think the devil made you do it, perhaps you really need to revisit who is responsible. And believe me I had feared being responsible for my own life. A consequence was that I let emotions boss me around.

Again, not being a doctor or scientist, but to affirm that notion, let me just name more of the capabilities and functions that; if you are normal, YOU ARE IN CONTROL OF. Providing of course, that you have lots of knowledge base which you added to the cortexes to base decisions and movements on.

Intuition	Analytical Processing	Deductive Reasoning
Motor Skills	Language	Hunches
Safety	Logic	Motor Use
Coordination	Dancing	Logical Use of Experience

All of this happens in a quick instance, a sudden twinkle. So, when someone insults you and asks if all the lights are on, it is that twinkle. And you want to hope you have fed and nourished the brain. On top of that, we add our strength, dignity and serenity. I don't even want to think about mind altering substances people purposefully take in to that beautiful and pure system! I love minutes where I am so involved my ephemeral passion for the moment muddles time and I just stay – for me, I pause at art work, children playing, nature.

So the brain's creation of love needs nurture.

You are so lucky! You live in an age where nutrition experts and scientists suggest to us a need for supplemental and readily at hand, vitamins and exercise and such. Your three pound, one hundred billion cell brain uses 30% of the calories you eat and drink. What are you feeding it? Twenty percent of your blood flow is used by the brain. Are you keeping your arteries clean? Are you breathing fully? Sleep apnea can damage your brain. Why on earth would you purposely take risks with this clever organ? I have had two brain concussions. Now I tell you, huh? I did not have damage, but they created swelling and pressure on some lobes for a year! I was slow witted, dull in thinking, said things wrong, lost some word finding. Those are only the errors I was aware of. Deprivation of air, and optimal space, or scary and traumatic events automatically rob the brain of correct metabolic status. Here's one recommendation for instance: People in Montana need Vitamin D. There are eighty-five thousand neurons sluffing off each day, please contribute to the replenishment with loving relationships and nutrition.

In medical terms, from Author Peter Strick, "...The Cerebral cortex influences stomach function – those parts of the brain are associated with emotional control (love) and mental activity and create an environment for helicobacter pylori. Neurons in the cerebral cortex contribute to harbor bacteria in the gastrointestinal system." It is well known that inflammatory bowel syndrome and dyspepsia are related to stress. There is much more in precursor GI episodes than we know.

Boosts are out there. Learn new things constantly (a language, travel). Eat more nutritional foods, such as smart carbohydrates. Take time to meditate and be quiet with nature. Practice an exercise that involves balance and coordination (dancing works). Give love truly and learn to accept love however given your way. Engage in healthy ways with healthy people. Laugh more. B6, B12, as well as Vitamin D have proven results in brain power.

All this will enlarge and support your capacity to give love.

Check out this chart made by Emotional Coder, Marsha Greene, Sonora, and Nan Potts, who find major health issues which emotion contributes to:

	Column A – Conscious	Column B – Unconscious Mind
Heart and Small Intestine	Abandonment . Betrayal Forlorn Lost Love Unreceived	Heartache Insecurity Overjoy Vulnerability Efforts Unreceived
Spleen or Stomach	Anxiety Despair Disgust Nervousness Worry	Failure Helplessness Hopelessness Lack of Control Low Self-Esteem
Lung or Colon	Crying Discouragement Rejection Sadness Sorrow	Confusion Defensiveness Grief Self-Abuse Stubbornness
Liver or Gall Bladder	Anger Bitterness Guilt Hatred Resentment	Depression Frustration Indecisiveness Panic Taken for Granted

Kidneys or Bladder	Blaming	Conflict
	Dread	Creative Insecurity
	Fear	Terror
	Horror	Unsupported
	Peeved	Wishy Washy
Glands and Sexual Organs	Humiliation	Pride
	Jealousy	Shame
	Longing	Shock
	Lust	Unworthy
	Overwhelm	Worthless

Did you know that a person with an untreated hearing loss loses an additional 1.2 cubic centimeters (size of a sugar cube) of brain tissue every year?

As well as talking about boosts, let me spend a minute on how you are damaging that greatest of all organs:

(Why would we damage the executive programmer of all of our life?)

Sugar and sweeteners
Exposure to plant and animal pesticides
Living in stress
Lack of bodily movement
Lack of exercise
Exposure to bad people

Obesity
Smog and environmental toxins
Use of drugs – all kinds
Follow doc's orders
Ignoring health issues even slight blood pressure
Processed Foods

Being abused
Use of alcohol
Sports that have common brain damage causes
Listening to chronic negativity
Thinking chronically negative!
Aging

People Who Hurt Us

Often the perpetrator of pain (I call them POP's because they POP up every day in our lives.), has no idea they affect us. Huh. The curmudgeon grouch of a clerk has no intention to throw your change in your hand or be lax in her assistance to your inquiry. She has plans for tonight, doesn't want to be late, and has a flat on her car in the snow-covered parking lot. IT WAS NOT YOU.

Now take this scenario to your home or church or meeting or next engagement. We all come from. Alice comes from a home with a suicidal father. George makes $12.00 an hour and has $200,000 in bills looming. Serious depression keeps Laura from her job way too often. Susie has been told there will be no Santa gifts this year. Mary has severe cramps seven days a month! Owen is healing from an arm break by his father's abuse. Three generations of the Jonses have been in jail repeatedly. Melody lives in a drafty house, sick all the time. Pam is on disability, and too blind to work. Shanae is afraid her husband is an alcoholic, gambler, addict. The horrible life list goes on and on.

We hang out among these folks every day. Their walks of life are currently full of struggle. Sometimes it is me. It is my struggle, disease, discomfort, etc. that drives me into necessary interactions with others. The only provenance, the only history, the only upbringing, the only exposures I have had, the only teachings I know are now my provenance – and I NOW believe all of that provenance is my truth. What if I was abused, what if I lived with a lying and betraying father, what if my teachers were

407

all coaches and cared little about what I absorbed academically, what if I was not exposed to religion, what if I did not have proper nutrition, what if my group of friends were thieves and graffiti damage doers? My truths and practicalities, my provenance as I know it and believe it, would be so skewed and I would definitely not be one of the world's honorifics. Could have been that way. And there are many folks with that kind of exposures, and we, we, take the right to have expectations that they 'know better'. THEY DON'T. Yet we contextualize their character, based on ours. You base my character on your provenance of life as you know it, so far. We might all be wrong.

Harm and hurt happen. Even ministers and priests do not escape that truth. Intentional. Some unintentional. Real, just the same.

What is your choice when in the midst of uncomfortability?

The attitude you carry is your choice.

The persona you signify and claim is your choice.

The harm you do along your way is your choice.

Yes, it is.

Yes, it is.

Yes, it is. See how our complete make up relies on limits on incoming knowledge and outgoing attitude?

A stimulus happened. YOU chose to REACT, not respond in a more pleasant manner. You chose.

Unless taught or mentored otherwise, you become the insular curmudgeon grouch, affecting people, perhaps infecting people with the Grumpy Cat virus, unknowingly.

Know who you are. Acknowledge reality only. Visiting the web site of grumpy, emotional reactions, or unpleasantness is sick. Choose. Choose the next RIGHT thing in every interaction. No excuses. No rationalizing. I will testify about a person very close to me who reads every political slant posted and I noticed that their factions and extremist attitudes are much more pronounced in any conversation. My nephews who are hooked on gaming, talk about almost everything they do as correlated to competition and shooting to win.

Their lives center on what they have chosen to pay attention and time to. Without a well rounding of input, they will be incomplete in relationships and thinking. Yet, they may insist that what they know is the only way to think and do in life.

I did not know what rationalizing meant when people dropped the bomb on me – "You are making an excuse for all your own behaviors". I was so busy in my reactionary emotion; I didn't get it. I was caught in dumb. I kept on going, obstinately stubborn and mad, even manipulating and fibbing to hold my ground. You know what I mean. You are not impervious to it. My egotistical and sapient pride wants to be right, no matter what. That is the kicker, holding on to pride, no matter what.

Lying, stealing, cheating, lusting, denying, envying, greedily taking, are never peaceful. Yet one half the population lives in a conniving manner of one of them. Gees. No wonder we get hurt and know how to loathe, hold a grudge, be vengeful, scheme against, and hurt back! The scam artists are permeating every facet of life and it puts us on the defense much of the time. These marketing and scamming slants are making us into a more fearful and untrusting society at a time we need to promote niceness! 'They' is creating a cultural problem.

I want to spend a couple of paragraphs on mental illness within our home or arena of daily functioning. We may view these afflictions as frightening or threatening. We often feel stigmatized. I am not qualified to elucidate about deficiencies or why they occur or birth disorders, etc. I suggest each of us research the illness near us to best know how our activities aid or help. Just a fact I want to include here: Did you know that women are more prone to develop Alzheimer's disease and men more so to Parkinson's? Know their limits as well as you know yours, and by all means, report to authorities when boundaries have been broken and harm is being done on either party. Thank you.

Appropriate impunitive boundaries do not control, attack, or hurt anyone; they only prevent that.

People who hurt us have their own opinion of us. Maybe they saw us jump ahead of them in line 10 years ago. They formed their opinion. We CANNOT change their thinking about that incident that hurt them. So, they are now unkind to us for no reason, we think. Or we might think, she was rude because she is disappointed in me. We could escalate this issue with more rudeness and and, and... Plus, some people's characteristics are like sandpaper. Let it go. Some people are incapable of forgetting former hurts and losses. Let go and let live. Why waste precious brain power and time on something that just doesn't matter. Accept her as she is. We cannot reshape the past. Her fear may be about me being rude first! Those are her feelings to own. My serenity is more important than this ludicrous thought game. Why let it take up time in that beautiful serene and Godful mind? We don't have to like the situation, but we need to embrace the moment we are in and like ourselves in the situations.

It is rare that we know exactly what is on someone else's mind. I have been miscommunicated with and felt someone was rude to me, though they had unearned that adjective. My lens needed full rotation.

I lacked compassion and made false judgements in many cases. I projected my unconscious thoughts onto their being. I selected who I wanted them to be in my mind, and then believed myself. LOL

Here's some truths I now process quickly through my mind when faced with the appearance 'that someone does not like me"

Perhaps they:

> Have recently suffered a break up
> Are on the first day back after a funeral and loss
> Are processing after occurrence of a trauma or great hurt
> Perhaps they are ill; or dealing with a close friend or family who is
> Have family commitments right now
> Need to find a calmness, instead of facing others
> Have financial difficulties
> Are overwhelmed with tasks or work or a deadline
> Are facing a life change
> Are tired
> Need to set up a boundary with you

Or any million other reasons. I no longer assume that I made them mad.

Sometimes folks unconsciously or consciously, know they are scamming us, hurting us, inflicting danger, or illiciting perplexing thoughts. Some folks work the game. A carnival worker I did research with (Yes, I did!), had so many soliciting remarks to hawk, based on people's clothes or handbags, handholding couples, men looking distraught, teenagers with pockets full of quarters, oh my goodness, he was scary in the facets that he preyed upon, all in the search of his end game – an apron full of quarters for the maestro at the end of the night. We easily succumb because our desire for more and better is on our shirt sleeves. Compliment me. Notice me. Recognize me as a person with money. I am vulnerable when it comes to friendliness. Most of us are. It may be that we have the smarts to not engage in manipulation, but our ego is stroked; and then you best lookout for what my ego and vulnerability can engage in: dishonesty, tedium, irritable circumstances – remember this is inflicted on us every day. Conscious vs unconscious thinking mediates our actions. We are in a world full of liars and dishonesty in oh, so many ways. Example: The markup on a head of lettuce is horrendous. Advertising is one of the biggest deceits, tricky and duplicitous. (I would secretly like to add a degree in Advertising to my resume just so that I could be fully aware of truth and counter the scams.)

Do the Footwork:

Perspectives change when I am COGNIZANT of my actions and aware of all that surrounds me.

Prayer happens only in a frame of mind which is open to God. Willingness to pray is mine.

Pain happens when I cling to the fact that there is a defect. Do I really like having pain?

Patience is right here. How arrogant am I to try to take control from God or destiny? Gees.

The Process of living MUST be done willingly and ready. There is no fight or denial.

Pay-offs are gifts to me, if I have done God's footwork. What feels good about what I am doing? Do I have a chance to change out of where I am?

Uncover – discover – discard - Pretty simple really:

Uncover: Disclose to myself and others the truth only

Discover how I am reacting and acting on truth

Discard untruths

I have been a control enthusiast! I've been in charge and at large, overbearing, foreboding to others, mostly when I think I am so entertaining, wise, and full of the insight they need. I thought martyrdom was normal behavior. I now know that Mom was not the only trusted servant in my house. I could have taken on helping her at any time. My mother was a martyr – she gave up her everything to care for us and keep us from harm and from our father's alcoholism. Her favorite phrase when we brought a problem to her: "Give it up to God." That was her only outlet. I had to learn that caring about people can be done without interfering. I did not need to take care of them in the manner I thought best for them. Care about others, not just for them. My best progress in recovery was overcoming the urge to get involved in others' lives. I do not know what to do for the best result *for them*. My responsibility is to focus on my behavior in situations. I learned that I do not know what is best for others and judgement of others is not my job. Ask yourself if the problem has your name on it.

Start with unlearning what does not serve us well. It DID serve to protect me in my fearful childhood desperation for safety, but not needed now. What is standing in my way of full usefulness now as an adult?

There is a difference between expressing ourselves and controlling others. I know that when I repeat myself, I am attempting to control. Notice how many times you say the same thing. – That is trying to get your way, maybe not the fair way. Leave the room if you have to. Stop controlling others. What they are to know will come to them.

If someone is not asking for help, it is not my job to do their job for them; I am there to assist, educate, help. I rob people of the dignity of their own experiences.

Go ahead, open the door on a different and better self. We often do not realize the successes God has in mind for us because we get in the way.

Why I Have An Absence of Calmness – Holding A Grudge

Remember this? If you have not done it yet, do it now. So much will be revealed to you. The last column is now your focus.

RESENTMENTS

I am Resentful at:	The Cause or Reason	What was Affected							This was Our Course:	Prayer:	The Exact Nature of Our Wrongs WHERE WAS I:					What Could I Have Done Differently?
		SELF ESTEEM	PERSONAL RELATIONSHIPS	MATERIAL SECURITY	EMOTIONAL SECURITY	SEXUAL RELATIONSHIPS	AMBITIONS OR I HAD MY OWN WAY	PRIDE	Realize at once that the people who have wronged you are spiritually sick... That they like yourself, are sick too. Can I now see what it was like in their shoes – with their fears, insecurities, and background experiences. Could I have done to someone what they did to me? (See page 62 in 12 x 12, Second paragraph)	Ask God to help you show them the same tolerance, and pity that they would cheerfully grant a sick friend. This is a sick person; how can I be helpful to him? God save me from being angry. Thy will be done.	SELFISH	DISHONEST	SELF SEEKING	FRIGHTENED	WHERE WAS I TO BLAME	

Educate Yourself - Ongoing Cranial Conversion

To educate: A vast expanse of memory filled.

In my city of over 120,000 folks only 15% of our students are projected to go to college. I wonder though, how many less will mature? What's that statistic? Growing up is a state of mind.

If we make it to age 18 or 21, or the 15%, who, fortunately graduate with a college degree and 'break' out of the home of our parents, we are adult! Yay! On our own! What we always wanted! Till cost of living and relationships, and challenges, and other people try to control OUR/MY world. Then we rely on the defenses, the immaturity, the redolence of our original people, our basic knowledge and gut instincts to make it in the world! How many times we each fail! It's disgusting how little we really know when we become the misnomer title of 'ADULT'.

I had defects which I could fix but I was not even aware of the many ways I used my habitual negative thoughts. I was fearful in relationships: What if they pull away? Should I pull away first? What if they are not as emotionally connected as I feel? What if they know my thoughts? I had fear of outcomes and insecurity about trying new suggestions made to me. I had guilt of not treating my mate better than myself or treating him better than myself and losing my self-respect. Do you see what a mess I brought to my relationships?

Our lovability, performance, including sexual performance, are not love. Our committed partners want to be with us for far deeper understandings. Our definition of love can be detrimental or fantastic, depending on our capability to love with listening, grace and unconditionability.

Here is a horrible habit I had. I would continue with my work, task, or forward movement when loved ones, friends or coworkers talked to me. Industrialist. Stays on task. Multitasker. I couldn't wait for my work evaluation! Instead, I found I was too busy to love. Don't ever be too busy to stop and love on people who bother to take a second for you! I realized I could be physically present with someone but not available to them. How would you like that treatment? Ouch.

I had a critical role in how all that went. I was side-stepping normal thinking – social expectations of conformity which have proven successful. I did not have 'normal' in my genes to draw from.

Maturity is an essence of our being. Without understanding ourselves and involving a bigger presence than our meager selves, we mutter through, struggle along, suffer break ups and ills and fall prey to bad doings.

If you are in the low statistic in my state, the 7% with a severe disability, or the 13% with special needs or even of those graduating from college, have 20% of a math or reading deficit; how on earth, and I mean, how on this earth, are you going to cut the mustard when you have my immature thinking besides??!

Well, 20% contemplate suicide! The rest (and this percentage is getting smaller and smaller), the saner portion of society, shop at Walmart and travel, and listen to political debates, and eat bagels and drive and vie for tickets for concerts, or can't afford insurance, etc. And then we claim we are as normal as they get. Oh my.

Don't shortcut the struggle to become a butterfly by cutting your cocoon: Meet challenges and walk through them. Do you really want the same ole, same ole forever?

One true goal of all higher education is to create a man who is continually educating himself, continually asking questions about life.

Instruction may end in the school room but education should only end when life does.

So a big part of education of self is learning the guidelines that are the unmitigated TRUTH. Now the first four of the Ten Commandments are religious direction; instructions from Exodus 20 in the Bible. Just another cue here, Bible stands for Basic Instructions Before Leaving Life. The Bible seems to be regarded as divine inspiration consigned to writing.

The rest of the Commandments are just a way to live, if you think about it. EVEN if you are not religious or follow a Christian methodology, read the other commandments. It is about us doing acts in life...the acts we already do every day; but the twist is that this set of instructions keeps us from doing harm, even emotional harm to our loved ones. We will emerge on the threshold of freedom from self-hate and rejection. Learning is the only procedure we find out how to put novel problems in correct alignment and perspective.

It is up to us to start a new wiser strategy as evolutionizing adults. Christianity is not an albatross. Exposure to the frozen doctrines coach us in a special way. Our intellectual and social integrity depend on the doctrines to give introspection to a way to live. The Biblical inhabitants who knew Jesus did their best to inform the world. Since, we have had Mandella, Buddha, and Ghandi and many others with ideals and perspectives. Jesus's life was an interruption to living but an eruption in the cosmic process. We cannot be naïve about Christianity and have a balanced life. God may fill a void in someone's life. Take a look into what Faith is about.

For you Rednecks, Commandment Ten says thou shall not covet thy neighbor's ass. So, whoever you are, in the range from elitist, egotist, anarchist, atheist to the poorest, homeless, criminalist, it would do you good to at least read these!

"A man is not complete who believes that his advancement depends on crushing others – or who worries about matters that cannot be altered – or who insists that a thing is impossible because he has not been able to do it. That man is lacking wisdom. Wisdom that can put aside his ordinary routine in order to refresh his mind with rest, change, and meditation. He needs much help who thinks he can compel others to do what seems right to him." – from <u>One Day at a Time.</u>

So all that these pages are asking of you is to change your heart. Educate. Sometimes, one must relearn how to love one another. If your father was an egotist, demanding or abusive patriarch (someone you hated sometimes) you were exampled that this is acceptable behavior, I don't care what argument you put up. It was a way to get things, to control everyone, and have it his way. (Ick) The belief here that you absorbed, is that some things DID come to him due to his aggressive conduct. I used to think that it was my job to protect, lead, and control other people. If either parent is abusive or aggressive, they do that by loud voice alone. I have no power. This thinking always leads to someone's misery – occasionally mine.

The opposite behavior is done with love. Relating with love and care and understanding satisfies so much more, I can't even tell you. Love is an action verb. Thus, we must learn appropriate actions. We <u>choose</u> to relate with love. Get this: Love heals pain, forgives, creates healthy relationships, dismisses engagement in conflict, allows divergence, and drives out fear. Whew. You choose.

Do you ever stop to think that Christ "is in" that other person too?

Relating with love lays a foundation of receiving and giving for when we are emotionally healthy, we also know how to receive love. Ain't nothing better than not only feeling love coming to you from others; also feeling nice, just sitting in the warmth and light of God's love, power, and glory.

Follow the directions, those.

The Difference between Habits and Developed Skills

We have great expectations of ourselves. We set the goal. We set the plan. We put a foot forward and a squirrel running by, in the form of an old habitual thought, prevents us from the change up we wanted.

Then, the cycle kicks in our own desire for betterment or expectation fulfillment, and we remorse because we didn't fulfill the new desire. Familiar? Guess what, you hold the steering bar on that cycle!

Our lower functioning brains looooooooooooooooove to rely on rote. If we could stay embalmed in our amygdala, we would do only what we reactively feel from our hippocampus stimulation. The amygdala, at the center of our brains, is the hub of emotional responses. A thought comes in directly to that part of the brain and if not processed to the frontal lobes, it stays in the reactionary rote (which is wrought with fear) mode. That first thought is based only on intuition and quick, not insightful or reasonable.

The only way to change a habit is to apprise our psyche and involve whole brain engagement. My mentees laugh but my best remedy from old rote is to cognizantly put up a hexagon shaped (STOP) sign with the word ABORT on it.

) I become aware of an incoming thought.

) Give it a pause - time to RESPOND, not react with old info, A B O R T that.

) Process the new vision, stimuli, voice, etc. through my logic and practical lobes up front.

) Make a conscious decision to take the next best action based on sensical terms, for the betterment.

After repeatedly practicing this, I eventually do this more automatically than rote reactions; RESPONDing to stimuli rather than re(perhaps fearful)action.

Willpower can be changed. Ha. Let me say that again. Through the above process, our willpower will be supported, altered, and come out wiser. Woo hoo!

Pause on that for a moment.

P.ostpone A.ction U.ntil S.erenity E.merges

Wait on this just a second.

W.hat D.o I T.hink? or,
W.hy A.m I T.alking?

HALT for the brain to think

H.ungry, A.ngry, L.onely, T.ired?

And think about it all for a minute.

Is it: T.rue, H.elpful, I.ntelligent, N.ecessary, and K.ind?

Abort action. Even second graders are taught: Stop, Look, and Listen. Abort current thought. Process stimulation through brain. Pause and think. Take an action toward the next right thing to say, do, etc. It may be outside the old comforts, however, extremely necessary for change. New aims with your willpower will surprise you. Business practices suggest a six second pause before responding. Sounds like a good length of time for me to give my brain time for a good outcome, rather than an impulsive nescient reaction.

The three P.s: Pause, Ponder, and Pray.

All this equals eventual self-correction, new healthy habits that become innate. We are going to implant good into your unconscious habits. We will act in a new habitually kinder, more thoughtful way.

When we become routinely kinder to ourselves, others benefit and more importantly, we like who we are and trust our intuition. Self-worth improves, and honesty projects itself into every aspect of our day. What great new habits begin. It all starts with cognition and a mental 'abort" sign to your first fearful urges. Stir. Repeat.

Here's the cool benefit you get from all the above - as you recognize your ability to process to fulfillment in a higher quality life, you will begin to see the process as it fails for others. They react. Their brains fire only so far. The hippocampus springs the fear marker on them. They react and stop moving forward. Cognitive dissonance occurs. They react and do the wrong thing. You sense them not understanding and returning to old behaviors and habits. Once you beat the odds and grab your steering bar, you never go back.

Thusly, bosses may yell, drivers may finger you, screamers may hurt your ears, but you now have the gift of honesty and wisdom planning every move you make. And 70% fewer regrets fall upon you. Yay!

You have got a good brain. Here's how to use it.

If you could picture your brain like a finger, or your hair, or nose, you would understand the functions better. Let's take a shot at understanding some of this obscure organ's functions. This requires application and thinking, which your brain organ can do!

Learning and memory happen there. Each piece of white matter plays an important operation in the factory of your brain. There are dense areas, there are interconnections employed, parts that rely on one another.

I got a real sense of how this Organ of Intelligence sometimes can skip a few beats. When I had a concussion, I hit my head again, the second occurred because I had lost some sense of balance after the first concussion!

I shook my neurons out of whack. It made me ACUTELY aware of what many with mental illness or a cognitive disability go through. I thank God that I am recovering, not everyone can come back.

For instance, word finding and crossword puzzles were still accomplishable, but slower than my earlier quick thinking. I would get a spoon, turn to the stove, return to the sink in a spin motion and be dizzy. I developed cluster migraines for the first time. I shied from riding in an airplane, even a car for months, due to the uncomfortable motion sickness.

This was not a week in bed - this was all summer of 2017 in bed for 2-4 hours a day.

Both hemispheres of my brain were affected. The clinical folks who aided me through this time said, slow down, be cognizant of your actions, allow time to heal. Those three instructions became my tether. I am nearly a Type A personality with latent television viewing. Slowing down to prohibit frustration with my own brain was extremely difficult. Time to heal was inhibited by every cut, cold, bronchitis, flu my body encountered, stressed by dividing my immunity. Cognizance of actions means, stop. Your brain network contains 100 billion nerve cells – that is a lot to control. Think about the application of nerves and sensations your fingers are making to hold a fork in your hand, pick up the soap, read a book, etc. That is cognizance of movement.

Motor skills, digital response, regular sleep all had to be conscious decisions. I told people my rote was gone during the recovery from the concussions. I could no longer rely on that sixth sense to open the door, solve the dilemma, put only a biteful on my fork.

Why am I including this? I was telling my mentees to be conscious and cognizant of their actions. I was learning the hard way what real cognizance was all about. Yet, those very patterns and habits were zig-zagging in my capsule called a brain.

So you tell your knuckles to bend when you grab ahold. You tell your toe to send the feeling of the tub water temperature to your brain. Reactions can stop in the hippocampus and leave you in fear of the next correct action. You pull the toe out. You send 'grasp' signals to the knuckles. Easy, right? If our 'nerves' could tell us the next right action emotionally, it would be so sweet.

Thoughts need ALL of the cerebral fluid, neurons, cortexes, lobes, blood, oxygen, fluids, etc. that are available for that brain capsule to interact. Only then can you take the next right action.

If you have stored up your mis-actions, retreat due to fear, wrongful habits, or inhibited memories, within those lobes, you are in trouble in relationships.

Could you expect your brain organ to spew out the appropriate information if stimuli sent to the brain from parents, teachers, abusers, politicians, aggressive individuals, impoverished living, bias, etc. have fostered a majority of more negative reactions?

Let me repeat that: How could you expect your brain organ to spew out the right information if stimuli sent to the brain (parents, teachers, abusers, aggressive individuals, poverty, bias, etc.) have offered negative reactions to your storage system?

Where do you get the next right action if it is not initially installed or retained there?

First, cognizance that others are living differently, acting with vitality and interest, fulfilling potentials, having successes, lives are filled with friends; and you are not part of that. They appear somewhat indifferent from your mode of life. That is the truth. This world was not made for you alone. It is as though an asset of others has floated just beyond your reach. Realization of that factualness can stop your heart for a nanosecond! Your Mom was on this earth for more reasons than to just raise you. She had a life! Be aware of others' purposes. So often, I hear voices react to the news in the media, verbally stabbing the messenger, the media or the scientist or forecaster or satellite module. Those people and things are helpers with communication. 'They' are not in connection with God to know everything, after all, "He's Got the Whole World in His Hands." Honor those who are fulfilling potentials differently.

I went as "They" with my mate one Halloween party because 'They' seem to get all the blame. We did not get egged but were repeatedly cussed at for insurance company failures and the high cost of electric bills, etc.

Second, recognize that your broken thinking brain sometimes puts you smack in the middle of distress, stress, despair, unhappiness, unmanageability, and on and on. We discover things about ourselves that we may have never suspected; like, it is possible to let go of old companions like failure, shame and guilt. The state of our minds in stress reverberates with suppression and immunity resistance via hormones that hamper those good cells.

So, let's heal that.

The intricate labyrinth components of the brain will charge the neurons, interconnect the tissue, file, store memory, etc. but WE MUST FEED it the correct impeti. Years of information and misinformation can make us good Christians, murderers, thieves, or slated for sainthood. Just like good or bad nutritional food works on many of the other internal organs - livers give out with constant alcohol induction, kidneys won't function without water, we will bleed out if an artery is severed or sugars affect diabetics; your brain requires intentional care and correct stimulus for output to be at its peak. Comprehendo?

Youngsters who grew up freezing, bitter, hungry, hateful, intense anxiety, or irreconcilable emotion, choose, as adults, to be victims, to avoid friction or to seek revenge; many times, are criminalistic.

Ok. Frontal lobes must be involved in thinking. The most common mistake is:

Reacting before we engage all the lobes. Those lobes are full of logic, repeated activities, rote calls, sensations experienced before, Mrs. Adams' English class, etiquette rules, correct infant care, balance, and on infinitively.

If you call on the frontal lobe, it will give you focus and forethought. It offers the planning and organization you do. Prefrontal lobes contribute judgement, empathy, impulse control and learning from mistakes. But it is up to us to pause long enough for the hippocampus to strike up the band in the front.

Eleanor Roosevelt quotes:

"The brain has got the answers and knows the resources to go get the unknowns and to stop when at risk."

Our reactionary state uses only the hippocampus - events react in the hippocampus sometimes and don't conduct the full study that we are capable of. Or sometimes there simply is not a conscious response yet inserted to choose correctly in the nodes.

Nature and nurture have a lot of effect on each personality. And the lack of exposure can effect us as much!

I don't know about you, but I do not like to expose myself to people and places or actions which are not for my betterment. Those things that put fear and doubt in my actions.

We can change that. Conscious behavior, conscious actions and responses replace REACTIVE FEAR and intimidation only take a pause to think. Simple, huh?

The little brain (cerebellum) plays a most important role in cognitive function. Use it. Attention, language, some emotional functions like fear or pleasure are there. The cerebellum does not initiate movement unless it is called upon! Timing (Pause) is important. Then intentionality penetrates through.

If you do not engage coordination and precision within your action process, you may go awry with your behaviors. Allow the lobes to suffuse into your conscious (pause).

The lobes located at the back of the brain and top side will process touch, special or directional sense, and perception. And just under the cerebral cortex are the emotional sensors which engage when bonding, sexual interests, nesting. See, the three full pounds of the brain need exercise. Just pause. While pausing, part of the thirty percent of the calories the brain uses in a day are burned.

Make sense?

Simple volition and determination without arousing all brain parts, well, you see the problem. How many folks walk around disengaged? Ya, you know what I am talking about. Don't be one of them.

Even kids do brain exercises designed to energize certain parts of the brain:

Rub your tummy and pat your head at the same time.

Touch your right elbow to left knee ten times; reverse

Smile while you pant

Shift your eyes to ten objects around the room, holding each for 3 seconds

Your executive function and your achievement of these simple maneuvers optimize your prefrontal cortex, shooting neurotransmitter dopamine which is associated with joy and pleasure.

You were God-given the gifts of many lobes, connective cerebral tissue, interactive hemispheres, brain fluid, arteries, and nerves to use. Make a conscious effort to act and respond in appropriate thought-out ideation.

Do not surrender yourself to self-chosen ignorance. - Confucius

Artificial Intelligence is intelligence exhibited by machines or software. And include reasoning, knowledge, planning, learning, natural language procession, communication, perception and the ability to move and manipulate objects. And is interdisciplinary with the limits of sciences and professions converging; so precisely can this be described as a machine which can simulate the sapience of Homo Sapiences? What about myth, fiction and philosophy? I read once that philosophy has no place against love or a toothache. Thank goodness, God created me. AI's robotics will always be dust between my fingers.

Storage and computation can happen at the same time through synapsing neurons through the dendrites, when they arrive at the next neuron, it is all computed (sorted into sense).

To reiterate what I am attempting to speak about, let's hear from experts at the Bozeman Science Museum;

A diagram from the Brain & Nervous System Health Center of Human Anatomy:

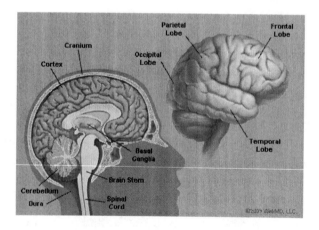

Our brains are divided in four major lobes, frontal, parietal, temporal and occipital. The skull protects the brain from injury. With 100 billion nerves running around connecting, ganging up in the ganglia there, it is no wonder we get confused and emotions sometimes win the descending vote. The basal ganglia coordinate messages going around. We depend on everything to run well. That requires us to pay attention to what we put in our bodies and give great care as to what we involve our thinking in.

So you have this brain. What a gift! So many properties. So many functions. It creates our conscience. As long as the balance of input is fed and enhanced, we will get positive production results.

Let's feed it right:

- ❖ Listen and observe experiences
- ❖ Listen and observe others
- ❖ Adapt principles
- ❖ Record common themes in occurrences
- ❖ Read, read, read
- ❖ Ponder and weigh thoughts
- ❖ Use history
- ❖ Be constantly aware, unless asleep
- ❖ Learn from experience
- ❖ Educate, educate, educate self
- ❖ Practice goodness
- ❖ Be still with self
- ❖ Use harmony of nature's vibration
- ❖ Allow grace and honor
- ❖ Practice integrity

Principles before Personalities

Do you have principles? I ask this because I really didn't. Of course, I mostly obeyed the law and didn't spit in public, etc. I had assets I had earned and learned. I had characteristics about my personality and likes and dislikes. I had old rules my parents endowed to me. I had values I had, up to now, invented and created from past experience. Did I have principles? Are those principles? I have things I won't do, or my fear is too large to overcome. Are those my principles of guidance?

Nothing in life is to be feared. It is only to be understood. – Marie Curie

I would more likely think that principles are good grace and sharing for all mankind. I am too self-centered to say that I embrace good grace for all others. I share, but not worldwide.

What does it mean to have principles? I contemplate for you: Do you have spiritual principles? Do you follow the Ten Commandments? Do you obey all the rules at work? How many of us know Hoyle's rules? How about Standard Bylaws for Meetings? Have you read the employees manual, the vision statement, mission statement, and follow all Osha standards, etc.? I bet not. Few people toe the line that well.

Principles and ethics. Sounds like a great way to live. But I clearly didn't know what they should be for me.

What are my morals? Could you write down 5 morals you live by? Or does ego lead your way?

1.

2.

3.

4.

5.

Are you fair with everyone? Or just fair enough...to those around...to those that need? If I am in need, will I only take my share? Does everyone in society get the same treatment from you? Do you believe everyone is deserving of the same? Or do evil and personal judgement or a frailness in others deter your fairness?

Do you believe everyone has a right to belong? Do you feel you have a right to belong? Or do you hold a bias against the elderly say, or a type of disability or green-eyed people?

Do you do your share of the work? The support each contributes makes the whole.

Does your soul feel in the right place? Or (does) Will Power and WANT lead you astray?

Are you agreeable? Do you preempt others' thoughts so you can speak first? What about just listening? What about learning from others? What about society's needs instead of your own? Be ready in conversation to spend time listening to the other person's response. That may gain you way more than trying to think what to say back. That is not listening fully. A basic principle – listening while others speak.

The question is not only, do you give honor and respect to others but are you worthy of theirs? Are you only equal when you can do that one function? Do others who fail at that one function get written off your friend list?

Do you do your civic duty? Are you involved in a unified purpose? Or stuck in the center of self?

Do you know all that you can before judgement? Or does impulse and 'looking good' determine your decision making? Are you consciously or unconsciously evaluating with pre-learned moral condescension?

Do you use your intelligence? We have all these senses at hand that tell us when to be fearful for our safety and when to take a risk. Do you think things through before responding? Or do you RE-act to life as it comes at you?

Do you ever say, "Why Wouldn't it be Okay?" and just let things be?

"Peace – It does not mean to be in a place where there is no noise, trouble, or hard work. It means to be in the midst of those things and still be calm in your heart." - JP

New Directions

Some of us are searching for peace.

It is not found in a search. It just comes to you, as if quantas change within your heart and soul.

My part is to learn to calm my heart through acknowledgement of God's existence.

What is the difference between peace and serenity?

When I got busy, I got better.

Alanon Books cost as little as 1 cent on line. From someone who said she wasn't sick, but as soon as I do get sick, I will read it, I was so naïve to stepping up. It astonishes and jump starts me, when attempts to get better, fail me. I learn from mistakes. Do the work, move forward and more will be revealed. Through action my thinking will change.

Act your way into good thinking. The promises materialize. Recovery follows the action, vigorous action.

"There ain't no Coupe DeVille hiding in the bottom of a Cracker Jack Box."

No action, no change. Practical experience shows that nothing will so much insure immunity from codependency as intensive work with other Al-Anons. It works when other therapies fail.

Here's how the world would act if we were all trained in 'good':

) Continued personal growth

) Unified kindness without exception

) Broad spread wisdom

) Responsibility for all with each of us

) Doing the right thing at all times

) Everyone participates

) Decision making balanced and fair

) Trust in your fellowman

) Good personal leadership

) Spirituality the foundation of all the above

) Belief that all souls are designed to live well

Song: "Change My Heart"

What to do when I am unhappy or confused or worrying and fretting:

Mind you, the United States ranks 18th overall, on the list of Happiest Countries. Let's make this statistic higher all over the world.

Listen to birds
Stare at clouds
Go watch planes at the airport and guess where people are going
Take a bubble bath
Read a fiction or joke book
Finish the crossword puzzle
Try to belly laugh without humor
Try different smiles in the mirror
Meditate
Pray
Watch for God to show up right where you are
Stare at the glass in your window for 2 full minutes
Drive up to a favorite spot
Take a walk
Audubon Center
Zoo
Sing
Visit any museum

Buy an ice cream cone

Have a giant cookie

Dance

Stretch

Breathe through your belly – you know how.

I will risk sharing my personal older BUCKET LIST from JUNE 2012

1. Print my favorite photos
2. Go see sister in Florida
3. Read novels
4. Zip line
5. Visit NE USA in fall
6. Learn a new language
7. Make love with abandon
8. See England
9. Just travel
10. Visit Rome and see the Masters
11. Skate
12. Balance on a bicycle
13. Boat as often as I can —sail?
14. Cruise
15. See Banff
16. Pray better
17. Get active again – Zumba or something
18. Write to be published
19. Entertain friends
20. Come up with 6 great dishes that I make
21. Assist the needy other than financial donation
22. Learn to drill
23. Learn to cut a wooden board
24. Dress up fancy for a dance
25. Read a beloved old novel
26. Make a cheesecake
27. New York to sightsee again and again
28. Lose dimple weight on stomach and thighs
29. Down load most favorite songs

30. Learn photo shop well
31. Create flowers for weddings
32. Get nature photos framed and sell them

Truth? There are 100 items on this list at all times. I have completed most of the items above but leave them on because I want to do them again!

What's on your list? Top my 100, would you?

Grateful, Not Hateful

I must daily say thanks to a power greater than me, God, for all the things I am blessed with.

Are you grateful all of the time, or only part?

If I constantly count what I don't have, I will have no peace, no moments of content. God may give me the moment, but I create the serenity, enjoyment and peacefulness of that moment, or my existence, or I may create the discontent. Same moment to use. Either way. Hmmm.

Which do you want?

Live that moment so well that you will want to see it again! Others will want to see what you lived and bring their friends. That's when friends are compulsed to join you in your journey – with you, the serene friend.

Take stock of what you say in that moment and how you say it. Is my attitude fair? Is my attitude nice? Is my attitude courteous? How could I possibly expect fairness, kindness, and courtesy if I am not giving it out? More principals.

So, say, I get food at a café. There are no forks at my table. To a wait staff, I could say, "Do you expect us to eat with our hands?" (And vibe her a negative glare.)

If I cuss out the waitress for forgetting silverware, what have I given out? What is my attitude? What is my mood? What do I expect back from a now upset waitress?

If I ACT in a positive appropriate manner so that we both are satisfied with the needs being met, am I not left happy? Why not do this at home, with those you profess to love the most?

I bring on most of my discomfort. Say that with me aloud. "I bring on most of my discomfort." Who feels my discomfort? Who usually speaks of it? Who takes on the discontent, upset and discomfort? Who spreads it to others? Who cops an attitude? Who expels the cuss words or takes on the 'poor me' victim attitude? Me, Me, Me, Me, Me.

If I meet raised voices, poor service, forgotten promises with ACTION – an action that is fair, well mannered and courteous, what do you think the moment will be like in now?

"Excuse me. (Smile) Looks like we don't have silverware. We will need some please." NOT, "You didn't give us silverware. (Blame).' Just a statement of the fact. No blame. No judging. Not belittling the waitress or cafe.

Once I learned what I value, I surrounded myself slowly with only that. I am surrounded with nice people, a healthier life style, pleasant exchanges, easy conversations, smiles, fair responses, and a better, more peaceful life. IT ALL CAME FROM ME AND MY ATTITUDE. HOW I LIVE WILL INFLUENCE THOSE AROUND ME TO TREAT ME WITH WHAT I AM GIVING OUT.

If I look at life as icky, one sad event after another, it is icky. It becomes my reality. My thoughts created ick.

If I meet life with a happy disposition, acceptance of who I am and where I am not, with what I know, and I live in positive action (not reaction), I get up every morning and do the right things, I see great things happening. Always know one thing: I am looking forward to today instead of looking at what I might dread. I even view a dental appointment from the other side – My teeth will feel so good after cleaning.

It's not really all our fault to jump to the negative or bad side of life. After all, even the newspaper owners will tell you, "If it bleeds, it leads." Ouch on that.

"We must find time to stop and thank the people who make a difference in our lives."
John F. Kennedy

The old me was sick in the head. I was not always grateful. I LIVED IN PAIN, JEALOUSY, ANGER, HATRED, JUDGEMENT, ENVY, GREED, SLOTH, in various forms. I would choose sitting on the couch to doing chores, like laundry. Then I would choose blaming my spouse for not doing laundry or dirtying more clothing. I would choose computer games over spending time with loved ones who were not communicative with me. Great ideas left me because I had no follow through or engagement. I lived in a selfish, non-gratifying life. I was filled with discontent – AT MY OWN HAND, OF MY OWN MAKING! I was caught in fear, like the dental nerves were sticking out. And beyond that, I thought I could offer to fix others. Why am I discordant with my own personal progress?

Once I learned that my attitude could be one of pleasantness, I reinforced the attitude with thank yous. Thank you for my family. Thank you for air. In the days before Jesus came to earth, our elders thought the air was a gift. Imagine being that grateful. They saw a loss of breathing when people died, therefore, air must be a gift. Imagine being grateful for the sky, the clouds, electricity, books, other people, fresh fruit, fish, air, shoes, and Walmart.

Imagine being grateful all the time. How would that feel?

I don't mean for you to paste a smile is on your face and go around thanking and dancing. I am talking about the kind of gratitude that makes your heart melt inside. Tears often well up when we stop and count our blessings. That kind of happy gratitude.

Imagine at the time of someone's death, being grateful for that person's livelihood and their sharing with me in my time on this planet. Imagine at the time of your car breaking down, being grateful for a friend that helps, a mechanic's skills to repair it, a job to earn the money to get the car running, a cell phone to get help.

How I think and act is a choice. I choose grateful.

In every situation.

With every communication and happening. Wow. I have a choice here. Take two steps toward progress or be an icky person? Which is it to be? I am trying to bring home that you make your heartbeat good or bad.

Imagine at the time of a spouse's, teenager daughter's or parent's angry or violent rage or stuck in stupid; being grateful it is not you raging out of control, it is not your rage or violence. I am thankful I am not in an awful mood. At that time, channel your power toward love and responsibility for self. Imagine at a time of violence being grateful for the symptoms presenting themselves, so we can choose not to live in that. It is an omen telling us that we need to change. OUR lives can only be changed by us, by taking steps in progress and solution.

These horrible experiences were given to us to grow, and they have strengthened us. We are growing to take care of ourselves. We are growing to love ourselves. We become more worthy of love. Do you take care of your own self with love? And do you accept God's love and guidance for yourself? It is a choice. Do you accept God's love? Do you love yourself? Why not start tonight?

Ephesians 4:30-32

"Let all bitterness and wrath and anger and clamor and slander be put away from you, with all malice. And be kind to one another, tenderhearted, forgiving one another, as God in Christ forgave you."

Let this reading remind you that eons before you entered this world, in the days of Christ's coming, the days when the Bible, Koran, or other books of nether languages were written, our foremothers apparently also experienced wrath, bitterness, anger, malice and dissing.

And all these many years later, we, we in this room, have been through the same painful emotions.

We can now go forth with wisdom of how to act.

God said, be kind to yourself, tenderhearted, forgiving, so that you can go forth and do his work.

That's why I disclose to you my story. I am going forth tenderhearted.

In Pursuit of the Good Life

We grope in pursuit of the good life the world has to offer. Yet we are unsatisfied.

Throw in deceiver and sinister and we get a quixotic image of life. Good life is fleeting. Simple desire flourishes and ebbs. We hide from our own hearts. Self-indulgence seems satisfying – till that 'thing' wears out or is past. Lust and desires of the flesh seem to get our motors going, even though our eyes 'look up the skirt and down the blouse', lust, is passing. Where is full time satisfaction with our lives? Not in lust. Worldliness complicates the heart. As we grow out of childhood, we egotistically and selfishly love what we love.

Lust is all GET—Love is all GIVE. –Unknown

An example: A teenager wants the privileges which age presents. They (Formerly, 'we' remember) can't wait to be on our own, to make our own choices, and use what we know to test against survival. However, some of that is tainted perhaps with our having lived under the roof of condemnation by an alcoholic parent; and the ill sought devotion we gave to that disease. What could we expect of ourselves once we take that headset into society? Our usefulness to others, our aspirations, and dreams were buried in muck-filled reactions to the people we lived with. We end up clawing for some form of self-worth and a reason for living, and generally feel most comfortable in the arms of another sick person, often an addictive personality or alcoholic. Distorted thinking.

Harvard Medical School researcher, Martin Teicher, found that brain alterations associated with language processing and depression do exist. Further, it was found that adults who had experienced bullying or verbal abuse as a child had significant brain changes. The phrase, "He comes by that naturally" comes to mind.

We are best off starting adult lives listing former reasons for our demise. It is not a healthy prognosis otherwise. Many people from alcoholic homes go into clinical and medical professions, to continue to give to what sickness needs.

That is not a bad thing. It is a statistic. And the world does need nurses, therapists and doctors, so we can even be thankful for our upbringings' result. As long as the medical training and knowledge has included self-examination and improvement toward healthy value-based judgement. Rationalization had been taught to us based on former untruths, maybe alcoholic thinking, and its weight was that of a dandelion puff.

However, deep cognizance of the truth within our choice without vindication is essential. Vengeance never proved useful. Guilt wears us out. Standing in a pity box (Look what I am doing. Look, just look at me.) casts 'wretched thinking' into our psyche. The head set of right things was not available to us, we remained polarized, gullible to recrement.

We perhaps lived in a fog, with lack of focus on reality, and alcoholic perceived notions which clouded our thoughts. At the end of this book, I can only hope that clarity comes instead of a being a codependent who chooses to sit in blind endorsement of the alcoholic's vomit of shitburger words and actions. We are only looking at symptom reduction in you. This will be long term therapy you apply on yourself. The diseased person has to heal and go forward on their own. I believed natural consequences to the alcoholic were not allowed to happen as long as I was on watch! Silly me, and I was *really* busy doing that. All the love in the world could not stop the disease from getting worse. I could only look existentially within me. I had to learn what parts of my husband, friend, and family I could detach myself from while maintaining my love and concern.

A God Box often helps us. Things I could not control but felt I NEEDED to have a part in, were written down and put in a God Box. I got so I mentally could visualize putting items in the God Box. The essence of a place to put things out of my control kept God in charge.

I hope you can sieve out the love and laughter filled times and tendernesses and be present in those. Then we shall weed our consciousness gardens and no longer live under the tendrils of malicious and benevolent behaviors. Let God's hand instead, grow in your garden of graciousness.

Let's examine our minds. Close your eyes if you want. Take a deep breath

If I were to expect an answer from you, how would you answer this question:

Is your self-pity fading? Are rage, martyrdom, and depression which were part of your everyday life, fading now? Was loneliness defining your life; and are you now allowing love and support in which others offer to you?

Have you experienced growth? Are you more accepting of human fallibility? Have you grown toward light, toward health, and closer to a Higher Power? Do you find more to be grateful for?

How did you get to this place you previously couldn't get to on your own? Hopefully the flow this book has mustered up some progress very gently, to the point of your adaptation without knowing what I was pulling here: Step by step gently changes in our everyday lives.

I have permission to reprint a Facebook Testimony from an Alanon woman I worked with some years ago. She fought me in the beginning, I nearly resigned twice from working with her and it took many sessions to stop talking about the 'other person who was causing all her angst'.

She sweetened up within two years and I cannot believe what a beautiful human being she is today with a new start and a relationship that is going many places for her. Her testimony:

"I'm not sure who all knows my history...but I was blessed yesterday in a way I never thought possible. Many of you know I was previously married and had my two oldest with a man who has the disease of addiction.

Being young, naive and thinking I could love someone better, landed me lost and codependent. I was in therapy and I found Alanon. I thought I was crazy, believed I deserved the things that took place in that marriage and it added to the continued narrative that I had established in my head at a very young age, "I was not good enough". Today I know that's not the truth. I can accept not everyone will like me; I can be a lot lol. I'm ok with that. I don't have to change who I am to be what I thought others wanted me to be.

My ex-husband asked to meet with me to make amends. In all the years I'd hoped for this, I had accepted it would never happen, but it did. I feel incredibly lucky and grateful for us to be in this place. It truly is a miracle.

I can't forget what happened but I let it go a long time ago and I can forgive him today for the harm and hurt from the past. I don't need to list those things in detail but it was enough to give me PTSD and still I stayed. I went through things that seem almost unbelievable today.

Honestly, I can't believe he is still here on Earth, but I am very grateful. It makes me so happy to see him rebuild the relationships he had lost with our kids. They deserve a healthy, honest, loving and sober Father. And as amazing as my soon to be husband is, it's just a different relationship he has with the older kids. It is not an easy road but he does an unbelievable job. He's been the Dad when Al couldn't be, and he continues to show up for all 4 of our kids no matter what.

We've been through getting sober with Al many times, but no matter what happens with his addiction, I'm so grateful for his sobriety, his relationship with our kids, and all of the amazing lessons I have learned along the way. I can't believe I'm even saying that. I'm proud of him. I also can appreciate the journey bringing me to where I am today.

I've been given another chance to grow my family with an amazing partner. I now know what unconditional love looks like and to have a man who will do whatever he can to make me happy (well, most of the time lol). My life is such a blessing and I feel very fortunate to be in this space within myself today and for the partner I get to marry in a few months.

Anyone struggling with addiction or codependency, reach out, go to a meeting, it can get better, I've lived it. Does this mean Al will stay sober? I don't know, but I can appreciate when he is and hope it continues. Does this mean life is perfect, of course not, but that sounds utterly boring anyway."

Give Yourself Permission

Today, I grant thee permission:

To stop acting on false or possibly untrue demands

Drop all of your own negativity – actions, words, and thoughts

Strengthen your sense of a worthy self

Live optimally with no worry, fret, stress, or anger

Speak on behalf of your own feelings always

Ask for things you need

Drop worry and fret

Recognize futility and drop its use

Stop relationships that are harmful

So what do you think of that? Look at that list again. If selecting a partner for your daughter or son, would you wish for them to have all those assets? Well Silly, go ahead, take them and run with them your ownself.

Talk It Over with Your Brain First

In this chapter, I will ask you to be in charge of changing your thinking. Is your thinking positive? Is it adult thinking? Is it compulsive? Is it opinionated and stuck in your imprudent opinion? Is it full of gratitude? Hopefully I have laid out some good argument for you to be of higher quality. I can do no more for you. It all now involves only you. The end of arguments and beginning of great communication is now on you.

Communication involves three acts: 1. Greet 2. Introduce Topic 3. Resolution, with simple reciprocation, return on investment.

Also - Why am I talking? Is my name on this conversation? Decision? Examine motives for becoming involved.

Next argument you have, stop and ask yourself this: "Do I want to be right, or do I want to be happy?"

Check your chakra. Is it green? Are you emanating green energy? Blue would be nice. When we head into an argument foray, we are already yellow, orange comes, and we almost breathe fire red when involved in head-to-head combat. Green is better. Watch your energy color.

What the characters bring onto the stage often becomes the topic. Their performance makes or breaks good results. One sour dolt, one biased mind, one attitude bearing beast, one stubborn ideation can ruin a marriage's performance.

Good communication has no star - no award for winning. Even for the one who has the most lines. Sometimes the lead orator is loud and demanding, an ass. If the rest of the players REACT, pretty soon the conversation fails.

Talking is not one way. Only if you have the dais, or a halo on your head, can you stop listening. That's the only time. Got it?

Elephants live in many of our homes, and they take up a HUGE grey space hovering over all people within the house. Ever have Uncle George visit and as he first sits down, he says, "So how is everyone responding to the news about your divorce?" after a week of noncommunication in the household. The elephant must be broached, always. The hardest topic must be brought up, not ignored. Bad feelings can destroy our brain cells. People do not thrive in an environment where elephants linger.

If there is a divorce, and illness, injury, terminal disease, death, abuse; discuss it. Plan your walk through the stages of the suffering. Explore each member's phase with them with your mind wide open. Seven stages of grief mean just that, seven different feelings of strong emotional reaction to the impetus of death or loss (**shock or disbelief, denial, bargaining, guilt, anger, depression, and acceptance/hope**). Let each person be in their phase as they need, and share where you are. Softness will descend upon you and your walk through the experience will be aided, as you empathize, compassionately with the other cohabitants until 'this too has passed'.

*The stages of grief and loss seem to be definite assignations to a post traumatic mind. The mix of feelings may cross over, one may be skipped, a 'wait' during long terminal illness uses some. It's a mix-match.

Another seven common with grief is shiva, the intense seven-day mourning period which the Jewish defer to. They then expect that most regular activities of your life will resume. Grief is a demanding companion.

Be willing to face emotions. Tell people of your need be it Hunger, Anger, Loneliness, or Tiredness; and then HALT your own conversation until the feelings you feel are met. Sad emotions create fatigue. Energies are expended. Do not expect to be up to par. Rest. Eat. Making drastic changes sometimes (moving, new job,) do not allow people to deal with loss of a loved one and make one vulnerable to psychological fatigue. Realize the truth and take care with self. Communicate where you are; or leave the room to process separately if that is what you need.

Take special care with how you word things. Don't you profess to love this person more than anyone else in the world? Then why speak to them in a lazy manner?

I get to be very loving about what I express. Even if it is as simple as, "Supper is ready." Better is, "Dinner will be up in five. Will you be ready?"

My new attitude - since learning how to communicate - is extremely more amiable. People always treat me well in response. I make friends as I function through my needs. Miracles happen for me in interchanges.

Da Nile

'Living in denial' - a phrase that takes some definition. It is nearly impervious to REALIZE that I am living in denial while I am in it! I have argued with many folks when the argument was really between themselves and themselves. Ego has a piece of your personality. Selfishness will hang in there till enlightened. Pride holds on to a raft of old opinions and misinformation. Greed summons our selfish nature (double whammy). Lust almost cannot be overcome. All these deadly sins have a part in our psyche's. How stubborn they are will create sooooooooooooooooooooooo much denial of the truth - reality - what is really happening here.

So, think of your last 'hardest' time, an emotional time, perhaps during a loss or fearful time. Deadly instincts of fear surround your every action and thought, overshadowing all else. RECOGNIZING that you are in fear is huge. Say, "I am scared. I don't know how to handle this." There. The cognizance that you are in an emotional reaction is your first step toward more superior mental health. You have just quit denying reality. Now perhaps you can start to walk into the feeling, cry, know that it is happening, know it is not within your control, and breathe and live in the experience, knowing now that this feeling can happen, and you will live beyond. Always, always, there is a gain here, most likely knowledge of a happening - a new wisdom, experience behind you leaving you unscathed for functionality, belief in your own strength, and hope that life goes on. God had it all along. Denial has no place in reality.

So, if I live in this moment, I am secure. Most of the time even in peril, we still have our home, we still have our family, and we are standing upright. That may be all I have during this moment but it is a lot! Make it the best moment this moment can be, with full attention and a loving attitude and willingness. Great gratitude is what I get to know for this time.

I had to turn what they call a rubber conscience and concrete heart over to God. The chief symptom of an alcoholic family is denial. I knew how to put things aside really well, to delay thinking of them till the scourge got bigger, the deadline landed, the elephant hovered.

If we have been habitual 'hiders' and 'deniers' of actual experiences, we have been suppressing our spiritual, emotional, and intellectual growth. Is that really how you want to spend your time on this planet?

I would rather, love to live with sensibility and wisdom. This path is very abstruse to summon up when faced with a crisis, but imagine that you have practiced this over and over, and the next trauma faces the new you, with a conscious and subconscious that jibe. You have prepared for a walk through the trauma, step by step in a manner that accords knowing peace will be a result.

Profound changes can be orchestrated through your psyche and personality and sense of serenity when you "Let Go and Let God". The last paragraph was an experience in that. Imagine how many other growth experiences there are that we have not let into our thinking.

When I offer, "Let me help you." "Let ME figure out what YOU need." - Are you paying for my ideas? Did you ask for my input? Unsolicited advice is criticism. Don't take anyone's inventory but your own. You can tell me, you have 'got it'.

Did I just volunteer because I am so wise, better than you? Do I need to be needed? Oh my gosh. That is not people pleasing.

In my rolodex of thoughts, I tried so hard to justify my actions! I could rationalize for you what I was doing and why. I could force you to listen and understand, right? Hee Hee. I now notice that people bug their eyes out at me, nod their heads to get me to nod with them in agreement, and move in closer with side talk meant to convince me. I was probably doing all of that myself until I learned that I am receiving and offering *only opinion* sometimes. I do not get to press my unfounded thoughts onto anyone. And I had... I still have a desperate urge to act and push my opinion on others. My persona, my ego of property or prestige or money is mine; not for pushing on others, or influencing their ideology. That Stop, and go get God, realization brought insight to the fact that others used it on me. They, many times, also offer a self-formed (halfcocked) opinion.

My opinion might not be wanted. Did someone solicit it? Did they ask for my opinion?

My Mom's way was the only way, and she mentored my everything - Yea, but back in the 50's and 60's. In the 2020's I am over 60 years of age. It is a new century – many old mentored ways are no longer in effect. Some of my head is still in that box. It feels different to change, so I stay in the box sometimes.

Recently while preparing notes for this book, I went through another tremendous challenge that would affect both my financial and love life. I went through every wrong emotion for about eight hours. Then I remembered that I knew better. (Click) I processed what the challenge was, what was honestly at stake (nothing major) and checked my emotional involvement in those hours that just passed. Oh, for heaven's sake, I was worrying and fretting again. I said a prayer with my loved one asking for guidance. I said thank you to God for my abilities to deal with this. Thank you for my emotional health and the wisdom to not harm anyone with my words. Thank you for the capability to face this with a solution in mind. Done and out.

I still spend time concerned about things that are no longer. Instead of noticing and taking care with things that work today. I did not set out to react wrongly. I was just built that way, so far.

Get out of your own way. The courage to change the things I can. We need to be teachable.

And have belief that more truths will follow as I go along in my new way of life.

Laugh Enough

———

Here's an exercise for happy right now:

Think of a chuckle. Let it come through the air in your nose and a "humha" in your throat.

Warm it up. Duplicating the hum ha hum ha, until it opens your mouth in a smile by itself

Unleash uncontrollable laughter. Start with Ha, HA ha ha ha ha ha ha ha. (Till your throat warms up.)

Shake with your laughter. Undo your shoulders. Laugh with your arms flying.

Laugh like there is a friend laughing with you. Eye to eye, shared laughter. Sound tickled.

Row your belly boat, grab your belly with laughs spilling forth from your mouth. Hee Hee Ha Ha Ha Hm Ha Hu Ha.

Roar with laughter. Bend at the waist and get loud. HA HA HA Hee Haa HA Guttural sounds.

Drool and cry with laughter. Think it. Bending and stomping. Breathless gulps Tears

Laughter, whether a one liner, a smile inside, or a spontaneous clap, or an uproarious take you to the floor guffaw, burns calories. As Nike says, 'Just do it!' Laugh every chance you can. Laugh when you are tickled. Laugh when you think back on a funny scenario. Laugh to cope. Laugh with someone, share. Chip away your own inadequacies with a chuckle. Bring the benefits of humor everywhere you go.

It is proven useful to smile when your heart is breaking. I discuss aborting your thoughts in this book, and this is a place to mention the word 'abort' again. During what appear to be our worst times, at the notice of bad news, at the death pronouncement of a loved one, when disappoints happen, when fights or arguments occur; just appease me for a second and think of a "smile" to curtail the bad behavior and allow love to penetrate the discussion or relationship or room. What if this moment were about God's control and the love among his people? Most likely, it is. Smile at the person you are arguing with, admit you are at differing points of view, in pain. Admit and share. Together grief can be divided by more sets of shoulders.

Because, this too shall pass. Everything in life is transitional, ephemeral.

This moment, this sadness, this great abomination will disappear. Maybe very slowly, but I guarantee it will disappear. Lightening your thoughts, reaffirming yourself that this is a passing moment, finding peace within your heart with the truth of the matter, is facing the truth. No one said: "You must live in tension." No one said "Stress. Stress now." You did that to your own shoulders and you gave yourself the ulcer by your behavior in these times. Happiness and humor decrease pain consumption. Make a choice. Stress prevents us from being objective about our stress.

Exercising, even your pinkie, can take your mind off negativity. Spend a minute in movement. Don't beat yourself up mentally or verbally. Give the sensation a title, a mood. Have a conversation with yourself, or with God or about the elephant that sits in front of you.

What is the real culprit: anger, my stress, another's words, my feeling of inferiority, loss, guilt? Those are feelings *I have chosen* to feel. I can also choose to not have those visceral feelings rule.

By all means, take in a funny movie, read light hearted fare, contribute to others' smiles. Hang out with friends who look at life lightly. Find a Laughing Yoga class, for God's sake. Shake the humdrum and isolation. Mirth is a great perspective. Give yourself a super brain in doing so.

Clint Carter in the Wall Street Journal propounds that with isolation, the gray matter of your brain actually can shrink! With more grey matter, we are able to have better judgment, stronger cognitive abilities, and more positive moods. Keep that gray matter fed and active. We need it for potential mechanistic actions ahead.

AARP recently did their own study in the Antarctica, discovering that the hippocampus shrinks 7%, that is seven percent, in isolated folks. I would not live there as that seems purposefully harming my brain which I am not using most efficiently already!

What's the opposite? Do you do that? If I cannot label my mood or mode, I wonder about the opposite of my funk, or sad, or disillusionment.

Here's some options for you to choose:

Mirth
Humor
Do Stand Up Comedy
Jokes
Physical laughter
Stress Relief
Laughter Therapy
Health Clubs
Laugh at Yourself

Friendships with Laughter Benefits

Funny Phrases

Get Tickled

Be Surprised

Read a Comic Strip

Be Amused

Bring Levity into the room

Increase Your Breathing Power through a laugh

Prevent Heart Disease

Be More Optimistic

Be Positive

Cut Up

Do Slapstick

Don't' under laugh your allotted amount before you leave Earth.

I AM NOT making light of your serious times, your losses, your fears, and our basic-needs-starvation. I am only saying, we have a choice in walking our walks, in both the good times and the time when the possibility of happiness seems unreachable.

Take The Steps

———

Jumble of further studies to add life to your each moment. Your life is not a dress rehearsal of your life... Here are some ways:

Reiki

Pressure Point Massage

Positive Attitude

Quiong

Full Spectrum Light

Quantum Physics

Walk Thru Fear

Avoid Gluten

Echinacea

Release Emotion

Doing for Others

Create Art, Music

Get Out of Self

Sing: Forget Your Troubles

Acceptance

Appreciate Yourself

See Beauty

View Nature

Remember Who is in Control – A Greater Deity than you, my friend.

Color Your Cells

Practice Forgiveness, even of yourself

Live a Big Life

But here's a follow up question to not leave this chapter on such a positive note…

If you COULD call God right now, what is your question?

Look at Yourself

Take a penetrating look through this list of bodily movements, or quirks if you will.

You will find within this list, the tics and motions that many acquaintances have. But let's also see if you or I do some of the actions unconsciously and actually shut ourselves off from others...

We Know Not What We Do - but others often do! In the study of body language, my attitude and most often, everyone else's is very recognizable before I utter one word.

Look at a teenager when they are frustrated. Look at an ill person when the nurse takes a long time. Look at folks on nervous edge. Their attitude is generally emotional; physically and mentally derived and strongly appearing with a physical presence.

Pretend try these – you know you will; and you will be surprised that most of these movements habitually come to you quite easily!

Eye movement directly at you generally means listening. It can be the truth, or practiced dishonesty by a liar! Eye movement upward right is almost always a tall tale!

Eye movement downward can indicate rationalization or trying to convince themselves of something.

Lip biting is almost always anxious and tense. Twisted smiles usually are sarcastic and intolerant of what is happening. Pursed lips are upset and disagreeing or doubting.

So many movements with our face and head indicate to the companion what is going on with the other. It would behoove you to check these out on line. It is fun to know what your pal is thinking before he/she even speaks.

There are some other unconscious insinuations we have learned to shut people out and express emotion without a word. Are you CULPABLE of these? Remember, it takes effort to do these, for the most part, sorry expressions. It will take <u>more work</u> to get them out of your reactionary attitude and the void of unconsciousness.

Sometimes the thinking mind says "No" while the emotional section of the mind screams, "Yes", exampled by affairs of the heart. That pain is self-created. Folded arms show definite non interest. Self hugging is most often fear.

Other signs that you are in someone's personal space or arousing discomfort: covering a body part, adjusting clothing, one arm hugged close to body, holding a drink in front, needless appearance of scratching or touching self.

Of course, there are a mazillion ways to give off positive body language. I only intend to change your life here from the bad. You will eventually learn good behavior by observation. Definitely go to the mirror for the above and see how ugly some of the negative body language you give to other people; especially family who you proclaim to love the most. Before you walk away, I want you to end this mirror session with a smile, being kinder and gentler to yourself and you will find it is easier to extend that to others when you watch yourself this way.

One more body language thing and I will let you go. But this is a biggie.

Okay, so just as you want to have your personal space unencumbered, especially by aggressive nasty people, remember that others do not want that in their space(s)! They do not want you in their hula hoop area with your bad body or vocal language. They yearn for full time peace just as much as you do. Kindness begins with **KI** and ends with **SS**. Who doesn't want to be treated with as much care as possible in every minute we exist?

"Do unto those downstream as you would have those upstream do unto you.

Wendell Barry

One more note I want to share about body language and altering wrinkles: Botox enhancements near the lips diminish ability to smile. Facial expressions are essential to experiencing joy! It goes deeper than the fact that others may not see the apparent expression of joy on your face. Brains do not involuntarily interpret facial involvement toward joyful neurons. It is a conscious effort. Not smiling is a loss to both parties.

You can do all the eye rolls, have judgement thoughts about someone, turn away from ugly, you want – IN YOUR HEAD ONLY – not out loud or visible!

Who Owns Our Conclusions?
Missed Opportunity
for Potential

Hopefully, we have reached an anagnorisis – the point in a narrative in which the principal character (you) recognizes or discovers another character's (you, again) true identity or the true nature of their own circumstances.

You have just figured out your methods of deductive thinking. Everyone has some of the pieces of your thinking but not all. QUIT EXPECTING EVERYONE TO THINK AND ACT LIKE YOU. Got it?

Do you perceive everything you hear just like the guy next to you? Your twin brother? Buddha?

Our personal histories (yes, you have a history), habits of our parents, forefathers, where we live, how we live, who lives among us, events, risks we have taken, all form this Personal History. George Washington was not your neighbor and did not have your parents, so get over the fact that people are acting weird or stupid or ungodlike, or whatever it is you judge them about! - Just because their history is different than yours.

Goes without saying, doesn't it then, that you should not only respect who you are, but (you fill in the blank):

List everyone else you encounter today:

_____ _____ _____ _____ _____

Two conceptual semantics to help you realize your present plight: happy and stable.

Adam was the first human to pass the buck: (Gen.3: 12-13) Adam said *"The woman you put here with me - she gave me some fruit from the tree, and I ate it."* *Then the Lord God asked the woman, who replied, "The serpent deceived me."* Eve was wrong, but she also did not force Adam to eat. He was seduced and he personally made the decision to eat. He tried to evade responsibility. And Eve blamed the snake.

Generations have grown up, I witnessed, while working in a juvenile detention facility, three generations of felons, who had watched and did the same lifestyle that had been exampled for them. If happy and stable were part of your home, you know how to do it. When abuse or neglect or any tense of those negative examples are present in our home, we learn how to do it. Our brains have this ingrained, logged, woven, and impressed us as a way of life.

A learned helplessness can worsen life experiences. An abused child grows up to believe they are helpless and get to show anger like dad or nanny; thus, act this way. Previous traumas can be relived. Exposure to similar put downs or abuse in adult life remind them of the situational experience before, to render them helpless. If I had a loss or major change to my life, perhaps a humiliation, I created my own trapped existence there because of my circumstance, and then 'holding on' to an attitude.

An unhealthy brain results from living in sadness, sickness, poverty, and lack of success, and is an impediment to living a jubilant and full life. We, the Baby Boomers and Millennials are at the precipice as a species to change thinking; to spur our young about upgrading their behaviors.

A blind friend who admittedly said she had been marginalized all her life listed these harms done to her, acknowledging of course, that she had not known better than to allow it.

Marginalization:

> Saps energy
>
> Builds up over time
>
> Makes assumptions about you
>
> Believes it is a hard world out there
>
> Judges our own thinker
>
> Weighs on you
>
> Never felt a day pass without being marginalized

And makes you feel:

> Problematic
>
> Disabled
>
> Like a victim
>
> Sickly
>
> Gimp
>
> Grotesque
>
> Deaf and dumb
>
> Out of focus
>
> Less
>
> Afflicted
>
> Needy
>
> Limited
>
> Incapable
>
> Tragic
>
> Less valued
>
> Malformed

ɔuld come of someone who experiences this during their formative

A healthier brain has been formed when exposed rather to happiness, wealth, success, and good health.

The resolutions society makes are, he is mentally ill, she doesn't know any better, diagnostic labels we know nothing about (ADD, Bipolar, Anxiety). Trauma and grief, etc., can alter 'normal' temporarily, even sometimes get stuck in our gullet. Grief is very demanding. Those are genuinely true of a small minority, not mine to label, however. "Take a pill" is something we say offhandedly and rudely. When we understand the brain more in an educated status, we relax our rude thinking.

Back to the topic, now you know that you cannot blame your heritage, your forefathers, your upbringing, or your nonmental illness for your actions! It is believed that sixty percent of positive emotions come directly from our genes. (Hopefully our ancestors had it to give!) The rest is learned from experience and process of our own thoughts.

The truth is IF you have a diagnosis, you are under treatment or medicine or guidelines, and are cognizant of precautions you must take, such as a diabetic monitoring insulin levels. It is established that most of us are of sound mind. <u>OUR OWN USE OF OUR BRAIN IS WHAT DRIVES US TO BE WHO WE ARE AND ACTING IN THE MANNER THAT WE DO.</u> So, sorry, but your negligence to care for your brain leads to negative and unprogressive lives; and most often disgruntledness. We all know people like that, right – stuck in disgruntledness?

You create the style of life you lead with your decisions. We must weigh out what parents taught us in an older time of less technology, science, and evidence to the contrary. Research propounds that we can only blame about 40-60% of our actions on genetics! Inventions and research have altered their future. We are in that. So why stay in an era where it's okay to have ten old cars and a recliner in the front yard and use the word fuck? One-word answer, SLOTH. These folks may be guilty of laziness of the mind.

Purposeless activity may be a phase of death. –Pearl S. Buck

Final word: YOU ARE NOT STUCK WITH THE BRAIN YOU ARE IN.

Let me quote Hippocrates from way back in 400 B.C.:

"And men ought to know that from the brain and from the brain only, arise our pleasures, joy, laughter, and jests, as well as sorrows, pains, despondency and tears. And by this, in a special manner, we acquire wisdom and knowledge, and see and hear, and know what is foul and what is fair, what is bad and what is good, what is sweet, and what is unsavory...And by the same organ we become mad and delirious, where fears and terrors assail us...All these things we endure from the brain, when it is not healthy... In these ways I am of the opinion that the brain exercises the greatest power in the man. This is the interpreter to us of those things which emanate from the air, when the brain happens to be in a sound state."

Preparation for Life

Pamela Satran sets out a fairly poetic list of life's needs. I notice she does not list 'wants' as prevalent as details about what we 'need' to get through singlehandedly in this life we got. I like her minstrelsy verse, however I will just haiku it for you.

Preparation for life includes:

> *Screwdriver, in fact a nice set of tools, some power if you can*
> *Black lace bra*
> *Eight matching plates*
> *Running friendships*
> *A place of our own*
> *Enough money*
> *One perfect outfit*
> *Old shoes for kicking dirt*
> *Three good jokes*
> *One nice piece of furniture*
> *A recipe for a crowd*
> *One friend who can lift*

Knowing:

> *How not to lose her/himself with a lover*
> *Can't change history*
> *Can't change parents*
> *How to live with yourself*
> *Who to trust*
> *Not to take anything personally*
> *We belong anywhere*

Improve The Human Condition

Take a few minutes to write down what you are feeling. And then what you feel next. As you write, a normal rhythmic function, your nerves calm. Brain activity while writing feelings can refocus thoughts toward good behavior while activating good chemical interaction in your synapsis, rather than stress robbing you of precious dopamine. It is also true that buying new shoes, a letter from a long-lost friend, or having your favorite muffin, are each only a nuance, a small release of the chemical dopamine. Joys such as a cup of hot tea, petting your pet, giving gifts, helping others, all lift the dopamine level. Be sure to live in moments fully to experience that little lift. It is known that when you have gratitude for life's treasures in moments, your entire neural structure gets stronger and healthier. It is like joy leading to more joy. Keep it up.

So, let's say you need to see a doctor about a chronic issue and you are putting that off.

Scared shitless, I watched the screen of my MRI scan staring at the inoperable, monstrous lipoma in my musculature wrapped all over and around my hip.

First thing I said to the doctor was a piece of information I picked up in research for this book: "Did you know that doctors often only make 40 seconds total, of eye contact with their patients in an office visit?'

A doctor needs to look at how patients are postured, their breathing, position on the edge of the chair perhaps, leaning in. Often a screen with our information is in front of them to stare at instead. Yet, what I need, especially in that moment, is to begin to trust him. I need emotional reassurance, physical care, mental recognition of my situation.

That my dear, is a way to improve the human condition – the name of this chapter.

Listening to others comes with the whole package of unselfish kindness. Do you give that? Listening with your heart and body?

We burn the candle at both ends. We sacrifice our sleep to keep pace with America or a teenager. We spend our bodies in a laborious day. Then, after days and days of this, we have a medical problem. You have the pain/condition/ache. You know you have it every day. You put up with it. It causes you to step back or not step up to a task/job/fun time. You can function, but you are weighing the cost of medical service. Your mind decides practically that money is more important at this time. You fear losing money. You fear what the diagnosis could be. You fear you will have to undergo a treatment. You fear a treatment. You fear you will have to take time away from real life to attend to this. You fear you will have to step back from life while you heal. Fear. Fear. Fear.

So, let's look at what is R E A L: Pain. Loss of function in your life. End of sentence.

All the rest of the above paragraph, you made up in your head. And then the pain got worse and then we got more stubborn. And then we neglected ourselves. And then we got grumpy. And then we condemned the people who were able to do life's task/job/fun. Then we didn't like ourselves. We were fearful and self-condemning AND still in pain.

Step by step to progress.

Take out of that paragraph only the true statements. "I have chi
A doctor may help now."

Step One: Cognizance of Truth Only

Step Two: Call office

Step Three: See doc. Take care of minor issue without anxiety.

WHAT! Waaay easier than the anxiety and mental stress for a long time, which we caused us.

If you are prone to mercurial anxiety, it might be worth your effort to carry a list of what to do when panic strikes. If unable to think yourself out of the panic attack, hand the note to another nearby.

Breathe deeply in, exhale as much. Shallow or rapid breathing messes with your metabolic level. Deep breathing boosts incoming oxygen for the brain.

Students in school who are taught breathing exercises and meditative moments show significantly better scores in attention and SAT scores.

Generally, staying right where you are facing the fear, and walking through the steps of acceptance of truth, assist in calming you. Step one, say: "This is true for me and happening now". Step 2, Realize you are here going through this, standing on earth with the truth. Third step is to stay cognizant in order to process the situation.

Next, journal. Write down some notes from your thinking. Take notes of what is told to you. Write down your reactionary thoughts. "My brain put me on Elm Street, the movie." Then laugh at yourself.

Receive a hug. Touch someone nearby. Let them hold your hand. My fiancé at the time, laid on top of me while I was nauseous and scared in a full-blown panic attack. It worked.

Lastly, be prepared if you know you are prone. Carry a medication or know a physical method to make use of; such as squeezing your eyelid muscles, watching your belly rise and fall with breathing, relaxing and slowing down the motion, wiggle your toes.

Joy to the World

This is uncomfortable a time or two, but the takeaway feel-good is so strong, you will be returning to the practice. It comes down to choosing between discomfort and comfort. Hmmmm.

Visualization of the best scenario will support the previous chapter. Here's the kicker however. You may only entertain progressive and positive thoughts. Visualization salted and peppered with fear, worry and fret are just plain sick. God forbid you have that element. Realize that worry is potentially mind-altering. Worry focuses all our thoughts on an unpredictable, unknown, and un-factual future. Worry, wait, weep and wonder will only take me/you down.

Here's a good time for my friend's story. A Bible thumper, a really good Catholic from birth, instilled with several nun's adages, smart, suave about trends and modern life, etc. etc. A good person, right? So stuck on the harbinger that a devil lives among us, she blames her own antics on the devil winning her soul. Yes, she lives in blaming a nonexistent creature, shouts blame, and points to another (the devil) for her own ship going down. She subscribes to that and will argue this point to her death. (Can you tell that I have had suggestive conversations of persuasion with her?) No doubt, we have suffered in the past and it may explain why we are like we are, but we must not continue to keep ourselves in bondage to prior entrenched thinking events.

o argue with a person who has renounced the use of reason is like administering medicine to the dead.

So no doubt, her visualizations include an icon of the red demon himself and SHE LETS HERSELF OFF THE HOOK for bad behavior. Guess what. She will repeat bad behavior, because someone else is to blame for her doing. (The Devil)

Visualizations MUST, I repeat, must contain good characters, pleasant surroundings, and a win-win attitude. The more pleasing, the better. Check where your attitude lies. If your visualization takes you into pacing the floor, or anxious preemptive feelings, get a book on meditation. There lies more help than I have for you.

A sensation that everything will pass, leans to heal us; i.e., this moment is only for a moment long, and moods change, people go in and out of our lives in different ways, trains pass by, a dandelion loses its head, and our grief, happiness or wealth may be here only for a short stay.

Now enter your visualization with a more open mind, clear of old habits, open for clear and honest vision, engaging all the tools of life, use your imagination toward an essential goal toward world peace. That, my friends, is a good mantra.

Guaranteed here is that this sense of freedom and trust in your own pure thoughts is unbelievably mood lifting and serene causing. Yes, sad and bad things happen again and again. Once you open the mind you have and live, really live the moments, you realize their length, and begin to deal with each sensation.

Believe me, I once lived in cope. Cope, not hope. EVERY single day of my life had dread in it. Not all day, but particular times, I foresaw sadness taking me over, and thusly, it eventually came, often with anxiety, graduated to panic. I'm never going back to that same headset. I've got the other recipe now. I use to function and react only; however now I rather give myself permission to have an epic day full of epic moments. I learned to ABORT many sad habits. If you have read this book to this point, you get it.

Where do you want to retire? Tell me about a day in the life of your retirement? Think about your favorite get away. Where were you? What did the sky look like, air smell like, who was around? What sounds did you hear? Take it further, focus on your best times - a moment of total relaxation, appreciation, applause, acclimation, achievement. How light was your heart? How high was your mind floating? Breathe in that memory. Pause in the feelings. See the surroundings. Let your face relax in re-envisioning the time. Take in the warmth and comfort and fulfillment of your physical being.

Next paragraph: Okay, now tell me out loud how that was for you. Can you even remember what our topic was? That, my friend, is meditation. Can you imagine an hour a day of that mindset? Once well practiced, you and God can visit these beautiful places in a fly by. Between the oral test and the essay, you can go there. Among the hordes of folks waiting in traffic, your face can release. When the news story sets others afire, you repeat to yourself, "This too shall pass". I am talking about that kind of mindfulness full of peace and fresh air. That place where your shoulders actually hold themselves up and your heart beat is within calm flux. Your nervous system releases sympathetic vibes, transcending into corrective synapsis. You are confident. You are blessed. And your epinephrine, cortisol, and dopamine all grew new cells while living through the experience of mindfulness.

Let the word 'setback' leave your vocabulary. As do words such as should, would, could, wish, if only, and I'll do that for you. More words to pay attention to and drop from your lingo: what if, yes, but.

A reminder from previous pages that is important: Just plain remove the words: Should, Would, and Could from your language. Listen to others who use those words around you. It's sick to think we want to control our life rather than letting God, and yet relentlessly, we condemn mostly ourselves, and much of the time, others, with finger shaking words. Gees. Who wins when those words are out in the air? No one.

What brings you joy? What inspires you?

List these items/people/activities here now:

_____   _____   _____

_____   _____   _____

Where are YOU in each of the joys? I would guess YOU are in an interaction with the people, attending to something in life, or participating in an activity. Am I right? You commit yourself to enjoying these people and events. You accept each of these. Am I right? You take an action, whether it be in your heart or with your hand or foot. You are involved.

What do you do first to find joy? Engage? Listen? Look? Feel?

Why not do that every minute of every day? Hmm? Why not? Answer on a separate paper please.

You learn to give yourself a voice by speaking, to study by studying, to run by running. Be a mere apprentice again and learn the power of love until you master the art.

THIS TOO SHALL PASS

Biblical, isn't that phrase? How many of the Biblical quotes and adages still prove true. That is a statement not a question.

Recipe for Love

We may not like ourselves, yet we CRAVE for another to respect and love us. Marilyn Robinson wrote, *"For when does a berry break upon the tongue as sweetly as when one longs to taste it...and when do our senses know anything so utterly as when we lack it?"*

Humility and/or humbleness – big difference.

Humility: I am not first, last or best. Nor are you.

God has us both. We are side by side, God's kids. You need wellness, love, and support and so do I. I cannot help you unless I take care of me, too. And do my part.

Think, in 10 years, is this decision, argument, worry going to matter? Why wouldn't what is occurring in your presence be okay? If it is not ours to own, step back, don't jump in.

Self Check:

What do you do when you feel foolish? I can make it easy sometimes for others to make fun of me. I now know to laugh with them.

Laugh? Hide it? Redden, shrug shoulders, go on and on, verbally condemn yourself, call yourself 'only human'? Work your thought process here. Know yourself. Know your physical and physiological reactions to acting foolish. Take this time to review your behavior and consider what you could do differently.

Would you love someone who gossips, threatens you or others, offers false compliments, is sarcastic or dominates the conversation, interrupts you? Are you attracted to people who talk nonstop, are insecure, are hostile, flatter, solicit or seduce others?

Okay, reread that paragraph. Do you do any of those items on the list? Uh oh.

How to Love:

- Own your own. Make everything you do lovable and gracious. But you can only take care of yourself and your part in a relationship. What you do for another is love. You have a role in every single moment of your life. Along with those moments comes responsibility for what you choose, what you watch, where you go, WHAT YOU SAY, what you think and how you act. If you only did what was easy, you will remain weak and gutless. There is no blame ever cast when you are involved. YOU are reacting or responding. It is absolutely true, "You cannot change someone in a relationship." Let there be no clouds around that truth. See your part, speak to it. You may have made a mistake. My tongue misfires! One of the biggest fights in my life with my spouse was about dirt and a bucket. My words got twisted in my head, and the first part of my oration was, "*I don't appreciate you*...putting dirt on top the red rocks I spent a lot of money on when you dig the hole for my new flowers in the rock garden." The only part he heard was "*I don't appreciate you*"! Learn, as I had to, do not blurt, do not cast blame, do not HURT anyone else, ever period.
- We <u>choose</u> someone we like to be with us. In beginning marriage, it is often lovey dovey, 'you go first, you have the larger piece, let me get you one while I get mine'. Somehow this wonderful

choice of a person, does things we like, shares, and thinks of us first. Let them make one mistake of going first or their ego step out of line, or thinking outside "OUR" relationship box for themselves, and woo hoo, we CHOOSE to feel 'hurt.' Oh, Lordy this is so ridiculous. Let the people around you be who they are! If years later their choices are not similar to ours, and the change is unacceptable to us, we then have another choice to make. But it's ours. NEVER TAKE SOMEONE FOR GRANTED. ALWAYS BE ON YOUR BEST. Tell me one reason you would not. That does not mean we live with anxiety for goodness sakes, that means we are considerate and thoughtful ALL the time.

- So *they* have a flaw we don't like – gum chewing, starting every sentence with "So," or gawking while they drive. Grow up! You certainly have a flaw (or twelve) and people still choose to like you. If you are focused or have an inordinate regard on their lack of etiquette or defects, where did kindness and love go? We must counterbalance the effect of their defect in our hearts. Gratitude that someone else on this planet will hang with you is your only course of action, or you are in imprecise thinking. Handle people as you would like to be noticed and acknowledged yourself; not with nagging or suggestions for them to *change*. That never was and never will be your job.

- When you don't understand why they did what they did, ask and listen. If you feel hurt by their action, you chose to own that hurt, that is yours, not their problem. Oh, ya. True. My intent with the dirt and bucket argument was to protect something I had spent money on. But look what I did with my words…hurt the person I love the most. When we listened to the motivation behind each comment and feeling, we came to a deeper love and understanding and learned a valuable lesson *ourselves*.

- If you always give in, just to have peace, you made yourself a victim. God won't even come to that pity party! You are wrong! You just usurped your belief in yourself, demeaned and disrespected your own being. Do I hear 'victim' here? Many people do this – are compliant on the outside and resentful on the inside. You are not alone. Very often, the spouse gives in, and later comes to resent that they always do what the other wants. WHAT? Read that sentence again. That, that right there is headed for divorce or abandonment, even murders by court history.

- My first boss was married thirty-seven years when I met her. It was common in that time to refer to the old lady or the 'ole man' or the nag. And as the years went by, guys thought it was the proper reference in speech. Or we rolled our eyes when one or the other of us spoke. My first boss, was different. She always spoke about: 'the love of her life, my dear husband, my sweetie', with endearments and gratitude and nice words. Which words do you want to hear from your spouse's mouth when they are with their friends? No brainer.

If wise, we have many facets of love to look at in a partner we intend to share life with.

Physical needs seem to be first in teenagers and young love. We want to be touched and caressed. We crave physical support when sad, tearful or have great joy, I want your hug. Experimental kisses are so fun and arousing, and teens need to learn about that. Affection has so many definitions. While shopping for a partner, you want to make sure that interacting, activity sharing, tenderness and welcoming acknowledgements are included in the physical department.

Emotional needs are monolithic for almost all of us. Acceptance on all levels of our flaws, truths, and spirituality is utmost in importance. Respect is so evident in a new relationship because it will change with comforts and duties in the home. You have no idea till you are there. Sometimes intimacy stops for unknown health reasons. While shopping, think about that possibility. Is this just wonderful self-indulgent lust? You absolutely must feel that you are made a priority in your partner's life, for a lifetime. I can't stress enough what part truth and honesty play. If you have an inkling of doubt about either, follow through on that. Special investigation will be withstood if love is strong. Ask the lover what his frustrations are? What is funny to them? Do you have the same view? My chicanery was only funny to me; how about to them? Observe behavior with his/her family and friends. Do you approve? Is it part of who you are too? Often what the future in-laws are doing now will show up in your possible partner eventually, I can almost guarantee it.

Why do I (or your parents) care whom you select? This, this is a huge contention more times than not. Your mother and father and I, by the grace of God, have totally been in your shoes. We were your age, we had friends for fun and events, we have lived through horrors and lovelies in our relationships, and we experienced pieces of the life that is ahead for you. All the learning we have done applies, like in school – you learn History for a reason. You could not commit a science experiment until you had your goggles and apron on and the teacher was present. In relationship, we do not want you to commit to a marriage experiment until you have certainty in your vision of life ahead and the right person is present. You took your own apron off when you grew up and atoms of shit might fall on you now. Are you prepared emotionally to handle that?

Insecurity and fear as an individual must be dealt with on your own. Big girl panties/tidy whities for both men and women apply. Take care of and steward yourself in financial, physical, emotional, social and spiritual matters before putting yourself in another's arms/home. If you are not a fully self-activated person, you will fight and most likely (50%) fail in the relationship. Finding another fully activated person for your partner makes a fun endeavor. The experiences in the search are learning tools. Let the wrong partners go. After all, doesn't your partner also want a fully self-activated person to live with? Are his/her living quarters similar to your style? Just a personal theory, but I see most of the couples who met in a vulnerable open learning environment (college) stay together long time.

There are many quizzes in magazines and on line about love. Do them. Avoid the superficial tests (Can you stand his gum chewing? Does he dress trendily?)

> *"What you love only matters to you.*
> *What you do matters to those you love"*

Movie quote from "The Last Kiss".

C.A.R.P. – Certified All Round Person

What do you do that causes a deep, recondite sensation of appreciation?

If you didn't say 'connect', I'll say it for you. Connect with nature. Connect with another. Connect with God. Be at peace within. Pay attention to the connection with your body and mind.

I will venture that if you had your spirit, mentality, and physical dimensions all connected that you would have peace.

Why don't you? Not 'Why don't you have peace?', but rather, 'Why don't you connect your dimensions?' It's your world and you have control of the actions you take within it. It is your fault if you are not in peace.

Weaving our innermost sensations can be hard ONLY when we are not tuned in. The to-do list interrupts, an illness rules our day or hours, work is challenging physically or mentally, squirrels take our attention, others demand attention, stop lights go out, a leak spews out of the plumbing. Oh, yes. We all have days of that. But some of us connect with our spirit, our senses, our intelligence and our whole being, even throughout the leak. Some people just call the plumber and wipe up the mess and smile. Yes, believe it or not. Would you rather do that or do you prefer cussing and swearing, calling the landlord and demanding, and cursing about ruination? Some people do. God help them.

See the choice you had? You have that every second. Habits often do us in. We habitually hear our parent's or bosses' or politician's voices in our own thinkers and use that judgement against things and others.

"Damn plumber." "Damn leak." "Fucking clock." "Fucking wrong size wrench." "Gees, there's water in my face." Who hasn't been in this world? Who hasn't listened to this scenario or similar metaphor play out?

Which do you want? Peace? Or do you choose the damning headset that goes with the above?

"The education of man throughout the world cannot fail to result in a more tolerant and peaceful life for all" - Anonymous

Change the habit. Change the attitude. Abort the thinking. Happy the life.

I want to lay out more about what your brain does so that you know what you damage and where you are stuck.

(Taken from <u>Change Your Brain, Change Your Life</u> by Daniel G. Amen.) I can't offer a better list than he.

Biologically:

> Brain Health
> Physical Health
> Nutrition
> Exercise
> Sleep
> Hydration
> Hormones
> Blood Sugar Level
> Supplements
> Genetics

Trauma/Injuries
Allergies
Toxins Environmental, Drugs, Mold, Caffeine, Alcohol
Infections
Physical Illness
Medications

If anything above is in ill health or a predisposition to wrong thinking, it will be further influenced by:

Psychological:

Self Talk
Self Concept
Dealing with Grief/Loss
Sense of Worth
Body Image
Upbringing
Development
Past Emotional Traumas
Past Failures
Past Successes
Generational Histories and Issues
Hope
Sense of Control
Sense of Power

If any of the above are occurring, you are likely to react, rather than correctly respond, based on their foundation.

Social:

Quality of Current Environment
Sense of Connection to Family and Friends and Community

Health and Habits of Friends and Family
Relationships
Stresses
Health
Finances
Work, School
Current Successes or Failures
Information

If the above are not fully satisfying, again, we are likely to be ill balanced in relationships and health.

Spiritual:

Who am I Accountable To
Sense of Meaning and Purpose
Why Does My Life Matter
Connection to a Higher Power
Connection to Generations Past
Connection to Future Generations
Connection to Planet
Morality
Values

Dr. Amen's publications are outstanding if you want to delve further.

Wow, now put these four factors, how your body functions – well or not well; developmental issues and how your mind thinks; your current life situations and social support and connections; and your sense of meaning and purpose – put them together and you have your own sweet package of you. I'd like you to run down these lists again and perhaps pick out where struggles or losses lie, and where you spend your time. Learn what your deficits are. Be aware that they are occurring in your persona in so many ways with so many disparate impeti.

Here are some deficits many of us do not even know we do:

- Obsess about someone's else's need or problem
- Overtalk our cause
- Repeat ourselves to get our way
- Hate ourselves, or something about ourselves
- Fear
- Have insecurity about so many facets of life
- Shy around others we made authorities in our silly mind
- Non-Acceptance of what is true
- Refusal to mature by taking responsibility for OUR actions
- Blaming others
- Judging, judging, judging
- Not using a pause for brain to work
- Opining untruths
- Angry face making
- Closed mind
- Ungrateful
- Small lies
- Being defensive
- Controlling others
- Whining to get my way
- Self-willed
- Rationalizing thoughts away
- Rationalizing my errs in reasoning for other people
- Forgetting God is in all our affairs
- Minimizing my errors
- Not recognizing we have potential to grow in wisdom
- Refusing to grow in knowledge or laziness about it
- Being lazy in our responsibilities
- Taking more than a fair share
  Stealing consequences from those who need to experience them

These are some of the things I found out in inventorying myself that I never had a clue I was doing! I was like a chunk of swiss cheese, with so many holes of defects, yet, I truly thought I was a nice person. I let my habitual thoughts rule my speech and action and they were faulty! These things got me nothing good. I let my brain malfunction on lazy purpose. I could not be a better person until I let this hypothetical stinking thinking go. Sick mind. Someone with a like mind, called themselves shortsighted. Oh my gosh. I was that too. How about you?

What I discovered after doing an inventory of who I hurt and who hurt me, the illusion I had created in my mind was greater than the reality. I was arresting my growth based with intangible considerations – worry or regret.

This is just what is happening in the brain! Spend a minute contemplating the input from other organs, say the health and flow of your bloodstream; hunger; senses, emotions. The limbic system surrounding the cerebral cortex pulls together some of the factoids that are occurring in your body and thought, such as dangerous or safe. From there we make decisions based on all of the above, such as fight or flight. A woman's limbic system is larger than a male's. Interesting. Women truly may 'feel' more strongly about emotional events.

I particularly like my limbic system, where thoughts are tagged and sorted to the various stages where the actors are; where comparisons with past experiences and events or consideration of thought is weighed. This all happens in a quick instant.

It goes without saying, whether you won an Emmy, wear a crown or were neglected/abused, those emotions will be imposed on our daily living. Your limbic system contributes greatly in relationships, how long severe grief lasts, how much 'it hurts.' A chemical composition or decompensation can change your whole day. Well, your life, as a matter of fact.

I'll just ask:

> Have you reacted to recent criticism?
> Are you moody?
> Have trouble concentrating?
> Lost interest in friends, hobbies, pleasureful things?

The combination of activities within your head actually does alter our mood and attitude, sometimes for far too long. It is okay to process through these.

What I am saying is, be cognizant that much is happening biochemically from impetuses around us. We are reacting inside. This book is about awareness of thinking, accepting what is true, and allowing time for the brain to put it all together; and when possible, add knowledge for both good and healthy actions that make up our days. Focus on gratitude and one step ahead toward progress and solution.

Here is one of my most pitiful habits:

Many personalities, alcoholics especially, will question what you are doing, when, and why. While those questions make me feel cared for and appear to be an interest in my day, I feel that that person does not love me or trust me and I am imperfect if I have to be checked or watched by them. That, my friends is an inappropriate reaction which displays no self-worth. I want you to employ a little trick I learned to help my self-worth. Use your own name often, speak loudly, take a step to introduce yourself first, spell it if difficult, etc. This is a first step beginning to own your self-worth.

I received a gift of a wallet sized card that offers females accountability questions:

o   Have I been a verbal testimony this week to the supremacy of the Lord Jesus Christ?

o Have I fantasized a romantic relationship with someone other than my spouse this last week or read or seen any sexually alluring material?

o Have I lacked in integrity in my financial dealings? Have I spent money recklessly?

o Have I honored my husband and children?

o Have I said damaging things about another person, either behind their back or face to face?

o Have I succumbed to a personal addiction? Explain.

o Have I continued to remain angry toward someone?

o Have I secretly wished for another's misfortune so I might excel?

o Have I been faithful to my daily devotions?

o Have I just lied?

o Is there anything I see in my life that could be dangerous?

Fellas, listen up:

Your female started in this relationship with you with her trust and love.

Eighty percent of domestic violence victims are women. Fifty percent (50%) of homeless women are homeless due to abusive circumstances. Thirty percent (30%) of all women are abused. A woman is abused every 9 seconds. Only 16% of assaults of women are reported! Staggering, as they say.

Withholding money, sex, using weapons, demanding sex are all aggressive acts of abuse. Withholding income, preventing them from work, threatening family and close friends, impeding ability to call for help. Those are all abusive. Thinking about escalating any of these scenarios is felonious. Violence actually blinds us to true beliefs.

Here are some patterns of domestic abuse to recognize:

Feeling trapped, hopeless and helpless

No self-esteem

Lack of access to bank accounts or money

Feeling of being controlled

Hurt or harm to your person

Keeping you isolated

Keeping you from air, water, and love

Feeling stripped of choices

Fear of capabilities to thrive

Feeling stripped of personal power

Feeling of being dominated over

Verbal bashing

Emotional abuse

Did you know that there is such a diagnosis as Nature Deficiency Disorder that can result?

Rebuilding from the above abuse is long. To repair the damage, phases of life that last longer than the abuse must occur:

1. Secure a safe living condition, often without monetary resources
2. Repair damaged goods, including skin and bones, houses, material possessions lost
3. Recognize that the abused did not ask for it
4. Recognize right from wrong anew
5. Believe in self-worth
6. Rebuild and collect a functional environment and materials
7. Belief in own

Many of us get caught in any one of the menageries in that list and never make it through seven times, or twice, or three incidents that occurred at a man's hands. Death occurs. Just sayin'.

Life is One Big Dodgeball Game

Jesus, take the wheel! God uses me. The truth is. I am just fortunate enough to have legs planted on Mother Earth and do some actions to follow His lead. My behavior and pervicacious stubbornness and desire mess with His greater plan!

I am responsible. But am I acting responsibly? Do I have some wickedness in my heart that comes out? Do I mentor goodness for children? Do I deny my own goodness? Do I choose to act in ways other than good? Have I allowed my emotions and feelings to rule my actions? Have I become a slave to others? To my reactions?

What do I do with my money? Do I put a nickel's worth (prorate your income here to 5%) away for retirement, the church, savings account, fun? What value do I put on my life? Why wouldn't I look at the full picture of my, plus or minus eighty, years of life? Never borrow for something that depreciates.

In our culture, we learn to be responsible for ourselves and responsive to other people. Kelly Addy with the Billings, Montana "Gazette" offers that:

> *"…we have free will. The trick is to know how to combine our freedoms to become something more together than we can be alone….Nobody else has read our script…Franklin D. Roosevelt said, "Remember you are just an*

extra in everyone else's play…In communities and relationships we learn to be responsive to others and responsible for ourselves. When individuals act responsibly, our community becomes stronger, the future brightens for all of us, and freedom grows."

"I want world peace, Bob." – Miss America candidates.

Wouldn't it be sweet if we had it? Where we all belonged. We each were welcome like bees in a hive or monks in a monastery, as brothers and sisters, caretakers of one another?

Once we realize that WE are not going to reorder the world to suit our wishes, no matter how well intended or sincere they are; nor can we change our personal, sometimes traumatic history, we will find hope in a power higher than ourselves. That stress of trying to carry the weight of our children, our jobs, our future, etc. goes off our shoulders. We cannot change the behavior of our alcoholic, a difficult challenge at work, grumbling or offensive clerks, or relationship issues alone. God creates chance happenings and long-term fixes if you let Him. We can let go of false problems and deadly sins and ridiculous fretting. There is no time in our lives for those. We enter into a novel way of thinking, minus those pressures. We must recognize that most things are beyond our power.

Here is what you have power over: Mindful behaviors and actions and words. You get to now be of good service to others and explore your own talents and skills.

What beautiful intelligence comes when we depend on the Lord. After turning our will to Him, we deepen our serenity and gain confidence that the Lord is guiding us through His plan. Lessons come to us in His time, not our rushed belief that we could have His power over things. Then, only then, can your heart and mind have connected peace.

A prayer which is said to never fail: *"Thy will be done."*

How to be Happier

There are actually tips (other than this entire book) that help a person get on target to love their lives:

Keep a list of what is ahead for you to do(tasks) or a calendar or phone with reminders

Step one is take a step in the difficult task – take the next right step, according to God.

Know how to prioritize.

Ask yourself: What is your goal in life? Everything will be much less tasking if goals are clear.

(My goal became simply, 'To be my best self.' In all my affairs.)

Organize your stuff.

Take care of yourself, laugh, pray, mooooove, learn to listen.

A reminder I like: The Catholics do a little action in reverence to the Lord, the Sign of the Cross. In asking for help or to keep ourselves connected always, we begin prayer with it. It is a tiny cross on the forehead (Minds), Lips (Words), and midchest (Hearts). At mass, we say, "Only say the word, and my soul shall be healed." My broken thinker needs little actions or rote prayers to keep me in God's good standing. To keep in human being good status, I must use my Mind, Words, and Heart in every action, so that I can go in peace, glorifying the Lord. Make sense to set up your own little reminder?

Happiness is enhanced when the above does not go wrong. It is a simple mind frame to refer to. If you face life calmer because you know what you want, the tendency for it to go well happens.

Pray Pray Pray

'God asks no man whether he will accept life. That is not the choice. You must take it.
The only choice is how."
Henry Ward Beecher

How do I celebrate God's gifts to me? Prayer, church, and on my knees. It all gives special warmth to me. Someone is taking care of me. God can get in there and do something. It is a shift in thinking that I could not have pulled off on my own, with my ineffective ways of thinking. Then I have a whish of joy; a woosh of serenity, and see peace in my life.

I could be Mormon as I live 3 blocks from the Mormon Temple. (FYI: The light from it does not 'bother' me at night.) Their tall steeple, actually is a beacon to find my house from the interstate.)

Stop in a Universalist Unitarian service to learn how the other half lives – not necessarily with a common deity, but with a commonality of doing good, living right, being kind to others, enjoying cultural meditation and "Shalom".

I have had wonderful arguments with agnostics, teasing them to defend their scientific beliefs. Start with a question like, "Would you contact me if you die first?"

Baha'i, Muslim and a few others require a lot of discipline and knowledge from what I observe – I am not that good yet...always more Bible reading on my docket.

Too bad the local 'Sprit Quest' group folded. I happened upon them about ten years ago in Billings, Montana. A delightful experimental group, learning about their touch with higher powers in their sharing, including a Pagan Priestess, three ordained ministers, a Native shaman; trying out hypnosis, Reiki, healing touch, intuitive measures, color auras, meditation, Tazing, my drumming therapy class and blind dancing. We discussed the afterlife, the mafia, what Heaven might look like and tried out a number of transcendental means. Transpersonal psychologists and psychospiritual explorers will site you hordes of liberating actions; such as, "If there were no beauty, how would we declare what is beautiful?" Spirit Quest had a pledge spoken at the beginning and ending of our 'meetings'.

> Our Strength lies in keeping an open mind and heart
> Our Honor lies in maintaining pure discussions
> without judgement or prejudice
> Our Character lies in the kindness we demonstrate to others
> Our Happiness lies in finding our own pathway to joy
> We are both student and teacher on a Spiritual Quest

What a fair promise to one another, don't you think?

I miss my southern friend, Linda McCloud, who recently took her ministry back home to the southland. Married to a Baptist minister, she was in Billings to initialize a new west side Episcopalian church. Her "Ask Me Anything" classes were the best; open, and Bible based. We discussed clothing – why the deacon knots his belt on a certain side to what color obis go with which religious feast. She gave me a delicious bread recipe... after I told her I lost my concentrated faith returning to my pew from communion. Yum.

Yes, I suffer from irreverence often – not of God, but of earthly methodologies and doctrines. It is the people of this planet- the people who have designed our practices of religion. With Jesus' leadership and teachings, 'the people' formulated, sected out and bisected religious worship. Ergo, I have the freedom to find my way for closeness with my God, in a plurality of religions. Religion, however chosen, is a word assigned to our imagination and the understanding of how best to reside in a spiritual connection to where our God is.

Know your spiritual self. Do you 'belong to a church' because three generations of your family have done so?

- Is your religious experience so far, buying into a dogma?
- Is your religion based on YOUR accepted doctrine, based on imagination?
- Is theology concrete within your mind?
- Do you feel you are intuitive in your spiritual life?
- Have you probed into other religious practices?
- What propositions have been offered to you in your drive to be spiritual?
- Is Biblical lore or scientific knowledge more prominent in your life?
- Do you have a story about a climactic moment, a miracle or an apparition that you base worship on?
- Does what you do, how you act and speak, match the commandments you say you follow?
- If a God spoke, would you convert to what he said?

The search continues for me, last week I enjoyed Humor Sunday at St. Andrew's Lutheran with Susan Barnes. Lettuce lay on the altar. ("Lettuce pray'.) A knock knock joke got us to open our billfolds with, "Phillip the baskets with all your heart can share."

Dave Thompson is most welcoming at the First Presbyterian Church with classes provoking involvement in Jesus's ministry with topics like, "Who moved the stone?" And "How do I get to Heaven?" Their Church and Society Class will keep you learning about 'ways we can help our fellow man' in Billings, Montana.

And of course, the Cathedral, can't say enough about the attention my heart pays when in a Cathedral or basilica. Entering under double spires seems to double how wide my heart opens to the messages during prayer there. Just love Father Houlihan's Question of the Week, sending us off to seek further fulfillment of our spiritual lives, soul searching as we circulate among His many.

My niece, her husband and a best friend paid ninety bucks each to become ministers on line - a business move as she owns a Bridal Shop near a beach with a Gazebo. (Sorry niece, this paragraph is just for literature sake.) For some wannabee Christians there is a bridge, a gap between being blessed, and/or living with God. It is a choice and it takes action on behalf of us.

A best friend each week, tries to cheerlead me into salvation. The most I get from that is to notice that she is exhausted from her good work.

Recently in Bible study at Faith Chapel (entertaining service if music lifts you to that higher plane of worship) I was reminded that we should love God above all, above my brother, was the message. That got me thinking,

Me? How am I making out? Occasionally my love for my fiancé, my sister, my brother, my friend; or that busy-ness of car repair, earning money, or household needs, comes before God in my mind. Even with all the worship I do. The best thing I do for myself is to invite God in to each moment and remember this is His Kingdom, His Power, His Glory. Remember, you can start your day over any time during the day! Try as I may, I cannot seem to control above Him! Ergo, Let Go and Let God. See you in (your) church!

Wouldn't this world be wonderful if 'compassion' were our middle name? I find when I strengthen my closeness to God, compassion comes easier. Don't laugh, but when God is in your every moment, it feels like you were just handed a soft teddy bear. See, it improves our disposition and attitude immediately and increases our degree of humanity.

Practicing gratitude is the highest form of prayer.

Gratitude has an internal cycle you are going to like, once you start using it more: National Geographic's 2020 edition on "Your Emotions" tells us:

"...you sit and reflect on what you feel grateful for – but it's now seen as an energizing emotion that can spur one into action. Research by UC Davis psychologist Robert Emmons finds gratitude motivates people to meet goals – for example, exercising more, getting better grades, or engaging more socially – possibly because it makes people feel more deserving of good things and instills an ability to go after them. Some research finds that gratitude – as well as watching someone be charitable – activates our brain's reward circuitry, which doles out feel-good, motivating dopamine. Just saying 'thank you' can trigger an attitude of gratitude, alerting one that kindness has occurred and reinforcing future generosity for the giver: Benefactors who are thanked for their contributions are more likely to donate more and work harder than those who aren't thanked."

Seriously, I'm glad mom gave me a base religion.

So you go to church every Sunday. Well, almost every Sunday. Except... when I am going boating or fishing, or the boys want to meet for breakfast at Sam's, or when I decide to sleep in. Well, some Sundays, I go to church.

Many Christians only get about one third of the way to mature Christian development which means they might be active in their congregation. Joining a financial board, mowing the lawn, or being a trustee may still leave an individual spiritually incomplete.

I call myself a church-goer. That makes me good, right?

Where in the hell did you get that conception??!

What makes you good is goodness. Purity of heart. Projected kindness. Love of life and what it offers. Sharing, caring, truth, and gratitude. If you add closeness to God, you are in like Flynn.

One of our greatest spiritual needs is to have the truth.

Going to church does not add God to your life. Are you fooling yourself, thinking otherwise?

Lies. Lies. Lies. Fibs. White lies. Intentional lies. Excuse lying. These are each the same sin. Can you be fully spiritual if you lie?

"How are you? Fine. And how are you? Fine." How many of those conversations have you had? Yet your friend is in the middle of chemotherapy, having finished radiation which burned his innards and caused horrible vomiting. During the chemo, his car was hit in the parking lot. Oh, and you…You got an overdraft notice, your uncle is dying in a nursing home, you have remission herpes, and just argued with your daughter over money. I'm Fine. Fine? Liar. We give a false allusion to our friend.

Do you think the front for the above dis-eases of life is "Fine?" Your 'friend' would love to have your support and human kindness to aid him in his journey to death. You, his friend, would love to have an ear to lighten your walk through the unsettled and fragmented pieces of your day. Disgruntled, unhappy, hurting hearts in each of you, part from each other with I'm Fine", but still hurting. Are you really friends? Hm…Did you just lie to yourself too? You are showing a conditional friendship.

Gosh, it would be awful to "appear" to be hanging on by a thread, it would be awful to lose face and pride by sharing hardships between friends, it would be awful to humiliate myself by saying, "I need your smile, hug or a prayer." Gosh, really? Would it be awful to walk away from that discourse with a hug and a lift in your step because someone listened, and someone else on this big ole' earth cares about little ole you?

So let's say you have just discovered that you lie to yourself. Ask yourself these questions:

Have you ever stayed home and called in sick? Told someone you could not attend a function due to an illness you didn't have?

Neglected to point out to a clerk that she undercharged you or gave you more change than due you?

In scorekeeping with your brother-in-law over work he did on your roof, did you do much less work for him?

Lied during golf?

Ever say "it was on the line" during baseball/volleyball when it was an inch either way?

Nodded that you understood, when you didn't?

Said this line, "I think I read that book, saw that movie, studied that in school, tried it before"?

Exaggerated?

So your sister smokes marijuana for her fibromyalgia, doctor prescribed. She drives her car into another car where a person is injured. Do you admit she was smoking at your house just before this occurred?

Your unrich daughter and her husband, with 3 small children and college loans still to pay off make an insurance claim for hail damage which they never intend to replace or repair and have a friend write up an invoice for them. Do you tell on them?

We get caught. We have Catch 22's occur. We are just a little wrong. We have accidents that affect others or possessions of others. We do stupid things. We speed just once in a while. We never put shopping carts back. We litter only once in a great while. Ever used the handicap spot, just for 5 minutes? Find something of value that could be traced to the owner but we don't trace? Keep something we 'borrowed'? Keep the casserole dish left after the picnic? Borrow your neighbor's tool and are just waiting for him to ask for it back – if he ever does? Take something you are not positive is a freebie?

Ever?

If we can rationalize away the above things, we are fooling everyone. We are making mistakes. We are committing greed, envy, thief, law breaking, coveting, rule breaking and harm. But we certainly don't see that little white fib or small harm as anything 'wrong' or unjustified in our minds.

That thinking alone is the sin. See it?

We ostensibly cover up our committed falsehoods. We rationalize away wrongdoings as 'what normal people do'. Who wrote the normal rules, after all? Newsflash: They have never been written!

Okay, it is a given that we each have harmed another. And that we have been harmed. We each have been involved in a wrong doing. And have been wronged.

So we consider what we do as just evening out the score. Really? Is it?

Can you have peace of mind when you have grievous faults in your past?

Can you have peace of mind after grievous faults are committed against you?

This book is about straightening out our thinking, so that none of the wrongdoing we create is okay with us, and to allow others to be just as naughty as we may have been, without hating or condemning them. We never solved a problem entering into the solution with the same level of thinking that created the problem.

That sounds more like "fair" doesn't it? Intensely scrutinize it from where God sits. Which practice would He like more? Which would He be prouder to see you do?

Sue Olp, Billings Gazette writer, recently related: *"Men explore spirituality in ways other than religion; and used the descriptor "secular humanist".* The article stated *"people need to create a space for doubt and question".* I agree. It is within us to search and know, through collective worship and/or personal value.

My quote shadows those above: *"As long as each person holds constant value in niceness to community, people, and world, we are within ourselves in everlasting peace."* That 'value in niceness' often originates from joint worship and belief in a good greater than ourselves - often God. Put simply, spirituality creates both inner peace, and a striving for world peace creates an energy of the desired serenity, happiness and brotherhood, church attendee or not.

The pageant contestant stood in her gown, "I want World Peace." A colloquial joke? Is it possible for a single person to be the impetus to World Peace? Yes.

What do you want, really? Left up to me, I would live in a world surrounded by love, support and personal happiness, and well, quite frankly, Peace.

Have you found an orthodox practice that leads you to peace, joy, and happiness?

No single religion or church has as yet shown me to be the ultimate altruistic method of worship. I church hop.

Heard of a crooked church accountant, abuse by priests, the stout Methodist tax felon, or an Easterner fighting over their understanding of Allah? No matter the denomination claiming perfect spiritual direction, individual members fail. It is up to us.

What belief system is right for you or me, two different beings?

By church hopping, I have found Bible verses the same, messages identical 'cept for a verbiage flare, hymns of exact humming, and the host, each slightly different.

My Islamic friend advocates her Allah is my God, except for semantics; yet our worship, the ism is worlds apart. Both with God-of-our-understanding purviewing our lives.

Catholicism is said to be orthodox, sacramentally driven, and formal; Methodists, sanctimonious; Mormons, private and followers. Certain marriages are not sanctioned by other's tenets. Presbyterians prove to be community minded and the nicest people. Some sects are Biblically minded, others not. Some take the Body of Christ. Some say that is devil's practice.

Is one more right than another in our diatonics?

Are Agnostics and Atheists really that? Should those words be capitalized? What about none of the above? The only other church in my home town was "Non-Catholic" - what a biased and non-Christian attitude my grandmother inferred to me. She even forbade me to go into it with my little friend who was a member.

I am reminded of Nicolaus Copernicus, the Renaissance mathematician and astronomer who formulated a model of the universe that placed the Sun rather than the Earth at the center of the universe. Now my grandmother was not as old as Copernicus, but she had beliefs and ideas up to her time of life; not mine. I could no more vote for her political affiliation than use her eyeglasses and expect MY eyes to see through them.

She was not closed-minded. She was bright and knew everything there was to know in her lifetime.

A buzzard put in a six foot by eight-foot pen open at the top is a prisoner. It will not even attempt to fly and remain a prisoner to what it knows. Closed minded individuals do not see a bigger picture. How can we have peace without educating ourselves, opening our minds to allow differences? Questioning our cage bars?

Spirituality allows my every thought in communication with a being greater than myself. Let the world be in an ecclesiastical ether oneness, and live within that atmosphere among all.

Can you do it? Be unbiased, nonjudgmental, follow a Word of God, according to the many who wrote or interpret the Koran, the Quran, and Bible, etc.? Can you be nice and live in peace? I mean, all the time? That, to me is spirituality, for anyone, religious follower or not.

A planet of spirituality with 'His' teachings within, where I do unto others as I would have them do unto me, that's peace. We create in our minds, the people we are. Striving to live in a graceful place is a thought provoking and intelligent, open minded choice. Allowing God to be in our hearts and honoring Him; and others is our best work.

Oh, and I would like to see world Peace.

Did you know that there are seven stages of spirituality!? Which one are you basking in? Deepak Chopra, an Indian-American author and alternative medicine advocate, will tell you much about this. I bring it up here only because many do not realize we have so much growth to do. Sorry, men, but I will go far as to say, that many men (yes, and women) who have been the bread winners retire from their careers/jobs, and sit on their laurels content. While you may be content with achievements, pension, grown family, and financial gains, the end is not here for Spiritual Development. Full contentment cannot be had until that is also addressed; I guarantee it.

The likes of Orpah and Dr. Phil have done much to promote these two followers.

If so lucky as to have had a loving family and fairly healthy upbringing, you have walked through the initial connection to the higher power of a divinity. Your original consciousness was subtly basked in God's light and your innocence of openness to a God developed healthily. Stage One was Innocence.

Deepak Chopra and Roger Gabriel deepen our understanding of oneness outlined in their Embark on the path to self-mastery with Deepak Chopra and Roger Gabriel in the Primordial Sound Meditation Online Course. I will only mention them for your curiosity, however, please refer to what they offer − a much deeper of our own understanding of our spiritual beings. There is so much to understanding our own spiritual beings.

Stage 1: Innocence
Stage 2: Fear, Ego
Stage 3: Power
Stage 4: Giving
Stage 5: The Seeker
Stage 6: The Sage
Stage 7: Spirit

In my adaptative thought, then you developed, unfortunately, challenges to sort out: Fear and Ego. Society (church, state, and people) emanate fear and we naturally evolve into survival of the fittest thinking. (Ick.) Our ego parts of our personalities mimic all those proposed mentors around us, and we just go ahead and get selfish, some due to fear of growth, fear of risk, fear of you-name-it and selfishness grows like a bad fungus. The ick is that it defines us! Gees. Subtly fed to us, unwittingly adopted as a characteristic. Oh, my ego, self prophesizes and strives for money and power, other's devotion, and acknowledgement. There is no end to its wishes. All those egotistical feelings keep me in a constant state of wanting, and then fear of not being enough or having enough. Very sick. Thank goodness, I realize this now.

In Stage Three of Spiritual Development, we try to overcome fears. Methods we learn only garnish the fear with more control. We, though precariously, doubt God's ranking in OUR personal lives.

False   Ego   Appearing   Real = FEAR

Some people stay in this thinking through full adult blossom, accumulating power, control, doubt of God, belief in their power over others, adding objects to their homes and lives. This is a tough life to live beside as a spouse. The stuck adult continues to choose selfishness and self-centeredness, evil and detrimental characteristics. As I surrender my *imaginary* power over others, I gained a more realistic view of my own life.

In Stage Three, you will, if lucky, realize choice. There is more to learn, more to society's offerings, more choices. Mother Nature seeps into your amygdala. Nature, learning, biologics, and spirituality evolve. Meditation and education and development for all, are welcome; rather than dismissed.

I pray you reach a day when you can say to yourself: *"I will not accept unmanageability, pain, or be fearful anymore. I want love, acceptance, hugs, understanding, even acceptance of my flaws."* That is giving a voice to feelings.

Sometimes in Stage 4 of Spiritual Development we get stuck again. The ego sees a way to live here. Stimied but BIG. I have things. I can get things. I can control others. I feel good about Me. (Oh, boy. Look out everyone else. Here comes the stinker; he owns the road, he has the bestest ideas, or so he will tell you, "See me. Be me' thinking. And consequently, he thinks he has self-love and maturation.)

Stage Four, if allowed to evolve can instead, think about and entertain, how good you feel with knowledge and self-growth, so much so that you want for others to know your peace, to know your fulfillment, and you take their hand and show them gratitude, respect, honor, and mostly guidance about what has been afforded to you. You give the love you have been given. But moreover, you realize you have been given a gift. If you are dang lucky here, you realize that it came from God, and that others who gifted you were also gainers from God. What a beautiful connectiveness is coming.

There will occur some disconnect with others; it is needed and will happen gradually as you get stronger. Soon you will discover you are staying within the healthy parameters you have set up in your life – in your own hula hoop, as they say. There is some need for growth in detaching from bad karma which must happen while associating with goodness. Those are steps we must make. Is the issue important enough to sacrifice our serenity?

I personally needed to abstain from alcohol-serving and related places; give up some of my comfort zones that were unhealthy. Today is the beginning of my beginning.

Someone actually made this grammatically poor statement in a conversation, but I get it and hope you will too: "*I cannot unchange what has happened negatively already.*"

You are adopting quality assets in your character. That lightness, that gratitude prays to a higher-than-me power.

You feel an internal happiness with your life, with others, with your standings and successes BUT you know it was through a power greater than you and historians, and mentors and leaders, and givers. Here, Stage 5, we think about seeking, not only to gain a method of training others as we have seen others train us, but to use compassion. The lightness of a soul becomes apparent. We begin to sort out and visualize good and bad. Choices are clear. Choose good. Always choose good. There is a better way with goodness. And as we become cognizant, we see our time when evil or selfishness ruled. Our Individual Life Purpose begins to show.

I'm crying as I write the next phase of Spiritual Development. Many call it "Mindfulness". Gurus, Yogi's and preachers, some in it for the money, will lead us if truth is an outcome.

This is not the stage of speaking tongues, knowing the Bible by heart or ministering. This, this evolution is beyond thinking. In fact, I'm not sure the brain has a part. There is a hover, an opaque blessing, visualized angel wings, a "spirit" across our physical earthly being that emanates glory. We are showered, if you will, with a language that isn't a language, a communication that is not describable, belief so glorious we can only act with in it. Have you felt this? Your soul shines out and dissolves into the Holy Spirit's palms.

The best side effect is that ego is no more. Selfishness is not an adjective you employ. I must admit, I want this place to remain forever. This state of consciousness feels SO GOOD, I am ready for eternal life. Take me, God, and use my arms and voice for goodness all around. Earth was just a place I existed with fellow patrons, using material goods. Stage Five is a mixing of the two planes with nothing but good being my intention. Intention can be motive or a block to progress, or can be based on expectations, not honest truth. Be of good intention.

I must share. I exist only to spread the good word. In Spiritual Development, my next lift is to blossom, to transcend, to take the conscious (which has been honed from bad behavior completely, which has given up thought of hurting others or being the biggest SOB in the corporation) to a place of shared happiness. The word happiness is not enough. Content is not the word. Connected with a Oneness of Universe sounds egotistic, seems to be the words. It is the do-no-harm Stage Six. Beware, however, of Stage Six. Our human habits know how to pretend in this stage; and portray that we have something special to teach others. We slip into the alter ego of "Come with me. I will show you the way; I am Buddha, I am the strongest soothsayer, I have ESP, I will reach the dead." Oh Lordy, that is so wrong when we let old habits rule. I acquaintanced the wife of a local minister who *bragged* about her ability to speak in tongues. The Lord's presence in your soul and the word brag do not belong in the same sentence.

Know. I repeat, just Know that you are not that. You have only seen the lift for yourself. Do not get into sales of braggidociousness, aggrandizement, and leading others to fulfillment. (Truly giggling as I type that.) Mentorship is allowed.

Know who you are. Know you are a disciple. We spiritually know what a gift we have in our mind and soul. We appreciate the plateau of consciousness we have found. Nothing more. Here, our walk in life, our habits, and our co-minglings - all of it – reveal more natural goodness.

So here, you ask: "Can dope fiends, felons, devil worshippers recover to this level?" I ask you, "Who are you to say they cannot?" Whoa. Think about your style of judgment just passed! Often my judgement of anyone is a reflection of my own deficits and inabilities. If I judge somebody, I let my one-up-menship have value in my thinking.

An interesting definition of criticism comes to mind. Repugnant sarcasm is more distasteful when we learn that it comes from the Greek verb "sarcazo" which means, to tear the flesh.

The tricky part right here, between Stages Six and Seven, is humility. Oh my gosh, I have had dictionaries and on-line lectures, and priests try to help me understand humility. The understanding is unattainable, no matter how tenured you are as a Professor of Literature. True Humility can only be an essence felt and/or lived.

People will offer that your chakras or hippocampus or unconscious state are the only paths to Full Spirituality.

Few humans have this knowledge. I've watched television evangelist Billie Graham, preachers of all sects, tongue speakers, and Sages firsthand, experience the ugly eye lid flutters and unexplained grunts. I'm pretty sure the only true sighting of Stage Seven of Spiritual Development was in my mother. Heh Heh.

Energy actually flowed. Observing Oneness instinctively lifted the hair on my arms. Earth is under your feet still. But Heaven (or your version of Oneness) is pulling, tugging you to its portal. Gosh, no, not ET or the movie version. Give me a break. Emersion into your belief, acceptance of greater 'force' than any other, and unconsciousness of the existence of the universe or anything with atoms, transcends you through Earth's gasses.

Here, the ability to think disappears. Your functioning mass enmeshes with the rest of nature. The hypnotic plane or blissful state is exact and true.

What you think in your brain is nothing; you are lifted to a plateau above consciousness.

No fear, no judgment, no wants-desire-greed-materialism, no egotism, no fear, no illusions about life, no unjustness, no hurt! Did I say no fear? Nebulous joy. We are aware of equality, truth, fairness, unbounded freedoms, peace. This essence spills over onto all we encounter. I give of my heart. I open my arms. I welcome others as they are. I am free to be true to self and expose gratitude and love in all my doings. The human purpose now is to journey, seeking knowledge and truth.

Pray incessantly. Actually, why not?!

Then,

Then I learned that there were Twenty-Five Kinds of Prayer from an on-line source. Oh gees. I wonder just how 'good' can I get? Here are some as I can recall them:

God Da Da (Arms lifted, eyes closed)
With imagination (write your own)
Adoration
Graditudinal
Supplication
Intercession (as if)
Prayer of Tears
Sorrowful
Cream-puffy
Bring me to religion
Ask for Mercy
Show me the light!
Mantra – (Mantranic?)
Visualization of the lamb
Psalms
Lament
Why don't I? pray
Breathe in God, Out with Evil
Hope He Sees Me
Help to accept life
Change 'my' will to yours
A listening God
Help with Belief
Rote
Effective and Deep
Collectively
Inviting God in
Conversational

Try six of the above right now. Set the book down and tell God something bothering you, through silent thought. Believe he is listening and interceding. Put your hands in prayer mode and deeply restate your ask. Show Him gratitude for your being. That was six.

Sometimes just living in the presence of God is a real testimonial prayer. See, you can be with God if you want to be. God reveals what is needed to stay in touch. He may show you a religious way.

I believe I must keep my thoughts with the Lord throughout my day. Every moment is an opportunity to be mindful and offer my heart to Him. A prayer is a 'state' we are in, not an action. It is just a single moment to share a moment with God, to spend time with Him. Just say, "I miss you God. I have made myself too busy and here you are trying to serve me." Thessalonians tell us to pray without ceasing. What a sweet place that would be in my heart if I didn't let all other bits of life take over my thoughts and actions.

Say a contemplative prayer right now. This moment will be like no other you have had. Center your mind with God. Offer your heart.

Ask Him to make us open to His direction so that we can do what is right and just, noble and lovely. (Philippians).

Those who pray don't worry and those who worry, don't pray. – Zeitgeist

Yeah, I am gonna tackle more about religion. We talked about sex. I even threw in a little politics. Ha. Ha.

The changed soul has direct access to God.
Oxford Group

Why, in the middle of a perfectly good book would I discuss the items I've listed? Because, to be well rounded individuals, we <u>must know the ways</u>

<u>of the world.</u> We must check out other ways of living to make our choices toward the best kind of life we can. Naïveté is the same as dumbness. It is a choice we make to stay in or not. If everyone were passive, we would still be cave men.

Check out religiosity from my side of the street, ok? Megamillions coalesce in many different churches for a reason.

If the light fell through a stained-glass window onto your physical being, causing an aura, would you be moved? Do you need an affirmation that it occurred?

Spirituality is all that is about. The world struggles all over with this sect, this ism, this belief, this god, that pagan, belief systems, nonbelief systems, theorems, and dogmas. Atheists say that worship is mass delusion. Now that line is funny!

Proclamation of atheism is often meant to proclaim and oppress others. Like the shin kicking Mormons suppressed women in their early stages, many atheists say our focus is like that of a football stadium full of fans. Is that hypocritical if the atheist is a humanitarian, believing in a greater cause? Hmm. Atheism is just a reaction. They claim realism and tell us that we can't 'reason' with God.

Actually, entertaining atheism is also good for us. It brings out their beliefs, and causes the rest of us to talk about and explore our thinking.

Wrap yourself around this theory: Religion is an extreme biological phenomenon.

Thinking about the supernatural is hard-wired in us. It is part of the human condition to invest in the supernatural.

We naturally explore scientific laws of probability to find our reasoning and logic. Does it make us atheists, if we are doubtful about God? Don't you automatically look for a worldly confirmation of happenings before forming a bias or buying into it? We look for evidence that supports what we think. If a priest, a rabbi, a deacon, a pope, or a witch are there to lead us, why wouldn't we explore that? Hey, yeah, let's explore that. And away you go with your beliefs. Ask a 6-year-old which church they want to go to. The one with the most colorful windows? Where they read a book by the altar? I myself prefer some Sundays, to listen to a good band, so I go to a Four Square that week.

Even airlines ask the question, "Are you carrying anything that someone else gave you?" My religion is like that, whatever I was given, shown, or exposed to, will go in my worship bag.

When something is illogical, do we not reach for causes, or make one up? Don't you think the cave men did the same? In the b.c. years, did they not worship the sun and the moon as idols of the unknown?

Religious followers just focus on a collective thought. No more. Don't try to make a big deal out of it. It is the church my pal took me to, or his mother read the Bible – that's why he goes to that church; or I grew up in the south, of course I am Baptist. I'm from Utah; what did you expect? If I am seven years old, Dr. Spock or Star Trek are my logical idols.

I rewrote the Lord's Prayer with a girlfriend who couldn't find her Lord. She believed in a supreme universe where earth, stars, and people were created rather than smashing atoms. (Who guided those atoms to smash? but I digress.) But she had a hard time praying. She wanted to join at funerals and events where the Lord's Prayer was going to be said. But her pragmatic hardline approach to life and subjection to abuse led her to deny existence of a god who had good designs for the world. Let THY kingdom come, not my will be done. The rewriting worked.

There are some of us that see Jesus as only a Roadside Mechanic – there when we are in trouble, and then, only then, do we 'pray'. John Lennon even told us to 'imagine there is no Heaven'. A Lutheran minister threatened me with being insubordinate on purpose if I went to another religion's worship house.

We started small. Here is a prayer without God in it:

Dear Existence. Help me to see and admit that I am powerless of the past and future. Help me to understand how my behaviors have contributed to discontent and unmanageable feelings. Help me this day to understand the true meaning of powerlessness of the world and others. Remove me from the pain of my part. Nema. (That's Amen backwards for you atheists.)

Ready for the Revised Lord's Prayer?

Our Higher Power, who are in the universe. The kingdom comes, and all will be done on this earth as it is out there in the Cosmos. We are given another day, and our daily bread. Forgive me my trespasses and help me to forgive those who trespass against me. And lead me not into negative temptation and delivery me from evil. For the power, the glory and the kingdom of this universe do not lie with me alone.

And there my friends, is a truth. Based somewhat on the molecular theory.

I only ask that I live well in the boundaries of humanity; and that for as long as I live, I keep learning how to live.

God doesn't call the qualified, he qualifies those who are called. If you are open minded enough to listen for the phone.

I love this adage,

"With Divine help, I will accept what I cannot change – with courage, composure, and good humor."

Without a belief that the world/universe is bigger than us, we are selfish egotistical bastards.

When you buy into the fact that you did not create the world or its living organisms, you will be blessed, at peace, and able to know happiness.

Whew! I am not in control of the world. Let me say, 'whew' again. Big job off my shoulders.

So goes with that logic that I am not in control of others. One person does not control another. No teacher, no pastor, no ruler, no tsar, no king, no pope. Nope. We each have a human body and a mind that decides our actions and thoughts. Read that sentence again, so I don't have to repeat it here, please.

That means, me, of course. But bigger than that, realize that every other person, clerk, driver, mechanic, coach, etc. has a mind and body that decides his actions and thoughts.

Okay, so you have habits, right? - Routines that you do. You have your mother's and father's mindset of right from wrong. You have formed opinions. Wow, I used to think that others were better at opinions than I. Guess what – we each get a vote.

In a literature writing group I led in the early 2000's, I assigned members to write a quick synopsis of a parent's legacy. A truth came in writing my mother's legacy.

"Martyr is my mother's middle name." Although today I associate that with being less than or shameful; and of course, always, always putting others' needs ahead of her own. I inherited that trait easily. It got me in trouble. "...I gave up my time, my needs, my wishes and desires and my serenity and health at the expense of my spirit for life. I lost myself being my mother. However, my legacy is my love for my children. I died used up."

When asked what genre of movie, food, activities, music and hobbies I liked, my brain was awash with his country music, a love of meat and potatoes (he was a farm boy) Harley riding (not driving) and how he wanted me to dress. Apparently, I interpreted martyrdom as giving up to another person and allowing hurt and loss to be my characteristics. I learned it well from my mother. I got deft at it. I got depressed and sad in retrospect now and I lived years in that state. Mom had eight (plus two second and third trimester miscarriages) children and gave up everything for us. I wonder if she ever felt she lost herself or is that just today's societal forte?

Everyone has their formed beliefs, histories, influences, stereotypes, and mentored ways. Joe Blo's thoughts below:

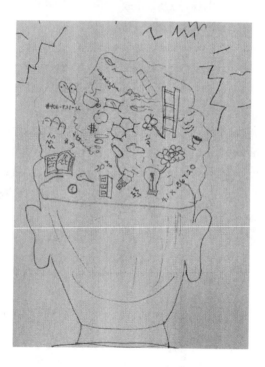

So has Joe. So has Sue, Atilla, Nemo, and Sasquatch. Their individual histories are not the same as ours. They formed opinions in their lives, very different from ours. Lots of people have a battery of opinions but if they are never refined with truth and God, then they don't even count!

Ever think about just letting them be? (Sometimes I "judge" that others are ignorant cuz they do not know what I know.) Hey, my head gets to have all the thoughts it wants. What comes out of my mouth or what steps my feet take do not have to correspond with their opinions or histories, but for the best of all, I need not condemn, judge, or be vengeful toward another. Words and thoughts can be so close together without the use of a pause to THINK it through.

Wow, what a concept.

That works for religions too.

If the Biblical story tellers, and there are many, heard right before they logged it, there are many previous lessons.

It is our choice to read, listen, or heed the lessons of others. It is our choice to abort negative thinking or actions also. Revelations come to us through listening to other people and their experiences. -JP

"The spirit of the Lord is on me, because He has anointed me to preach good news to the poor. He has sent me to proclaim freedom for the prisoners and recovery of sight for the blind, to release the oppressed, to proclaim the year of the Lord's favor." Luke proclaims that Jesus said this.

Lessons from elders have clout. Above, Luke writes that someone stepped out of Heaven to lead us.

So if you want to believe that God is waiting for us to get our act together; to think about freedom for all, recovery of sight for the blind, stop oppression.

And here we thought God was going to make us get our own act together. Hm. Our actions in his staid will be right in His time, not mine.

Are you pretending to always be in the process of that?

I will let you in on a little secret...We cannot complete that on this side of Heaven.

Oh, we punt a lot, hoping for a miracle.

Grace is the message of Christianity. Peace is the result. So what's wrong with believing in that?

Are you an atheist? I heard atheists are just agnostic wannabees. (Joke)

Or are you a follower of Nature's God? Divine Intervention? A Higher Power? Mother Nature? The Fifth Dimension (not the musical group)? We go with our knowledge habitually, as we know it thus far.

All I am asking, is let others do the same. We all come with pockets of humanitarianism. Granted some come with utopian views, but that is their cross to bear, according to me. And I can let that be.

Answer me this, Batman. What does every individual on this planet want? Beside creature comfort, silly. I venture it is Love and Support.

Why not give it? If Mr. Universe made that a moral order, Wow.

What if anything you said was not condemned, berated, argued, criticized or held against you? What if you could be vulnerable at all times and trust that another's arms were there? What if you could always lay your heart out?

Why not leave your arms open at all times? If your heart gets stomped on, do it again! Stop arguing. Try inspiring and supporting. Dazzle.

Who named them a trinity, anyway?

Growing up Catholic, praying to individual saints was a practice drilled into us repeatedly. And each saint has a special purpose, and they would help us in the event of our need of them. So we had to learn their names and their divine purpose.

Faustina aided us with 'mercy'; Christopher would help with travels if sought through prayer; St. Ann was about aiding mothers. And on and on.

Most of my youth, I had trouble with Mary and Joseph, Adam and Eve, Jesus and God, and where did the Holy Ghost come in? Who thought up that word 'trinity'? I was a Catholic girl who was more interested in playing outside than memorizing a name and a divine purpose.

I will have questions my whole life. No one knows all the answers. I don't even know all my questions yet. What I am offering here is that we need to continue to wonder. We have freedom to ask any question we want.

Key to Happiness? Open to the Truth in Everything.

———

I guarantee you will not feel the same after reviewing this list. I guarantee you will be happier, lighter, and take a deep breath. I'll put money on it. Call me.

List here what makes you happy; what makes you smile, what stops your thought pattern with joy?

Here's mine:

Friendly people who speak to you
Laughing till tears leak out
The smell just after rain
Simultaneous responses with someone close
My father's bubbling, then boiling short giggles
Light wet April breezes
The smell under a tree of musky dropped leaves
Warmth in the car seat on a cool but sunny day
E-mail from family
Thoughts of a former success
The smell of a new car interior
Branson, Missouri
Going through old photos
A rare cup of truly good fresh coffee

Quick notice of a cigarette puff

The moment in church when you know

Homemade soup

Grass under my bare feet

A patio, a friend, and a margarita

Traveling

Every day that is not in a hospital

The smell of a baby's head

A great writing pen

The boss's handwriting: 'Good work!'

Homemade vanilla ice cream

Hearing a group singing 'Happy Birthday'

Loose clothes that once were tight

The sparkle of a diamond, or any gem

Great song from the past coming on the radio

My sister's voice on the phone

The look when you both know what you are thinking

The first bite of a good strawberry

Health in every aspect

The great genes I inherited

Putting a smile on the face of someone with tears

Incredible sunsets

Having everyone who counts alive

Cherry coke

Smell of yeast dough baking

Thoughtful people are a thrill

Friends

Smell outside a steak house

Dots of salt that enhance flavor

Using my talents to help someone

"It" working the first time

Hearing others good luck stories

A good night's rest

Raspberry

My brothers' voices

Praise

A family gathering

Checks in the mail

The heart of a watermelon

That special place in your sweetie's neck

White teeth

Toddlers that make you smile

Giant snowflakes

Hearing laughter

Better yet, being in on the laughter

Gold jewelry

Reflections from a prism

Unexpected hugs

A new magazine and time to read it

A good haircut

Planning a vacation

Pleasant people, even overly

Crisp dollar bills

Birthdays – mine or anyone's

My sister-in-law

Every U.S. flag hurled

Saying the word, 'catalpa'

Being first to discover a rainbow

Sundays

A good hair day

Stepping into the ocean

Snowcap mountains in my view

Mountain air

Being close to the clouds

Spending time with a sibling

Somebody calling me their buddy

Speaking with people from another country
Oprah
Newly cut pine
Floating on an air mattress
Walking the white sands of a beach
Feeling good
Riding in a boat.
Floral deliveries
Feeling flat stomached
Ripples in the lake water
Geese in flight
When you realize "God did that"
A tiny hand taking yours
Getting pictures back from the developer
Clown shoes
Ideas for having fun
Crisp Chinese vegetables
Hand carved Jack-o-Lanterns
An old friend's voice on the phone
Seeing the shoreline of Malibu
The first sight of your friend
A line up of grade school kids
Getting wrapped up in a hobby
Hearing your stiff back 'pop'
Getting a smile 'back
Someone making a c.d. for you
The look in a toddler's eye when they learn
A perfect fit in the dressing room
A secret discovery how to please someone
Misty sunny mornings
Perfect finish on a wood piece
The fuzzy things inside an iris
Massage that gets that spot

A bubble bath

My brothers-in-law

Blue-Green

Persistent friendship

The rush after exercising

The phrase, "I trust your judgement"

New furniture

Free stuff you can use

Orange shades of a sunset

Roses on my table or desk

Taking time to notice an intricate pattern

Reading a list of happy things

"If you imagine less, less will be what you undoubtedly deserve," Debbie Millman

Because I'm A Gonna
Die Anyway

Most of the poem below comes from a Tecumseh quote:

Attitude toward Death

Live your life that the fear of death
can never enter your heart.
Trouble no one about his religion.
Respect others in their views
and demand that they respect yours.
Love your life, perfect your life,
beautify all things in your life.
Seek to make your life long
and of service to your people.
Prepare a noble death song for the day
when you go over the great divide.
Always give a word or sign of salute when meeting
or passing a friend, or even a stranger, if in a lonely place.
Show respect to all people, but grovel to none.
When you rise in the morning, give thanks for the light,
for your life, for your strength.
Give thanks for your food and for the joy of living.
If you see no reason to give thanks,
the fault lies in yourself.
Touch not the poisonous firewater that makes wise ones turn to fools

and robs the spirit of its vision.
When your time comes to die, be not like those
whose hearts are filled with fear of death,
so that when their time comes, they weep and pray
for a little more time to live their lives over again
in a different way.
Sing your death song, and die like a hero going home.

The present is a present!

Can you control the future? Can you mentally live life in the future? Physiologically?

We love to worry and think that if we itinerate well enough, we have control. Ha! We are not all knowing and all seeing. Who is? God is. Things will happen in God's time, not mine. The nature of events will fall how they fall, regardless of man's control and planning.

With all my yelling, crying, self-righteousness, suggestions, ideas, and other attempts, I was sure I could control the world – at least my world, his world, and anyone else who I thought needed my advice to live right. I wasn't an ogre, just a neat, tidy, clean individual with well-grounded ideas I thought were best for you to learn. Hee Hee Hee. See, I was forfeiting my own peace of mind over something not done to my standards. My part in that is yelling when I created my own discomfort. Expectations are just disappointments waiting to happen. If I am the only one that likes a clean bathroom sink, I am the one to keep it at "my" standard. Get it?

Was I going to yell him into believing that I was worthy and wonderful and right, damn it?

What kind of respect is that for ANOTHER HUMAN BEING? Yelling them into submission? ...to my expectations? (Key word there is 'my'.)

Ideas for Playing / Learning to Love Your Life Again

———

Make cookies for the neighbor

Make your Mom's chocolate chip cookies

Bake anything that grandma did

Go for ice cream

Buy a new nail polish

Bounce a basketball

Hit a wall with tennis ball

Do squats on an elevator

Have your favorite cookie!

Have a pedicure

Have a manicure

Walk a new trail

Walk

Get down with a toddler and play

Read a book you loved

Read a book

Buy a magazine and read it

TAKE A NAP

Take a nap in a sun ray

Wiggle

Invite someone to play cards

Invite someone to coffee out

Clean out one drawer or box or closet

Put your hands through sand (go to a beach if you have to)

Swim

Wade at Lake Elmo

Call a friend

Call a sibling

Look at photographs

Go shopping

Spritz

Take a bubble bath

Make a grass angel

Play with your pet for ten minutes

Lay in the grass

Relax in hot tub

Park in a cemetery and Thank God

Stare at nature:

    A spider's web

    A busy ant

    Aspen leaves shaking

    Colors of the season

    Cloud formations

Drum on something hollow, make up a beat

Wear sparkles

Create

Paint

Knit

Crochet

Learn to make rag rugs

Take yourself out for lunch

Hire a housekeeper for two hours' worth

Visit an antique store

Get out of town

Go take photos of nature

Fish

Walk along the river

Ride a bike

Skate

Paint an old candle stick or furniture new color

Read a bible passage

Make a goodwill run with old clothes

Play games on line

Stare at an old photo

Cry till you are done

Pray

Look at an old photo album

Watch a sunset

Find a constellation you know

Eat fresh berries

Put lemon in your water

Stargaze

Do an outdoor hobby

Visit someone

Kneel down to pray

Eat a bonbon

Wear the good perfume

Have a latte

Boat, Canoe, Kayak

Just try on a prom gown at the store

Curl up with a love story

Pick or buy yourself a bouquet of flowers

Sniff a rose

Take a day off

Make a snow angel

Build a snowman

Do a craft

Go see a movie

Get a new pair of shoes

Wear a hat

Soak your tootsies in bath salts

Switch purses

Visit the art museum

Visit any museum

Park on the rims and start

Walk on the rims

Visit a chapel at St. V's or Billings Clinic

Hug a stuffed animal

Make a want list for Christmas

Write a letter to Santa and mail it

Read the comics

Color with crayons

Deeply breathe

Yoga

Listen to your fav music

Visit the animal shelter

Name the top 5 people you love

Play an instrument, even badly

Sit on the patio, just sit

Take an exercise class

Go somewhere you have never been

Write your hubby a love-note

One further note about playing with your pet, there is direct correlation that, even if isolated (like with Covid 19), interaction with your dog or cat or other pet, raises self-esteem! Generally, it offers more exercise and movement, satisfies that attachment need we all have, and expands conscientiousness.

Wisdom, Knowledge, IQ, Lore, Habit

I absolutely did not know what I did not know!

Thoughts bear fruit.

Let's examine your thoughts in a day:

If my brain processes negativity, what will my attitude be? Simon and Garfunkel had a wonderful little song that included: *"A man hears what he wants to hear, and disregards the rest."* How true is that for you? When the teacher in grade school said we would line up alphabetically... I was defeated (last name started with U). When the teacher said we would line up alphabetically after we sorted by height, I was one of the tallest and my mood lightened. What voices do I tune out, what voices do I hone in on? All of them form us, some taint us. I hope that we all communicate to support, uplift, and strengthen each other.

My self-talk includes: (I would like to say this is all in the past and I have learned to counter my negative thinking but I have not yet aborted every thought that leads to these. Besides these have been habits for 50 some years. It might take a while longer to learn to not do them.) I would call myself names when something did not go well for me, Idiot, Stupid, Clumsy, etc. Stop that from this moment on. We are none of those

My character defects included:

> Feeling the victim to other's chastisement or opinions
>
> Anger inside which I bury or create feelings of resentment
>
> Resentment which I have negative vengeful thoughts to counter
>
> Attitude of sadness or hurt
>
> Sadness because of all the above
>
> Judging people because I need to feel like I am worthwhile,
> I put them down
>
> Lack of trust because I myself am not always trustworthy,
> I create lies
>
> Bitterness because I feel you by-passed me on purpose
>
> Obsessiveness with getting my way, dammit
>
> Diminishing myself because you are better or did better, or taking
> on shame for same.
>
> Believing what others say regardless of their IQ on the matter

I really needed to unpack all these traditional taught guilts and beliefs. I had to ask, "What do I get out of rehearsing these feelings over and over?" Who owns the resentment? Who is suffering? And I had to stop allowing myself this stinking thinking to lead me through my life.

Our minds are bombarded every day with disguised thoughts. We are clever! When fear rises, what we often do is grasp onto it and go through shakes, tummy tugs, and being unnaturally subdued. We can you know, learn to pause, process, and respond to fear, suspicion, doubts, or negativity appropriately.

When I don't expect anything good to come into my life, I won't have to go through disappointment when it doesn't! SICK! Believing that you have a negative cloud above you, will make bad things appear and veritably, no one wants to be around you. You are a burden to their personal joy. Repeat after me, "I want to change." Repeat louder. To change you must build the connecting Lego system of your brain to act fluidly with knowledge and wisdom. Let's go. There's more...

Dear God, I Don't Ever Feel Alone Since I Found Out About You!

———

I just love communion.

I'm a church hopper. I seek multiple reminders I am not all that and a bag of chips. Never mind the religion, I am going through any open door to fill me up with methods of being the good girl my mother wanted, treating my fellow man kindly, and quizzing myself always, WWJD?

Catholics still have me by tenure but my soul has expanded in this journey to churches around town. A born-again Christian whispered to me last week, "You can join several churches at once, you know." Is that in the rule books or is it a non-rule?

Father Steve Z. at St. Thomas Parish will give you yesterday's ball scores at St. Thomas, if that's what pulls you in the door.

To further discuss this neglect, during the Super Bowl last, 5.6 million dollars was spent on a 30 second ad. It used as truth, "Normal is wanting and obtaining." And it went on to show its car or beer or whatever. Really? We have come to that? Playing on our personal choices? Gaining material things is our normal? Oh please. An onslaught of antichrists write these ads, did you know that? Be mindful of deception; rebelliousness and lawlessness begin to sound normal, as they speak. I always ask, 'could I invite God into this setting'. Can I still be called a child of God after I do this?

The message this day in the sermon was to reach out your hand. God is reaching His to you! I love this. The passages below remind us to let others be themselves and to keep our thoughts on a higher plain.

Scripture from Isaiah 55:6-13

6 Seek the LORD while he may be found; call on him while he is near.

7 Let the wicked forsake their ways and the unrighteous their thoughts. Let them turn to the LORD, and he will have mercy on them, and to our God, for he will freely pardon.

8 "For my thoughts are not your thoughts, neither are your ways my ways," declares the LORD.

9 "As the heavens are higher than the earth, so are my ways higher than your ways and my thoughts than your thoughts.

10 As the rain and the snow come down from heaven, and do not return to it without watering the earth and making it bud and flourish, so that it yields seed for the sower and bread for the eater,

11 So is my word that goes out from my mouth: It will not return to me empty, but will accomplish what I desire and achieve the purpose for which I sent it.

12 You will go out in joy and be led forth in peace; the mountains and hills will burst into song before you, and all the trees of the field will clap their hands.

13 Instead of the thornbush will grow the juniper, and instead of briers the myrtle will grow. This will be for the LORD's renown, for an everlasting sign, that will endure forever.

Do we live our lives as God called us here to do? Here, let's find out. Assignment below.

I'll help you with your letter:

Dear God:

Please admit __(Your Name Here)___ to Heaven.

(Your Name Here)____ has helped this world in many ways and the people here have benefitted toward better lives because of _____ .

   (The worthy and graceful actions taken in life go here)

1.

2.

3.

4.

Signed,

(Your Name Here)_____

Lord, you know better than I know myself that I am growing older and will someday be old. Keep me from the fatal habit of thinking I must say something on every subject and on every occasion. Release me from the craving to straighten out everybody's affairs. Make me thoughtful, but not moody. Helpful, but not bossy. With my vast store of wisdom, it seems a pity not to use it all, but You know, Lord, I want a few friends at the end.

Keep my mind free from the endless recital of details; give me wings to get to the point. Seal my lips on my aches and pains. They are increasing, and love of rehearsing them is becoming sweeter as the years go by. I dare not ask for grace enough to enjoy the tales of others' pains, but help me to endure them with patience.

I dare not ask for improved memory, but for a growing humility and a lessening cocksureness when my memory seems to clash with the memories of others. Teach me the glorious lesson that occasionally, I may be mistaken.

Keep me reasonably sweet. I do not want to be a saint - some of them are so hard to live with. But a sour old person is one of the crowning works of the devil. Give me the ability to see good things in unexpected places, and talents in unexpected people. And give me, Lord, the grace to tell them so.

Amen

Do we live our lives as God called us here to do?

Did you know that God's love never fades?

We are smart enough to know that partnership connections and love wane and wash. We know that people die and the love we have is registered solid in our hearts, but their activities on earth no longer fill our thinking as much.

But God, He has a transcendence into our hearts. The belief that we can transcend love right back to him is pretty satisfying and outstandingly fantastic!

What if… we could love our fellow man with that open feeling? Could we at least try? The reason for religion, the reason we practice religion, the reason we go for an hour once a week, the reason we get on our knees is to open up that passage way for communication with God.

What if…we spent more of our one hours a week locked eyes with God, in the transcendence of goodness and fairness with all mankind? What if we spent all every day, all day, with God in mind?!

Does that blow your mind? It should! And better yet, it is possible! One moment taken in at a time…

Meditation —
"Zen there was None"

It is so simple:

You are asked to go to a quiet alone setting to meditate. This will not be weird. That is simply because in our brains, the human voice trumps anything visual. We only are asked to think quietly.

You feel much younger, a lighter flux in your head, when you meditate regularly!

1 Minute, 1 Thought at a time.

Three minutes spent in meditation can fight an urge.

Right now, think of a word or phrase you can use for a mantra. I said, do it.

Hum   Purr   Say a word, like: 'breath', 'peace', 'I am'

Say it slowly ten times with your eyes closed deep breath between each pronunciation of the word. Think of the colors of the rainbow in order. Do it a second time, third. This will clear your head of day to day busy.

Emotion will pass. Take a walk. Sit in the sun. Sit anywhere, preferably a nonstimulating arena, i.e., park, your car, on a hill, in the woods, at a cemetery, find a bench, sit in an empty chapel.

I have never known anyone to walk in a beautiful, ambient, nuance filled and resplendent floral garden and not feel that stillness. If you are in a city, take in a garden store.

Endorphins actually have altered in your body. Only good can come from that.

Abraham Maslow, one of psychology's forefathers on the hierarchy of needs and priorities and self-actualization, says to us that high moments occur in life where we joyfully find ourselves beyond the confines of ordinary – in a glimpse of the eternal realm of Being. Eckhart Tolle, spiritual teacher and author, reflects this level of thinking as talking about meditative states where it seems another door is open in our minds which "is bathed in luminescence" and we are catapulted into a stunning mental place, other than here and now. Tolle further explains in these advanced levels of spiritual maturity, extraordinary capacities begin to blossom of love, vitality, personhood, bodily awareness, intuition, perception, communication, and volition.

Who doesn't want this!!!!

Conscious levels and subconscious levels – You know you have them. Ever been caught staring during a lecture, or called on during a meeting or class when your head was 'somewhere else completely'. That is a form of detraction. We need discretion as to when we go into 'off site thinking'. We can actually talk/walk ourselves into these places. So put yourself in a safe place. I often park on a hill overlooking my city. And come out so relaxed and invigorated on the other side. Yet, we fight taking t i m e to meditate. We love that relaxed place. It is as rendering as REM sleep. We can travel there under our own direction.

> *Many go fishing all their lives without knowing that it is not fish they are after.*
> — Thoreau

I am in hopes that this book transcends you in that direction; so much so that you desire to live in the moment and love your moments. If you could live in infinity, it would be now. Imagine if this moment, right now were a photograph. Is it beautiful? You, you are in charge of only that – where your thoughts are. Be where your feet are. Let go, let life happen – that gives you peace and gratitude. It is not a huge thunder clap of great glee and rainbows that always arrive with the joy. Sometimes, a cup of coffee, or a meal shared, or sunshine, just sunshine is the joy to live in. Wouldn't you rather, always prefer to be favorable to or promoting health in a salubrious air?

The best advice I ever received was to live in the moment.

So if I want quiet time; if I want peace of mind; if I want to enjoy life, I must find it in this moment that presents itself. Or it will disappear without joy.

No one can gift me with peace. No one else can live this moment I am having. If I did not have peace, happiness, enjoyment in that last moment just past – I did it to myself. I, me, myself, and I, gave up the chance. That is a pretty powerful statement. Read this paragraph again aloud with theatrics. Peace can only exist in one moment at a time, as the moment occurs.

You lie to me when you say, "I don't have time to think like that." There is a very good principle in the simple replacement of "get to" for the words "have to". I get to take the kids to school or I get to do the dishes. It is a privilege to live this moment with these children. It is with gratitude that I have a set of dishes and a place to cook and enough food to dirty these dishes. This mental training changes your life. Mental intention to harness that moment of life. This becomes skillfully effective!

One of the best stress relievers I ever took part in was actually active Zen! We played an upbeat instrumental in the background that we all knew. A group of twenty folks in a Spirit Quest group circled together and laughed to the song instead of singing. The united catharsis at the end of this effort was amaz-sing!

See, Zen, or reflective meditation, demonstrates for us that we can center our conscience. We direct that to happen, using our own power of consciousness. Meditation of itself proves to us that we can fully think! We have the capability to clearly find an inner voice that is guided with wisdom. Proof we have control of our minds. We can change our minds toward only positive and progressive ways. We proved it to ourselves. Heed that consciousness. Allow pause time. Allow the guidance and direction to happen before responding. It will be a thought out and more desired outcome in relationships also.

> *"I think that I shall never see,*
> *A poem as lovely as a tree.*
> *— A tree whose hungry mouth is pressed*
> *against the earth's sweet flowing breast.*
> *Poems are made by fools like me.*
> *But only God can make a tree."*
>
> - Joyce Kilmer

I am asking that the next time you see a tree, you study it. The greatness of it. The height. Check out the type of bark. Is it a uniform shape? See its many shades of greenness. How did the planting happen? Who made this? Think about how old it is? It is a thing of wonder and awe. So are each of your moments. This practice of grasping joy must be fondled, conditioning of your mind, till you get it. You are malleable.

It is going to take some human development. Are you ready for that? Yes, I am saying that we, you and me, have not evolved to that great state of transcendence in our walk abouts. Connecting with our greater Spirit, and I mean, God, when I speak; seeking always into a transformation to a gentle and agreeable self. As we well know, it takes more than a click of our fingers. I wonder (if) a hypnotist who put me in a trance died while doing so, if I would stay in an instinctive phase, petulant, smiling, in enjoyment of my being? We are the only keepers of that key. What part of o p e n m I n d e d n e s s don't you want?!

Cathartic [ca·thar·tic] *adj.* Producing a feeling of being purified emotionally, spiritually, or psychologically as a result of an intense emotional experience or therapeutic technique. "The strength of the movie had a *cathartic* effect on her."

That man is the richest whose pleasures are the cheapest. – Thoreau

I thought for years that deep breathing was just a way of relaxing, of calming down. This is true but one further note: you breathe away brain fog or irritability while inhaling oxygen which allows more energy into your body.

I want to offer some alternatives to zoning in on meditation because as we know, we are not all prone to jumping off the anxiety, obsessiveness, busy train.

Try these:

Sort something: your books, recipes, photos

Paint an old garage table or a room

Color or paint

Give your pet a shampoo

Sort out anything too small/big/you dislike from your closet

Pump air in a basketball and dribble, as long as you want

Write a note you never intend to send

Do everything more slowly for a few minutes.

Rest your hand on your stomach or your heart and feel the warmth inside

Plant a new flower

Observe the sky

Visualize flying above your space; glide on an air current

Revisit mentally, the last time you felt peace and joy

Play your music. Set up new speakers in your favorite area of the house.

Knit, sew, cross stitch

Help someone, anyone, anywhere

Smile and hold it on your face as long as you can

Rearrange one drawer or cupboard

Dance by yourself

Fix something

Try a cool shower, or a contrast shower – hot, then cold, then hot

Experiment with different laughs, loud, exuberant, giggle

The emotion of wonder occurs. Bliss and the quietness from chatter and traffic, offer our thoughts to change perspective - on all other things in our life. That transcending moment takes us far beyond the daily chores. We can frolic within the meditative state to amusement, solutions, calmness, recreating moments, create ideas, see our goals clearly; to awe, to wonder. Criticism is quieted. Ego disappears. New experiences pop in our minds, thoughts of tasks accomplishable happens. Zen can happen during reading, creating art, riding, exercise, with music, while staring at ocean waves or wildlife. Thoughts ride aloft and we relax.

CLOSE YOUR EYES (Well, read through this exercise first and then close your eyes, silly.)

Close your eyes.

I am in the forest; I hear no noise.

> No cell phone vibration or blaring tune
> No traffic whirring
> No voices, no ping ping of any machine, not even a halogen bulb buzz

In the forest, I hear the startle of a branch breaking below my foot. Snap! Now there are two pieces where there was one. Another, six where there were two. Step. Step. Snap. Snap. I stop.

I hear only a fly (pause) whirring wings swoop by my ear. (whisper) "Just a fly".

Just like that, I heard wings with child-like excitement. I heard wings!

I hear breathing, mine… and my dog's. In with the air, out with a wind, in with the rush of air, out open-mouthed with a soft gush. My dog's pant, quicker, and liquid (pant with your own tongue a bit out).

As I listen,

> I hear a water fall   perhaps a mile away   I listen.   Just listen

I hear the takeoff of a large bird – the branch shakes its leaves in a bow, the birds feathers flog together, and a fading "caaawww" "kaaaawwww" sound as it leaves my space of air, then a more distanced cawing.

I listen, just listen.

A quick chirp, chirp, = small chickadee? a baby frog? a cricket? 'Do it again, do it again' I think, so I can discern.

Chirp. Chirp. Still, I am not quite sure.

Do I actually hear the dew falling from leaf to leaf as it pools and drops its heaviness from one to the other?

I'm conscious of a din in my ears. If I listen, I hear a duck far away quacking to locate its brother.

I hear a horse snort, maybe two simultaneously.

A rancher's tractor putt-putting steam to seed its land.

I can listen to silence if I want, or tune in. Tune in to the sounds of the land and mother nature.

No cell phone tune, no traffic in the distance, no other voices, just my breath.

And my dogs. (soft pant heh-a-heh-a-heh)

While in a meditative state, there is a maze of neurons reconnecting, seeking dopamine. These surges allow a fire-up of awakenness to a sense of self unlike any other sensation. We like the ecstasy and the God center we find there. Subconsciously, neurologic activity clears the way for a euphoric or spiritual happening. Serotonin and dopamine are released to lengthen the experience through a parietal lobe, which houses our perception of time. We never even know what work is going on, we only meld into the encounter with peace. What a gift Zen is.

Yet many refuse to relax. Anxiety and control are so embedded in their persona, there is no letting go. You probably know a few folks who suffer from this fierce control. I am sorry for their loss.

Girls (and Boys) Just Want to Have Fun

Happiness gets all twisted up sometimes. Do illicit drugs make you happy? Does someone falling down make you happy?

How we chase our happiness factor can be as different as night and day. I took Valium and Xanax, each for a while because it took me to a place of synthetic serenity. I drank alcohol quickly to gain the 'high'. None of the abusive items helped to give me a more serene life. Some of them actually worked on frying my liver and made me obnoxious or forgetful of behaviors I did while blacked out. It's pretty plain to see that that kind of happy is harmful, short lived and of no benefit to anyone. Unless, of course, you stay high and continue to self-medicate; then you have a shorter, more painful life, where no one wants to be around you and you are worsening your health with every dose.

Let's talk about denial of self-fun. Take the test below to see how fun you are!

The top advantages to my being 'no fun' are:

1.
2.
3.

Having fun would force me to:

The thought of having fun makes me feel:

If I had fun, my life would be:

The ways I sabotage my ability to have fun include:

I use sadness for:

I use my sadness to deal with or avoid:

If I were fun, people would:

The most common reason that I give to people for not having fun is:

But really, I know the reason is:

Three advantages to being happy include:

    1.
    2.
    3.

People who are fun are:

If I quit being sad, my family and friends would:

If I were fun, how would I use sadness differently?

If I were fun, I would have to give up:

If I were fun, I would gain:

The message I would give to others if I let myself have fun would be:

In my heart, I want to be fun because:

The only thing between what you are feeling now and happiness is in your mind. We all should laugh often and loud, till we are gasping for breath.

Read BEATITUDES when you find you are sitting in judgement of others. After all, who are you to judge? Perfect?

My mother's favorite prayer:

Blessed are the poor in spirit:
>   For theirs is the kingdom of heaven.
Blessed are they that mourn:
>   For they shall be comforted
Blessed are the meek:
>   For they shall inherit the earth.
Blessed are they which do hunger and thirst after righteousness:
>   For they shall be filled.
Blessed are the merciful:
>   For they shall obtain mercy.
Blessed are the pure in heart:
>   For they shall see God.
Blessed are the peacemakers:
>   For they shall be called the children of God.
Blessed are they which are persecuted for righteousness sake:
>   For theirs is the kingdom of Heaven.
Blessed are ye, when men shall revile you and persecute you, and shall say all manner of evil against your falsely:
>   For my sake.
Rejoice, and be exceeding glad:
>   For great is your reward in Heaven:
>   For so persecuted they the prophets which were before you

What I Want from Others So Shall I Give Them First

---

1. Pay attention
2. Acknowledge others
3. Think the best
4. Listen
5. Be inclusive ("Come with us." is the best phrase to hear)
6. Speak kindly
7. Don't speak ill
8. Accept and give praise
9. Respect others' opinions
10. Mind your body
11. Be agreeable
12. Keep it down and rediscover silence
13. Respect other people's time
14. Respect other people's space
15. Apologize earnestly
16. Assert yourself
17. Avoid personal questions
18. Care for your guests
19. Respect even a subtle "no"
20. Be a considerate guest
21. Think twice before asking for favors
22. Refrain from idle complaints

23. Accept and give constructive criticism
24. Respect the environment and be gentle with animals
25. Don't shift responsibility and blame

From *Choosing Civility* by P.M. Forni:

> *We never touch people so lightly that we do not leave*
> *a trace. Our 'state of being' matters.*

Hurting people will hurt people.

Last time you were sick, were you kind with your words? Or were your words, "Just leave me alone" "I think I am going to die" "Bring me the remote" ...our good and considerate manners went out the window. Hurting people lash out. Hurting people will slap you if you touch them in the wrong place. Conjure up that pain when you see someone lash out. They may have mental pain. You do not know their history, or their day's occurrences leading them to be as they are, maybe they are even in nefarious thinking from an abusive history. It is not mine to pass judgement, say correcting words, or make change occur in them. Try this on: "We judge ourselves on intentions to do; and we judge others by their actions." Hmm.

Intend to do good:

Take care of any health issue
Golf/Roller Skate/Ski/Swim
Try a new direction to and from work
Wear your good clothes
Scent up
Test drive your favorite auto
Volunteer where they need help
Ask for/Hire help with a major stressful job
Wave any time you can
Think of a new way for your next celebration
Write a journal of today
Check out a new business
Write a story for a child
Visit a library
Close your eyes during the day
Treat yourself
Make a new work contact
Shut off tv/electronics for an evening
Dine by candle light
Take a bubble bath
Buy a treat for someone
Throw the golf ball around the holes
Welcome people at church
Walk
Learn a clean joke
Clean out one shelf
Color
Get up and move every hour
Mind your posture
Try a new spice while cooking
Dance by yourself today

Sing

Daydream

Plan for your next trip

Cut down on sugar

Stretch

Ride a bike

Make up a poem or palindrome

Watch the sunrise

Watch a sunset

Take someone out for lunch

Go to the aviary/zoo/pet store

Help at the pound

Buy a new vegetable to try

Listen well

Laugh

Make up a new prayer

Sit in different seats

Attempt deep yoga

Hide something fun for someone you love

Be gentle with yourself

Walk a new path

Smile at everyone

Risk it

Change your view – travel, go for a ride

Read Fiction

Sit next to lapping water

Visit with someone

Try a different type of mint

Watch a good TED talk

Try a new exercise

Call an old friend to chat

Let someone know you thought about them

Learn about something new

Get comfortable shoes
Be really nice
Make new friends
Just be you
Sit in the sun's rays
Try it a new way

You have God's permission and my support to get better. Give it to yourself. You deserve better from the world. You have so much worth! You can have exactly the life you imagined. You get to stop just growing older and be the star of your life.

My Day in Reflection

Set this by your bedside until you have reviewed it so many days you have this memorized:

Leave space to write percentages of true for yourself:

Was I resentful today?

Was I selfish?

Was I dishonest? With myself?

Was I afraid?

Do I owe anyone an apology?

Have I kept something to myself that I should have discussed with another?

Was I kind?

Was I loving?

Was I thinking of myself most of the time?

Was I thinking of what I could do for others?

Was I thinking of what I could pack into my stream of life?

Did I pray?

Did I let go and experience serenity?

Describe feelings about any of the above. Then ask yourself, 'Do I owe an apology or discussion'?

Do you think happy will finally come when you get control of it all? When you get that last letter written? The lawn mowed for the last time? Your child raised and safely on his/her own?

Hee Hee Heh Heh Ha Ha Ha Ha.

There is always challenge. There is always an opportunity to become tense. Bad behaviors or action or thoughts steal from you; steal time and thoughts from your very precious life.

You are not powerless over you. What if I could rocketship you into a peaceful place? Would you buy a ticket?

With the new understandings of what role you play in your own life and how to be in a relationship with others, you will have the dynamics to go to a peaceful place.

I have talked with many, many people who were ready to give up. Anonymously to you of course, but in our trusting client space, people shared their innermost thoughts and feelings of suicide. I used to think that enough love from another could keep anyone alive. Well, my husband of almost 40 years succeeded in his pursuit of suicide. All I have to give them is hope, a warning, and perhaps inspiration. Just love doesn't do it. I offered to others, post my husband's death and after much training and research, how to say "no" to the act of suicide. See, everyone deserves to make peace with the insidiousness that makes them think 'I'm at fault for too much. I see no way out.'

Wait, is this the Happy chapter or not?

Therapists ask, how happy are you on a scale of one to ten. What they know that we don't, is that we still think we are in control of people, places and things. We even have failed to cure our own minds of negative thoughts, let alone another's. We have failed to cure other's lack of respect for us. We feel we have caused our own demise, another failure. Perhaps we think we caused others to ruin some part of their future. Therapists know we are trapped in T H I N K I N G wrongly. So I can contribute to negativity by accommodating others' problems. I can't cure everything, I didn't cause others' actions, I can't control all things.

So the opposite of all that is Happy. Let's get on with it.

Here is the list of instructions on how to be happy

DO:

- Do forgive
- Do be humble
- Do take it easy — tension is harmful
- Do play — find recreation and hobbies
- Do keep on trying whenever you fail
- Do learn the facts about alcoholism
- Do attend Al-Anon meetings often
- Do pray

DON'T:

- Don't be self-righteous
- Don't try to dominate, nag, scold and complain
- Don't lose your temper
- Don't try to push anyone but yourself
- Don't keep bringing up the past
- Don't keep checking up on the alcoholic
- Don't wallow in self-pity
- Don't make threats you don't intend to carry out
- Don't be over-protective
- Don't be a doormat

Also, I like to follow the A's:

Aware – be aware of my thinking

Admit – Admit to my part in all action and communication

Accept – Accept truth only

Act – Act appropriately at all times

Ask – when you don't know so you can be smarter.

Ta Da. Now you could tape this to your wall and think, 'I'll see this and remind myself every day to be happier because I read how.'

You don't know the principles involved yet in practicing each of the above. It is coming. Keep reading. See, the previous are titles to chapters in your life where you have had problems and challenges. You kept doing the same thing each time they occurred and got the same results. Sit up now and take heed. The principles you practiced in each challenge might have been part of the problem. Oh boy, whack on the side of the head. You have been part of the problem. Own it. Your dilemmas are self-created. Now, don't would of, could of, if only, or should at me. Own your action, words, and thoughts. Your moral life needs cleaned up.

Challenges are just opportunities to grow. I continue to evolve. I know I lack in areas, which is a means of stimulus for growth. Surrender to the error and learn anew. Do you realize you can begin your day again any moment of the day you want? It is a new 24 hours from this second on out.

Challenges and problems have a purpose. The problem has surfaced, brought me to my knees, and has provided me an issue to learn to solve!

See, if you even think, 'I was biased once.' You are feeding your negative side. When your first thought is rather, 'Everyone has a right to be under

God's eyes.', you are still biased and your old judgement has determined someone was unusual – in your opinion! Acceptance of people where they are with a smile in your head is peacefulness and happiness. Acceptance takes realistic humility. Without humility, no genuine advance can even begin.

Learn to live a life of honest poverty, if you must, and turn to more important matters than transporting gold to your grave. – Credenda

When this change in thought process occurs, I am constantly awestruck by its powerful transition.

My ideas so far, and how they were affecting me and how they were blocking me were not gaining intelligence. Do I hate myself that much that I want to keep my old ideas and defects?

Example: I asked a woman to write down some names of people she had hurt in her life, with her words or deeds. Of course, she added her ex-husband's name. When she eliminated the 'but he… if only he…I did it because he...' She was left with <u>her</u> actions. After two hours of discussing her part in the disagreement, her raised voice, her own opinions, her nonacceptance of his humanness, we were getting someplace. An opinion is only a myth that looks like a truth. Even though he had been the betrayer, the drug user, the 'cause' of their marriage declining, SHE had negative actions to own. By her own admission, she had escalated, judged, belittled, and dismissed another human form just traveling through his life at a time when they no longer saw eye to eye or loved one another. She chose to stay in his arena. When her light bulb went on, she realized, with this neo thinking, she had hurt him and was probably aiming to do it again to others; because she knew how. Secretly, I was so happy she realized her part and that she had a part. She could now move on to practice NOT acting the same way in future difficult discussions. Powerful transformation. Her pupa was testing its wings.

She realized if she had time to complain, she had that *same* time to change herself.

Women apparently are the better sniffer-outers of intrigue and betrayal. Women are more predisposed to suspicion and we do not give up probing for details. We have no shame when it comes to sniffing out proof of problems in our marriage. I am ignoble of all the investigative measures one could take to prove another (my spouse, most often) in the wrong. If suspicion comes into my heart, I will be ugly in my blame and finger pointing. I will not look for my own faults, just his.

I would bet that if we had a mirror in front of our face at all times, we would be totally surprised at what our face reveals about our thinking. I know when my tongue searches for food bits, it is very unbecoming - well disgusting actually. Bet if I saw my image when I am angry or not accepting what others say or do, I would not like the face that shows in judgement or mad. This is that hard. To control your face requires thought. To change your face requires thought. To change your thinking requires a pause in your thought. I really don't want anybody to have to look at me while cleaning my teeth with my tongue after I have a bite. I am the only one that can be aware, think about how I look, and stop the image others see.

Wear your good clothes. Use the good dishes. Light a candle. You are worth it.

Today's Media: He Touched Me Inappropriately

I CAN HARDLY WRITE as I begin this chapter, I am laughing so hard at the Me-Too movement toward aggressive men. Hear me out. Oh, yes, rape and sexual abuse are ugly, deadly, and rampant! Children are not to be touched inappropriately. Girls are ripped from the streets and abused in trafficking. I am not talking about the unfortunate aggressive crimes against us. I do not deny that is a horror in too many lives.

However, why is it that wealthy and famed men are often the object of the lawsuit? Girls with loss of self, or girls who never learned their worth, will shout out with rigor, that someone else made them feel. If I absorbed every piece of news put out, I would have a lot of insignificant lore. News items do not tell scenario as it played out – no way they could. Rape and sexual abuse occur in one in every five women! This is not a light matter.

Women need to be taught a strong "No" regarding others touching their bodies. Aggressors will continue to be visible in societal news, but perhaps date rape would be less. Teenage hormones will continue to thrive. Correct protection can't be done if we are not mentors in this. Something few mothers talk about with daughters. Teachers must address this in Junior High, to my thinking.

I'll restate my thought about why I am laughing. In the past two to three years, a number of politicians, very rich men, counsels to the president, and sports figures have been lambasted with previous and former rape charges. It seems much of the inappropriate touching and suggestions were made years before the person got famous and in the twilight of the news. Now that they have fame and money, women are stepping forward with old stories, not spoken to before. What is this about? It looks ironic that the fame or the possibility of promoting a book or obtaining a settlement has NOW made the earlier 'intercourse' – exchange of communication, sexually inappropriate. I get that there is often a sequential method for liability to come out later. It is also attention seeking and may have monetary reward for the person charging another with this.

Yet, I want us all to be *perfectly* honest about our charges! Most women or men act in a flirtatious manner at some point, <u>consciously or unconsciously,</u> putting it out there, that they will give up something of themselves to gain - it could be anything - your attention, notice, a job, a part in a movie or on stage, your approval, another's love, another's possession. There is an assigned term – necromancer – for people who believe this false crescendo works. People who have no power often use an aura of spiritualism, maybe secretism to dominate, using romantic behavior; i.e. sweet or cute voices, eyes that look up into another's, a helpless gesture. It works in many a couple.

However, my laughter rises because, I would bet that many false charges are being filed by people who were once necromancers and NOW as an older, smarter person, don't want what they now call 'rape or sexual promiscuity' to be their fault at all! And there is a benefit by screaming, "Monster. He made me." Let us not get mixed up on what has really happened. Own your part in any affair involving a physical exchange if you have been a participant. I am not saying tell the world you had an extramarital affair, but know in your heart that you too were involved and stop harassing the opposite sex with blame.

I've done it... You have done it... Flirtation. Seen wives who still use their 'cutsey whims' to get husbands to do something?

Further, when a young person does not know better, they do it.

Adolescent... sounds like 'Adult Lessons'...Adults give lessons... Teens get lessons from Adults...Adult Lessons! Non-Adults learning the hard way through lessons of consequences...Adolescence.

When a young person has not been exposed to understanding something YET; it all bodes like a challenge. Touch that yellow flame. Taste that green blade in the lawn. See how fast this car can go with the pedal way down. Explore the tongue of someone who likes me. Give in to the good sensation in my pants. How can I get that person to like me better? I want to belong. Adolescents rarely say "I don't know how." Unless it involves a chore. (And that may be the truth.)

As younger, unwisened people, we test the waters. We test everything - our boundaries, the rules, and laws, even our physical prowess, and unfortunately sometimes with one-ton metal hunks and alcohol.

We can't know until we do know.

Most of us, when really honest, have explored our vibrating sexualities. We cannot know another's acceptance of our forwardness, until it is out there, too late.

Men and women and men and men and mix and mix as it goes, all test the above. Some mature untimely, some pubert early, some late; some of us are witness to right and/or wrong mixes, some have been abused, some have been taught prudishness. Who in the Hell has had a perfect exposure to the sexual activities that they needed to know at the time? I mean, come on. Experimentation is a part of growing up.

So, the ensuing result in the media today is blame. I used to be really good at finger pointing. I was the good girl. I was always 'talked into it', passing blame on to the current 'fast' boyfriend. Or it looked/sounded too exciting to pass up. Yes, I too, wanted the boy to notice me, ask me out. I wanted to be invited to the keg party. I wore short skirts and heels, in fashion but also known (to) catch a boy's eye. Maybe I would giggle more, look softer, wear makeup. Most of the time, my conscious at age 13 – 20, did not know what would come of the way I dressed, talked, and walked.

Maybe I would act prudish, be unexposed to pornographic literature, maybe I in truth, was not yet physically mature, and someone took advantage of my naiveite to 'show me theirs'. I truly had no idea that I was accountable for my actions. I played around.

If we each stepped up to our half of the event, if we honestly owned up to our lack of knowledge or a boisterous personality; if we owned our behaviors, as did other parties, do you think as many folks as say, are truly violated? Now, I do know that the World Health Organization in 2021 released a report that shows one in three women worldwide experience physical or sexual violence in their lifetime. I have. I was molested at 13; slapped on a first date because "I wouldn't"; and my husband, who had seen his father hit his mother, who had been abused and neglected himself by his father, followed his father's footsteps in throwing me around several times. I know wrongful abuse happens to people, I am not naïve. I am only addressing here that women who are flirts, and women who need attention for their own self-esteem, accept that they had a part in leading someone on. Yes, a perpetrator is breaking a law.

Recently to the date of publication, Scott Baio, a teen television series heart throb (Happy Days) with his satin unruly black hair, now 60, has his character defamed by a woman in her 50's, saying they messed around behind the set as teenagers. I mean, come on. Everybody's All-American image of a good boy. Thirty-five to forty years later? Media said he took advantage of a younger, more naïve girl. Did he do so with intent to ruin her emotional health or physical being? Did you expect more of your bad self at that age? Sexual urges create themselves. Young brains do not have enough information to review when a fire rises in their groins. I have no right to pass judgment on any other human being. I grew up when the rumors about 'girls being sent away for a few months' was a part of conversations. I worked with sixteen-year-old prostitutes and thirteen-year-old pregnant gang rape victims. What events were they the outcome of? Blameless? The connotations others assign young female victims are often not their fault.

John 8:7 *He that is without sin among you, let him first cast a stone at her.*

I will add, that I have been, in my past, very quick to pass blame because of my own guilt by participation. Just ask my older brother about our physical fights. My little innocent eyes, always said, "He did it." I learned early to pass the buck to avoid facing a consequence for my actions! It's easier. It didn't take away my self-blame but it got me off the hot seat for a spanking. It blames another for my lack of knowledge. "I guess maybe my teacher or parents forgot to talk to me at the right time". Blame. Point the finger. Another thing our parents did to us. Gees. Step up to the plate. Add forgiveness to your repertoire. Forgive others and forgive yourself. Be a God-like person already. You will see that forgiveness collapses the passage of time. Proverb 16 includes a passage about the Lord touching a man who said "Woe is me, I am doomed." And God said, "Your wickedness is purged." My belief that this can happen is of the utmost.

That unpredictable staining or making judgements of others gets in the way of having an amazing life. They do not augur well in to your new more fulfilling lifestyle. Why waste my time assigning judgement to things and people that are not my business? And then carry the judgement or gossip about it. Noooooo.

I parallel this movement to what our legislators ALL have done. We elect them because WE think they are full of idealized hope with all their promises and campaign rhetoric. They are flirting with us - with our heads, environment, pocketbooks, emotion, and future. They really got me going, fire in my belly, excited, loving their words and promises! But statistics about those very same men and women candidates show that once elected, a first, primary obligation is their selfish selves! They take care of any bills that give them better or more benefits, and set a cost of living raise or two and determine how many weeks they will work this year. Our basic human needs often over rule any common sense we have – so far. In sex or politics.

I've been raped by someone who promised me the moon. Sound familiar? Just days before he was married to his college girlfriend.

Wiser and Better

How exciting to think that I could be wiser and live better if I just grabbed onto the guru's advice! So I trudge through my next few days after each lecture, sermon, or enlightening class; only to find I am doing just that, trudging as I always have.

Hmmm... Perhaps you will realize, as I am now, that CHANGE takes decision and then action. It requires, well... altering our thinking first. Here is a guru I like, telling us what to do.

Don Miguel writes his Four Agreements.

The Four Agreements are:

1. Be Impeccable with your Word: Speak with integrity. Say only what you mean. Avoid using the Word to speak against yourself or to gossip about others. Use the power of your Word in the direction of truth and love.

2. Don't Take Anything Personally

    Nothing others do is because of you. What others say and do is a projection of their own reality, their own dream. When you are immune to the opinions and actions of others, you won't be the victim of needless suffering.

3. Don't Make Assumptions

> Find the courage to ask questions and to express what you really want. Communicate with others as clearly as you can to avoid misunderstandings, sadness and drama. With just this one agreement, you can completely transform your life.

4. Always Do Your Best

> Your best is going to change from moment to moment; it will be different when you are healthy as adverse to sick. Under any circumstance, simply do your best, and you will avoid self-judgment, self-abuse, and regret.

"Super. Sounds good. Tomorrow then." "I will get up and start these practices." "Yeah. I am on my way to a better life and everyone will love me."

But often I get stuck in trudging. Doing the same thing as before. Same attitude as yesterday. Thinking negative thoughts. Not including God any more than I did last week. These are all the killers of self-improvement. What makes you think that your life will change miraculously in front of you while you practice the same behaviors and thoughts? Let me say, "Duh!"

One must adopt a new style…in every notion, movement, thought, idea, action!

Are you up for that? I know many of us are ready for that! So far, what we have done has not brought us our desired satisfaction.

The potential for higher wisdom levels far beyond my current status excites us, probably the most. Others told me that my friends will change up. My attitude will be great all the time. I will stop indicting and judging others.

I will stop lying to myself. I will have no false hopes, only truth. I will be loved and accepted more. I will no longer regret, or resent, or rationalize, or hurt anyone. I will be doing God's work as He designed when He blessed my parents with my seed.

The possibility to enjoy all people and every minute of this short time on earth with fulfillment and happiness is here. Now.

Don't miss this opportunity. I did. I did for thirty years living as an adult. If I held regrets anymore, that would be the one I would speak to. I missed 30 years of happiness because why? Because I didn't change when my mind said I would.

For 30 years, I more often than not, responded to impeti and others. Today my new mantra is ensuring that you know I will not 'sit back and take it'.

"YOU cannot hold on to what I have been. I have changed. I have a new way to understand. Let old me go. You, nor I can go back."

Here are Some Things I Wonder

Wonder - Get back your sense of wonder! Best decision I ever made.

Screaming "Yahoo", down Route 3 on the back of a motorcycle on a perfect day, I felt embedded with a rush like no other. Not like ferris wheels or bungie jumping thrills, but that feeling of relief, easing out from a dark hole, or like the wash of a deep breath when semester tests were over. You know, a profound sense of growth and being 'done with that' piece of life. A huge dose of fresh air can do that.

The celebration of living is so rare. Why do we not do that for ourselves? Our personal Edens usually come at great cost and stay only temporarily. I may have found the path to serenity - giving up! Giving up stress, letting go of trepidation, opening my soul, heart and mind to a greater existence; letting go of things that are not in my control and trusting in something way bigger than me. I recently heard these words from a guru of health.

"Why not live every moment in awe? It is after all – awesome that we get to live." Wow, huh?

It's time to stop the madness of stress and comparison, stop carrying burdens, go ahead laugh and ridicule your schedule.

From Hazrat Inayat Khan, I offer this Sufi poem:

PARADOXES OF PRAYER

I asked God for strength, that I might achieve;
I was made weak, that I might learn humble to obey...
I asked for health, that I might do greater things;
I was given infirmity, that I might do better things...
I asked for riches, that I might be happy;
I was given Poverty, that I might be wise...
I asked for power, that I might have the praise of men.
I asked for all things, that I might enjoy life;
I was given life, that I might enjoy all things...
I got nothing that I asked for – but everything I hoped for-
Almost despite myself, my unspoken prayers were answered
I am among all, most richly blessed!

Think about this: We have visceral feelings and sensitivity we cannot ignore. Like excitement and a desire for happiness to enter into all interactions. We cannot deny our feelings. We can alter our feelings with intent - to stay positive, to look for good, to act in a legal and mindful way, given those facts and truths.

Analytical and critical thinking help us to decide what is best. Where we get into trouble is when we act without incorporating all lobes, those of memory, aesthetics, values, feelings, truths, impact, and deductive reasoning.

Why would we go into battle without that army? Because our amygdala operates on fear and fear responses. The amygdala sends signals to the reasoning and logistics lobes, through the center where memories wait for processing. Without engaging our brain, we would REACT based on fear. That is not a way to live. God gave us a whole brain to make conscious chosen responses. (I call to mind here, what my dad often said to me, "Use your brain!") Scientists recommend waiting three seconds before responding to allow for your brain to systematically go through the thinking steps.

It will change the way you live.

Without using our brains in this full manner, toxic instincts govern our lives. Ick. Concepts and principles were not even consulted.

Put It All Together, It Spells: Peace

Do you really know what is important in your life? Do you really know what you have on your mind a lot that is unimportant? Woo, I hit a nerve, didn't I? Let's qualitize your thinking.

1. Are the things you are spending your time on going to be of value to you?
2. Do you have a mindset to value what is first on your first things first list?
3. Are you driven by someone other than yourself to do things?
4. Does urgent or pressing always matter?
5. To what do you tie the urgency?
6. What activities do you do that will have positive results in your personal life?
7. What activities do you do that will have positive results in your career/vocation?
8. Would you have wanted this in your life when you were a teen dreaming of being an adult?
9. Does this have historical value but not now?
10. Would your mother approve of your decision?
11. Does God want this for your life?

(I) Important   /   (U) Unimportant

____ Preparation or planning

____ Fun activities

____ Incoming mail

____ Bill paying

____ Favorite television shows

____ Cleaning

____ Crossword Puzzle

____Junk mail

____ Email

____ Messages from friends

____ Messages from the boss

____ Safety

____ Security

____ Meditation

____ Messages / Email from office

____ Playing

____ Tennis, volleyball, pickle ball, etc.

____Attending children's game/event

____ Reading for leisure

____ Hole in roof

____ Gas on one-fourth full

____ Work/school deadline

____ Laundry

____ Rest/Nap

____ Hydration

____ Nutrition

____ Gizmo usage

____ An essay/report due

____ Time with family

____ Meeting other's priorities

____ Reading a novel

____ Reading to learn

____ Listening

____ People stopping by

____ Meetings

____ Professional development

____ Media games

I won't leave you hanging. 'Important' refers to feelings of confidence, fulfilled and on track. Words like meaningful and the offer of peace seem to apply.

'Unimportant' or 'Urgent' typify stress, unfulfilled, or worn out by. These feelings reveal much about why we are not getting the results we want.

I will also tell you that there were trick questions. See, deciding what is important in our lives is a grey area. There is cross-over between the degree or perhaps timing in some of the items on the list. How do we know? Urgent refers to addiction to that 'thing'. Urgent can mean we are trying to please another, keep our job, beat the crowd, be on time – often it is about racing with a clock. Our clock? Someone else's clock? My only question here is, is there peace on your heart after the race? Sometimes we are the only one's thinking, 'this must be acted on now'. Everybody has that same clock – the casino player, the homeless person roaming streets all day, the person in a pew praying, or you on a race to get to softball practice.

Does the environment control you: Mow the lawn, do this or that before nightfall, time enough for hobbies, eating before the kids' ballgames? It can fool us. Reclaim your peace here also! Are you being deceived by your own reaction to life? What is your capability in the matter? Use peaceful time in the decision.

Personal example: I spent too much time on 'to-doing', but not enough on family and friends. Result: My house always looked brand new and trendy, but no one ever saw it! I was tending to a lifestyle that was inefficient with fervor toward a selfish, urgent, and irrelevant need within my head, rather than a principle I knew I wanted to develop.

Is there a crisis that involves you? First question is, is it a crisis to YOU? Are you mistakenly calling it a crisis based on real time and event size? Can the solution be put aside for now? Are you losing time having an anxiety attack or reacting and involving others unnecessarily? Is this just unique to you or has it been resolved before?

Are any of the items on the previous page just things? "Tangible things' never require our feelings. They may affect organization or structure, money, control, and efficiency; however, they are not urgent. They will come up again if worthwhile.

Items that require relationships, people, and your mission in life are moral principles and truth. They ask you to apply discernment, time, service or your vision.

Your life depends on these questions. Forget anything insignificant. Be mindful of HALT (Hungry, Angry, Lonely, and Tired) in all things. These all change relevance of doing. Stop and respondfully address any part of HALT.

Peace: The decision to reclaim our use of time or thinking we are doing something important, rather than losing time to the deception of reaction, which is self-created.

Most folks first, want relationships with God, friends and family to be their priority. That includes communication with each of those. Better care of self is right up there, as it applies to being the best you can in the relationships previously listed, and in the next priority. Personal growth in however many ways it happens seems to be next and it varies on what you need to improve: upgrade skills, new opportunities, preparation, planning and organization.

How'd you do? I leave you with one phrase: 'Nothing happens without you acting on it.'

Mercy is Deep

A wave of relief is coming your way.

This too, shall pass.

God is going to help; you just have to be willing to understand what richness and depth of relief you can have.

His mercy is deep, deeper than our sin.

He helps us change our way of life so that what we do is good, what we love is freely loving, and what we need is through Him.

> *Let us treasure up in our soul some of those things which are permanent…, not of those which will forsake us and be destroyed, and which only tickle our senses for a little while…* – Gregory of Nazianzus

Read a Nate Poetzl lecture on a new way to be human. It's a good read. Nate has got it going on! From the Thessalonians, Nate interprets that there are instructions by the authority of God. Now we all know Biblical stories were told in a time when writing was not even invented and no one recorded Jesus. However, Christian ethics rely on the graphai descriptive words of our forefather's to be as close to true as we are every gonna get.

So say we have instructions from God:

1. As for other matters, brothers and sisters, we instructed you how-to live-in order to please God.

Not a bad idea! Nate interprets: Be purposeful about the way you live. If you go with the flow – what is normal and acceptable, you will end up somewhere that doesn't please God. We often do what *seems* right, what is easiest or what is the path of least resistance.

2. God's will…that we are sanctified.

Most of us need interpretation here. Sanctified means set apart for a unique purpose. (Wow, people. That is a glorious charge to be put upon us!) God's *will for us is that we are dignified*. (Oh my gosh, I love this idea.)

3. Avoid sexual immorality.

It is God's will that you should be sanctified: that you should avoid sexual immorality. (Porneia)

Nate states further, this is: "Any form of sex outside the covenant of marriage between a husband and a wife." So this my friends, is simply mind over matter. A new and better way to be human. Social Equality for all sexes. Pleasing our God has to do with both the mind and the body. What a gift sex is. We are allowed to experience orgasm and procreate. Another of God's beautiful beings has allowed us to join in consensual consummation. Honor one another with respect and gratitude under God's request. If you are not doing that, start at the beginning of this book and read it over again.

4. Learn to control your body

Each of us should learn to control our own bodies in a way that is holy and honorable, not in passionate lust like pagans, who do not know God. For God did not call us to be impure, but to live a holy life. For anyone who rejects this instruction does not reject a human being, but God, the very God who gives you his Holy Spirit. People can be wronged in this way.

Well said, Nate. Thank you. His words so contribute to society's reckoning with truth.

So, you are challenged to answer the questions below.

) Do you really know what is best for everyone and everything?
) Do you trust what you believe in your spirituality so far?
) Do you trust what is in your heart?
) Can you let others live their own lives without interfering with your words?
) Are you fully aware of the difference between physical actions and what your soul/hear feel?
) Do you allow yourself to be led into temptations?
) Do you believe in a Higher Power greater than yourself?
) Do you admit to your sins? Do you apologize and feel humbled?

Here's a factoid: Sin lives in our hearts. Our minds cannot will it out. UNLESS we let God abide in our heart and we in Him. And you know by now, that I believe your Higher Power may not be my God. That is a big bite to chew. Read it again. A life that is lived righteously must be our habit. Am I enslaved to laziness and sloth? Temptation? Omission of purity? Sin can simply be lack of love. Are we carrying guilt? Have we fallen asleep on our faith? If we are a child of God, it will affect our lives. We will be restored. We can cleanse and refresh our faith. The quality of our heart will get purer by the beauty of His grace over and within us. We are in His cosmic redemption. What a wonderful time to be born into.

As children, we are wide eyed looking for light and purity. Was it always shown to us? No. Sometimes the fear of God or fear of the 'debil' were put in us. It made me shirk from God's coming. I was damned for fighting with my brother over a ball. I am glad the Catholics saw the light since I was in Sunday school some 50 years ago. When I discovered that I knew of God more than I knew of my sister or my spouse, I believed in His daily redemptive powers. What a close feeling. God wants us to know Him in our hearts and then use that light as an extension of Him. Jesus came to earth to tell us how to be pure through accounts in the Bible, gospels, and sermons. Add prayer to normalize pure living.

Here's the kicker: We can waltz through repentance, only by asking and then listening. We can become aware of our disobedience to His word. Do you trade His glory for that dang TV box? Could I make better use of my time and rather than selfishly get numb, ACT in honor of my self as a child of God?

A truth I do not like to be aware of is this:

In 2004, 78% of the world claimed to be Christian

In 2020, only 65% claim this

26% claim at any time to be 'unchurched'

We may read and study the Bible. We take heed to some, some not, of the printed word. We choose of our own volition what to belief, what to follow. We are not remembering that to partake in His divine nature is a privilege. Peter said it.

We each seem to long for eternity; however, it could come. Upstairs, or here on land. Yet the instruction manual to have that is slight. Grace and sanctification, not human satisfaction, are already ours. We are the ones that mess it up.

Rich Beyond Your Wildest Dreams

Dr. Seuss said: "You are you."

Who is 'World Class' in your life? To entitle that assignation to a person we trust in their purpose and potential. Now sir, (or ma'am), why wouldn't that assignation be given to you? Aha, that got you thinking, didn't it? You were born to a role on purpose. You are given potential. Let's not underperform! Spirit lives within us. You have hope already given to you by God.

What does it take for us to 'getoffourass'? Action by us? Encouragement from another? Life's happenstance?

Jesus asked Saul, "Why do you persecute me?" Did you ever think that perhaps you are persecuting yourself from your potential? (This right here, this, is a mortal sin called 'Sloth'.) You are your own disciple as well as a disciple of God. Are you taking the right steps to act in that manner? Woo. That is quite an in-depth look at how your persona engages, huh?

Do your best. Contribute to the world. Be an encourager. What the heck do you think you are doing here? Were you created on earth to have another beer, to sleep in till 10 or later, be rude, demand things of others? You got another 'think' coming if that is your pissy mindset. Grab back on to that HOPE that God gives you every day you wake up. He has a vested interest in our emotional and spiritual growth, why don't you?

Maybe, just maybe, your predecessors set you up...their exhibited behaviors performed indulgent or unethical acts. Did adults or authority figures, teachers, mentors, etc.:

1. Teach you to worry and fret?
2. Embarrass and shame you?
3. Upset and cancel plans?
4. Tell lies to cover things?
5. Break laws?
6. Threaten you?
7. Create fear in you? Sometimes great fear? Fear of other people? The public? The government?
8. Live with money problems or relying on government and people to support them?
9. Make you feel a failure/less?

We took advice from people who didn't know their direction or purpose in life sometimes. That was misdirection. So what now are YOUR underpinnings?

Sometimes, the family unit though, looked competent and successful from the outside. Sometimes we grew up thinking this is normal: Look good, fake it, lie; or within the home/office/marriage, abuse is okay. That statement gives me shivers. And abuse comes in all forms, verbal, physical, mental, emotional, expectational and punitively.

We actually 'get used to this'. Did you know there is a soothing kind of lifestyle with inner calmness? If that sounds boring, you need to read a couple more chapters. Just a glimpse into what it can be is to say that when you have 'time' in your mind, your thoughts are no longer fear, how to lie your way out, worry, or act shamefully; but instead, you fill your time thinking with positive ways, progressive thinking, and beautiful actions that benefit you.

Well then, how could you feel otherwise? Stick with me kid and we will find in you, your potential and hope and work your way out of the above sick ideations cast upon you. Opportunity is knocking.

Consider that when we were young, modern developments in science and theory were just on precipice and all those new awakenings and new ideas were trickling down into our lives, adding new education every day. See, every generation is shaped by what is known, only so far. We were born into our family's religion, environment, economic status. There may not have been much growth in our earlier times and we were forced to be only as much as our parents knew. Buddhists will tell you that we are born seeking novelty and of a certain temperament, and seeking earthen vibrations to lead them, their fates inevitable. No one chooses their path in Buddhism; it has been set before you were born. Many, rather have no idea what we are doing on earth and listen to every nuance exposed to them; why wouldn't we? Those of us who were in families with great wreckage as a way of life, have much more to overcome than old scientific beliefs. Spiritual, cultural and mechanical, industrial, technological and medical neo-nuances of thought were edging into our lives. In Freud's time, he showed the world a visit into the human psyche of our control belonging to primal urges and driven by the brain nodes. Thank God we had leaders in science and biology to take us to where we are now. This book would have been of great use back then. And I am hopeful that it will be useless in 10 or 20 years. That brings with it the thought that behaviors and thoughts will be purified someday.

So here's something to try-on: The key to peace within you (serenity) is cognizance of behavior and of others' behaviors, a willingness to change, and then practice, practice, practice, and have patience with yourself. And lastly, don't fight the feeling, when complete abandon of worry happens – when serenity knocks on your door, embrace it.

A miracle happens within you. When we surrender our will to the care of God, limits we developed from the past drop. That allows great things to happen in our future possibilities.

Apologies
Amends

I want you to get this right, so I am repeating words to clear your mind of a clutter you do not realize is living up there.

"I was wrong."

Say it out loud. "I was wrong." There is kind of a fizz happening in my throat and my mouth gets momentarily dry. It seems like it is hard to spit out in audible syllables. If I hear someone else say it, I have a similar bodily reaction happening empathetically. It is important to notice your physical senses. Cognizance just happened. Something is un-easy. There, If you realize (are cognizant) that there is an uneasy feeling, something must have been noticed by your progressive and positive thinking as not quite right. If another is involved, they probably noticed also. Is an apology needed?

As I write this, my husband called me to show him what I wanted fixed on my exercise equipment. We talked it through. He doubted that it could be done. I picked up the tool and began to repair it. "Here, let me do that." Came out of his mouth. My sassy kicked in with, "Oh, you can do better than I can?" I apologized for sassy and he apologized for insisting that he take over. I wanted him to do it as it required more endurance than I had in my arm muscles. We smiled as I walked away. A quick amends is better than walking away with guilt or remorse for words uttered without thought.

It is emotional to admit wrong doings: I deviated from my own principles. I told an untruth or stretched truth. I acted or reacted poorly. I have to own up to something done in a poor manner. I have to say to someone else that my head didn't opt correctly, most likely with full knowledge and intent. What I did affected you in a negative manner. I was wrong.

No justifications. No rationalization. I apologize. I was wrong. I have learned the error of my way.

Perhaps you can forgive and say so. But neither of us forget this. A black mark has been made. I condemn myself and then, on top of that, I condemn me on the fact that I have also hurt you in my action, non-action, or reaction.

The fact that I get to apologize to you, though, has great power. I got to admit, instead of beating myself up in the coversive activity, I told you - I am not perfect - I slip - my mouth speaks before my head - I react instead of thinking. I spoke also to myself. There, there was an error. A mistake. I have retracted as best I could, I have made amends, and I am paying it forward in a better manner. I learned and will not harm in this manner again. Tell the person you harmed. Go on, step up.

I am a better person for my being cognizant of my previous ways, admitting to my mistake and promising to correct the errors of my ways. Cognizance alone, takes courage to admit to. I found that many of my discoveries were in God's time, put before me as the challenge to negotiate differently. I now needed to discern truth and accept the things I cannot change and stop controlling and interfering with what is just God's, not mine.

Heard the term I.C.E.? It applied when I was interfering, controlling and/ or criticizing, and escaping.

Another recommendation: Learn how to apologize!

Ease into it. Allow your mind to put yourself in their shoes.

Instead of: "I'm not going with you." How about, "Thank you for asking. Shoot, I have an engagement at that time. I'm sorry." (Your engagement could even be to relax!)

Or "Unfortunately, I can't make it. I'm sorry."

Or, "Thank you for that opportunity. Homelife comes first."

Or I'm torn - I made another obligation. Guess I better do what I promised. I'm sorry."

Don't leave friends feeling rejected. Leave them knowing your sincerity. Be up front and honest as you can be, always being kind in the say so.

Or "Haven't been home all week. I'd love to do that with you next time. I need to make my family know I love them too. I'm sorry."

Be good with asking. Demanding folks and louder people might get attention, but they often leave a negative note in the exchange of communication.

Honesty works best here too. "I lost my sense of direction. Which way to the door, with a smile" takes you much farther than, "Where in the hell is Gate 9!"

Body language walks in the room before you do. People give you 1/8 of a second and if that persona is not amiable, you have lost one-half your communication, coldly.

Talking with your hands is essential. It helps listeners comprehend so they can respond well.

An actress recently tweeted an apology for "...being unnecessarily difficult. It was my immaturity," It is also strongly encouraged that you do not make that kind of irrational excuse. Oh, she is off the hook because she can blame something? That is just sick. Did some persona within her act in a negative manner? Is she blaming her psyche, not taking ownership of her wrong doing? How about, "I acted immaturely."?

'Mind your own business' was a popular shunning phrase we used in junior high – a time of high insecurity when we knew just enough to pretend, but were so unsure about most of life. Staying in my own hula hoop was the last thing I wanted to do. You *just had* to have a clique, even if it were the musician or the book clique.

At that time, we did not know boundaries. We did not know people obsessed on things. We knew nothing about true respect or holding onto our own dignity. We did a lot of unacceptable behavior. It was a natural thing because we did not know boundaries or earned respect yet.

I'd like to ask you if you think you take responsibility for the cleanliness of your soul? That is a cool concept, huh? The choices we make with attitudes and beliefs, whether values, desires, or behavior; our soul is the filter. Run your next decision passed your soul. How does it shake out?

What we didn't have before follows here, and I am afraid to say, some adults still do not grasp these things about life:

1. Acceptance of what is not like us
2. Knowledge enough to make good choices
3. Allowance of others to make their own decisions
4. Commanding/demanding behavior often gets us nothing more than disliked
5. That our minds are still small, stuck in old thinking; exposed only to a hundred people like us
6. Realization that we are not in control of others
7. Learned empathy

We were so subjective, caught in what little we knew.

Namaste Moore offers this insight: *"True healing can only occur when you become less attached to how you received your wound and more attached to your desire to be healed from it."*

Paradise Every Day – Open Your Mind

Best decision I ever made:

Choosing a positive life every day. The celebration of living is so rare. And why do we do that to ourselves? Our personal Edens usually come at great cost and stay only temporarily. I may have found the path to serenity-giving up! Giving up stress, letting go of worry, opening my soul, heart and mind to a greater existence; letting go of things that are not in my control and trusting in something way bigger than me.

I personally love not worrying. I no longer have to have all the answers. I no longer have to live anywhere but in the present moment. As I learned to let go of the nuisance of worry, I found more time in my head and happier thoughts could fill that void. We are not responsible for all the answers. It was revealed to me repeatedly that no one knows the outcome ahead; God has got it all and he has a plan, not yet given to me.

So this moment is knocking on your door.

With whatever you are doing, are you living toward your legacy or destiny? Are you even happy? Have you settled?

Are you coping? Is your connection with God all the time? Are you a good girl/boy in Mom's eyes? Have you grown up into the person you always wanted to be? Are you chasing dreams? Do you have a garage full of broken dream attempts?

OPEN YOUR EYES.

Are you lying to yourself in any of those answers?

Do you sometimes feel restless and stressed? Sure, you are getting that way because (blame) of work, kids, marriage, events, tasks, and toils. Wait, who said to you: "Feel stressed right now."? Oh, you did. Oh?

If you consistently engage in activities to the point of stress or tension, perhaps there is one more thing you can do. Stop thinking of it as stress. Take in the moment you are in. Only once will this moment be in your day or any day. One chance at this moment of engagement with life. What is the essence? What is this moment's quality based on for you? It is your one existential moment in life. It is exponential – never to be seen again. We could process through every second to just get through it, and on to the next, and the next ball game, don't be late for church, what's for supper, what time does bowling start? OR, we could embrace what is in front of us. Want to be the life of the party? Then live while at the party, live the moment.

Stress, feeling impatient, feeling empty inside, feeling indecisive, are all THIEVES of happiness. When the truth is, you did not want to miss the ball game. So be there when you are present. Abort the push which other moments purport to have on you. Aren't you in control of your own thoughts? Impatience is a sign of pride – that your time is more valuable than another's time. Sometimes I want God to work like a microwave – fast. He does my wishes, but in a slow stewing crock pot, allowing me to get ready for the reality of what I am about to do. To pretend you are involved in wrong choices or other's problems, is useless and you leave feeling empty. To worry means you are not enjoying this moment. Hm. Are you getting it?

Indecisiveness has its own issues; there are too many points of view. This is real. Wikipedia offers Seven Types of Ambiguity (by Ember):

1. A metaphor occurs when things seem alike but have totally different properties to consider.
2. Sometimes two meanings of the same wording.
3. One context but two ideas occur through wording.
4. Simultaneous connection of two ideas.
5. Two meanings do not agree.
6. Written word and idea comprehended are different
7. Empty statements must be interpreted by the listener

Jonathan Swift said, *"Whoever is out of patience is out of possession of his soul."*

Your chance to live in extraordinary happiness is here. Tune in to your purpose: to listen all the way through their sentence, to show compassion, to know love, to be in the now. If you are not attuned to what your legacy will be, you are not honoring yourself. One sometimes feels like we are dragging ourselves around. It is said that an overview of your day at night, will quickly tell us when we engaged with life. When we have misgivings about what we did or feel a need to apologize or make up, we failed ourselves. Pay attention to the list of light, good, and happy moments. After days and weeks of nightly review, you may find you are eliminating stressors and setting good boundaries as to how to fill your moments, and thus, your mind.

Stay quiet when anyone else is speaking, anyone else. Do this with intentionality.

Another counter to stressful moments is to see them differently. I have a friend who always says, "God gave me a challenge to live up to today." I love her thinking. She put her mind's energy into solutions and outcomes, I guarantee if you were to take a poll of your family, coworkers or volunteers, or people on the street, only twenty percent would truthfully tell you they do not have a headache, or feel overwhelmed, or are depressed or sick. We have become oriented to outside forces and problems that seem big, or without solution. In response, we lash out or fight or flight, and a whole other list of negative thoughts and behaviors. If you see the reaction as energy, convert it to positive energy use. The first question to ask yourself is whether _your name_ was even in the mesh. Did someone ask you to solve this? THEN YOU HAVE NOTHING TO SAY AND CAN STOP FROM INVOLVING YOUR ALREADY OVER USED HAPPINESS SEARCH.

Pablo Picasso on computers... – *"But they are useless. They can only give you answers."*

We are working with real brains and looking for solutions. Computers give us facts but cannot think for us or use emotion and feeling. We are in charge of our humanness.

You already know this, if you exercise and eat healthily, you like yourself better. Parallel this with thinking positively (brain exercise) and putting healthy thoughts in your head. You will like yourself better. And a side effect is that others will like you better and want to hang with you in your happy and serene place.

Physiologically, when you run a race, you prepare. At the time, your adrenaline and cortisol hormones rush into the blood stream. It synergistically combines to get your vision, brain, muscles empowered and ready to react. You mindfully have a mental trick happening, energizing your body to succeed.

Optimize the rush of those good hormones every day, every hour. Just with *thinking*. It takes some training just like a marathon: alternative practices, dedication to what you want and positive thoughts about the action.

Live Greatly

See there are choices in your path – Integrity is one choice.

Integrity [in'tegradē] NOUN

> the quality of being honest and having strong moral principles; moral uprightness; moral and undivided, approaching the mission of the moment with peace, good character, and knowledge

It is distinguished over other choices. It is the only correct path, from which you can never get lost.

Think for a moment about the incorrect path: I became a lonely, selfish, sad, individual; clawing at manipulative ways to change somebody else; to my demise with nagging complaints, lost happiness, and vengeful hatred of my lot. Add that I had great doubts about any recovery from this. But I eventually healed and wrote this book, didn't I? And if you are reading it, you do not have a low comprehension factor, I'm just sayin'.

All organisms have the ability to produce more offspring than can survive. I'll risk a statistic, about twenty-five percent of human conceptions were never known about, but sluffed off. Organisms do not survive because the resources are limited that supply them; and they were fighting for resources. There will be systematic selection by nature.

The competition there will be predictable. Traits will be carried forth from weak and strong resources.

Those traits, good or bad, will be carried into the next generation and fight again.

So, with that in place in your mind, we also have spiritual evolution.

Our ancestors had more ideas than survived. There again, was scarcity of resources for survival, but this was in everyone's heads. Competition happened, and traits were carried forth; and systematic selection happened in the population.

They were recounting experiential (to them) and essential methods of believing when lives were at stake. And we continue to perpetuate their historical ideation. Based on your current life in the current day! Do you fight to survive each day? Do you hunt rabbit for your table tonight?

Where is your integrity in living applied?

Wrap that around your Christianity, your Muslimhood, Jewish ideation, or agnostic thinker. Heritage of ideas, Missouri River Lutherans, Presbyterian Christian, Universalist Unitarian (I can pronounce that three times in a row), and on and on. They made it up as they went, People. And we followed. It was inherent, or at least, intuitively immediately what religion or non-practice our 'parental authority figures' showed us.

If their dogma was rigid, we chose not to follow or to follow, for twenty years and more. Am I whistling dixie in your case? In recent times, were the white people of Ferguson, Missouri, to be discredited because one of the so called 'righteous' among them did something wrong? Is Buddha right or wrong? Did Jesus have brothers just as pious as himself? Who knows this information absolutely? Is it just to say if you are Midwestern, you are middle class? Who judges and who says and why do you buy into it? Do you think about this, or do you just punt and pretend to be on a team?

Can religionists impose their doctrine on the secular state? How many will fall?

If their dogma was loose, we had no selection criteria and were ripe for the influential clown or Southern Baptist minister who knocked on the door. We probably didn't worship or take communion, or vote or read the Bible quotes. Does that make us bad people?

Aha, but when you list the seven deadly sins, is your behavior in there: greed, jealousy, envy, sloth, couch potato, and valium use? Are you scheming or scamming? I had so much imagination to justify my morals. So, you must buy into a creed of some sort. Or do you just want the rest of us to be Christian and honest and believe rather? These rules do not apply to all inhabitants, meaning me?

What are you doing there? What is your spiritual thinking? Was it a concentrated decision? An inherent given? An aggressive influencer? Still enmeshed in a grandparental description? What are you doing there, there where you are in your head? How did you get there? Yet, you thought you made the decision as an adult. (Adult definition in Chapter on Maturity.)

Or are you involved in Reactionary Religion? Any few people can be a group, negative and unhealthy or true and generous; rigid or placid; stable or rabblerousing; slow and with little information; helpful or dangerous. Are you a thinking follower or a historical pillar? What is your motive to think in a (fill in name of religion here) manner?

Perhaps, just perhaps unlearning patterns, habits, and rote-following is in store for you?

Do you believe in something that is absolute? Then, think about this: Is anything absolute?

Someone once told me the difference between rural or urban is whether or not you ever defecated on the ground and used a leaf. How different are we really? Are your noble values so real compared to reality?

These are lead-in questions to clarify your hook-up to a star. Who/What is your idea of a higher power, if not God? Is it an autocratic, demanding patriarch? A demanding or inflated egotist? I ask, because I want your 'hook-up' to be of moral purity.

Are you falsely sanctimonious? Now really, who isn't, is more likely the question. Have you grown balls of integrity yet?

Is what is coming out of your mouth ALWAYS true enough that it could be written?

Controversy only happens when I express my opinion with persuasion. Otherwise, I would never have controversy. Pause and think about that. Is there integrity in my speech?

I bring on my unhappiness when I allow others to persuade me into their nonfactual opinions. I bring on unhappiness when I react to stimulus rather than act on the truth.

I always know my discomfort and/or guilt. I always know when I am compassionate with myself. Pick one or the other in all places.

Love, or not at all.

Advice for People in their 20s

1. Getting good sleep is super important. Like, really, really important. Make it a priority, as it affects every aspect of your life. That whole "You can sleep when you're dead" line is **BS**.

2. People over technology. Always.

3. Travel now as far as you can and as much as your finances allow. Life will soon bring you commitments that will likely make travel much more cumbersome.

4. Learn how to cook at least a couple really good meals.

5. Your 20s may take you far from family, both physically and perhaps emotionally, but work hard to keep connected with them as they will become even more important to you with each passing decade.

6. Sunscreen. Sunscreen. Sunscreen. (Also water, water, water!)

7. Marry someone with your same sense of humor. You will need laughter throughout your lifetime, in both the good times and (especially) the bad.

8. Don't waste more than 15 minutes on a new show or movie. If you're not feeling it, move on. You have endless choices.

9. Some people never, ever mature. You will meet 50-year-old mean girls and 60-year-old dudes who haven't grown out of high school locker room mentality. Cross to the other side of the street and keep walking.

10. Always be open to advice and criticism from others but take it all in with a filter of self-knowledge. What might be effective for someone else, may be meaningless to you.

11. One drink of alcohol is usually enough. Special occasions may warrant two, but more than that usually just results in regrets.
12. Exercise. Regularly.
13. Read at least four good books a year.
14. Don't stay in a job, relationship or city that you have to convince yourself you care about.
15. With fashion and in your home, spend money on quality basics in neutral colors. Accessorize on the cheap.
16. Seek out friends with differing viewpoints and backgrounds so you can listen and learn from them.
17. Always read the entire article, not just the headline or the tweet.
18. Educate yourself on issues and candidates and get in the <u>lifelong habit of voting</u>.
19. Never be afraid to ask a stupid question. Because it's almost certainly not stupid.
20. There are multiple reasons to be grateful every single day. Acknowledge and focus on them.

Who's Gonna Die Last Off this Earth?

Attitude toward Death
By Chief Tecumseh

Live your life that the fear of death
can never enter your heart.
Trouble no one about his religion.
Respect others in their views
and demand that they respect yours.
Love your life, perfect your life,
beautify all things in your life.
Seek to make your life long
and of service to your people.
Prepare a noble death song for the day
when you go over the great divide.
Always give a word or sign of salute when meeting
or passing a friend, or even a stranger, if in a lonely place.
Show respect to all people, but grovel to none.
When you rise in the morning, give thanks for the light,
for your life, for your strength.
Give thanks for your food and for the joy of living.
If you see no reason to give thanks,
the fault lies in yourself.
Touch not the poisonous firewater that makes wise ones turn to fools

and robs the spirit of its vision.
When your time comes to die, be not like those
whose hearts are filled with fear of death,
so that when their time comes, they weep and pray
for a little more time to live their lives over again
in a different way.

If we build our character on honesty, morality, goodness, kindness, and oneness, we then have great spiritual values.

There is a seventh step prayer used in AA that I want to quote for you here:

THE SEVENTH STEP PRAYER

My Creator, I am now willing that You should have all of me, good and bad.
I pray that You now remove from me every single defect of character
which stands in the way of my usefulness to You and my fellows.
Grant me strength, as I go out from here, to do Your bidding.
Amen

Faith without the work is dead.

At the very least, I would ask if you take the action to welcome His presence in your heart and soul? Then, do you take the action to reflect it out? Those are conversion moments.

Yes, part of what I am asking of you, is to abandon what we call our own power. It helps to keep things between me and God. I want to be useful to you and my fellows. I want the dichotomy within me of good and bad to lose the bad. I have found when I dismiss the devil from sentences and thoughts, the demon doesn't ever show up. It is so fun to live a clean life.

I would have said, that fixing other people is what I do and controlling is how I care, ten years ago. And those are painful to change. Feelings are not shortcomings; we need accept that we have feelings and choose what to do with them. Anytime I am giving advice, I am condemning or criticizing another for not having the good sense that my ego has, can't you (LOL) see? See we are *giving* advice, but it is rarely accepted as a gift! I have relied on my intuitive vs reflective part of my brain in the past. Usually intuition kept me safe, but I also gave it clout to have everyone's else's decision made in MY brain, and that was wrong. Here, I learned that to allow others freedom and respect, no one has fodder to use against me! I have time now to maintain my own interests and allow others their autonomy instead of controlling them. People have a right to their opinion.

"Let" is an action verb.

Death by Chocoholism

———

Here's a plan. Write your obit. Only one instruction. Don't let your obituary say that you did not dance to the song you love.

Rather, write about being reborn. Contemplate within this creative writing where you want to be when you die. Will you turn your body functions over to others to decide to kill you? Is that plan in place? Who or what are you waiting for to get on ahead with the rest of your life? A second coming of you? Hee Hee Hee Hee.

Who do you want to see before you go into the beyond? Why? Where do you want to die? Where do you want to be spiritually? Socially? Emotionally? Tell us when you start looking forward to death, then we will know you are ready. Who do you want to sing? Do you want music? Do you want a minister to talk? If there is a legal way to take your life in the end, do you want assistance? What cemetery would you choose? Where do you want those ashes and crushed bones to be tossed?

Did you ever look up your grandmother's maiden name? Did you try to catch a falling star with your grandchild? Did you drive out of town like you planned, to see the Northern Lights? Do you want just one more Fourth of July to have that party of a lifetime? Did you write a will? Did you get a witness to your note? What if you are in denial of your own ill health? You have already had many miracles, now your life is up to you. Call that place to donate your organs. Write your messages. Tell people you love them all the time. What are you waiting for? I have such peace since I have plans made for after I die

May the angels lead you to paradise.

"To die will be an awfully big adventure". – Peter Pan

May the Martyrs come to welcome you. Death of you will happen at the end of your lifetime on earth. Know this and you will be wiser during that life time.

You see, it is all happy in the end.

Think about a loved one friend or relative maybe whom you have personally known and lost.

Everyone has lost someone, relative, friend, close, near, through battle, accident, trauma or disease. As one of the living, we haven't had enough of them yet. We resist in our hearts, the letting go. It is OUR desire, our need, for one more time with them, one more human touch, hug, sharing, experience with them doing the same things they did with their warmth of sun and face we knew. Not the absence of life. That is our loss. They are tranquil. Why deny them that peace in your mind?

Picture them serenely dead, expressionless. If you must, go back to the accident or the emaciated illness exhaustion of a body lying where it last did. Know that their reactionary mentality is not awake. Feel their quietness. See their limpness as a complete release of pain from this side. Allow them to pass into death, just like it was a dark photo they enter. Allow their passage and honor their going home.

I stumbled on this unknown quote: *"Go ahead and grieve, but do not engage in lingering despair."*

We on this side, we will know puppy licks, receive hugs, hear jokes, feel the warmth of the sun. We must be brave and walk through sadness in these times. If we picture our loved ones as they were in life, we will have their photographic journey in our lives and on our minds. That is an honor to them. That is enough. It hurts but it will be enough. Life is. Death is.

Who's gonna die last off this earth?

On Death: You go first. No. You go first, please.

See, we have been talking about our fears. Fear of death sounds good for a last chapter, don't you think?

> *"Even though I walk through the valley of the shadow of*
> *death, I will fear no evil, for you are with me;*
> *Your rod and your staff, they comfort me."* - Psalm 23:4

I'm going to talk about walking through this valley of death - not my own, of course, but walking with someone who is going through their dying process. See, we are in a life relationship with someone until they are gone. Let's do it right.

The dying have rights: The right to walk through this valley of death, the right to have no fear as they go, the right to realize they are dying and that ahead is a walk with God; and finally, they have the right to comfort as they go.

Let's not stop them from doing any of those things. This will help you to accept the reality of their dying.

Laughter is okay with the dying. Emotions are charged anyway, why not add memories of joy and retrace strains of past joys and laughter? The impassive, repressed emotions, stressed concern, deathly talk is all too visible at deathbeds. I have suggestions how to incorporate a more peaceful passing during the inevitable cross over.

In this final end to any relationship, let us remember what we have learned and offer what we can to help die.

Cognizance of Our own Feelings
Understanding and Care
Retraining Our Thoughts and Subsequently Our Words in Regard to Dying People

I am not a neurosurgeon or a psychiatrist, but I have been there with those who knew they were headed into death. I have been on the walk, as a friend and family member, with people who want to die suicidally and in dire straits, people who are near death, and those who just received their terminal notice from a doctor.

Here's why I wanted to share with you.

I have worked with Hospice, the Suicide Prevention Coalition, and have mentored abused women and imprisoned women; I also worked with the disabled. – therein lie several groups whose members wish they were dead. I worked with thousands of juvenile delinquents who made suicide attempts weekly. And I have had losses: a brother, my husband, and my parents and their ancestors. I lost a great friend to a murderer.

As a layperson, I have experienced deep, deep grief, after sudden deaths. The need to understand death and grief through God's eyes brought me to where I am today. After all, as Christians, we are only in the awakening phase of our being.

We have all watched siblings and friends face losses. Our grief and our mourning periods were so dissimilar that I delved into the reason for the difference in our walk with terminal patients.

Unfortunately, we are in a culture that doesn't prepare for or talk about death much, and it makes it that much harder.

Some folks believe killing a sinner (in their opinion) will gain them 72 virgins in afterlife.

People believe demon worship is the truism we are otherwise forgetting on this earth.

People denounce that Jesus ever had existence, though testimonies and stories abound. Good that the majority of folks believe in Him and live their lives with Him in their plan.

A truth-based decisiveness had stupidly given way to fear in our minds of the unknown results and insecurities.

People claim to hate death, they question God, or, perhaps we remove ourselves - turning emotionally cold from what is actually happening, and we become unable to help or cope with the person who is dying.

We, the "okay, the "healthy" - the family or friend, we go through much of our grief before - our terminal patients pass on.

Simple Definition of Grief: Deep mental anguish, a wellspring of sorrow, frustration.

Knowing that, cognition that we are in that stage of grief is ESSENTIAL. It is a truth. Many of us deny our own feelings when someone is dying around us, and then we react on those buried feelings.

When it comes to dealing with the dying, there is no prewritten script; and we are caught up in our innate or cultured concepts, our own fear, and reactionary emotions; and of course, act in the manner which those emotions dictate. <u>PERHAPS NOT</u> in the manner which the dying person needs!

Physiologically, our hippocampus reacts to our fears, not waiting the time it takes to get to our common sense and logic part, in the frontal lobes. I like to compare the acts of the hippocampus to a real surprise. We are stymied until filters engage and we can speak or blink or think. Words come out from automatic pilot! WE MUST FEED THOSE LOBES knowledge for the logic and sense to be honed, rehearsed and practiced and thus, change our habitual responses.

Your awareness and your appropriate part in another person's dying - comes from the heart.

So, first cognition of our feelings is essential.

I want to foster a change in people so that WE, you and I, KNOW what not to do (!) in the presence of someone dying.

See, we are in our own depression of great sadness, with anxiety over loss of OUR formerly 'unterminally diagnosed person' who now is labelled a terminal - loved one. These are real feelings. I am going to talk about acting within this interim period of life, rather than just existing - within that period of time.

AND about some better ways for US TO BE OF HELP to the ill family or friend -while grieving and mourning and resisting their death!

We need to behave in a manner that helps, not hinders comfort and the walk to the pearly gates.

As we die, as others die, we have a Bill of Rights. How many of you have heard of this?

I was very manipulative with my mother's death. I tried very hard to "skirt" the issue of her dying, wanting everything to appear back at normal; manipulating doctors, talking her out of her signed 'pull the plugs' declaration(!), keeping her in nursing care rather than allow her to go to her dangerous - in my opinion - own home. I was greedy for my needs for her rather than her needs in dying: talking for her, interpreting for her when she couldn't speak, angry with God for taking her so harshly, creating chaos with nursing staff, pharmacists, caregivers.

Others' agendas can SO hinder "dying with dignity and grace!"

Our feelings cannot get in their way.

*Death is imminent. That is a truth. Feelings and thoughts are not truths. Let's lift the fog that clouds that confusion at the time near death.

Here are some common feelings WE have:

Denial about the disease and the extensive effect on the person diagnosed! Anger, frustration with the person who can no longer do things for themselves; or anger with the fact that they are stubborn and grouchy, is also useless.

I love this quote by a male geriatric caregiver to a patient:

"Oh, I bet you're sweet as pie, Mrs. Smith, under all that 'grumpiness'."
She threw her daily vodka shot over him.
'You'll never know", she replied, unable to find her former sweet-as-pie personality.

Other common feelings:

Anxiety about our future and facing and our own lack of capabilities without THEM

Our own Depression

Exhaustion and sleeplessness, irritability, negative responses and lack of concentration in our daily duties.

•

Okay, so if that is going on with us, WHAT ON EARTH IS GOING THROUGH THE AILING LOVED ONE with what they are facing?!!

People, let's get a grip. Be aware of your thoughts and actions. Walk through them, as moments... given to us by God... to know loss and understanding in those very days and moments. I was guilty of many sins listed in Proverbs 6-16: (I paraphrased for brevity.)

Proverbs 6 – 16, in the Warnings Against Folly;

"Go to the point of exhaustion, allow no sleep to your eyes, no slumber for your eyelids. (What good was I to the terminally ill if I was tired and grumpy?)

Passage # 12: A troublemaker and a villain, who goes about with a corrupt mouth - he always stirs up conflict.

Stirs up conflict???? (Arguing with doctors, blaming them, begging my loved one to go through all treatment efforts - painful and killing as they may be! Telling them not to speak of their own death because I DID NOT want to hear it! I stirred up conflict.)

I DID NOT recognize the true value of dying. I wanted MY old relationship with MY mother, my husband, father, friend and brother. I wanted their "normal" to come back FOR ME – I prayed wrongly for that to happen – for MY benefit. Was I pushing control of MY life onto someone else to do?

Cognition is important!

The brain must allow the hippocampus to 'LISTEN' to the frontal cortex.

Rather than live in "reaction" to death; let us rather "act" in a likeness of God.

Thinking about reality, and what we all know in truth – WE WILL ALL DIE. And we need accept that is God's way.

Think about this…in the acknowledgement of history, we each have 2 ½ million ancestors, all whom our forefathers and now us, must let go, as they have died.

Let's offer more wisdom now to our loved ones in their walk through the valley of death, with acceptance rather than resistance.

You want to die with dignity and grace; so does every man and woman!

So if you want to try something new, say dancing lessons, whittling, or cooking with rutabaga, and your best friend or spouse says,

"You don't want to do that, do you?"

How do you feel right now?

Listen to these comments:

"Dad, you don't want to sign that document to unplug life support. That's like killing yourself!"

Or to your just diagnosed friend, "Aren't they going to try chemo and radiation?"

And how often is this said? "Oh, Honey, promise you will NEVER send me to a care facility.

Imagine you have an illness and have no control over its erosion to your body? And someone says, "You don't want to do that, do you?"

It's a berating sentence and our emotions are eroded as is our physiological BEING, which is already BEATEN AND EATEN UP BY TERMINAL ILLNESS AND DEATH'S ONSET.

Let's be careful, people of what we say and do. Dying people have rights.

'Rest in peace' the sign over the cemetery gate says.

But on their way there...let us be most helpful to them so they know they will have peace.

Some things to say to afford that grace and dignity:

(Have someone you love read these to you while you close your eyes.)

"I do not want you to go, but I want you to know peace, and I want you to be pain free; so, I will share with you what those who actually knew Jesus before me, wish for you:

(Soften voice:)

Matthew wrote, "See, as angels, always, the face of our Father who is in Heaven"

From John: "In my Father's house, there are many rooms, one prepared as a place for you."

And in Revelations:

"Worthy are you to take the scroll and open its seals, for you were slain. You ransomed people for God from every tribe, language, people, and nation."

"Worthy are you to receive power and wealth and wisdom and might and honor and glory and blessing in Heaven."

"He will wipe away every tear from your eye. Death shall be no more, neither shall there be mourning, nor crying, nor pain anymore. Former "things" have passed away."

Also from Revelations:

"Then the angel will show you the river of the water of life, (soft lightness in voice) bright as crystal, flowing from the throne of God and of the Lamb through the middle of the street of the city; no longer will there be anything accursed, but the throne of God and of the Lamb will be in it, and his servants will worship Him. You will see His face, and His name will be on your foreheads. Night will be no more! There will be need no light, of lamp or sun! for the Lord God will be your light, and He will reign forever and ever where you are."

"Death is how He paid the price, in the garden His earthly blood was also spilt."

And from John 16:22,

You will have sorrow now,
But I will see you again
And your heart will rejoice.
And no one will take your JOY from you.
- John 16:22

-

Just two more...

Isaiah reminds us:

"But they that wait upon the Lord shall renew their strength; they shall mount up with wings as eagles. They shall mourn and not be weary, and they shall walk and not faint."

From Psalms 116: "Precious in the sight of the LORD is the death of his faithful servants."

Aren't those precious comforts?

Here's your education today:

*From the Dying Person's Bill of Rights: I have the right to be treated as a living human being until I die.

** From the Dying Person's Bill of Rights: I have the right to be cared for by caring, sensitive, knowledgeable people who will attempt to understand my needs and will be able to gain some satisfaction in helping me face my death.

> *"It's true, I suffer a great deal–but do I get to suffer well? That is the question."*
> — St. Therese of Lisieux: Her Last Conversations

We can help those suffering to suffer well.

Number 4 in Dying Person's Bill of Rights:
*I have the right to express my feelings and emotions about my approaching death in my own way.

Here's how we can assure those rights:

Just be there. Share your time. Last chance to do so.
Let them guide conversations.
Talk to them in a space that is comfortable, where you won't be interrupted

Listen to their words, these are the last.

Ease into conversations - they may not be ready to hear what you have to say. Allow time to hear - Denial is our first response to turmoil.

Communicate in a straight forward manner. One topic at a time.

Be aware that not accepting the PROCESS of dying causes its own great suffering.

Though WE have guilt for not "saving them" with our love, it is not our fault they are ill and we can wear no weight in this. It will show.

- Avoid prying and check yourself, 'is my question to the patient appropriate?" Is it really your business whether they have had a bowel movement?
- Do not press them for conversation, but give them longer pause, opening an opportunity to talk.
- Do they have regrets in life they want to verbalize now? Open the door for those hard conversations.
- We may all ask - "Was my life worth dying for?" Tell them how theirs was so!
- Take notes for children if they desire to pass on loving words.
- Continue to talk with them about family, weather, easy conversation, what is happening in the community.
- Reflect on what gave their life meaning.
- Keep speech at age level, not baby talk, like
  o "Open your mouth a little bit more, Honey" or any treatment like a child. Keep in mind that illness has nothing to do with intelligence. Avoid talking louder. Silence is okay.
- Be aware of their confusion or upset with what truth you might say, allow it to flush through their thoughts.
- Be sincere in care and easing pain - follow through with the care.
- WE ARE truly sorry they have pain and aches. Warmth and comfort are welcomed.
- Do not assume you know how they feel.

- Encourage them to remember what they are most proud of in their life and their inherent uniqueness, their expressions of self.
- Show respect for their method of communication, speech, hearing losses, or their search for appropriate words.
  In fact, if I am speechless, I want these signs over my bed!

  'If you want to talk about already dead people, my hearing went first.'

  "My coffin is in the shop. Let's still talk about life."

- Ask, "How can I help?" They may need a blanket loosened, or are waiting for you to leave to go to the bathroom, or want to send a nurse flowers, or pray with someone special.
- Ask them about their fears. Do not try to assuage them, only acknowledge their feelings.
- Cry all you each want to!
- Recall hilarious times, make new laughter together.
- Pray with them that they may forgive themselves for discretions, as God already has.
- Acknowledge that the control of their or anyone's, destiny was never ours.
- Acknowledge 'their passing' whenever it is broached. Help them to walk through their sadness. They get to do this as best as they can - last chance at it.
- Tell them of unspoken love you and others have for them.
- Tell them what a gift it is to be with them in these moments and as they pass. It can leave us with a lifelong intimacy which inspires us.
- Even Jesus had to suffer and die to be ascended into God's hands, to divine love.
- Remember that God's love is the utmost healing.
- If open to it, massage their feet. Hands on, touch, can be comforting to some. Ask first.

- Encourage their freedom from deep mental anguish and constant sorrows: Point out, 'would they wish that upon us'?
- As we look to the moment rather than the future, we will find blossoms of beauty that will help us feel love.
- Remind them of the joy they have given you.
- If they want to discuss our future, share dreams. Agnostics seem to have that curiosity especially.
- Acknowledge the death they are facing in words - it is the elephant in the room, address it.
- Entertain asking them what they want to have included in their eulogy.
- Offer that we must grieve, it is a part of living.
- Thank them for living for Jesus.
- And lastly, ask them if they remember.

Last February, a pastor I listened to asked us the question:

"How DO WE GET TO Heaven?"

One of the answers was:

"We get to Heaven by dying to ourselves after living for Jesus."

Things not to say. Avoid these platitudes:

- "Just pray about it", dismissive of our obligation to pray with them
- "You need to look at things differently." Inflicting guilt about the way they feel?!
- "Everyone feels that way." - Wow, ouch.
- "You are so stubborn." - Not funny.
- "You have the same illness as Gertrude, my uncle, cousin, friend." - They hear that they are nobody special.
- "Yes, we all forget or misplace things sometimes." - Pretending they are not losing faculties, when they know they are slipping.

- "Let's not talk about death." I don't want to face that. Many people believe that if they don't think about death, it won't happen. (Denial and setting oneself up for shock of grief!
- "We all are a little crazy now and then." - Negating their anxiety.
- "We all have aches and pain." Really, you think ours could match what they are feeling?
- "You're strong. You will get through this."
- "You are so negative. Where is your hope?" Well, truth is, my hope was gone the day the doctor used the words, Stage 4."
- "You'll be okay." - Oh my God!
- "Why aren't your children seeing to radiation therapy for you?" another 'friend' asked.
- "I know a case where..." more friends offered undoable alternatives.
- The Want-To-Do-Gooders-in-Life know not what they do.

From the Dying Person's Bill of Rights"

*I have the right to not be judged for my decisions which may be contrary to beliefs of others."

I just exampled that for you.

Truth be told, WE would have done anything, anything, to have Mom forever. But God had made that decision.

*From the Dying Person's Rights: I have a right to attempt to "put my house in order" by myself.

Unable to get out of the care facility bed, we were instructed by our mother not to touch her sewing room, or the quilting squares. In fact, she wanted the fabric and lamp brought to her. She couldn't work with them, we knew, but she had a desire to finish her project regardless of our insistence that she could not do it! I have a right to attempt to "put my house in order" by myself.

This next story was the worst, most heart-rendering occurrence and broke a law in the Dying Person's Rights:

There were no masses held at Nursing home. Mom had prayed every morning, night and day of her-before-cancer-life. Now, she was stricken not only with cancer but denial of the right to worship. She walked in to the nursing home chapel during a Congregational service.

"You can't come in here, Marie," the lay minister told her.

An aide, a little forcefully turned my Mother around and headed her back out the chapel door.

"I just wanted to pray with you." Mom softly told the minister.

"But this is a Congregational service and you are Catholic, Ma'am," the aide told her.

She just wanted to pray.

*From the Dying Person's Bill of Rights: I have the right to discuss and enlarge my religious and/or spiritual experiences whatever these may mean to others.

On a Sunday, after mass, we told Mom that she was crazy. It was the only way that it would concretely set in. Much more gently said, a brother-in-law had to tell her that she was doing things that were a danger to her and she needed to be watched constantly, and be constantly medicated to stay alive. 'She was doing 'crazy things' he informed her.

*I have the right not to be deceived. From the Bill of Rights for the Dying

Also on the Bill of Rights:

*I have the right to have help from and for my family in accepting my death.

Telling her was the right thing...

*I have the right to be free from pain. - From the Bill of Rights for the Dying.

It is my personal belief that everyone, when the time comes, MUST involve Hospice. Good people. Good things. Godly people.

Hospice convinces doctors to ease their pain.

And all I can do is stand here. Dammit. Just let her have peace. And hold her hand.

There I said it: The peace, the peace of dying. Dying.

*I have the right to die with peace and dignity. From the Bill of Rights for the Dying.

I am standing upon the seashore.
A ship at my side spreads her white sails to the morning breeze
And starts for the blue ocean.
She is an object of beauty and strength.
I stand and watch her until at length she hangs
Like a speck of white cloud
Just where the sea and the sky come to mingle with each other
Then someone at my side says:
"There, she is gone."
"Gone where?"

"Gone from my sight.
That is all."
She is just as large in mast and hull and spar as she was
When she left my side
And she is able to bear her load of living freight to her destined port.
Her diminished size is in me, not in her.
And just at the moment when someone at my side says,
"There, she is gone!"
There are other eyes watching her coming,
And other voices ready to take up the glad shout:
"Here she comes!"

The Dying Person's Bill of Rights

- I have the right to be treated as a living human being until I die.
- I have the right to maintain a sense of hopefulness however changing its focus may be.
- I have the right to be cared for by those who can maintain a sense of hopefulness, however changing this might be.
- I have the right to express my feelings and emotions about my approaching death in my own way.
- I have the right to participate in decisions concerning my care.
- I have the right to expect continuing medical and nursing attention even though "cure" goals must be changed to "comfort" goals.
- I have the right not to die alone.
- I have the right to be free from pain.
- I have the right to have my questions answered honestly.
- I have the right not to be deceived.
- I have the right to have help from and for my family in accepting my death.
- I have the right to die in peace and dignity.
- I have the right to retain my individuality and not be judged for my decisions which may be contrary to beliefs of others.
- I have the right to discuss and enlarge my religious and/or spiritual experiences whatever these may mean to others.
- I have the right to expect that the sanctity of the human body will be respected after death.
- I have the right to be cared for by caring, sensitive, knowledgeable people who will attempt to understand my needs and will be able to gain some satisfaction in helping me face my death.

Walking through the Death of A Loved One

The abruptness of death is so disarming. My routines were all broken. My turn-to guy is no longer sitting at the kitchen table, so easy to turn to. "What's the forecast?" was always answered by him. I never had to read the paper or listen to weather forecasts on t.v. news or radio. He had my answers.

"What's the psi on your tires, Maam?" Gees, I don't know.

"Where's your valve for gas turnoff to the house?" Gees, I don't know.

How much do you have left to pay on your mortgage? I.D.K.

And yet, none of that mattered. My tears, my loneliness – they were now my life. Yet the material things kept flying at me to become solely responsible for.

Take the trash out on Thursday morning. Where's my key to lock the gate? It's just my gate now. No longer our gate.

And I don't like that. I don't want to be solo.

I'm screaming inside, "Why me, God?" Why? Why him first? Why not me? What good am I going to be alone? It's just not right.

Yes, when you ask if I want the air filter changed. I don't know.

Don't you know that the abruptness for death is disarming me? What air filter? I couldn't care less.

Tomorrow can't help, nor will a new oil filter. I'll cry till I'm done.

Most of us respond to death of a loved one with a momentous loneliness, called yearning. We are in disbelief that this could happen; furthermore, happen to us. Sometimes that includes being mad at God or with the world and people because they still have their "loved ones". We get angry about that sometimes even. Being vitriolic with someone we love is too close to the bone – it makes our physical being sick too! Walking through the stages of grief must be done. Take yourself from the anger, loneliness, and jealousy, by walking through, accepting life on life's terms. After all, did you believe that that someone would not die? Of course not. So the only course of action is to accept the fact that everyone dies. From that, the greater course now is for us to live, and to live like life will be taken away any minute. We get one chance. There is no do-over for this moment, or this day or this week. Good intentions weigh zero. And then we too, will be gone. So live in it, smile during it, but embrace what life is giving you now. Lamenting and self-pity are not attractive, even to yourself. Change out of those pajamas.

Grief is in the Eyes of the Beholder

Wow. I chose once to stay in grief. It had a name for a period of time in my life, so I could put the cap on with the logo, and wallow in grief. I got medication for depression. I excused myself from 'things'. I was in grief, a hollow dark hallway leading to sadness.

One night a miracle happened. I was sobbing. I had gotten down on my knees to pray and have a talk with God about how He was running my life – not so good by my account. Instead, I choose that time to cry and cry over my lot in life. Like a toddler checking to see if you know he is being naughty, I peeked out from my palms full of face, and Nobody was there. Nobody came to my pity party. Not even God.

Boy, was I self-centered. My ego thought I could call God and get my behaviors changed. Heh Heh. (Ego: Easing God Out) Actually, I am pretty sure he had his hand in that moment.

It was as though lightning struck. I realized I was the only one there. I was the only one at the party, the only one stuck in the pitiful grief. And I wasn't going anywhere from that moment if I chose to attend the party continuously. My behavior sucked. So while I was still down on my knees, I thanked God for the insight. It was up to me to change what I was doing, what was going on, my behavior, who I listened to, who I talked about or to, if I celebrated life again or had more parties like this.

.

I recall from history, even Columbus had a bad day when his journal entry was only, "This day we sailed on. Course WSW."

More help was needed than even the most supportive friends and family could 'give' to me. God gave me an idea. What I did with this higher level of thinking was either my demise or became a change in my thinker. God gave me a healthier sense of self – IF I grabbed onto it.

People had been talking to me about 'walking through my grief'. I understood that I would have to live again among the throngs, grocery shop, walk in snow, get new glasses, play ball with kids, but it could all wait until 'after', I had hitherto rationalized. With God's knock on my brain, I realized that I could start living again right now. I continued to walk through grief, but I participated in life. I now allowed sad moments, said to myself, "That's a sad moment.", was gentle with myself, and kept walking. My RSVP list to my pity parties didn't even include me!

Helpless Me, Helpless You,
I'm Dead Now

You all will think that I am not as recovered as I say, with these chapters about death included, but to my point of view, I could not let you leave this reformation in progress without warning you that death is a real thing for you!

Were you not to realize your ending, you could not promise change in your 'during'. There is no one more chance at this moment. You have used up all your priors. There are only a certain number of days left in anyone's life. Count yours. Estimated average age at this writing is 76 for a man, 81 for a woman. Figure out the days you have spent and the number ahead. To me, why would anyone stay as their former self after knowing this?

Average retirement age is currently at 64 in the United States

Life expectancy is 80 in the United States

That gives you 16 years (5,840 days) to enjoy life, if you are postponing enjoyment!

And if you are reading this book to the end, you MUST be informed about suicide probabilities. The information shared with you thus far, are methods to keep you from the horrors of life, from thinking in a traumatic, anxious way. Much of the time, living a life of so much hell can lead one to suicidal thinking. Such simple occurrences which can be fixed or altered, lead people to suicide, i.e., nightmares, sleeplessness, anxiety, college woes. So I am including a lot about suicide in order to inform you of preventative measures. If not for your own recognition, so that you may save the life of another. Thank you for granting me time to share this.

Some people are more at risk for suicide than others. Did you know that thirty-seven percent of suicides in the U.S. are teenagers? True. Look at historical factors in the family, which depict a tendency. More considerations a friend should review:

Behavior	Mental Health Conditions	Environmental Factors	Their Talk
Anxiety	Prolonged Stress	Stressful Life Events	Depression
Psychosis	Mood Disorder	Substance Abuse	Loss of Interest
Aggression	Withdrawing from Activities	Sleeping Too Little or Much	Humiliation
Rage	Feeling Trapped	Isolating from Family	Agitation

Listen to their talk, in private. Show understanding, absolutely no judgement, only reflect their words in question form. Take their concerns seriously. Work with them to keep them from lethal means and drugs. Don't wait for them to reach out; discuss their elephant in the room. Ask pointed questions. Do not minimize their feelings – they are real to them and deadly serious. Do not give advice. Do not discuss with them the value of their life; they already have a fixed idea of worthlessness and YOU are not the one that needs to change them. Get them to a hot line, then follow up. Get them to a health professional.

If it is you struggling, reach out. Do not wait for someone to discover how you truly feel.

National Suicide Prevention Hotline: 1-800-273-TALK (8255)

I do not want you to go on living without recognizing your worth and potential. Your personal worth is not only the concern of those who lack it.

Fill your days and fill them well, for the poem below was written by a presuicidal person dead inside.

You wouldn't believe what is inside me.
You only see my quiet, or sometimes my anger.
as I seem to constantly fight with you...and life.
I cannot find comfort in my own skin.
So much so, that I cannot offer ease to the you I love.
You have NO idea of the real war.
...inside me

The emotion and mental pain
I am reeking on myself
is using every fiber of my body's tissue
to barely function in the light of day.
Among others of you who are in life's reality.

You try it on, not sleeping...
for days, something overtaking your rest.
You try, not caring about anything
for months, that caring piece of you void.

There is no gratitude, or peace within me.
Ever. Yes, I smile once or twice
but it hurts to drum it up for you...it's a lie.
My insides would rather not.

Somewhere in here, I know
You want to see the old me.
It's not that I don't care about you -
my soul just can't respond.
I can't offer care about anything or anyone;
the world, hell, the universe, are a bothersome fog
In my head.

My ability to care is deeply sad and broken.
Together, we throw an antidepressant at it.
But it laughs like a devil in ownership of sad.

A wretched vacuum fills my brain.
and seeps between my heart and soul.
Your help, manipulation, treatment offers
are useless against me. My 'want to'
left the building. It is no more.
I cannot respond. I cannot act.
I care not to move. I fight offers
of anything I would have to 'work' at.

If I am lucky, you take me to
the right doctor, rarely a match,
him and me.
If you are lucky, you find
a pill to throw at my
already depleted chemicals. Little notions
of the old me may sneak through
on drugs.
You are happy to see them, but always watching.
Will I slip? Inside I have.
Self-torture keeps me alive.
I hate me.
Adrenaline juice is all that looks like stamina.

...Those healthy cells that have not yet given out.
It's just a matter of time for the others.
Infighting is a constant.
I want release, relief from
the war between what I call
feelings and conscience, heart and mind.

Did you know that the drug,

the alcohol, or sleep

give me only momentary,

temporary relief. I leave myself

for as long as the abusive drug or nap lasts.

Abusive drugs have destroyed me

after their snapshot of a moment's fake euphoria.

What you want for me and what

I crave - are grand canyons apart.

Do you know for sure there is no life after death?

Cause I would like a do-over. I'm ready to get out of this one.

So what can you do?

You are the one that wants me alive.

Currently, I am not. I want out.

Out of body because in here

it is twisted, raunchy and pathetic.

You want your selfishness for me.

Are you really allowed to try to live my life

under God's authority?

Here's what you can do, while I'm here.

Continue to hold me, when I coldly buck you off.

Continue to talk to me, lovingly only.

When you point out the sick actions

I am involved in, chastise me for it, it is only more

ammunition for me to hate myself,

knowing you now condemn me too.

Just like I do every fucking minute.

I need warmth and a safe space,

where nothing is needed of me but

to rotely function, to see others like me

in pretendville - treatment,
shuffling around in and out of hate fog.

There exposed to their angry outbursts,
their wrist scars, their malfunctions,
I become cognizant of what you see,
my visibility.
And I know it is not right
while on this earthly planet.

Yet, I need to be there; there, where
nothing is expected of me. It is safe.
The fighting within me stops - there is no
premise that I must be happy like you,
must go to work, or socialize – or buy bread.

I am only required to "be" in a place like that.
Leave me there. Keep trying to visit me,
show me loving faces, things I loved, photos
of loved ones, faces needing my presence
in their lives.

It helps. Somehow. To calm me.
Keep me warm, let me be.
Then don't wear yourself out with
hope and worry.
I'm ok within here. You are good out there.

Life as we knew it might be over, but
there is existence for each.
And it is now our reality. Let it be.
You have saved me from hurting you and others worse
Emotionally, verbally, with my lashing out.

Hippocrates made doctors promise that
they would do no harm first.
In my case, that of those of us wanting to die,
I need the severest form
of treatment they have, less a lobotomy!
But they are bound by laws and oath
to try, oh, this and that – just do no harm.

While hours of nausea, headaches, bodily
rejection to the this's and the that's they try.
As they overtake my original natural cells, are only
additional torture,
maybe I will be alright.

We don't know.
It is like air hockey - lots of punch only for it to maybe return,
maybe hit the pocket, be returned and
continue the game of life for a bit more.

Can you give up the ghost?
Can you give up YOUR ghost?
Of who I was to you?
For I am not, no more.
Why stress yourself with manipulation, thinking
you could make me live forever?

I am just here biding time. Why don't you use YOUR time more wisely?

*Death by suicide is more common than death due to homicide or motor vehicle accidents.
There are 25 attempted suicides for every one completed death.* – Psychiatric Times,
Maria A. Oquendo.

Of suicide attempts which occur every minute in America, every 14 minutes
today, a loved one will complete their own death.

Promotion of Suicide is out there and working:

1. Music, internet, books, antichrist groups offer suicide as a solution. Some of you remember these lyrics from the television show, MASH: "Suicide is Painless / It brings on many changes / And I can take it or leave it if I please."
2. In front of a live Web cam, a college student completed suicide by taking a drug overdose while some users egged him on.
3. Pro-Internet sites give detailed information on the most effective ways to commit suicide.
4. A not so fun fact found on Google follows. There has been a variety of ways revealed in the media: including swallowing poisonous spiders, power-drilling holes in their heads, sticking hot pokers down their throats, choking for a high, injecting peanut butter into their veins, crushing their necks in vices, and hurling themselves into vats of beer.
5. Influential and well-known people, along with the media, have unknowingly glamorized suicide: Sigmund Freud, Cleopatra, Mark Antony, Brutus, Virginia Wolf, Adolf Hitler, Ernest Hemmingway, Vincent van Gogh Pontius Pilate, Socrates, and possibly Tchaikovsky, Elvis Presley, and Marilyn Monroe.
6. The most common types of suicide include copycat methods.
7. Earmarked phrases are offered, even with the mist of idolatry: Do it for honor and martyrdom!
8. 'Death by cop' has become a buzzword.
9. Suicide notes have been published, speaking about the pain of existence, and the attraction of death.

We have got to counter this!

In the book, Biathonos, John Donne stated suicide is <u>not</u> incompatible with the laws of God, reason, or nature.

Voltare and Hume led the way to abandoning legal punishment of attempters.

A book titled *Suicide, mode d'emploi* is both a how-to manual and a political manifesto encouraging readers to exercise their right to die.

Both books and the internet sites contain information about prescription drugs that ensure a "gentle death" along with how to calculate a lethal dose.

Some familial ancestry or nations of origin suggest preferential modes for suicide. Russians prefer hanging. The English and Irish prefer poison. Italians prefer firearms, and the Americans prefer firearms, poisons, and gas. The Sac and Fox Native Americans were notoriously known to lie on railroad tracks. Proclivities for certain methods tend to travel with immigrants wherever they go. Offering to young people, here is your way. The first woman to die in the Chieftains family will be chief's wife in the afterworld.

Guns kept in the home double odds for potential adolescent suicides.

They were in spiritual agony, and they sought a physical solution. Their thinking was compromised by lack of chemicals and transistors; there was a disconnection inside the brain. The overwhelming feeling is alienation from self; and an isolation like no other – a darkness and war inside. Addiction on top of these feelings creates a sense of no way out of this darkness. Sometimes that is true. Synthetics cannot bring back what is destroyed, gone. As was my husband's case.

What was immediately apparent, was that none of them had truly wanted to die.

They had wanted their inner pain to stop!

They wanted some measure of relief.

There is promotion. It is there. Done by parents, friends, peers, our news. I read that if your parents did not think they were worthy of Heaven, you will undoubtedly share that pitiful belief and be prone to suicide.

Media spews the commonality of suicide with noteworthy facts: "For every homicide, there are 1½ suicides".

In a suicidal crisis, it's all about time. They're going to grab whatever is available. Determined suiciders don't change gears if their attempt is thwarted, because they have rigid thinking in that moment. They're not thinking about dying. They're thinking about ending the pain.

Suicide is the tenth most common cause of death in the United States.

Over 38,000 Americans took their lives in 2010, the most recent year for which we have data. *Suicide* accounted for 12 deaths for every 100,000 people in the United State.

All of a sudden, they didn't want to die, but it was too late. Ones who are determined, succeed on their 4th or 5th or 25th try. The very fact that someone kills himself we regard as proof of intent. Know that we cannot change, cure and we did not cause the suicidal feeling.

So Live Life While
You are Here

I think Henry David Thoreau summed this book up so well with his words written long before its making:

"Go confidently in the direction of your dream! Live the life you've imagined. As you simplify your life, the laws of the universe will be simpler."

And,

"Men ought to know that from the brain and from the brain only, arise our pleasures, joy, laughter and jests as well as our sorrows, pains, despondency and tears. And by this, in a special manner, we acquire wisdom and knowledge, and see and hear, and know what is sweet and what is unsavory. And by the same organ we become mad and delirious where fears and terrors assail us. All these things we endure from the brain, when it is not healthy. In these ways, I am of the opinion that the brain exercises the greatest power in the man. This is the interpreter to us of those things which emanate from the air, when the rain happens to be in a sound state."

Hippocrates

Is who you are, who you are meant to be?

'BROKEN DREAMS'

As children bring their broken toys
With tears for us to mend,
I brought my broken dreams to God
Because He was my friend.
But then, instead of leaving Him
In peace to work alone,
I hung around and tried to help
With WAYS THAT WERE MY OWN.
At last, I snatched them back and cried,
"How can you be so slow?"
"My child," He said,
"What could I do?"
"You never did LET GO."
- Biblical Prayer by Georgy

After one plants seeds, we must allow time for them to grow. This book was full of seeds. Parts of it may need rereading while you pause to let 'better' happen to you. We repeated our bad habits for years. Don't you think it might take some time to now repeat our good habits, maybe equal time? This was all about quieting our minds and opening our hearts. What a great way to live. I am proof!

I am so grateful to have recovered from my former self. My connection to my spirituality has allowed me to regain my spirituality, for in doing so, I have regained an essential part of myself. As a result, today my life has a sense of purpose that makes each moment a precious gift.

Live this moment. Treasure it. Do it right. Give this 60 seconds the integrity it comes with.

The future of civilization depends on our overcoming the meaninglessness and hopelessness that characterizes the thoughts of men today. —Albert Schweitzer

Bibliography

The Big Bang, The Buddha and the Baby Boom by Wes "Scoop" Nisker

Eight Stories Up by Dequincy A. Lezine with David Brent

Tying Rocks to Clouds by William Elliott

Words to Live By Edited by William Nichols

Battle of the Mind by Joyce Meyer

Change Your Brain, Change Your Life by Daniel G. Amen

Anatomy of the Spirit by Caroline Myss

The Brain by Seymour Simon

The Bible

Numerous AA and Al-Anon literature

The Optimists Creed

To be so strong that nothing can disturb your peace of mind.

To talk health, happiness and prosperity to every person you meet.

To make all your friends feel that there is something in them.

To look at the sunny side of everything and make your optimism come true.

To think only of the best, to work only for the best, and to expect only the best.

To be just as enthusiastic about the success of others as you are about your own.

To forget the mistakes of the past and press on to the greater achievements of the future.

To wear a cheerful countenance at all times and give every living creature you meet a smile.

To give so much time to the improvement of yourself that you have no time to criticize others.

To be too large for worry, too noble for anger, too strong for fear and too happy to permit the presence of trouble.

- Optimists International

Repeat after me:

> "I am larger, better than I thought, I did not
> know that I held such goodness."

About the Author

_____

I lived in a Post Office. When my mother disciplined me for fighting with my seven siblings (I mean, who wouldn't need to discipline that crowd?), she 'sat' me for time out within the view of all the town's postal patrons. I grew up humbled but always looking for a way out. Those characteristics coupled with an alcoholic and an A+ codependent family set me up for self-condemning and shameful doom. Add early Catholicism. Sprinkle with enough psychological education to make me dangerous, baby's place in the family, and, and, you get an author of this book, learned by default.

Stories from my experiences, self-deprecation and egotism mostly, led my path, late in life, to a development (latent they call it) after the fact of most of my shortcomings and defects of character guiding me astray, coming into spirituality, enlightenment of people skills, and a cognizance beyond my wildest dreams. Fulfillment, acceptance, happiness and joy fill my days. Serenity is within my grasp each moment. Good luck with the steps I proposed.

An acronym that catches me every time I realize my ego is talking...
Easing God Out – EGO.

AN UNHEALED PERSON CAN
FIND OFFENSE IN PRETTY MUCH
ANYTHING SOMEONE DOES.

A HEALED PERSON UNDERSTANDS
THAT THE ACTIONS OF OTHERS
HAVE NOTHING TO DO WITH THEM.

EACH DAY YOU GET TO DECIDE
WHICH ONE YOU WILL BE.